SWEDISH–AMERICAN BORDERLANDS

NEW HISTORIES OF TRANSATLANTIC RELATIONS

DAG BLANCK *and*
ADAM HJORTHÉN, EDITORS

UNIVERSITY OF MINNESOTA PRESS
MINNEAPOLIS
LONDON

Published by the University of Minnesota Press
111 Third Avenue South, Suite 290
Minneapolis, MN 55401-2520
http://www.upress.umn.edu

ISBN 978-1-5179-0751-8 (hc)
ISBN 978-1-5179-0858-4 (pb)

Library of Congress record available at https://lccn.loc.gov/2021058758

Printed in the United States of America on acid-free paper

28 27 26 25 24 23 22 21 10 9 8 7 6 5 4 3 2 1

Contents

Acknowledgments

This book is a collaborative effort and the result of work of a transatlantic academic community. We are first and foremost indebted to our authors for their dedication to this project during the past several years and for their willingness both to contribute their own research and to shape the ideas of the project as a whole.

Our ideas about Swedish–American borderlands evolved through discussions within an international and interdisciplinary network of scholars in the field of Swedish–American relations. Our meetings at Uppsala University in 2016 and at Sigtunastiftelsen in Sweden in 2017, where most of the authors participated, were particularly important. They were made possible through two research initiation grants from the Swedish Foundation for Humanities and Social Sciences. Beyond the authors in this volume, we also recognize the participation of Petter Bengtsson, Bo G. Ekelund, Lizette Gradén, Arne Lunde, Oskar Nordell, Linda H. Rugg, and Ann-Kristin Wallengren.

The contributions to *Swedish-American Borderlands: New Histories of Transatlantic Relations* were significantly strengthened by scholars who read and commented on the chapters. Thank you to Jennifer Eastman Attebery, Anders Bergström, Ulf Jonas Björk, Anne Brædder, Ulla Börestam, Carl-Henrik Carlsson, Richard Evans, Ola Johansson, Anna Källén, Jim Leary, Helena Mattson, Magdalena Naum, Magnus Rodell, Ann-Sofie Rossholm, Jonathan Skinner, John Wilson, and David Östlund. Thank you to Harald Runblom for succinct feedback in the early stages of writing and to Jørn Brøndal for close readings and constructive criticism of the complete manuscript.

We gratefully acknowledge support from Erik Anderson, our editor at the University of Minnesota Press, who enthusiastically believed in our idea from the beginning; to David Thorstad for his meticulous copyediting; and to the editorial team at the Press who shepherded the manuscript through production.

Adam Hjorthén would especially like to thank all friends and colleagues in the history of ideas at the Department of Culture and Aesthetics at Stockholm University and at the Department of History of the John F. Kennedy Institute for North American Studies at the Free University of Berlin. His work on this book has been made possible by a grant from the Swedish Research Council and by tireless support from Nevra Biltekin. Dag Blanck expresses his thanks to the Swedish Institute of North American Studies at Uppsala University and to the Swenson Swedish Immigration Research Center at Augustana College in Rock Island, Illinois—his two academic homes for the past several decades.

Introduction

Conceptualizing Swedish–American Borderlands

Dag Blanck and Adam Hjorthén

This book offers a reconceptualization and redefinition of the study of Swedish–American relations. Rather than focusing on one-way processes or specific national contexts, this volume revolves around contacts, crossings, and convergences. The focus on boundary crossings—on the back-and-forth movement of persons, ideas, and goods—results in new understandings of what we perceive as Swedish, American, or Swedish-American. We suggest that the concept of borderlands is highly useful in this pursuit. Borderlands, with a long past of its own in American Studies and North American history, has the potential to advance our understanding of Swedish–American relations, and might serve as a fruitful model in the study of other forms of transatlantic contacts.

To talk about Swedish–American borderlands might sound like a contradiction in terms. Sweden and the United States are, of course, geographically remote, located in different parts of the world. They do not share common borders, and their starkly different size and global power makes the relation inherently asymmetrical.[1] Despite the geographic distance, there have been significant patterns of transatlantic contact. Over the centuries, different events and processes and large-scale movements of individuals have resulted in a nongeographic proximity between the countries. The relations have been shaped by colonization, migration, tourism, commerce, and ideological, religious, cultural, academic, and technological interchanges.

The mass migration of the late-nineteenth and early-twentieth century thoroughly reshaped Swedish society, and had a considerable effect on certain areas and regions of the United States. This book, however, does not retell the common narrative of Swedish-American history that begins in the 1840s—the decade most often presented as the starting point for the history of the Swedish emigration to America—or in the year 1638, when the short-lived New Sweden colony (1638–55) was founded on the banks of the Delaware River. Doing so would not reflect the current state of the field. The scholarship on Swedish–American relations was long dominated by the study of migration and ethnicity. Today, the field is much broader and more diversified. Rather than simply reiterating the significant contributions made by scholars ever since the early twentieth century, this volume offers an alternative way of studying the history of transatlantic relations.

Swedish–American Borderlands brings together scholars from a wide range of disciplines within the humanities and social sciences in explorations of different, and sometimes unexpected, aspects of Swedish–American relations. We do so with two ambitions: to produce original research that suggests new ways of understanding its character, and to offer inspiration for further studies on transatlantic relations. By placing interactions, entanglements, and cross-border relations at the center of the analysis, the volume seeks to bridge disciplinary divides, joining a diverse set of scholars and scholarship in writing a new history of Swedish–American relations.

Introducing Swedish–American Borderlands

The study of Swedish–American relations has a long history that can be traced back to the late nineteenth century. The ways that scholars have explored the relations have changed significantly, in terms of the questions asked, the topics studied, and the analytic perspectives applied. It is possible to conceive of the field's historiographical paradigms in different, yet partly overlapping, themes: from the lay history writing among Swedish-American immigrants, over academic immigration research by American scholars, to emigration studies by historians in Sweden. Since the 1980s, the field has broadened considerably to include studies of, for example, ethnicity, popular culture, and cultural diplomacy, resulting in a diversified scholarship that has largely proceeded along separate trajectories.

The mass migration emerged as a topic of study when nineteenth-century Swedish Americans began documenting and writing their own history. A high degree of historical consciousness existed among the Swedish Americans in the second half of the nineteenth century. In 1869, the Lutheran Augustana Synod, the largest Swedish-American organization, appointed pastor Eric Norelius as its official "historiographer."[2] Many of their early publications focused on different settlements and organizations created by Swedish Americans. They were descriptive and compilatory in nature, usually keeping very close to the source materials.[3]

Early Swedish-American historiography strongly emphasized the positive character of the Swedish migrants, often exaggerating their contributions to the United States. This "filiopietistic" way of writing Swedish-American history sought to establish an early Swedish presence in North America, giving the group a privileged status. The leading author in this vein was Johan Enander, longtime editor of the prominent Chicago-based Swedish-language newspaper *Hemlandet*. Enander placed the beginning of both American and Swedish-American history in the eleventh century with the Viking journeys to North America, and objected to what he saw as "Catholic attempts" to suppress the fact of the Viking "discovery" of America in favor of that of Columbus.[4] The New Sweden colony became another central dimension of Swedish-American history. The Swedish-American filiopietists were eager to give the Swedes the status of an American colonial people, on the same level as the English and the Dutch, and to create a continuity between the Swedish colonists in seventeenth-century Delaware and the nineteenth-century immigrants in the Middle West.[5]

During the first part of the twentieth century, the filiopietistic history writers were replaced by professional historians. George Stephenson from the University of Minnesota is a good example. Born in a Swedish-American milieu in Iowa, he benefited from the cultural and linguistic backgrounds of his ethnic heritage as he pursued a successful academic career in major American universities. He established important contacts in Swedish universities, and his research was based on extensive archival work in both the United States and Sweden. Even though he seldom used the word *assimilation,* the larger story relayed through his work dealt with the conditions under which Swedes and Swedish Americans over the course of a couple of generations were integrated in American society, and how their ethnic distinctiveness gradually disappeared.[6]

It took time for academics in Sweden to begin studying the migration and the development of Swedish-American history. A few important works appeared in the interwar period, including the geographer Helge Nelson's important analyses of Swedish settlements in North America, and the church historian Gunnar Westin and the ethnographer Albin Widén's studies of Swedish-American religion and social life.[7] Nelson had also been a part of the government Commission on the Emigration, which between 1907 and 1913 published twenty-one volumes analyzing the reasons for the migration.[8] Swedish historians in Lund, Gothenburg, and in particular Uppsala took up the topic in earnest after 1960. For a decade and a half, they published a great number of articles and books, many emerging out of the "Emigration Project" at Uppsala University. Theories and methodologies from quantitative social history dominated—often inspired by the social sciences—and questions about the causes, volume, chronology, and composition of the migration were central.[9] With some exceptions, many of the questions emanated from Swedish scholarly perspectives. It is noticeable that American history and historiography played a relatively small role in this scholarship.

The Uppsala project broke important ground in its comprehensive approach to the study of the migration. Scholars were able to systematically use the extensive and unique Swedish population records, giving a rich and nuanced study of the Swedish migration to North America. One important conclusion of the project dealt with the significance of the myriad of migration links established across the Atlantic. These links sustained the migration over time, connecting particular sending and receiving areas even at times when the social and economic conditions that originally fueled the migration had improved.

Scholarship on the migration was empirically and analytically broadened in the mid-1980s, as scholars inspired by the cultural turn began to focus on the cultural dimensions of the migration, addressing questions of ethnicity and identity. While the Uppsala project had focused on social history, the creative literary and cultural output of Swedish Americans was now studied, not least through the Swedish-language press in the United States. Influenced by gender history, scholars also began studying the particular experiences of immigrant women.[10] In many studies, historians highlighted the question of what it meant to be Swedish American, both on an individual and a collective level, and explored the emergence of a distinctive Swedish-American culture. An important dimension of this process was the Swedish language in the United States, which often survived into the second generation but took traits influenced by English.[11]

The historian Kathleen Niels Conzen has noted that by the 1980s Scandinavian-American history had become a "victim of its own success." Its volume and strength had resulted in a feedback loop where the Scandinavian ethnic experience most often was treated within its own historiographical tradition. According to Conzen, there was a need to situate Scandinavian immigrants "within a more general context."[12] This long-overdue development had taken place by the turn of the twenty-first century. For example, scholars have begun to investigate the role of Swedish immigrants in the westward expansion. Studies have shown how Swedes who emigrated to the United States in the nineteenth century, and even into the early twentieth century, settled and farmed on Native American land.[13] In a similar way, the history of the New Sweden colony—which had long been framed as a form of "early migration"—has been reinterpreted in a global historical context of concurrent European colonialism. Instead of emphasizing Swedish agency in maintaining peaceful relations and trade, scholars have demonstrated the crucial role of Lenape Indians in upholding peace and stimulating knowledge exchange.[14] Finally, historians have also begun to situate Swedish immigrants in the larger American ethnoracial hierarchy, analyzing how Swedish Americans related to other European ethnic groups and African Americans in urban environments. Compared to other ethnic groups, Swedish immigrants—together with the Norwegian and Danish—benefited greatly from the developing pseudoscience of racial biology, which framed their "Nordic whiteness" as racially superior, thus awarding Swedes sociocultural privilege in American society.[15]

Since the 1980s, a diversification of the study of Swedish–American relations has taken place, with scholars following research trajectories unrelated to the history of migration. Influenced by international American

Studies research, cultural historians and political scientists have addressed the question of American influences in, or the "Americanization" of, Sweden. The presence of American culture in Sweden has been noteworthy, with U.S. literature, music, television programs, and movies exerting a considerable impact on the Swedish public, in particular in the post–World War II period.[16] Another research topic has been "images of" or narratives about the United States in Sweden—and, to a lesser extent, about Sweden in the United States. This line of inquiry has longer roots, reaching back to the first part of the twentieth century.[17] In art history, scholars have focused on the interchanges between the Swedish and American art scenes, studying the lives and careers of individual artists such as the painter Anders Zorn or the sculptor David Edstrom, or of the artistic exchanges between New York and Stockholm in the 1960s.[18]

Historians and sociologists have also studied the links between the reform movements in the two countries, particularly by focusing on the role of individuals, such as Gunnar and Alva Myrdal, and on the exchanges of ideas. Beginning in the 1930s, Sweden underwent major political and social transformations, linked to the long political dominance by the Social Democratic Party between 1932 and 1976. The emergence of the Swedish welfare state—or *folkhemmet,* the People's Home—was closely linked to a sense of modernity.[19]

As the United States became a dominant political and military power after World War II, it has become increasingly important for Swedish security and military policies to relate to the United States. Scholars have studied political and military relations between the countries during World War II and the Cold War, and Swedish–American relations during the Vietnam War.[20] The special position that Sweden had as a neutral country during most of the twentieth century has been of particular significance in this context. The experiences of both world wars left the country in a precarious situation vis-à-vis the United States, and historians have traced the Swedish efforts to improve relations after each war.[21]

It is clear from this historiographical overview that, over the last century and a half, there has developed a set of separate research traditions dealing with Swedish–American relations. By adopting borderlands as an analytic concept, we aim to bring together, and thus make use of, these different traditions in an analysis that centers on transatlantic crossings, convergences, and contacts.

Scholarship on borderlands has a long past in American Studies and American history. Although the concept in recent years has been applied to multiple studies of the Eurasian landmass—including the borders of the Russian, Ottoman, and Habsburg empires—borderlands scholarship remains historiographically anchored in the study of the early North American past.[22] By drawing from its extensive historiography, it is possible to isolate two different but complementary dimensions of the field, which we suggest can be used in analyzing histories of transatlantic relations: geographic and conceptual borderlands.[23]

The first dimension is rooted in the writings of Herbert E. Bolton (whose 1921 book *The Spanish Borderlands* was formative for the field of borderlands studies) and focuses on geographic spaces in the history of early America, mainly from the sixteenth-century arrival of European settlers to the consolidation of U.S. continental expansion in the mid- to late-nineteenth century.[24] While Bolton and his students focused their work on the northern edges of the Spanish Empire in America, scholars in more recent decades have also studied other cases where European settlers and Indigenous populations came into contact on the North American continent. In Jeremy Adelman and Stephen Aron's definition, borderlands are "the contested boundaries between colonial domains."[25] Within this tradition, borderlands are situated historically in time and space, connected to the boundaries and frontiers of the expanding Spanish, French, British, and U.S. empires, and negotiated by Indigenous populations in the face of dispossession and depopulation.[26]

The second tradition adopts borderlands as a way of studying cross-border relations, cultural encounters, and ideological exchanges. An early influence came from Chicano/a studies and Latino/a studies with the 1987 publication of Gloria Anzaldúa's *Borderlands/La Frontera: The New Mestiza.* In Anzaldúa's rendering, borderlands "are not particular to the [U.S.] Southwest." Rather, borderlands are "physically present wherever two or more cultures edge each other, where people of different races occupy the same territory, where under, lower, middle and upper classes touch, where the space between two individuals shrinks with intimacy."[27] Beginning in the 1990s, this tradition was also related to the growing interest in transnational history, which further contributed to the detachment of borderlands from its American geographic moorings. In the words of Pekka Hämäläinien and Samuel Truett, "What was once the marker of a particular place has become a way of seeing the world."[28] Following this line of thought, historian Kathleen DuVal has described borderlands as "a methodology" that "questions what happens when distinct societies rub against each other or contest lands in between."[29] This notion of borderlands can be used in the study of phenomena that are not necessarily situated geographically, such as studies of identity, ideas, or knowledge.

By drawing inspiration from these geographic and conceptual traditions, *Swedish-American Borderlands* seeks to reshape the study of Swedish–American relations. Our overall intention is not to contribute to the theoretical, methodological, or empirical discussion within borderlands studies, but to find new ways of writing histories of transatlantic relations. We thus use "relations" to outline our empirical field of study. It aims at opening up for studies of all sorts of phenomena—patterns, cultures, contacts, and ideas—that somehow involve the United States and a European country. Although transatlantic relations often involve individual movements and often have been preconditioned by pasts of settlement or migration, the study of relations does not always account for such movements. This, then, is in contrast to a borderlands analysis, where meetings, crossings, and entanglements are the center of attention. The volume's chapters adopt the borderlands concept in slightly different ways depending on the author's disciplinary tradition and chosen methodology. While some authors engage the concept theoretically, others draw inspiration from its interpretative potential. What unites all contributions is that the borderlands concept changes the analytic interpretation and thus the empirical and theoretical results of the studies. The book offers studies of borderlands as physical, social, and cultural spaces. It deals with life along borders and boundaries of the expanding American empire shaped by settler colonialism and Indigenous relations, it investigates cultural and religious dimensions in social interactions, and it addresses how patterns of transatlantic exchanges and entanglements have been shaped by a range of factors, including capitalism, consumerism, and geopolitics.

Although the book constitutes a significant departure in the study of Swedish-American history, it is important to acknowledge the ways that we build on intellectual traditions from previous scholarship, some of which dates back to the early twentieth century. Already in 1938, the Swedish scholar E. H. Thörnberg emphasized the close links between the two countries, discussing religious connections and the back-and-forth flow of ideas and persons. "A Sweden is growing in America. An America is growing in Sweden," Thörnberg argued, the first through the migration of Swedes to the United States and the second through religious and political thought. Transatlantic contacts, he wrote, had "advanced and cross-fertilized" the Swedish religious and temperance movements of the nineteenth century with "an extraordinary power," concluding that "innumerable threads of an American spirit and culture were woven into the tapestry of Swedish everyday life."[30] More recently, scholars influenced by transnational historiography have studied how conceptions of Swedish modernity have been shaped through—direct and indirect—cross-border relations between Sweden and the United States.[31] Expanding on these intellectual traditions through the notion of borderlands is a way of building on knowledge already gained and developing an analytic way of understanding Swedish–American relations.

Histories of Sweden and the United States

The consequences of the borderlands concept for Swedish–American relations are clear by looking at the history of individual movements between Sweden and the United States, the oldest and largest research tradition within the field. In Sweden, the "emigrant" and "the emigration" have occupied a central role in both the historiography and the popular imagination, while in the United States "the immigrant" and "immigration" have been fundamental building blocks for an understanding of American history and identity.[32] These concepts limit the migratory experience within the geographic borders of the sending or receiving country. The notion of borderlands changes our view of this aspect of Swedish–American relations. By rereading previous scholarship through the lens of borderlands, we suggest a different chronology and interpretation of the movement of Swedes to North America and of North Americans to

Sweden, adding settler–Indigenous relations, cross-cultural contacts, and processes of entanglement and liminality to our understanding of the nature of these processes. Our conceptualization also avoids the emigrant/immigrant dichotomy by emphasizing the significance of different kinds of individual mobility over a long period of time on both sides of the period traditionally studied in immigration/emigration history. In doing so, three categories of movements emerge as central: settlers, migrants, and sojourners.

Settlers

The first geographic Swedish–American borderland was located in the Delaware Valley. The region was home to the Lenape and Susquehannock, who lived in villages throughout the area of the Lenapewihittuck (nowadays called the Delaware River), growing corn and other crops. There was a steady stream of European colonizers during the seventeenth century, but the Lenape continued to dominate the region up to the 1681 formation and large-scale settlement of Pennsylvania. After the first survey of the Delaware River by Henry Hudson in 1608 and the brief Dutch settlement and whaling station of Swaanendal at the mouth of Delaware Bay in 1631, the Lenape encountered a succession of Swedish, Dutch, and English regimes. When the first Swedish settlers arrived in the spring of 1638, the Lenape had lived in close proximity to the English of the Virginia colony to the south and the Dutch of New Netherlands to the north for more than two decades.[33]

Led by the former director of New Netherlands, Peter Minuit, two ships outfitted by the New Sweden Company and backed by Swedish and Dutch financiers entered Delaware Bay and sailed up the Minquas Kill (now the Christina River). After having made a treaty with five Lenape sachems, the colonists sought to consolidate control of the area. The New Sweden colony was one dimension of the Swedish so-called Great Power Era of 1620 to 1720, when Sweden expanded geographically around the Baltic, participated in several wars on the European continent, and became recognized as a significant power in European politics. Although the Swedish Crown had settlement plans for the Delaware Valley, the colony's population never exceeded four hundred persons. This can be compared to the number of Lenape, which despite heavy losses from epidemics and smallpox counted at least four thousand by 1650. The settlers' contact with the homeland was weak. Only a dozen expeditions left Sweden during the colony's existence, two of which never reached America. The Swedish and Dutch financiers believed that the colony could bring Sweden into the growing transatlantic mercantilist trade in the seventeenth century, but it did not become the financial success its backers had hoped for. Given its small size, the colony became dependent on the Lenape and Susquehannock.[34]

When the colony fell to New Netherlands in 1655, most of its settlers remained in the area, eventually creating a noticeable presence. They built several churches in present-day Delaware, Pennsylvania, and New Jersey that, for seventy-five years beginning in 1696, were staffed by ministers from the Church of Sweden.[35] Even though the immediate imprints of New Sweden on North America were limited, H. Arnold Barton has observed that it did create a Swedish interest in North America, and that a number of accounts and reports from the colony were published in Sweden. In particular, the different Swedish church ministers were important in transmitting information and awareness of the colony back to Sweden.[36]

As the United States expanded its territorial claims westward across the continent during the nineteenth century, Swedes became one of many European and Anglo-American agents in the process of settlement. They moved to territories in the West and Midwest that had been newly incorporated by the United States, staking claims to land that was, or until very recently had been, dominated and controlled by Indigenous groups. These movements followed a settler-colonial logic. It was a form of Indigenous replacement, grounded in long-term elimination of Native Americans, that was premised on the idea of sovereign entitlement to "open" or "virgin" land where settlers could establish a new (or better) polity. In the definition of Lorenzo Veracini, whereas settlers are "*founders* of political orders . . . migrants can be seen as *appellants* facing a political order that is already constituted."[37] This logic was further stimulated by the 1862 Homestead Act, which Blake Bell aptly has described as "the first accommodating immigration law." It was a way for Congress to "build an agricultural nation by encouraging immigrants to settle the public lands of the United States."[38] As Harald Runblom has pointed out, the 1841 Preemption Act—which allowed the claim of federal land as individual property—and the Homestead Act were central "legal instruments by which many Scandinavians gained access to inexpensive land."[39]

A significant proportion of what previous scholars have described as "early immigrants" were such settlers. This comprises all of the "pioneer settlements" frequently taken as the alleged starting date of mass emigration, including Gustaf Unonius's Pine Lake settlement in Wisconsin in 1841, Per Cassel's settlement of New Sweden, Iowa, in 1845, and Erik Jansson's settlement of Bishop Hill, Illinois, in 1846, as well as settlements in the territories and states of Minnesota, Kansas, Iowa, and Nebraska.[40] Agricultural land claims continued to be the principal objective of Swedish migrants into the 1870s.

Most Swedish settlers had moved farther west from the 1840s to the 1860s, following the movement of the "frontier," and also relocating within the frontier areas to find better agricultural land. In the 1880s, immigration patterns started to shift, with urban migration increasingly replacing rural settlement. This period also accounted for the largest shift in the number of Swedes moving to the United States. Around 160,000 persons left Sweden in 1820–78, and a full 103,000 of these left during the famine years of 1868–73.[41] Looking at a rural area of Wisconsin, Hans Norman noted that the years 1868–69 constituted the largest in-migration to this agricultural district.[42] Indeed, as Karen V. Hansen has demonstrated, Swedish and other Scandinavian settlers continued the process of Indian dispossession well into the twentieth century. Similar to other Scandinavians, up until the 1920s Swedes took advantage of the 1887 Dawes Act that divided Indian reservation lands into individual allotments and made it available to white homesteaders, thus ensuring that Swedish settlers would continue to live lives close to, and entangled with, Indigenous communities.[43] Swedes were one of the European groups that benefited from homestead land, making them an agent in the long-term U.S. project of Native dispossession.

The period of Swedish settlement in the United States is thus long and partly overlapping with the subsequent era of migration, beginning in 1638 and continuing to the 1870s, in some areas even stretching into the 1920s. While many Swedes moved to North America as part of a settler-colonial logic, however, the vast majority of individuals relocated through another logic, namely, that of urban migration.

Migrants

The people of the mass migration were "the children of capitalism," to use the phrase by John Bodnar, and were part of the simultaneous movement of individuals that led to domestic urbanization in Sweden.[44] The logic of urban migration differed in significant ways from the settler-colonial logic of land taking: it was directed at industrial centers that provided greater opportunities for wage labor; it was considerably more voluminous; it consisted of a higher proportion of single men and women, rather than of whole families; and it was associated with a significant degree of return migration. By applying this distinction between settlement and migration, it becomes clear that Swedish migration began in the late 1870s, rather than in the 1840s, as is commonly argued. Nor did it end with the end of mass migration in the 1920s. It continues, we suggest, to the present time.

The late 1870s were crucial as the patterns of migration began to shift from primarily rural to increasingly urban, and it was a period that accounted for a significant and persistent surge in the sheer number of immigrants. From 1879 to 1930, roughly 962,000 Swedes immigrated to the United States, with more than 50 percent of those arriving between 1879 and 1893. The peak was reached in 1887 when nearly 46,000 Swedes immigrated.[45]

A number of urban areas received a particularly high number of Swedish immigrants, many in the Midwest, but also on the East and West Coasts. In 1910, Chicago, Minneapolis–St. Paul, and New York City were the three largest centers. Other cities where Swedish immigrants left significant imprints included Worcester, Massachusetts; Rockford and Moline, Illinois; Duluth, Minnesota; and Seattle and Tacoma, Washington.[46] These, and other American cities, offered Swedish immigrants a possibility to enter the growing American industrial economy and gave them experiences distinct from that of the settlers in rural areas. Certain industries, such as Washburn & Moe in Worcester or John Deere in Moline, became significant places of employment for Swedish workers. Although Swedish immigrants in general benefited from their background as white, Protestant, and Northern European, many were also found among the urban poor.[47]

Unlike the period from the 1820s to the 1920s, which has received significant scholarly attention, the Swedish emigration to the United States of the following century has so far not been the object of a coherent study. There are, however, data, provided by the U.S. Department of Homeland Security, that demonstrate that the migratory flows have continued after the 1920s. The migration changed both in volume and in kind, but—with exception for the 1930s—the annual number of Swedish migrants has been in the vicinity of, or sometimes higher than, the statistics from the pre-1878 era. While 6,500 people immigrated from Sweden in 1930–39 and 9,000 in 1940–49, the following two decades saw a significant increase to 21,400 and 18,800, respectively. After a slump in 1970–79, when 6,400 people immigrated, the numbers for the following three decades were rather stable at 10,100, 12,600, and 14,000. Although conclusive data for 2010–19 are not available, it appears that the numbers from the previous decades hold steady.[48]

There were, in other words, more persons from Sweden who obtained permanent residence in the United States between 1950 and 2000 than the total number of people who immigrated in 1820–67. The rate of migration was lower in the 1840s than in all but one decade in the post–World War II era. Indeed, with the important exception for the surge of migrants during the famine years of 1868–73, the yearly averages for the 1950s and 1960s match the number of immigrants during the period 1850–78 (an average of ca. 2,000 individuals per year for 1951–70, compared to ca. 2,400 per year for 1850–67/1874–78). Of course, owing to the smaller size of both the U.S. and Swedish populations in the nineteenth century, the earlier migration had a greater proportional impact on both societies. These figures do show, however, that throughout the twentieth and twenty-first centuries there has been a continuity in the flow of migrants from Sweden to the United States. The idea of a period of classic Swedish migration to America with some 1.3 million migrants between 1840 and 1930 formed by the Uppsala Emigration Project and popularized by scholars, authors, journalists, and others thus needs to be reconsidered and seen in a more extended perspective.

While most agricultural settlers remained on their American land claims throughout their lives, it was common for urban migrants to eventually return to Sweden. Between 1880 and 1930, the return rate for

Swedish immigrants was not quite 20 percent. Few of the Swedes who emigrated to America before 1880 returned to Sweden. When immigration became more urban and industrial, the frequency of return migration became increasingly connected to the state of the American economy, with the return rate rising during times of economic depression.[49] "As the trio of concerns of *journey, job hunt,* and *employment* became more predictable, [and] less dangerous," writes Mark Wyman, "the trip to America could then be viewed as something other than a lifetime change.... It was not so much the start of a new life as another step in the process of social mobility."[50] The increase in return migration was partly connected to the transition from sail ships to steamships, which began in the 1850s, picked up speed after the Civil War, and became the standard means of transportation in the mid-1870s.[51] Faster, cheaper, and more convenient transportation also encouraged repetitive migrations, where people made multiple crossings as workers on a transatlantic labor market. Of the passengers leaving Sweden on the Swedish American Line in 1922–23, close to 11 percent had previously been to America.[52]

Few studies of the return movement exist, but we do know that the returnees brought material wealth back to Sweden, mostly to buy property. A study of returnees to the Bjäre peninsula in southern Sweden observed notable social mobility, and the so-called Långasjö study, a remarkably complete compilation of the out- and in-migration from a parish in Småland, showed that the majority of the returnees sought to either buy land or expand the size of their ancestral farm. This strategy was successful, and significant capital was invested in land purchases in the parish.[53]

The impact of returnees on Swedish society was not only limited to social mobility or the purchase of land. A number of ideas and impulses, skills and know-how, were also brought back from America through the returnees. Technological inventions, techniques, and tools are some examples that became prominent in, for example, the agricultural sector. A number of Swedish businesses were established by Swedes who had spent significant time in the United States.[54] Some scholars have even characterized the baggage the returnees brought back as a different American "lifestyle," suggesting that the time in America had given them a different outlook on life. "There came with him something of a fresh breeze from the land of the West," a contemporary observer remarked about a Swedish-born minister from the Swedish-American Lutheran Augustana Synod who had returned to his birth country to pursue a career in the Church of Sweden.[55] The Swedish Americans became a well-known and often respected category of inhabitants in local communities in Sweden, together with the carpenter, schoolteacher, or local shopkeeper. The title "Swedish American" seems to have become an honorific, and it often followed the person until the end of her life, which many tombstone inscriptions testify to.[56]

The migration has left significant imprints on the two countries. The impact has, however, been asymmetrical; for Sweden, between a fourth and a fifth of the population was involved in the movements whereas in the United States the Swedes were dwarfed by much larger European groups. The character of the migration meant, though, that certain regions of both the United States and Sweden were particularly affected and drawn into the migration networks. In the United States, noticeable Swedish-American communities were established, particularly throughout the rural and urban Midwest and in the Pacific Northwest and, to a lesser degree, on the West Coast and in certain industrial areas in the Northeast.[57] Especially in the urban settlements, the group interacted and competed with other immigrants for a space in the American social fabric. By the end of the nineteenth century, however, these white, Protestant, Northern Europeans had found a privileged position in the American ethnoracial hierarchies. A rich ethnic life developed, based on cultural, religious, and educational institutions. Numerous personal and institutional ties were created, leaving a long-lasting network across the Atlantic.[58]

The Swedish-American community changed during the decades following World War II. The Swedish language gradually disappeared as a vernacular, and by the end of the twentieth century few members of the ethnic community spoke Swedish. It had instead assumed a symbolic role and had, like other Germanic languages in the United States, become a "heritage language."[59] Still, several million Americans continue to self-identify as Swedish Americans in the U.S. Census. The sense of American Swedishness today revolves around perceived Swedish cultural traditions, a sense and affirmation of a common Swedish-American history, and an interest in the culture of the ancestral homeland. A particularly vibrant and widespread area of contact is genealogy, where ancestral tourism to Sweden for decades has played an important part.[60]

The smaller flows of migration after World War II have resulted in new Swedish-American organizations. The most notable is the Swedish Women's Educational Association (SWEA), which was established in Los Angeles in 1979 and today has more than seven thousand members in seventy-two chapters in the United States and around the world. SWEA serves as a network for Swedish women and emphasizes the use of the Swedish language and the promotion of Swedish culture. Its members are often well-educated professionals, who focus on modern Sweden and in many ways work in the area of public diplomacy.[61] The contemporary migration patterns are often less permanent than earlier movements, as many relocate for shorter periods of time and move back and forth across the Atlantic. In that respect, the migrants today resemble and sometimes overlap with the final category of movements between Sweden and the United States, the sojourners.

Sojourners

Not everyone who made the journey across the Atlantic can be labeled settlers or migrants. There were also people who traveled for other reasons, such as leisure, education, science, or business. Similar to the patterns of settlement and migration, most of these sojourners have traveled westward from Sweden, even though a significant number of Americans have traveled east to Sweden as well, especially since the mid-twentieth century.[62]

The sojourners include Swedes who have traveled to the United States since the late eighteenth century to observe, analyze, and report on conditions in the New World. One of the earliest travelers from Sweden was the botanist and naturalist Pehr Kalm, who visited North America in 1749–51. One of Carl Linnaeus's students at Uppsala University, his task was to describe and collect plants from the New World. His journey is described in three influential volumes titled *En resa till norra America* published in 1753–61 by the Royal Swedish Academy of Sciences. It was also translated (in parts) into English—published in London in 1772 as *Travels into North America*—as well as in German and Dutch, and has become a part of the canon of European accounts of North America from the eighteenth century.[63]

A significant proportion of all Swedes who left for the United States in the first half of the nineteenth century were sojourners. In his summary account of "early migration" between 1820 and 1844, which only amounted to some 563 recorded passengers, Sten Carlsson noted that "many of these Swedes came for the purpose of tourism, business or studies and were not emigrants in the true sense of the term."[64] The most prominent example of these nineteenth-century sojourners is the celebrated author and feminist Fredrika Bremer, who spent two years in the United States and Cuba between 1849 and 1851, where she met with leading American intellectuals such as Ralph Waldo Emerson and Nathaniel Hawthorne. Her book *Hemmen i den nya verlden (The Homes of the New World)* from 1853 provided a generally positive view of the social and political conditions in the new republic. The exception was slavery, which Bremer condemned.[65] It was immediately translated to English and in fact appeared in London and New York a few weeks before the Swedish edition was released in Stockholm. Its impact was great, and Lars Wendelius has observed that "no Swedish account of the United States is better known."[66] A persistent testament to Bremer's impact in the United States is Bremer County, Iowa, which received its name during her American travels in 1850—despite the fact that the author herself never visited the area.[67]

After the end of the Civil War, an increasing number of Swedes traveled for shorter or longer stays in the United States. A number of these individuals had an occupation, education, socioeconomic status, and—most important—writing skills that enabled them to not only observe but also publicly report on their American experiences. Quite a few of them were journalists. According to H. Arnold Barton, these sojourners, including the growing number of Swedish Americans who could afford the time and money to visit Sweden, came to express the "growing cleavage between those who left the old homeland and those who stayed."[68] These Swedish and American observers' appreciation and critique of the United States and Sweden evolved over time.

In 1860s and 1870s, most Swedish writers, such as Hugo Nisbeth and Isidor Kjellberg, had a positive view of the United States, providing added justification for emigration and critique of the conditions in Sweden.

Moving in the opposite direction, Swedish American travelers to Sweden, including Hans Mattson in the 1860s and Ernst Skarstedt in the 1880s, reported indignantly about Swedish class society, institutions, traditions, and the monarchy. The period 1889–1903 was, according to Barton, marked by contrasting views by Swedish visitors to America. As most prominently highlighted by the 1889 visit of theologian and free church leader Paul Peter Waldenström, many of these observers were critical of American commercialization and mass culture, and associated the country with immorality and frivolity. The first two decades of the 1900s were marked by antiemigration debates in Sweden. Reflecting the notion that Sweden could learn from the United States in order to modernize and thus stop the flow of emigration, the majority of Swedish sojourners showed a high estimation of American life and society.[69]

Marked by the rise of the United States as a global power after World War I and the end of the mass migration in the 1920s, there was a shift in the pattern of and response to transatlantic sojourning. Swedish travelers paid less attention to Swedish Americans, who, in the words of Barton, "in Swedish eyes were increasingly regarded as relics of the past, even more out of touch with modern Sweden as the years went by." Instead, these observers discussed American economic and social life as well as mass culture, reflecting doubts that Sweden still had something to learn from the United States. It was also a period when all the more high-profile Swedes traveled to America, including Archbishop Nathan Söderblom in 1924 and Crown Prince Gustaf Adolf and Crown Princess Louise in 1926 and 1938.[70] In the eyes of official Sweden, Swedish Americans had been a national problem but were now becoming a foreign asset, providing not only a historical and cultural but also a purportedly biological connection to Sweden.[71]

Beginning in the 1920s, but more intensely after 1930, observers from the United States took a considerable interest in conditions in Sweden. Coverage of Sweden's social modernization spread through American journals, spurred by the 1932 election of a Social Democratic government led by Per Albin Hansson. The most consequential of these writings was *Sweden: The Middle Way* from 1936 by the journalist Marquis Childs.[72] Childs had traveled in Sweden, and the book presented to an American audience the attempts that had been made in Sweden both to combat the effects of the Depression and to modernize society in general. Its central message was that the country had found a golden "middle way" between capitalism and communism, and described a situation where "[t]he state, the consumer, and the producer have intervened to make capitalism 'work' in a reasonable way for the greatest good of the whole nation."[73] Sweden became known as a social laboratory, attracting visitors interested in learning about the reforms in the country. There was a positive image of Sweden as a country that had solved many social and economic problems, especially in the 1950s and 1960s. Critical voices also emerged from American conservatives, who branded Sweden as a socialist country with high rates of alcoholism and suicide.[74] More attention was paid to Sweden in the American public debate than to other small European nations, and the country turned into an argument adopted by both liberals and conservatives in the United States.

Travel between the two countries was facilitated in 1915 by the establishment of the Swedish America Line (Sverige Amerika Linien), which made it possible to travel directly from Gothenburg to New York. It resulted in increased tourism between Sweden and the United States, especially after World War II. Many of these travelers were Swedish Americans going on summer visits to friends and relatives. The direct connection also facilitated group travel. The three journeys in the 1920s and 1930s of children of members of the Swedish-American fraternal organization the Vasa Order of America to "the country of their fathers and mothers" received a great deal of attention in Sweden.[75]

Following the end of World War II travel resumed, and the numbers of travelers increased significantly.[76] The coming of commercial air traffic revolutionized the possibilities to travel. In 1946, Scandinavian Airlines System (SAS) was formed, through which Denmark, Norway, and Sweden joined forces. The United States was a key market from the beginning, and on September 17, only six weeks after the pan-Scandinavian agreement had been concluded, the somewhat dramatic inaugural SAS flight for New York's LaGuardia airport took off from Stockholm, stopping in Copenhagen and Gander, Newfoundland, on the way. The arrival of the *Dan Viking* was celebrated with a banquet at New York's Waldorf Astoria with Trygve Lie, the Norwegian-born Secretary General of the United Nations as the guest of honor. Soon there were daily connections between

Stockholm and New York.[77] In 1954, SAS was the first airline to establish a much-talked-about transpolar route, connecting Copenhagen and Los Angeles; in 1964, traffic to Chicago began, and in 1966 Seattle—also using the transpolar route—was added to the list of the airline's U.S. destinations.[78] As air travel became an increasingly affordable alternative to the ocean liners, travel agencies and ethnic associations began to organize transatlantic charter travels, partly to bypass air-traffic regulations. An example of highly publicized charter tours were the 1950s and 1960s family visits to Sweden by the Chicago building contractor and millionaire Ragnar Benson.[79] The increased frequency of sojourning in the postwar period was accompanied by a steady stream of travel accounts being published by Swedish writers.[80]

The growth of Swedish tourism to America, and vice versa, after World War II has added a special layer to Swedish–American relations. In the decade between 1954 and 1963, 118,000 Swedes visited the United States, the majority of whom were so-called Temporary Visitors for Pleasure. Travel from the United States to Sweden also increased. In what appears to be a very optimistic estimate—one that likely did not differentiate between tourists, business travelers, and return migrants—the semiofficial Swedish Tourist Traffic Association suggested that more than one million Americans had traveled to Sweden between 1914 and 1963.[81] Although the number should not be taken at face value, it is clear that there was a significant movement of individuals for nonimmigrant purposes throughout the twentieth century, and it accelerated after 1945.

Although statistics are hard to come by regarding American visits to Sweden, a sizable number of Swedish Americans who travel have, since at least the 1960s, visited Sweden for genealogical purposes. Looking at statistics from recent years, visitors from the United States were reported to be the fourth-largest group of international tourists in Sweden in 2018. It is not known how many of these traveled for ethnic reasons, but it is reasonable to assume that they constitute a significant proportion.[82] The volume of Swedish visitors to the United States has also soared during the last decades. Between 2008 and 2017, Swedes accounted for an average of 536,000 arrivals to the United States under nonimmigrant status, the peak being reached in 2015 with 624,000 arrivals (these figures, however, only account for the number of total entries and not for the number of individuals, which is lower). The United States, and in particular New York City and Miami, has for years been among the top foreign destinations for Swedish tourists.[83]

Unlike the settlers or most of the migrants discussed earlier, the traveling of the sojourners is part of a network of exchanges where individuals move back and forth as easily as travel technologies allow. Their volume has been significant. In 1887, the peak year of Swedish mass emigration to the United States, the number of migrants represented slightly more than 1 percent of the Swedish population. As a comparison, the number of Swedish arrivals in the United States in 2015 amounted to more than 6 percent of the population. Over the past century, sojourning has thus become an increasingly important part of Swedish–American relations and a notable dimension of the individual movements between the two countries.

Movements and Circulations: New Histories of Transatlantic Relations

The chapters of *Swedish–American Borderlands* offer studies that move across four centuries and two continents. The volume is structured into two parts, one grounded in borderlands as primarily geographically situated, and the other based in borderlands as chiefly conceptually oriented. The first part of the volume, "Across Waters and Lands," builds on the geographic tradition of borderlands studies and contains studies of settlement histories and of Swedish–Indigenous contacts. Attesting to the impact of the concept in drawing together seemingly diverse topics and disciplines, it also includes chapters on migration, jazz music, genealogy, academic exchanges, and industrial design. This section thus centers various dimensions of movement between Sweden and the United States, placing settlers, migrants, and sojourners at the forefront of the studies. The volume's second part, "Exchanges and Entanglements," is grounded in the conceptual approach to borderlands studies and analyzes how ideas, cultures, knowledge, and images have circulated across the Atlantic. The chapters in this part cover studies of visions of the New Sweden colony, cookbooks and heritage language, the concept of political correctness, architecture and design, Civil War reenactments, heritage tourism, movie directors Ingmar Bergman and Michelangelo Antonioni, and the memorialization of Civil War engineer John Ericsson. It focuses, in other words, on dimensions of transatlantic circulations.

The unexpected combination of contributions shows the width of the field, but also results in an understanding that differs from previous attempts at providing an overview of Swedish–American relations.[84] Although migration is—and will always remain—a major aspect of the field, it is no longer a dominant theme. Rather, what emerges is a notion of two countries that have grown close by way of heterogenous patterns of interpersonal contacts. It paints a picture of a long history of interactions where people, for different reasons, with different objectives, and through different means, have moved back and forth across the Atlantic, carrying with them both tangible and intangible resources.

Although governmental and diplomatic work has been important, the volume presents a set of relations that have not primarily been shaped by state agents or agencies but rather by organizations, associations, businesses, and individuals. Most important, a common theme in all chapters is the transatlantic movement and mobility of individuals that has been closely associated with the cross-border circulation of knowledge, ideas, and culture.

Collectively, the contributors to *Swedish–American Borderlands* demonstrate that individual movements have been significant, but also that their importance and effects have shifted. The chapters should not, in other words, be understood as moving progressively from a geographic conception of borderlands toward the study of borderlands as pure metaphor. On the contrary, the individual chapters demonstrate the intricate ways in which the movement of individuals have always been connected to circulation. Notions of spatial attachment might therefore be most productively thought about in terms of foreground and background; while geographic borderlands center on land in a topographical sense, conceptual borderlands are set against a spatial backdrop. They are not opposite to one another, but are rather set on a sliding scale.

An illustration of the former is Karen V. Hansen's study of Swedish settlements on Native American reservations in North Dakota, while two examples of the latter are Franco Minganti's exploration of postwar kitchen design and Maaret Koskinen's analysis of the works of directors

Ingmar Bergman and Michelangelo Antonioni. Movement and circulation are significant in all of these studies, but where Hansen puts movement in the analytic foreground and circulation in the background, Minganti's and Koskinen's studies do the opposite. The overarching result about the importance of movements and circulations, present to various degrees in all chapters of the book, can be refined into a more fine-grained set of results. We will detail these results through the various kinds of movements (settlement, migration, and sojourning) that have shaped and informed Swedish–American relations, and the different sets of circulated visions (of the past and of the future) that have become entangled across the Atlantic.

The first aspect of movement deals with *settlers*. While there have been many historical studies of the New Sweden, we know less about the ways that Swedish authorities and travelers thought about the colony and its geographic place in the world. This question is explored in a chapter that looks closely at colonial maps and travel narratives, showing that New Sweden was imagined simultaneously through notions of territorial affinity with and geographic distance from Sweden. These dual conceptualizations affected the colonial administration's work, as well as the experiences of the individuals who traveled to and lived in the colony. While New Sweden is the most obvious example of how Swedes through colonial settlement encountered, and lived lives entwined with, Indigenous populations, these processes continued as long as into the first decades of the twentieth century. Complicating the narrative about Swedish emigration to America, one chapter shows that Swedish settlers made use of the 1887 Dawes Act to homestead Native American reservation lands into the 1920s, long after the supposed "closing" of the frontier, so famously proposed by Frederick Jackson Turner. Being neighbors on the reservations, Swedes, Dakotas, and the Arikara-Mandan-Hidatsa lived lives that were socially and economically entangled yet profoundly unequal, their everyday proximity forcing them to continuously negotiate each other's traditions of culture, religion, and language.

Like settlement, *migration*—the second aspect of movement—is a collective process that involved economic, demographic, and juridical dimensions, but that also had a significant impact on the lived experiences of individuals. It might be, as one chapter argues, that the crossing of borders, the oft-resulting feelings of in-betweenness, and the will to ground the memory of one's life in certain places are central dimensions of the migratory experience. It is proposed by one of the volume's contributors that the concepts of liminality and topogeny go a long way in explaining the anxiety, loss, longing, belonging, and becoming of many Swedish-American immigrants as they moved across geophysical spaces. As discussed in another chapter on legends from the American West, these movements also had a generational effect. The stories of the migrant's passages and boundaries have lived on in local lore. The very act of migration itself, as well as the subsequent efforts to make sense of it, have had ramifications in the twentieth and twenty-first centuries. This is the case in chapters that deal with Swedish-American genealogy—which is grounded in tracing migrant ancestors—contemporary heritage tourism to Midwestern Swedish pioneer settlements, the biographical promotion of migrant heroes, and the linguistic hybridity displayed in cookbooks. Although settlers or migrants were not themselves active agents in most of these processes, their movements have conditioned the possibilities and limitations of latter-day heritage work.

The majority of the volume's contributions deal with movements of a less permanent nature. These *sojourners* make the transatlantic crossing for shorter periods of stay and then return (often repeatedly), carrying impulses and ideas across the Atlantic. While immigrants can be credited with creating long-lasting transnational bonds, many sojourners have, through their professional occupations, had a significant and immediate impact on cultural, economic, or political life.

Examples of the impact of sojourners are provided in two chapters that study mid-twentieth-century industrial design and welfare housing, and the movement of academic scholars. The travels of American architects and designers to Sweden, and vice versa, were significant for both countries' urban and industrial modernization. The decades from the 1930s through the 1960s were particularly vital in this respect, marked by intense conversations and exchanges between important figures in Swedish and American industry. While advocates such as Catherine Bauer in the 1930s gathered knowledge about public housing in Sweden, industrial designers like Johan Munck in the 1950s developed the work on ergonomic industrial appliances through visits to the United States. The far-reaching impact of individual sojourning is also exemplified by the U.S. stints of Swedish students and scholars. Their periods at American university and college campuses have been consequential on both an individual and an institutional level, wielding a noticeable impact on the social sciences and (although to a somewhat lesser extent) the humanities in Sweden. Through their extended experiences of American academia and social life, individuals such as Olof Palme, Gunnar Myrdal, and Alva Myrdal became carriers of U.S. experiences that came to reverberate in Swedish political life.

Sojourning appears as a critical aspect of the spread of ideas and cultures that over time have grown to become naturalized in Sweden, to the effect that they sometimes have been brought back to the United States. This is exemplified by the diverse topics of jazz music, first introduced in Sweden in the 1920s, and the concept of political correctness, which found its way into the Swedish public in the 1990s. In both of these cases, individual sojourning was key for the transfer of these phenomena and, in both cases, it set in motion a process of transatlantic discussions and cultural exchanges that is still today ongoing. Further examples of the long-term impact of sojourning are the chapters on the twenty-first-century tourism in the small Illinois town of Bishop Hill, and the trajectory of the riding whip of nineteenth-century Modoc leader Captain Jack. The history of Bishop Hill, established in 1846 by Swedish settlers, demonstrates how a seemingly localized story is bound up in intricate transatlantic networks. A central figure in the 1960s heritage preservation of the town was Olof Isaksson, the director of the Swedish National History Museum. Similarly, while the whip of Captain Jack is inseparable from the discussions and discourses about Native dispossession and Swedish and Swedish-American fascination with the American West, its transfer to Sweden is likewise conjoined with the acts of Swedish traveler Hugo Nisbeth who carried the whip across the Atlantic.

In some instances, sojourners do not act individually but become agents in larger networks of exchanges. One such case is the twentieth-century history of Swedish-American genealogy. The search for migrant ancestors developed during the twentieth century through a network of individuals who were motivated by a wide range of interests, including religion, academic scholarship, the local heritage movement, local politics, and tourism. Together, these agents developed practices and cultures—including the production of registers, microfilms, and archives—that have served the writing of family history. An unexpected case of the impact of networks is U.S. Civil War reenactments in Sweden. Gathering hundreds of Swedes each year, these reenactments are connected on cultural and personal levels to their more established American counterparts, developed through both individual interactions and social-media exchanges.

The reasons for and consequences of the individual movements of settlers, migrants, and sojourners can be explored through two types of circulations. These circulations are set in a temporal nexus centering on the ways that individuals have envisioned a common past and a shared future. The first aspect, *visions of the past,* includes studies of cultural heritage. Memories of the mass migration constitute a prominent aspect of the ways in which Swedes and Americans have looked to their shared past. The will and need to make sense of their movement to the United States was manifest already among the immigrants themselves, as they negotiated a place in the new land. As immigrants grew increasingly removed from the experience of migration, the stories of emigration and immigration, of overland travels by train and on foot, were relayed across generations. By using common motifs and story patterns—such as narratives of disembarkation, of transplantation, and of exposure to the American landscapes—immigrants and their descendants negotiated their encounter with unfamiliar lands, and their feelings of vulnerability.

During the twentieth century, memories of the immigration were slowly but steadily transformed into cultural memories, detached from immediate experiences and instead relayed through institutionalized practices and cultural scripts. Today the most widespread practice through which these memories have been nurtured is genealogy, which has grown enormously popular since the 1960s. For at least half a century, the culture of tracing ancestors in Sweden or the United States with deeper roots and more branches of the proverbial family tree has produced a sense of ancestral relations with a significant grassroots impact. The grassroots awareness of Swedish immigration history is actively nurtured in sites of rural Swedish settlement, such as Lindstrom, Minnesota; Lindsborg, Kansas; or Bishop Hill, Illinois. By tracing the heritage history of the latter, one chapter demonstrates that as tourists today visit the town, only a fraction of the fraught history of the religious settlement in Bishop Hill seeps through. Engulfed in a tourist economy that feeds on a lure of purportedly "simpler times," the ethnic heritage of the community is offered for noncontroversial consumption together with the offer of dining and shopping.

Language and food culture are important components in ethnic everyday heritage and have been crucial to the maintenance of Swedishness in the United States. By analyzing recipes in Swedish-American cookbooks from the 1930s to the 1990s, one chapter shows that although the Swedish language has more or less disappeared as a vernacular among Swedish Americans, it has continued to fulfill significant roles as a heritage language. The linguistic and culinary heritage represented through the cookbooks has, however, not been static, but is dependent on new impulses from Sweden and Swedish food culture.

Some visions of the past concern histories that have unfolded on the North American continent but have been transposed to Sweden through interpersonal contacts. One such case is Captain Jack's riding whip, which ended up in the National Museum of Natural History in Stockholm in 1874. The trajectory of the whip, from the western United States to the Swedish capital, provides the focal point for investigating how knowledge about Swedish–Indian encounters and Native American history evolved through late-nineteenth-century transatlantic exchanges. Another example is the seemingly quintessential American memory of the Civil War. Through reenactments during the last decades, a number of Swedes have reached a sense of proximity to this major event in the U.S. past, at the same time as their geographic and cultural distance has enabled them to represent contemporary Swedish ideals. What emerges are Civil War reenactments where notions of race are seemingly unimportant, but where issues of gender equality—being a prominent theme in Swedish social and political life—heavily informs the performance of history.

The ways in which memory is shaped by the different contemporary contexts of Sweden and the United States is also discussed in relation to another Civil War history, concerning the engineer John Ericsson. The legacy of the inventor of the Union Army's ship the *Monitor* has been the object of many commemorative activities on both sides of the

Atlantic, resulting in monuments and memorials in Stockholm; Gothenburg; Washington, D.C.; and Brooklyn, New York. Centering on two biographies published shortly after Ericsson's death in 1889, one chapter shows that although Ericsson's life was rather differently framed in each country—highlighting his military achievements in the United States and his social mobility in Sweden—the different narrative strategies display a similar image of Ericsson as an individual embodying an entwined transatlantic life.

The second type of circulation concerns *visions of the future.* This category involves notions about technological, cultural, and political modernity, which forms a significant aspect of the twentieth-century relations of the two countries and shapes ways in which people have envisioned development and progress. An example is the case of mid-twentieth-century streamline design, ergonomic design, and welfare housing. The ideological optimism about technological innovation, urban development, and the accompanying transformation of social life affected areas far outside the Swedish-American nexus. A chapter on interior design in late-1950s Italy, specifically centering on the kitchen, shows that during the Cold War era both Swedish and American designs and design ideas were negotiated through specific Italian cultural needs and traditions. Rather than directly importing kitchen designs from either country, the 1950s Italian kitchen was imagined through an amalgamation of both Swedish and American notions of modernity.

In the mid-twentieth century, ideas about technological modernity were coupled with representations of cultural modernity. Music and film were two notable areas where American and Swedish cultural influences mixed and merged. One example is the transfer and transformation of jazz music in Sweden between the 1920s and 1960s. Initially considered a "fad," or even a "disease," by Swedish cultural critics, jazz eventually developed into a hybrid genre shaped by both American and Swedish influences. In a chapter exploring the work of Ingmar Bergman and Michelangelo Antonioni, the entanglement of ideas about what constituted modern culture in the postwar period is analyzed from the vantage point of Bergman's film *Tystnaden* (The Silence) and Antonioni's *La Notte* (The Night). As part of a late-twentieth-century auteur culture, both directors worked and were critically received in a European-American context. Both filmmakers, moreover, also portrayed women, sex, and urban cityscapes as displays of what it meant to be modern.

Some visions of the future were not primarily expressed through material renderings or concrete images of modernity, but rather through hopes and prospects for different sets of futures. One aspect of this future vision has been the production of knowledge, something that in Swedish–American relations predates the founding of the United States. Already the seventeenth-century colonizers of New Sweden were occupied with making sense of the spatial relation between the colony and the homeland. Swedish officials conceptualized New Sweden as being in "another world," yet understood the colony as their rightful possession and as a part of the Swedish realm. A much more recent form of knowledge production that also had the effect of pulling the Swedish and American imaginary closer together is twentieth-century academic mobility. As the twentieth century progressed, the United States became the most important academic reference point for Sweden.

Yet another aspect associated with the prospect of better futures concerns participation in politics. An important dimension of political life is the question of economic and political autonomy, and its uneven historical distribution. The early-twentieth-century Swedish settlements on Native American reservation lands in North Dakota were connected to a Swedish prospect of economic incorporation. Unlike their Dakota and Arikara-Mandan-Hidatsa neighbors on whose land they lived, the Swedes also had a clear path to U.S. citizenship. This granted Swedish settlers a privileged position in their chosen homeland. Today, a significant dimension of political visions for the future relates to the entanglements of Swedish and American far-right movements. An expression of these ideological exchanges is the notion of political correctness, which for the last twenty-five years has been a consequential concept in politics and public debate. As a tool by which right-wing and far-right movements have challenged—or even attacked—liberal society, today it serves to connect populist groups and individuals on both sides of the Atlantic.

There are several themes and topics not covered in this volume that we believe would be productively studied through a borderlands lens. They include food culture, where the American and international career of chef Marcus Samuelsson would provide a fitting case, but also studies of Nordic(-American) cuisine in general, the U.S.-stimulated latte coffee culture of the post-1990s, and the twenty-first-century increase in American-style food trucks and hamburger joints in Stockholm. Other topics deal with fashion studies that, beyond well-known global brands such as H&M, also concern smaller brands such as Lexington (founded in Sweden) and Gant (founded in the United States but sold to Swedish owners in the 1990s), both of which have reached international success through adaptations of New England–style designs. And sports, finally, where Swedish and American athletes have practiced, competed, and lived their private and professional lives in both countries, such as Swedish athletes Ingemar Johansson (boxing), Björn Borg (tennis), Peter Forsberg (ice hockey), Annika Sörenstam (golf), Zlatan Ibrahimović (soccer), and Armand Duplantis (pole vault), but also a trove of lesser-known U.S. athletes who have become local stars for Swedish ice hockey and basketball teams.

There has been a multitude of transatlantic religious contacts between Sweden and the United States, with a lively exchange of religious ideas across the Atlantic— within the Lutheran denominations on both sides of the Atlantic but in particular among the "free" or nonconformist churches that arose as alternatives to the Church of Sweden. This also includes the growth of Pentecostalism and Mormonism in Sweden. Another area of inquiry would be the music industry, with examples such as contemporary EDM (Electronic Dance Music), embodied by the success of Swedish House Mafia and Avicii, but also Swedish *dansbandsmusik,* which ever since the 1950s has been a widely popular style of American country-influenced rock that in some cases has been transposed to the United States through productions made in Nashville, Tennessee. Many other examples of both popular and highbrow culture, including film literature, theater, and arts, could also be productively included.

Prominent aspects of contemporary Swedish–American relations would also be suitable cases to study through the borderlands concept. Two examples include the discussion about and policies intended to combat global warming, highlighted by the 2019 Atlantic crossing of youth climate activist Greta Thunberg, and the transatlantic ramifications of both the Black Lives Matter movement and the aftermath of the killing of George Floyd in Minneapolis in May 2020. Another aspect concerns practices connected to the development and culture of the Internet, digital technologies, and social media in the twenty-first century. Although only some of these areas are discussed in this volume, all of these themes occupy the broad landscape that constitutes transatlantic Swedish–American relations and could be explored through a borderlands perspective.

A couple of general observations can be made about the empirical contributions to the volume. It is possible to detect a temporal development across the chapters. While the studies covering the seventeenth to the nineteenth centuries emphasize how circulations of knowledge and ideas are dependent on geographic situatedness—linked to settler-colonial land claims—the studies that focus on how different forms of practices and technologies contribute to these circulations are all set in the twentieth or twenty-first century. This shift is, in a sense, not very surprising. The importance of individual transatlantic movement also means that we need to acknowledge the development of technologies of Atlantic crossings. This includes the changing nature of individual travel (sailing ships, steamships, and airplanes), communication technologies (mail service, telegraph, telephone, and the Internet), and popular media (newspapers, literature, television, music, film, and social media).

Rather than studying Swedish–American borderlands as an existing place or site, the volume demonstrates how borderland relations have been created by individuals and groups active in a transatlantic nexus. Together, they have both made and manifested the proximity and distance between the countries—socially, culturally, politically, intellectually, and technologically. It is clear that borders are meaningful, perhaps particularly for political relations, but *Swedish–American Borderlands* shows that the borders between Sweden and the United States have not been lines of separation and containment but rather of porous contact zones, resulting in interactions and transgressions. This is largely a result of long-standing amicable and privileged relations between Sweden and the United States; compared to many other European countries, there have been few overt obstacles—of race, political regimes, or warfare—preventing the movements or circulations between the two countries.

The longtime perspective, spanning the seventeenth century to the present, shows the necessity of thinking about contemporary Swedish–American relations with a temporal depth. It is overtly deterministic to claim that old relations beget new, but it has clearly been the case that new relations have benefited from the relations of the past. The geographic distance between the two countries has meant that the awareness of historical borderlands has not been a given. This awareness has thus been actively produced through the hundreds of thousands of individuals who have traversed the Atlantic, or who have made efforts to initiate and uphold long-distance contacts. The volume's broad pallet of studies paints a picture of the vastness of these transatlantic relations, showing the great impact of settlement and migration, the significant role played by sojourners, and the entangled visions about the past and the future produced through cross-border exchanges. By treating borderlands as spaces of mutuality, our understanding of Swedish–American relations has become both empirically and analytically more complex and encompassing.

Notes

1. Dag Blanck and Adam Hjorthén, "Transnationalizing Swedish-American Relations: An Introduction to the Special Forum," *Journal of Transnational American Studies* 7, no. 1 (2016).

2. *Protokoll hållet vid Skandinaviska Ev. Lutherska Augustana-Synodens 10:e årsmöte* (Chicago, 1869), 17.

3. Robert Grönberger, *Svenskarne i St. Croix-dalen, Minnesota* (Minneapolis: Stats Tidningens Tryckeri, 1879); Eric Johnson and C. F. Peterson, *Svenskarne i Illinois: Historiska anteckningar* (Chicago: W. Williamson, 1880); Eric Norelius, *De svenska lutherska församlingarnas och svenskarnas historia i Amerika* (Rock Island, Ill.: Augustana Book Concern, 1890).

4. Johan Enander, *Nordmännen i Amerika eller Amerikas upptäckt: Historisk afhandling med anledning af Columbiafesterna i Chicago 1892–1893* (Rock Island, Ill.: Lutheran Augustana Book Concern, 1893).

5. Amandus Johnson, *The Swedish Settlements on the Delaware: Their History and Relation to the Indians, Dutch, and English,* 2 vols. (Philadelphia: University of Pennsylvania, 1911).

6. George M. Stephenson, *The Religious Aspects of Swedish Immigration: A Study in Immigrant Churches* (Minneapolis: University of Minnesota Press, 1932).

7. Helge Nelson, *Nordamerika: Natur, bygd och svenskbygd,* 2 vols. (Stockholm: Bergvall, 1926); Gunnar Westin, *Emigranterna och kyrkan: Brev från och till svenskar i Amerika 1849–1892* (Stockholm: Svenska kyrkans diakonistyrelses bokförlag, 1932); Albin Widén, *Svenskar som erövrat Amerika* (Stockholm: Nordisk rotogravyr, 1937).

8. See Gustav Sundbärg, *Emigrationsutredningen: Betänkande i utvandringsfrågan och därmed sammanhängande spörsmål* (Stockholm: P. A. Norstedt & Söner, 1913).

9. Harald Runblom and Hans Norman, eds., *From Sweden to America: A History of the Migration* (Minneapolis: University of Minnesota Press, 1976).

10. Anna Williams, *Skribent i Svensk-Amerika: Jakob Bonggren, poet och journalist* (Uppsala: Avd. för litteratursociologi, 1991); Ann-Sofie Ohlander, "Utvandring och självständighet: Några synpunkter på den kvinnliga emigrationen från Sverige," *Historisk tidskrift* 103, no. 2 (1983): 140–74; Joy Lintelman, "'On My Own': Single, Swedish, and Female in Turn-of-the-Century Chicago," in *Swedish-American Life in Chicago: Cultural and Urban Aspects of an Immigrant People, 1850–1930,* ed. Philip J. Anderson and Dag Blanck (Urbana: University of Illinois Press, 1992), 89–99; H. Arnold Barton, *A Folk Divided: Homeland Swedes and Swedish Americans, 1840–1940* (Carbondale: Southern Illinois University Press, 1994).

11. Williams, *Skribent i Svensk-Amerika*; Nils Hasselmo, *Amerikasvenska: En bok om språkutvecklingen i Svensk-Amerika* (Stockholm: Esselte Studium, 1974); Dag Blanck, *The Creation of an Ethnic Identity: Being Swedish American in the Augustana Synod, 1860–1917* (Carbondale: Southern Illinois University Press, 2006).

12. Kathleen Neils Conzen, "Commentary," in *Scandinavians and Other Immigrants in Urban America: The Proceedings of a Research Conference, October 26–27, 1984,* ed. Odd S. Lovoll (Northfield, Minn.: Saint Olaf College Press, 1985), 196.

13. Karen V. Hansen, *Encounter on the Great Plains: Scandinavian Settlers and the Dispossession of Dakota Indians, 1890–1930* (Oxford: Oxford University Press, 2013).

14. Gunlög Fur, *A Nation of Women: Gender and Colonial Encounters among the Delaware Indians* (Philadelphia: University of Pennsylvania Press, 2009); *Colonialism and the Rise of Modernity: Small Time Agents in a Global Arena,* ed. Magdalena Naum and Jonas M. Nording (New York: Springer, 2013).

15. Harald Runblom, "Swedes and Other Ethnic Groups in American Cities," in Anderson and Blanck, *Swedish-American Life in Chicago*; Dag Blanck, "'A Mixture of People with Different Roots': Swedish Immigrants in the American Ethno-Racial Hierarchy," *Journal of American Ethnic History* 33, no. 3 (2014): 37–54; Erika Jackson, *Scandinavians in Chicago: The Origins of White Privilege in Modern America* (Urbana: University of Illinois Press, 2019).

16. See, for example, *Networks of Americanization: Aspects of the American Influence in Sweden,* ed. Rolf Lundén and Erik Åsard (Stockholm: Almqvist & Wiksell International, 1992); Erik Åsard, ed., *Det blågula stjärnbaneret: USA:s närvaro och inflytande i Sverige* (Stockholm: Carlsson, 2016).

17. Harald Elovson, *Amerika i svensk litteratur 1750–1820: En studie i komparativ litteraturhistoria* (Lund: Gleerup, 1930); Nils Runeby, *Den nya världen och den*

gamla: Amerikabild och emigrationsuppfattning i Sverige 1820–1860 (Uppsala: Studia historica Upsaliensia, 1969); Gunnar Eidevall, *Amerika i svensk 1900-talslitteratur: Från Gustaf Hellström till Lars Gustafsson* (Stockholm: Almqvist & Wiksell International, 1983); Martin Alm, *Americanitis: Amerika som sjukdom eller läkemedel; Svenska berättelser om USA åren 1909–1939* (Lund: Nordic Academic Press, 2002); Amanda Lagerkvist, *Amerikafantasier: Kön, medier och visualitet i svenska reseskildringar från USA 1945–63* (Stockholm: Institutionen för journalistik, medier och kommunikation, 2005); Jeff Werner, *Medelvägens estetik: Sverigebilder i USA*, 2 vols. (Hedemora: Gidlund, 2008).

18. William Hagans and Willow Hagans, *Zorn in America: A Swedish Impressionist of the Gilded Age* (Chicago: Swedish-American Historical Society, 2009); Rolf Lundén, *Man Triumphant: The Divided Life of David Edstrom* (Uppsala: Acta Universitatis Upsaliensis, 2014); Annika Öhrner, *Barbro Östlihn och New York: konstens rum och möjligheter* (Gothenburg: Makadam, 2010).

19. Byron Rom Jensen, "The Scandinavian Legacy: Nordic Politics as Images and Models in the United States," PhD dissertation, Aarhus University, 2017; Werner, *Medelvägens estetik*; Jan Olof Nilsson, *Alva Myrdal: En virvel i den moderna strömmen* (Stockholm: Brutus Östlings bokförlag Symposion, 1994); H. Arnold Barton, "The New Deal and the People's Home: American and Swedish Perspectives from the 1930s," in *Migration och mångfald: Essäer om kulturkontakt och minoritetsfrågor tillägnade Harald Runblom*, ed. Dag Blanck (Uppsala: Centre for Multiethnic Research, 1999).

20. Yngve Möller, *Sverige och Vietnamkriget: Ett unikt kapitel i svensk utrikespolitik* (Stockholm: Tiden, 1992); Leif Leifland, *Frostens år: Om USA:s diplomatiska utfrysning av Sverige* (Stockholm: Nerenius & Santérus, 1997); Charles Silva, "Keep Them Strong, Keep Them Friendly: Swedish-American Relations and the Pax Americana, 1948–1952" (PhD diss., Stockholm University, 1999); Mikael Nilsson, *Tools of Hegemony: Military Technology and Swedish-American Security Relations 1945–1962* (Stockholm: Santérus Academic Press, 2007); Mikael Nilsson, *The Battle for Hearts and Minds in the High North: The USIA and American Cold War Propaganda in Sweden, 1952–1969* (Leiden: Brill, 2018); Wilhelm Agrell, "Den neutrala bundsförvanten: Svensk-amerikanska säkerhetsrelationer i medgång och motgång," in Åsard, *Det blågula stjärnbaneret*.

21. Steven Koblik, *Sweden the Neutral Victor: Sweden and the Western Powers 1917–1918: A Study of Anglo-American-Swedish Relations* (Lund: Läromedelsförlagen, 1972); Nikolas Glover, *National Relations: Public Diplomacy, National Identity, and the Swedish Institute, 1945–1970* (Lund: Nordic Academic Press, 2011); Ulf Bjereld, Alf W. Johansson, and Karl Molin, *Sveriges säkerhet och världens fred: Svensk utrikespolitik under kalla kriget* (Stockholm: Santérus, 2008).

22. Steven Seegel, *Mapping Europe's Borderlands: Russian Cartography in the Age of Empire* (Chicago: University of Chicago Press, 2012); Alfred J. Rieber, *The Struggle for the Eurasian Borderlands: From the Rise of Early Modern Empires to*

the End of the First World War (Cambridge: Cambridge University Press, 2014); Paul Readman, Cynthia Radding, and Chad Bryant, eds., *Borderlands in World History, 1700–1914* (Basingstoke: Palgrave Macmillan, 2014); John W. I. Lee and Michael North, eds., *Globalizing Borderlands Studies in Europe and North America* (Lincoln: University of Nebraska Press, 2016); Mihai I. Spariosu, *Intercultural Conflict and Harmony in the Central European Borderlands: The Cases of Banat and Transylvania, 1849–1939* (Göttingen: V&R Unipress, 2017); Elisabeth Boesen and Gregor Schnuer, eds., *European Borderlands: Living with Barriers and Bridges* (London: Routledge, 2017).

23. The isolation of these traditions is based on the historiographical overview by Pekka Hämäläinen and Samuel Truett, "On Borderlands," *Journal of American History* 98, no. 2 (September 2011): 343. For a similar categorization, see John W. I. Lee and Michael North, "Introduction," in *Globalizing Borderlands Studies in Europe and North America,* 1–2, and Alexande Drost and Michael North, "Future Directions in Borderlands Studies," in Lee and North, *Globalizing Borderlands Studies in Europe and North America,* 251–57.

24. Herbert E. Bolton, *The Spanish Borderlands: A Chronicle of Old Florida and the Southwest* (New Haven: Yale University Press, 1921).

25. Jeremy Adelman and Stephen Aron, "From Borderlands to Borders: Empires, Nation-States, and the Peoples in Between in North American History," *American Historical Review* 104, no. 3 (June 1999): 816.

26. See, for example, Brenden W. Rensink, *Native but Foreign: Indigenous Immigrants and Refugees in the North American Borderlands* (College Station: Texas A&M University Press, 2018); Jeffrey M. Schulze, *Are We Not Foreigners Now? Indigenous Nationalism in the U.S.–Mexico Borderlands* (Chapel Hill: University of North Carolina Press, 2018).

27. Gloria Anzaldúa, preface to *Borderlands/La Frontera: The New Mestiza* (San Francisco: Spinsters, 1987), n.p.

28. Hämälänien and Truett, "On Borderlands," 341, 344.

29. Kathleen DuVal, "Borderlands," Oxford Bibliographies online, last modified June 8, 2017, https://www.oxfordbibliographies.com. See also Jared Orsi, "Construction and Contestation: Toward a Unifying Methodology for Borderlands History," *History Compass* 12, no. 5 (2014): 433–43.

30. E. H. Thörnberg, *Sverige i Amerika, Amerika i Sverige* (Stockholm: Bonniers, 1938), 20–21, 100–101, 135.

31. Kazimierz Musiał, *Roots of the Scandinavian Model: Images of Progress in the Era of Modernisation* (Baden-Baden: Nomos Verlagsgesellschaft, 2000); Glover, *National Relations*; Carl Marklund and Klaus Petersen, "Return to Sender: American Images of the Nordic Welfare States and Nordic Welfare State Branding," *European Journal of Scandinavian Studies* 43, no. 2 (2013): 245–57.

32. It should be noted that the terminology in the Uppsala "Emigration Project" shifted over time toward "migration," and the term is part of the subtitle of

the group's final report from 1976 ("A History of the Migration"). See Runblom and Norman, *From Sweden to America.*

33. Jean R. Soderlund, *Lenape Country: Delaware Valley Society before William Penn* (Philadelphia: University of Pennsylvania Press, 2015), 1–11, 43–44; Mark L. Thompson, *The Contest for the Delaware Valley: Allegiance, Identity, and Empire in the Seventeenth Century* (Baton Rouge: Louisiana State University Press, 2013).

34. C. A. Weslager, *New Sweden on the Delaware: 1638–1655* (Wilmington, Del.: Middle Atlantic Press, 1988), 11–55; Gunlög Fur, *Colonialism in the Margins: Cultural Encounters in New Sweden and Lapland* (Leiden: Brill, 2005), 88–99; Soderlund, *Lenape Country,* 18.

35. Gunlög Fur, Magdalena Naum, and Jonas M. Nordin, "Intersecting Worlds: New Sweden's Transatlantic Entanglements," *Journal of Transnational American Studies* 7, no. 1 (2016): 4–6.

36. H. Arnold Barton, "Clio and Swedish America: Historians, Organizations, Publications," in *Perspectives on Swedish Immigration,* ed. Nils Hasselmo (Chicago: Swedish-American Historical Society, 1978), 5.

37. Lorenzo Veracini, *Settler Colonialism: A Theoretical Overview* (New York: Palgrave Macmillan, 2010), 3.

38. Blake Bell, "America's Invitation to the World: Was the Homestead Act the First Accommodating Immigration Legislation in the United States?" (n.d.), https://www.nps.gov.

39. Harald Runblom, "Nordic Immigrants in the New World," in Hans Norman and Harald Runblom, *Transatlantic Connections: Nordic Migration to the New World after 1800* (Oslo: Norwegian University Press, 1988), 151.

40. Sten Carlsson, "Chronology and Composition of Swedish Emigration to America," in Runblom and Norman, *From Sweden to America,* 115–16.

41. Runblom, "Nordic Immigrants in the New World," 146–55, 159–63; Carlsson, "Chronology and Composition of Swedish Emigration to America," 115–30.

42. Hans Norman, "Swedes in North America," in Runblom and Norman, *From Sweden to America,* 256–61.

43. Hansen, *Encounter on the Great Plains.*

44. John Bodnar, *The Transplanted: A History of Immigrants in Urban America* (Bloomington: Indiana University Press, 1985), 1, 8.

45. Carlsson, "Chronology and Composition of Swedish Emigration to America," 115–30.

46. Harald Runblom, "Chicago Compared: Swedes and Other Ethnic Groups in American Cities," in Anderson and Blanck, *Swedish-American Life in Chicago,* 70.

47. Sune Åkerman and Hans Norman, "Political Mobilization of the Workers," in *American Labor and Immigration History, 1877–1920's,* ed. Dirk Hoerder (Urbana: University of Illinois Press, 1983); Hans Wallengren, "Svenskarna i Hooverville: Svenska immigranter i Seattles största kåkstad under den stora

depressionen," in *Mellan Malmö och Minneapolis: Kulturhistoriska undersökningar tillägnade Lars Edgren,* ed. Victor Lundberg and Cecilia Riving (Malmö: Arkiv förlag, 2018); special issue on Worcester, Massachusetts, *Swedish-American Historical Quarterly* 47, no. 1 (January 1996); Dag Blanck, "Immigrants by the Mississippi: Ethnic Relations in Moline, Illinois," in *Swedish Life in American Cities,* ed. Dag Blanck and Harald Runblom (Uppsala: Uppsala Multiethnic Papers, 1991); David Lanegran, "Swedish Neighborhoods of the Twin Cities: From Swede Hollow to Arlington Hills, from Snoose Boulevard to Minnehaha Parkway," in *Swedes in the Twin Cities: Immigrant Life and Minnesota's Urban Frontier,* ed. Philip J. Anderson and Dag Blanck (St. Paul: Minnesota Historical Society Press, 2001).

48. *Yearbook of Immigration Statistics* (Washington, D.C.: U.S. Department of Homeland Security, 2017), 6–11. From 2010 to 2017, 9,550 Swedes had immigrated to the United States. If the averages remain constant during the period, the total will reach about 12,000 for the decade. Note that these figures are not directly compatible with statistics from 2004 and older, because the U.S. Department of Homeland Security—and its predecessor, the U.S. Department of Immigration and Naturalization—previously configured their statistical brackets differently (as in 1931–40, compared to the newer system, 1930–39).

49. Lars-Göran Tedebrand, "Remigration from America to Sweden," in Runblom and Norman, *From Sweden to America,* 201–28; Lars-Göran Tedebrand, *Västernorrland och Nordamerika 1875–1913: Utvandring och återinvandring* (Uppsala: Studia Historica Upsaliensia, 1972). It should be noted that it is methodologically impossible to accurately measure return rates for emigration to the United States. Apart from inconsistent, or lack of, record keeping on the returnees, the statistics gained are also somewhat unreliable. Of the individuals statistically noted as return migrants in 1880, for example, most had likely emigrated before that year. On problems with statistics, see Mark Wyman, *Round-Trip America: The Immigrants Return to Europe, 1880–1930* (Ithaca, N.Y.: Cornell University Press, 1993), 7–10.

50. Wyman, *Round-Trip America,* 12, 193; emphasis in original.

51. Ibid., 5–6; Raymond L. Cohn, "The Transition from Sail to Steam in Immigration to the United States," *Journal of Economic History* 65, no. 2 (June 2005): 469–95.

52. Tedebrand, "Remigration from America to Sweden," 226.

53. Magnus Persson, *Coming Full Circle? Return Migration and the Dynamics of Social Mobility on the Bjäre Peninsula, 1860–1930* (Lund: Sisyfos, 2007); John Johansson et al., *En smålandssocken emigrerar: En bok om emigrationen till Amerika från Långasjö socken i Kronobergs län* (Växjö: Långasjö emigrantcirkel, 1967); Ulf Beijbom, *Mot löftets land: Den svenska utvandringen* (Stockholm: LTs förlag, 1995), 51.

54. Per Clemensson et al., eds., *Göteborgs-Emigranten 6: Rapport från symposiet "Amerika tur och retur"* (Gothenburg: Göteborgs-emigranten, 1997); Ingvar Henricson and Hans Lindblad, *Tur och retur Amerika: Utvandrare som förändrade Sverige* (Stockholm: Fischer, 1995), 234ff.

55. Sten Carlsson, "Augustana Lutheran Pastors in the Church of Sweden," *Swedish-American Historical Quarterly* 65, no. 3 (July 1984): 246.

56. Beijbom, *Mot löftets land,* 51.

57. Helge Nelson, *The Swedes and the Swedish Settlements in North America,* vol. 1 (Lund: Gleerups, 1943).

58. Blanck, "'A Mixture of People with Different Roots'"; Jackson, *Scandinavians in Chicago*; Anita Olson Gustafson, *Swedish Chicago: The Shaping of an Immigrant Community, 1880–1920* (DeKalb: Northern Illinois University Press, 2018); Anderson and Blanck, *Swedes in the Twin Cities.*

59. Angela Hoffman (Karstadt), *Tracking Swedish-American English: A Longitudinal Study of Linguistic Variation and Identity* (Uppsala: Acta Universitatis Upsaliensis, 2003).

60. Dag Blanck, "Being Swedish in America Today," in *Hembygden & världen: Festskrift till Ulf Beijbom,* ed. Sune Åkerman and Lars Olsson (Växjö: Svenska Emigrantinstitutet, 2002).

61. Catrin Lundström, "Transnationell vithet: Svenska migrantkvinnor i USA och Singapore," *Tidskrift för genusvetenskap* 1–2 (2010): 23–45; Nevra Biltekin, "Mellan migration och diplomati: Svenska emigrantkvinnor som kulturdiplomater i USA, 1980–1990, in *Tillit och diplomati: En diskussionsbok om personliga relationer och diplomatiska processer,* ed. Susanna Erlandsson and Siri Nauman (Uppsala: Opuscula Historica Upsaliensia, 2019).

62. Mark Wyman also describes the return migrant as a "sojourner," in the capacity of being a "temporary immigrant" (*Round-Trip America,* 204).

63. Pehr Kalm, *En resa til norra America, på kongl. swenska wetenskaps academiens befallning, och publici kostnad*... (Stockholm: Salvius, 1756–61); Pehr Kalm, *Travels into North America: Containing Its Natural History*... (London, 1772).

64. Carlsson, "Chronology and Composition of Swedish Emigration to America," 115.

65. Fredrika Bremer, *Hemmen i den nya världen: En dagbok i bref, skrifna under tvenne års resor i Norra Amerika och på Cuba,* 3 vols. (Stockholm: Norstedts, 1853–54).

66. Lars Wendelius, *Fredrika Bremers Amerikabild: En studie i Hemmen i den nya verlden* (Stockholm: Almqvist & Wiksell International, 1985), 15; Åsa Arping, "'The Miss Austen of Sweden': Fredrika Bremer's Transatlantic Triumph in the Age of Reprint," in *Swedish Women's Writing on Export: Tracing Transnational Reception in the Nineteenth Century,* ed. Yvonne Leffler et al. (Gothenburg; Lir Skrifter, 2019).

67. J. F. Grawe, *History of Bremer County, Iowa: A Record of Settlement, Organization, Progress, and Achievement,* vol. 1 (Chicago: S. J. Clarke Publishing Company, 1914), 90.

68. Barton, *A Folk Divided,* 4.

69. Ibid., 44, 59–61, 90–91, 187–88.

70. Ibid., 283–84.

71. Adam Hjorthén, *Cross-Border Commemorations: Celebrating Swedish Settlement in America* (Amherst: University of Massachusetts Press, 2018), 137–43.

72. Barton, *A Folk Divided,* 315–17; Merle Curti, "Sweden in the American Social Mind of the 1930s," in *The Immigration of Ideas: Studies in the North Atlantic Community,* ed. J. Thomas Tredway and J. Iverne Dowie (Rock Island, Ill.: Augustana Historical Society, 1968).

73. Marquis W. Childs, *Sweden: The Middle Way* (New Haven: Yale University Press, 1936), 161.

74. John Logue, "The Swedish Model: Visions of Sweden in American Politics and Political Science," *Swedish-American Historical Quarterly* 50, no. 3 (July 1999): 162–72; Carl Marklund, "The Social Laboratory, the Middle Way and the Swedish Model: Three Frames for the Image of Sweden," *Scandinavian Journal of History* 34, no. 3 (2009): 264–85.

75. Algot Mattsson, *Vägen mot väster: En bok om emigrationen och Svenska Amerika Linien* (Stockholm: Askild och Kärnekull, 1982); Johannes Hoving, *Vasabarnen från Amerika: Trenne resor i fars och mors land 1924, 1929, 1933; Minnen och intryck* (Stockholm: Saxon & Lindström, 1935).

76. H. Arnold Barton, "Editor's Corner: The Summer of '46," *Swedish-American Historical Quarterly* 35, no. 1 (January 1984): 3–5.

77. Anders Buraas, *Fly over fly: Historien om SAS* (Oslo: Gyldendal Norsk Forlag, 1972), 69, 73.

78. Anders Buraas *The SAS Saga: A History of Scandinavian Airlines System* (Oslo: Scandinavian Airlines, 1979), 161–62.

79. Dag Blanck, "'Very Welcome Home Mr. Swanson': Swedish Americans Encounter Homeland Swedes," *American Studies in Scandinavia* 48, no. 2 (2016): 107–21.

80. Lagerkvist, *Amerikafantasier.*

81. Emory Lindquist, "The Swedish-Born Population and the Swedish Stock: The United States Census of 1960 and Comparative Data with Some Concluding Observations," *Swedish Pioneer Historical Quarterly* 16, no. 2 (April 1965): 89–90.

82. "Gästnätter 2018," Tillväxtverket, February 7, 2019; accessed December 2, 2019, https://tillvaxtverket.se.

83. The large majority of these individuals traveled under the Visa Waiver Program. See *Yearbook of Immigration Statistics* (Washington, D.C.: U.S. Department of Homeland Security, 2017), 70, 79; "Resiabarometern 2019," Resia, https://www.resia.se; accessed December 3, 2019.

84. There have been relatively few attempts at writing syntheses of Swedish-American histories, and the examples that exist have focused on immigration and ethnic history. See Beijbom, *Mot löftets land*; Lennart Pehrson, *Utvandringen till Amerika*, 3 vols. (Stockholm: Bonniers, 2014–15). Runblom and Norman, *From Sweden to America*, would also fit the description as a summary of the Uppsala emigration research program.

PART I

Across Waters and Lands

1

Reservation Borderlands

Gender and Scandinavian Land Taking on Native American Land

Karen V. Hansen

Contrary to popular myth, a reservation is not a section of Native peoples' ancestral homelands that has been set aside for them as a place where they could continue their traditional way of life. Instead, a reservation is a geographic space defined by the United States and imposed on Native peoples through the exercise of military power and treaty negotiations. It represents invasion and conquest. Indigenous people who had survived protracted conflicts and brief, but intense wars were confined to them in order to make way for white settler colonists. Bounded via negotiations between Indian nations and the United States and legislative fiat, reservations are legally defined and socially recognized. Their boundaries have been enforced by bureaucracy, surveying technology, and strategic use of resources. Ironically, reservations became new and different homelands for Native peoples, even with their restrictions on mobility, racialized hierarchies embedded in law, and constant surveillance by government agents.

Today, most Americans are entirely unaware that whites, whether U.S.-born or foreign-born, were invited to homestead public land that had recently been taken from Native nations *on* reservations. In 1887, when the U.S. Congress passed the Dawes Act, it specified that individual tribal members be allotted land that had been held in common and then the "surplus land" on reservations be opened to white homesteaders. In effect, it converted spaces reserved for Native Americans into public land that allowed white settlers to homestead and live in integrated contact zones. This essay explores this seldom considered path to cultural and economic incorporation in the United States: homesteading on Indian reservations, using the case of North Dakota.

Such was the case for two young Swedes whose lives intertwined shortly after World War I. Independently, each claimed homestead land on the Fort Berthold Indian Reservation. Their land taking and eventual marriage did not unfold quite as the dominant narrative about Swedish migration would have predicted.

Two Swedish Cases

Axeline V. Johnston

Axeline V. Johnston was born to Swedish immigrant parents in 1894. The third daughter in a large family, she lived with her mother and two sisters in a modest house they owned in St. Paul, Minnesota. By 1910 when Axeline turned sixteen, her father had died and her widowed mother was the head of household. Her older sister Julia worked as a milliner, while Axeline was employed as an "errand girl" for the same wholesale milliner in Minneapolis.

Initially, this portrait seems entirely consistent with Swedish historiography that notes a great proportion of Swedes migrated to the Midwest and concentrated in urban centers, particularly neighborhoods with other immigrants from Sweden.[1] Axeline's mother, Thelma Johnston, had arrived in 1878, then aged twenty, at a peak of nineteenth-century migration waves from Sweden.[2] With her husband, she found sufficient wherewithal to purchase a home and could claim to speak English (according to the census). Two of her daughters earned wages in millinery work, an industry considered "respectable" that employed lots of young women.

A few years later, Axeline's story takes a less predictable turn. She headed west to North Dakota and filed a homestead claim on the Fort Berthold Indian Reservation. Few women left urban centers to homestead and farm, although it was not unusual for homesteading women to practice seasonally a trade such as schoolteaching or millinery while they were clearing land and farming. The land Axeline claimed was still legally part of an Indian reservation, her presence made possible through the Dawes Act of 1887, which applied the principles of the Homestead Act of 1862 to this Indian land. Importantly, an adult woman could file a homestead claim as long as she was single. Married women could not claim land.

In western North Dakota, Fort Berthold was (and is) home to the Three Affiliated Tribes—Arikara, Mandan, and Hidatsa Nation. The reservation was formally established near Fort Berthold in 1870, totaling almost three million acres. In less than a generation, it was subject to the Dawes Act. By the early 1900s, when officials began allotting land to tribal members, it had already been reduced to less than a third of its original size. In 1910, 227,504 acres that had not been allotted were opened to white homesteaders.

The region had for centuries been a major crossroads for multiple Indian nations as they fished and traveled the Missouri River, traversed the northern plains, and harvested its bounty. The Mandan and Hidatsa built villages and farms on the north side of the Missouri at least since 1100, the crossroads of trade between Indian tribes and later with European and American fur traders.[3] Lewis and Clark famously wintered with the Mandan in 1804–5 as they made their way west on their "voyage of discovery."

After moving to the reservation, Axeline's life intersected not only with members of the Three Affiliated Tribes, but with a Swedish migrant who would alter her life path.

Ernest August Nelson

Ernest A. Nelson came in a later wave of Swedish migration, arriving in 1907. He was born in Stockholm in 1891 to Johan Fredrik Johansson Hagelin, a carpenter age forty-on, and Ida Charlotte Gustafsdotter, a child minder age thirty-four. Klara parish records reveal a query by Pastor Lindstrom.[4]

In 1907, at the age of sixteen, Ernest made passage to the United States and began working as a day laborer in eastern North Dakota. The young men and women who migrated from Sweden after the turn of the century were more likely than their predecessors to be poor and unmarried.[5] Motivated by the prospect of escaping poverty and gaining a modicum of self-sufficiency, Scandinavians arrived as voluntary migrants to the Middle West. In Sweden, those emigrating had primarily been farm laborers and industrial workers. They came with few resources, but sought out those who spoke their language.

What appears less common about Ernest's journey is that he was born as an urban dweller in Sweden and once in the United States he headed to a rural state with a primarily agricultural economy. Like South Dakota and Montana, North Dakota did not have large urban centers that attracted Swedes.[6] Most Swedish rural settlers had farmed in Sweden before emigrating.[7] After statehood in 1889, North Dakota acted as a magnet for large numbers of first- and second-generation Scandinavian Americans, especially Norwegians. In 1910, foreign-born whites and U.S.-born whites of foreign or mixed parentage comprised 70.6 percent of the population of North Dakota. Twenty-nine percent of the state's foreign-born residents were from Norway, with 8 percent from Sweden and 3 percent from Denmark.[8]

While living in Cooperstown, North Dakota, in 1912, and working as a servant for Per and Ellen Kindso, Swedish immigrant farmers, Ernest filed papers declaring his intention to become a naturalized citizen, a precondition for homesteading. Later that year, he responded to the opening of homestead land in the western part of the state on the Fort Berthold Indian Reservation, more than two hundred miles away, and staked a claim. He married the Kindsos' American-born daughter, Minnie Cornelea, two years his senior, who had been working out as a housekeeper. They took up residence in McLean County on his claim in 1913 and began having children.[9] On the reservation they lived among multiple Norwegian settlers (in North Dakota, most Swedes clustered in Norwegian communities),[10] as well as Hidatsa, Mandan, and Arikara members of the Three Affiliated Tribes who called Fort Berthold theirs.

Through the ups and downs of clearing the land and cultivating flax, barley, wheat, and oats, Minnie gave birth to two children. Before finalizing the homestead process, Ernest Nelson had to foreswear his allegiance to his homeland. That he did in 1914. In accordance with principles of the Homestead Act, to make his final proof and take title, he had to improve the land by living on it, building structures, and cultivating crops. Ernest filed final proof on the claim on June 30, 1917.[11] He registered for the draft soon after the United States entered the Great War, but at the age of twenty-seven and as a farmer producing much-needed agricultural products, was not called to serve. Two months later, their fortune took a different turn.

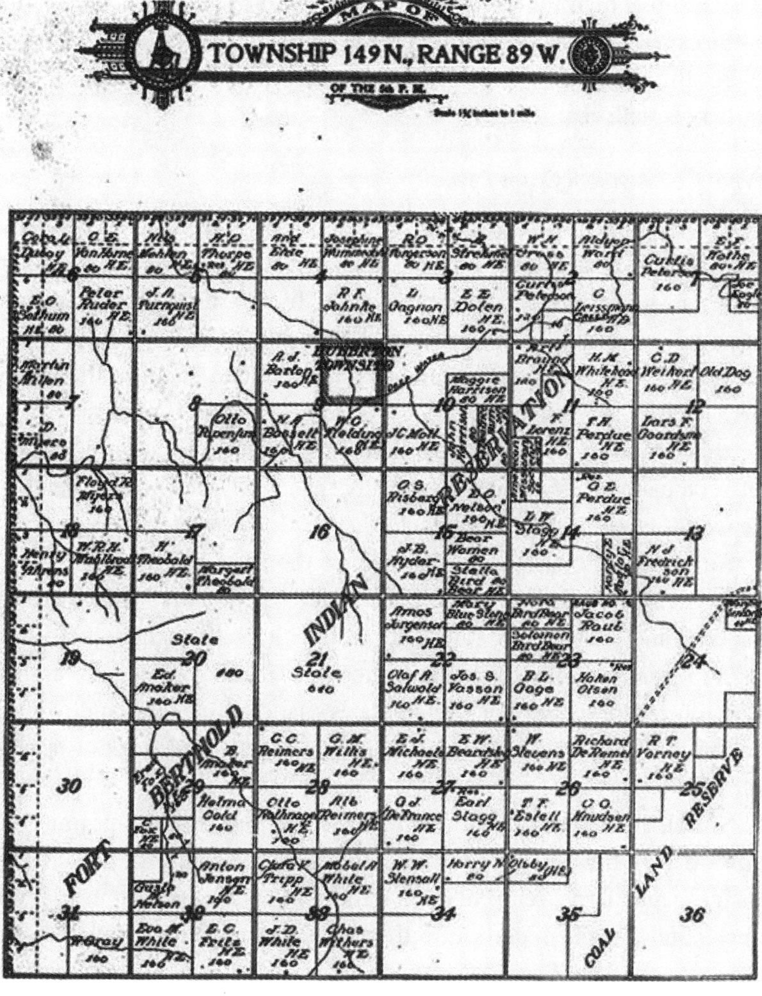

Plat map for Loquemont Township, North Dakota, on the Fort Berthold Indian Reservation, 1917.

Shortly after giving birth to their third child, Minnie died (August 24, 1917).[12] With two small children and an infant, no farmer partner, and title to 160 acres, Ernest had to find his way forward.

His story of loss unfolded in the context of the tragedy of cumulative land loss for members of the Three Affiliated Tribes. The land-taking opportunity that drew Swedes and Norwegians, spurred them to give up citizenship of their mother country, and yielded ownership of land came at the expense of dispossession of those who already lived there.

But this is not the typical story told about Swedish migration in the early twentieth century.

What Can Atypical Cases Reveal?

The cases of Axeline Johnston and Ernest Nelson make visible a regularly ignored historical process typically assigned to the colonial era. Rather than a historical precursor or mere aside, Indian dispossession was an essential precondition for immigrant recruitment and a fundamental part of the success of agriculturalists in the United States in the twentieth century. As historian Gunlög Fur argues, a separation of the two is detrimental to an understanding of the processes of migration, ethnicity, and colonialism.[13] Viewed concurrently, it becomes clear that settlement depends on removal or displacement.

Furthermore, homesteading is part of the Swedish-American story, even in the twentieth century. Ernest and Axeline, first- and second-generation Swedish Americans, both from cities, set up a household and began raising a family on the farm they were making. Theirs represents agricultural success in the United States—land taking and landowning among Indigenous people, and the use of land as a strategy of family support.

Not all migrants were drawn to urban centers and the promise of upward mobility. They could seek a rural way of life, with advantages such as reputational reinvention and the capacity to support oneself and one's family. In his migration to the United States, Ernest could escape the question of his illegitimacy. In her venture west from St. Paul, Axeline was pursuing a means to make a living and support her mother and sister, something she could not do easily or effectively with only female wages in the Twin Cities.

Theoretical Framework: Reservation Borderlands

Borderlands at the heart of what Frederick Hoxie calls "the red continent" reveal multiple contradictions.[14] As European settlers discovered when they arrived, North America was and continued to be occupied and used by Indigenous people. The vast reservation system constructed and coercively implemented in the nineteenth century did not *reserve* land for Native people, it progressively and systematically shrank it. As the examples of Axeline and Ernest demonstrate, Indian land dispossession did not stop with the end of armed conflict at the end of the nineteenth century.

The history of North America has been fundamentally shaped by settler colonialism and Indigenous dispossession. Swedish migrants who settled in rural areas of the Midwest were part of that process. While some accepted the description of the land as "virgin" and vacant, others had to come face-to-face with Indigenous inhabitants. In the early twentieth century, Swedish immigrants and their American-born children took up public land on Indian reservations, which was made available to white settlers by the federal government. In homesteading land on Indian reservations, they had direct encounters with the Native Americans and materially benefited from the process of their dispossession. The consequences of their land taking were immediately and concretely visible.

The clash over land as a resource and commodity in the context of U.S. territorial expansion resulted in the continued dispossession of Native people. It was a precondition for the opportunity for white settlers—both immigrant and U.S.-born. Settler colonialism, "an inclusive, land-centred project," in the United States was promoted by the railroads and facilitated by the federal government.[15] Once immigrants began arriving in large numbers, their settlement placed them in unequal and often oppositional legal, economic, and social positions to the Native Americans who had lived here for millennia. White immigrants were legally privileged because they could become naturalized citizens, which Indian peoples could not.

Fundamentally, as Evelyn Nakano Glenn argues, settler colonialism intertwined reproductive labor with land taking, making women central to the endeavor. Settlement was imagined not as an extractive enterprise, but as a long-term, multigenerational project based on having and raising children.[16] In addition to their reproductive and productive labors, women also took land. A gendered perspective illuminates the division of labor and the essential role of women in the success of the enterprise. Landownership was "the foundation for family security, political-economic autonomy, and cultural continuity."[17]

If immigrants were not always celebrated in the United States, they were recognized as a necessary part of the U.S. labor force in the aftermath of the war over enslaved labor. Congress and the railroad companies facilitated their entry and recruited them into the project of populating the continent and developing agriculture in the heartland, the ever-shifting borderlands. The Homestead Act of 1862, which mapped out a plan for white settlement through land taking, can be considered the "first accommodating immigration legislation in the United States."[18] Twenty-five years later, a post–Civil War, post-Reconstruction Congress, still overseeing armed conflict with Indian nations, passed the Dawes Act, formally titled the General Land Allotment Act of 1887, in an effort to assimilate all tribes into the agricultural economy and further expropriate Indian land.

Intended to separate Indian nations from the United States and contain their territorial claims, Indian reservations became borderlands of a peculiar kind. At the edges of competing nations, they were transnational spaces with boundaries structured by racialized laws designed to subordinate Native Americans and privilege white settlers. The Dawes legislation aimed to integrate these bounded places, Indian and non-Indian, with a clear eye to dispossession.

Using a borderlands frame, Indian reservations can be understood as what Pekka Hämäläinen and Samuel Truett call a "multiethnic point of confluence."[19] They define borderlands as "spaces marked not only by violence but also by cultural transience, mobility, and intermingling."[20]

For Gloria Anzaldúa, borderlands are a juncture, a nexus of people, cultures, and economies.[21] She points to "the emotional residue of an unnatural boundary," such as the boundary that in one fell swoop incorporated Mexican territory and its inhabitants into the United States.[22] Borders of nation-states, legally claimed but regularly contested, mark geography not visible to the naked eye, but drawn on a map or perhaps enacted through social action. A border is an edge, an invisible line that sometimes sports a fence, survey markers, signs, or marching soldiers. It can be created by natural geographic formations such as rivers and lakes and imposed by a dominant society. It can also be breached by acts of nature such as flooding lakes or human constructions such as roads, bridges, and relationships. Artificially constructed, the borders of an Indian reservation stood ready to be transgressed.

North Dakota Land Taking

For the Three Affiliated Tribes, the vast expanse north and south, east and west of the Missouri River, that great trading nexus, had long been their domain.[23] For Spirit Lake Dakotas, for several hundred years their homeland had been southern Minnesota. North Dakota had been a hunting territory, and home to Ojibwe people, but not until the aftermath of 1862 did it become a place to permanently reside. Borderlands imply fluidity and mixing, destabilizing "the logic of national incorporation."[24] The residential, economic, and social integration of settlers and Indians did precisely that; land that had ostensibly been "reserved" for Native people was "opened" to white settlement.

On the northern Great Plains, Congress turned reservations into swaths of land for white settlers, including those arriving from Scandinavia and other parts of Europe. In 1887, Indian reservations encompassed more than 136 million acres for a population of approximately 250,000 enrolled tribal members. Passage of the Indian Reorganization Act of 1934 ended allotment. It also terminated homesteading on reservations. By then, reservation land had contracted to fifty-two million acres while tribal enrollment had grown to approximately 328,000 people. Within those legally defined and contracted spaces, Indian people controlled much less land than before. Some well-documented cases, such as Melissa Meyer's study of dispossession at White Earth Indian Reservation in Minnesota and William T. Hagan's exposé of the Jerome Commission's allotment process in Oklahoma, point to the federal and local, political processes that systematically removed land from tribal hands.[25]

But to investigate the particular foothold that white landowners gained on reservations, it is essential to look at homesteading. In the twentieth century, homesteading on reservations reveals the convergence of the processes of immigration and dispossession. At Spirit Lake, where I documented the transformation of landownership from 1910 to 1929, Dakotas' land contracted by half from 1910 to 1929. In that same period, Scandinavians' land acreage doubled, making them the largest landowning group on the reservation.[26] This expansion of that research reveals that Spirit Lake was not the only reservation where that happened.

In North Dakota, homesteading fit a particular pattern that Richard Edwards, Jacob Friefeld, and Rebecca Wingo call the Dakota Pattern, because, unlike earlier periods of homesteading in Nebraska and Colorado, for example, "homesteading was intimately tied up with dispossession."[27] Dakota Territory, which later divided into North and South, had the largest number of homestead claims in the United States.[28] Those statistics include reservation land.

Of that vast homesteaded land, Edwards estimates that "no more than 10–15 percent" of it was on reservations.[29] I would argue that while homesteading on reservations was not the most common, it nonetheless had an enormous impact on tribal territory. It has been an invisible component of these statistics because reservation land only became "public land" after a tribe was allotted. It is a significant part of the twentieth-century Indian dispossession story, even if it is a lesser part of the homesteading history.

The Cases of Spirit Lake and Fort Berthold

Because Fort Berthold and Spirit Lake were the two largest reservations entirely within the state, were opened to white homesteading about the same time (1910 and 1904, respectively), and shared a political and demographic landscape, their comparison is illuminating. Using land records, plat maps, homesteading files, and census records, we systematically gathered information about gender, nativity, acreage, and timing of land taking in order to understand who was claiming land, when, and with what magnitude on reservations.[30] This analysis has focused on white homesteaders rather than tribal allottees.[31]

Of the 2,651 total homestead claims and commutations on the two reservations, 12.6 percent were made by women.[32] Strikingly, Scandinavian women constituted 53 percent of the female homesteaders. They were a smaller percentage of women who commuted their claims (37 percent). To commute a claim one had to pay a fee per acre and needed live on the claim only fourteen months as opposed to five years. The calculus of labor versus capital had to be assessed in relation to individuals' ability to pay and in the context of perceived risks and future market values. That Scandinavian women used sweat equity to take land spoke to their use of the resource they had—labor power—rather than the capital they lacked.

When we ask whether there was something distinctively Swedish (in contrast, say, to Norwegian or Danish) about their agency in land taking, the answer is no. This is a Scandinavian story, not a distinctively Swedish one. The observable behavior of those Swedes who founded and remained on farms in North Dakota differed little from that of their Norwegian counterparts. The primary difference that emerges among Scandinavian homesteading groups is the collective zest for landowning exhibited by Norwegian women. As Hansen and Leonard find, "Three times as many Norwegians as Swedes claimed land. Danes were a demographic minority in the state and in the land taking."[33] They disproportionately took advantage of the opportunity to make claims and take title at Fort Berthold and Spirit Lake.[34] While they may not have been the dominant group, some Swedes and Swedish Americans discovered this path to opportunity and economic incorporation.

Scandinavian Lives on the Reservation

In the early twentieth century, Scandinavian immigrants and their American-born children took up public land on Indian reservations along with other settlers. They had the most direct encounters with the Native Americans who had been continuously and recently dispossessed, but not entirely displaced. Moving to and homesteading on an Indian reservation gave full meaning to the notion that the land belonged to Native people.

Reservation homesteading brought immigrants face-to-face, neighbor to neighbor with Native American people. When Ernest Nelson filed a claim, he had to acknowledge that "no Indian uses that place." Two of Ernest's neighbors in Loquemont Township (T149N, R89W) were tribal members: Stella Bird-Bear and Mrs. Bird Bear (also known as Bear Woman), who had been allotted eighty acres and taken title (the patent) to their land in 1910. Invisible to the historical record is how the Bird Bears interpreted or received their Scandinavian neighbors. Did they, as Dakota at Spirit Lake, exercise reciprocity in times of need, during harvest, childbirth, or harsh weather? Did they tolerate them, resent them? Trade with them? Work with them?

Although we do not know how they met, by 1920 Ernest and Axeline had married. He was a widower who needed help with his small children, she was a homesteader who had not yet proved up her claim. The enumeration of their household by the U.S. census lists Axeline's widowed mother Thelma Johnston and one of her sisters, Freida Johnston, as belonging to their household. Also listed were Ernest's three young children ages eight, five, and three, and a hired man from Germany. Ernest was identified as a farmer and head of a household; Axeline's occupation was listed as "none," the common designation for housewives who were partner farmers. Not having the title of "farmer" does not mean that Axeline or any woman living on a farm was not involved with farm labor. As a partner farmer on homestead land, women's reproductive labors made farming viable. The census also listed no occupation for Axeline's sister and widowed mother, both of whom were presumably helping to take care of the children, the housework, the barnyard, and the garden, if not the fields.

The census locates their residence on Ernest's land in Loquemont. Axeline had not yet taken title to her homestead, three miles away. Even though the Homestead Act stipulates that only single women could homestead, the General Land Office, recognizing that women's marriages jeopardized their claims, issued clarifying circulars in 1900 and 1904 that specified that "so long as a woman remained eligible and did not abandon her claim," a woman who married could "retain rights to her land."[35] That presumes that the claimant continued to improve and cultivate her land. Axeline's land patent, for 158.72 acres in Township 149N, range 88W, was not issued until 1929, a decade after she married.[36] She received the patent under her married name, Axeline Nelson, although the document also referenced her maiden name, Johnston. Together, Axeline and Ernest held title to 320 acres on the Fort Berthold Reservation.

For those Swedish women who sought independent landownership, homesteading provided a meaningful, although demanding, path. We need only look to the example of Axeline Johnston Nelson to see evidence of someone who sought land with the aim of supporting herself, her kin, and a family enterprise. She prioritized landownership in the process of establishing a household and family. With an eye to agriculture, she followed a path that would best ensure food and a place to live for her widowed mother, her older sister, and now three young stepchildren in addition to the three biological children she would bear in the next several years.[37]

Once Scandinavians and other white settlers began homesteading on Fort Berthold and Spirit Lake reservations, they accumulated more land. The consequence was continued Indian dispossession. As Scandinavians embedded themselves on the reservation, intent on multigenerational ownership, they acquired more land from Indigenous people, not just through homesteading and commuting, but by leasing agricultural land from Indians and buying it on the open market. On these reservations, the massive land transfer under way undermined Indians' efforts at farming and economic autonomy.[38] Their dispossession thus made possible the Scandinavians' staying power. In the borderlands' multiethnic confluence, white landownership shifted the balance of power even though the reservation continued to "belong" to the Three Affiliated Tribes.

Reservations as Transnational Spaces

Reservations were a nexus of cultures and economies, a fluid crossroads of people. Like other kinds of borderlands, they were at once central to the continent and the making of nations, and marginalized by historical narratives. They are local and particular and yet transnational. Because entire Indigenous nations often do not reside on a single reservation, many Native Americans of a common tribe or nation are linked to multiple reservations through kinship, trade, religious worship, and mobility. Native people traveled to reservations where they were enrolled, where their relatives lived, and where they had kin to visit. Sometimes those connections traversed the borders of nation-states (for example, over the border or "Medicine Line" into Canada) as well as states in the United States. This makes bounded reservations transnational not only in their formation—with the Native nation and the United States—but in their twentieth-century incarnations as well.

With the potential for land taking, reservations became immigrant destinations. In North Dakota, that meant reservations were sites of American incorporation. For newcomers from Sweden, Norway, and elsewhere, Fort Berthold and Spirit Lake became spaces of opportunity, places where those with more labor than capital to invest could own land. Reservations were defined by the continuing presence of Native Americans, controlled and managed by white U.S. federal officials, and inhabited by a multitude of Scandinavians.

The U.S. Constitution explicitly excluded Indians from citizenship and denied them naturalization. As Frederick Hoxie demonstrates, Indians were at best "partial citizens"; they "could be jailed without trial, barred from performing religious rituals, and removed from participating in the disposition of trust property assigned to them."[39] For Indian people, reservations were confining, more like refugee and internment camps or prisons than like sanctuaries. Indians' land remained in trust with the federal government, which also controlled their travel, marriages, and the education of their children. These legal distinctions point to essential differences between the groups: Who can own land, buy land, mortgage land, sell land? Who pays taxes? What court has jurisdiction over this land? Who is a citizen of what nation? What rights do people have to practice their religion and culture?

Scandinavian settlers exercised economic and political autonomy and were eligible to own land outright. They could mortgage their land or sell it at will. In the economic exchanges between Natives and newcomers that occurred in the early years of reservation homesteading, white settlers were advantaged: they could lease land allotted to Indians with the permission of the federal agent, hire Indians as seasonal and day laborers, and buy foodstuffs and handcrafted goods from Indian neighbors. In turn, Natives received rent, wages, and cash, none of which was enough to enable them to develop farms rather than merely subsist. Over time, property and citizenship offered Scandinavians and their descendants an economic foothold in their new country and a measure of inclusion in political life that remained unavailable to Dakotas and members of the Three Affiliated Tribes.

We have to ask, even if we cannot answer: What did it mean for Swedes to encounter America in this space? To be incorporated into the dominant culture? Even when Scandinavians established their own enclaves on reservations, they necessarily interacted with Native Americans as well as with white Americans and other immigrant groups. Although their own ideas about what they were doing on this land may have had little to do with the dominant American ideology, they nonetheless homesteaded land and lived on it in an Indian space. The meanings of "American" were shaped by this transnational, multiethnic context for incorporation.

A borderlands frame highlights the entanglement of immigrants and Indians. Like immigrants, Indians were also subject to Americanization efforts.[40] Scandinavian immigrants arrived as economically and politically marginal but nonetheless exercised the privilege of whiteness with potential to become citizens. That privilege of access to landownership enabled them to participate legally in dispossessing Native people, whether or not that was their conscious intention. An agricultural foothold gave them a place to live and a means to support themselves and an extended family.

Reservations are places of Indigenous endurance as well as sites of dispossession. Concurrent histories in common places brought Native Americans together with Scandinavian immigrants.[41] With each other and separately, they exercised agency and asserted power in a bounded space and became more interconnected or distant with each interaction. In landowning and the agricultural economy, immigrants' and Indians' lives intertwined. On the patchwork of land parcels that made up a reservation, Scandinavians' homesteads and farms were interspersed with Indians' allotments. Proximity facilitated interactions and shared work, but rather than subsume one culture within another, the two groups had to come to terms with their mutual distinctiveness, differences in ancestry, language, ways of worship, and citizenship status.

At Fort Berthold and Spirit Lake, Scandinavian Americans—first- and second-generation men and women—arrived, homesteaded, proved up or commuted claims, and purchased land, then lived among Indian people. Others kept moving. Some Swedes even returned to their homeland.[42]

Occupying a space legally designated as Native American, Scandinavian immigrants had to be aware of the racialized legal hierarchies that affirmed their differences even as they encountered each other in the everyday.[43] Borders involve daily negotiation and human interaction in the context of structural asymmetries in access to land and legal status.[44] The boundaries of community, buttressed by legal privileges of landownership, shaped social engagement between groups and affirmed the white privilege of immigrants. Natives and newcomers moved to identify, mark, and interpret the edges of their social lives.

At the same time, in a place where the dominant culture was Dakota or Mandan-Hidatsa-Arikara, Scandinavians and other whites were foreigners, whether or not they were foreign-born. When they ventured off the reservation, Scandinavians might be treated by U.S.-born whites as belonging to the dominant group, as non-English speaking foreigners, or stigmatized for their residence among Indians, whom they regarded as racially inferior. Regardless, reservations were an international nexus.

Because of the interpersonal as well as property entanglements on Indian reservations, both boundaries and borderlands operate as useful concepts. The asymmetrical status of Indians and immigrants translated into unequal relationships. Scandinavian homesteaders were members and even representatives of the surrounding nation-state and enjoyed rights to property and standing in ways that Native Americans did not.

Reservation borderlands challenge the seamless narrative that describes the march toward assimilation, upward mobility, and homogenization of cultures—Indian and Scandinavian-American. The borderlands frame evokes contingency and invites the search for turning points and surprises in a colonial logic. Because borders were not always boundaries, human action could blur, shift, or transgress them.

In the borderlands, laws configured opportunities and constraints differently for men and women, depending on their race-ethnicity. From the vantage point of 1910 looking forward, Axeline Johnston had profoundly different options than Ernest Nelson, even though reservation land was opened to both. As a U.S.-born single woman, she could homestead 160 acres. She was spared neither reproductive responsibilities nor hard labor in making the land productive. As a woman, she could remain a citizen when she married a foreign-born man only if he had naturalized. She could not vote in national elections until 1920.

Had Axeline been Hidatsa rather than Swedish-American, her prospects would have been profoundly diminished. With her tribe facing continued dispossession, poor health, and poverty, even with her own allotment she would have faced the consequences of the U.S. destruction of her people's historic way of life.[45] Instead, as a white citizen, second-generation Swedish-American, woman, and even wife, she was able to own land and provide for her family in the reservation borderlands.

Notes

I would like to thank Samantha Leonard and Grey Osterud for help with research design and conceptual insights, and Aina Lagor for scouring Swedish birth and migration records. Richard Edwards read an earlier version of the manuscript with a generous and critical eye. I am grateful to Adam Hjorthén and Dag Blanck for creating the conditions for this synergistic intellectual exchange.

1. Philip J. Anderson and Dag Blanck, eds., *Norwegians and Swedes in the United States: Friends and Neighbors* (St. Paul: Minnesota Historical Society Press, 2012); Helge Nelson, *The Swedes and the Swedish Settlements in North America* (Lund: Gleerups, 1943), 47; Hans Norman, "Swedes in North America," in *From Sweden to America: A History of the Migration,* ed. Harald Runblom and Hans Norman (Minneapolis: University of Minnesota Press, 1976), 242.

2. The facts of Thelma Johnston's life derive entirely from the U.S. manuscript census, as she reported them to census takers in 1910, 1920, and 1930.

3. Cheryl Elman, Kathryn Feltey, Barbara Wittman, and Daniela Jauk, "Drawn to the Land: Women's Life Course Consequences of Frontier Settlement over Two North Dakotan Land Booms, 1878–1910," *Social Science History* 37, no. 1 (spring 2013): 27–69.

4. Klara kyrkoarkiv, Stockholm, Födelse- och dopböcker, 1891: https://sok.riksarkivet.se/bildvisning/00008094_00266#?c=&m=&s=&cv=265&xywh=-302%2C-382%2C5942%2C4448.

5. Sten Carlsson, "Chronology and Composition of Swedish Emigration to America," in Runblom and Norman, *From Sweden to America,* 140.

6. Ibid., 228.

7. Nelson, *The Swedes and the Swedish Settlements in North America,* 71.

8. Steven Ruggles et al., Integrated Public Use Microdata Series: Version 5.0 [Machine-readable database], (Minneapolis: Minnesota Population Center, 2010).

9. The northeast quarter of section 15 in the township 149N, range 89W, Bureau of Land Management records; patent serial number #623119.

10. William C. Sherman, Playford V. Thorson, Warren A. Henke, Timothy J. Kloberdanz, Theodore B. Pedeliski, and Robert P. Wilkins, eds., *Plains Folk: North Dakota's Ethnic History* (Fargo: North Dakota Institute for Regional Studies, 1988).

11. On March 3, 1918, he was issued a homestead patent. Homestead Entry Patent (under 12. Stat. 392), Document Number: 09219, BLM Serial Number: NDMIN 0009219, Accession Number 623119, issued March 27, 1918.

12. Death Certificate, ND, 001882989, filed August 29, 1917.

13. Gunlög Fur, "Indians and Immigrants: Entangled Histories," *Journal of American Ethnic History* 33, no. 3 (2014): 55.

14. Frederick E. Hoxie, "Retrieving the Red Continent: Settler Colonialism and the History of American Indians in the U.S.," *Ethnic and Racial Studies* 31, no. 6 (2008): 1153–67.

15. Patrick Wolfe, "Settler Colonialism and the Elimination of the Native," *Journal of Genocide Research* 8, no. 4 (December 2006): 393; Richard White, *Railroaded: The Transcontinentals and the Making of Modern America* (New York: W. W. Norton, 2011).

16. Evelyn Nakano Glenn, "Settler Colonialism as Structure: A Framework for Comparative Studies of U.S. Race and Gender Formation," *Sociology of Race and Ethnicity* 1, no. 1 (2015): 52–72.

17. Karen V. Hansen, Grey Osterud, and Valerie Grim. "'Land Was One of the Greatest Gifts': Women's Landownership in Dakota Indian, Immigrant Scandinavian, and African American Communities," *Great Plains Quarterly* 38, no. 3 (summer 2018): 267.

18. Blake Bell, "America's Invitation to the World: Was the Homestead Act the First Accommodating Immigration Legislation in the United States?" In *White Paper:* Homestead National Monument of America, 2012: https://www.nps.gov/home/learn/historyculture/americas-invitation-to-the-world.htm.

19. Pekka Hämäläinen and Samuel Truett, "On Borderlands," *Journal of American History* 98, no. 2 (2011): 352.

20. Ibid., 341.

21. Gloria Anzaldúa, *Borderlands—La Frontera: The New Mestiza,* 4th ed. (San Francisco: Aunt Lute Books, 2012).

22. Ibid., 25.

23. Mandan Hidatsa Arikara Nation, https://www.mhanation.com/history, accessed July 12, 2020; Wendi Field Murray, Maria Nieves Zedeno, Kacy L. Hollenback, Calvin Grinnell, and Elgin Crows Breast, "The Remaking of Lake Sakakawea: Locating Cultural Viability in Negative Heritage on the Missouri River," *American Ethnologist* 38, no. 3 (August 2011): 468–83.

24. Hämäläinen and Truett, "On Borderlands," 360.

25. Melissa L. Meyer, *The White Earth Tragedy: Ethnicity and Dispossession at a Minnesota Anishinaabe Reservation* (Lincoln: University of Nebraska Press, 1994); William T. Hagan, *Taking Indian Lands: The Cherokee (Jerome) Commission, 1888–1893* (Norman: Oklahoma University Press, 2003). For other studies of reservation dispossession, see, for example, David A. Chang, *The Color of the Land: Race, Nation, and the Politics of Landownership in Oklahoma, 1832–1929* (Chapel Hill: University of North Carolina Press, 2010); and Emily Greenwald, *Reconfiguring the Reservation: The Nez Perces, Jicarilla Apaches, and the Dawes Act* (Albuquerque: University of New Mexico Press, 2002).

26. Karen V. Hansen, *Encounter on the Great Plains: Scandinavian Settlers and the Dispossession of Dakota Indians, 1890–1930* (New York: Oxford University Press, 2013).

27. Richard Edwards, Jacob K. Friefeld, and Rebecca S. Wingo, *Homesteading the Plains: Toward a New History* (Lincoln: University of Nebraska Press, 2017), 111.

28. Ibid., 33.

29. Richard Edwards, personal communication, May 26, 2019.

30. With able research assistance of Samantha Leonard, I began compiling a quantitative database of homesteading on all reservations in eleven states.

Digitized land records are part of the Bureau of Land Management's General Land Office. We used plat maps and survey maps, including the 1902 Letter to the Secretary of the Interior on Agreement with the Indians of Fort Berthold Reservation. From the universe of women homesteaders and land purchasers on each reservation, we selected *all* women landowners and a *proximity sample* of male homesteaders and commuters. Using a combination of U.S. census records, state census and marriage records, state naturalization indices, and World War I and World War II draft registration cards, the place of birth, marital status, and parents' place of birth was established for these individuals.

31. Presidential Proclamation 1311, Woodrow Wilson, September 17, 1915; Presidential Proclamation 1367, Woodrow Wilson, April 7, 1917. Once Fort Berthold opened to white homesteading in 1910, more land was added when the federal government, in 1915 and 1917, recategorized coal lands as first- and second-class agricultural land and grazing land (U.S. Department of the Interior, "Report of the Commissioner of Indian Affairs" [1912]: 103, 114).

32. The alternative to homesteading and living on a claim and "improving" it, was commuting. Claimants who commuted could take out a mortgage, which homesteaders could not do; nor could Indian allottees. Borrowing money with their land as collateral allowed farmers to expand operations, invest in machinery, and clear more land. Also, if a claimant had to travel away for an extended period to work or care for a family member, as women often did, their absence might violate the residency requirement and jeopardize their homestead claim. Richard Edwards conducts a systematic comparison of the relative merits of each approach (Richard Edwards, "To Commute or Not Commute, the Homesteader's Dilemma," *Great Plains Quarterly* 38, no. 2 [spring 2018]: 129–50). To his list of advantages, we add that a single woman who took title through commutation could marry after fourteen months, which as a homesteader (with a five-year residency requirement) she could not. Although Edwards reports that, on average, about 20 percent of homestead claims were commuted, we find twice as many acres commuted as proved up. See Karen V. Hansen and Samantha Leonard, "Reservation Homesteading: Norwegian Immigrant Women and Indian Dispossession, 1887–1934," special forum: "*Immigrant Land Taking and Indian Dispossession,*" *Norwegian American Essays.*

33. Ibid.

34. Ibid.

35. Edwards, Friefeld, and Wingo, *Homesteading the Plains,* 216.

36. On her patent, the land is described as lots three and four and the east half of the southwest quarter of Section 19 township 149N, range 88W of the Fifth Principal meridian on Fort Berthold reservation, McLean County.

37. Hansen, Osterud, and Grim, "'Land Was One of the Greatest Gifts.'"

38. Hansen, *Encounter on the Great Plains.*

39. Frederick E. Hoxie, *This Indian Country: American Indian Activists and the Place They Made* (New York: Penguin, 2012), 273.

40. Samantha Leonard, Mikal Eckstrom, Karen V. Hansen, and Gwen N. Westerman, "Immigrant Land Taking and Indian Dispossession," in *Norwegian-American Essays 2020: Migration, Minorities, and Freedom of Religion,* vol. 16, ed. Terje Mikael Hasle Joranger and Harry T. Cleven (Olso: Novus Press, 2020), 21–73.

41. Diana Brydon, Peter Forsgen, and Gunlög Fur, eds., *Concurrent Imaginaries, Postcolonial Worlds: Toward Revised Histories* (Leiden: Brill Rodopi, 2017).

42. It is estimated that one-fifth of the Swedish emigrants returned to Sweden. See Lars-Göran Tedebrand, "Remigration from America to Sweden," in Runblom and Norman, *From Sweden to America,* 201.

43. Hansen, *Encounter on the Great Plains.*

44. Karen V. Hansen, Ken Chih-Yan Sun, and Debra Osnowitz, "Immigrants as Settler Colonists: Boundary Work between Dakota Indians and White Immigrant Settlers," *Ethnic and Racial Studies* 40, no. 2 (2017): 1919–38.

45. Gilbert L. Wilson, *Buffalo Bird Woman's Garden* (St. Paul: Minnesota Historical Society Press, 1987).

2

Borderlands and Lived Encounters

The Swedish Immigrant, Interiority, and Home

Philip J. Anderson

The study of any group, community, organization, institution, culture, or nation involves the aggregate stories of people. Every individual narrative embodies the unique complexity of experience, an identity representing physical, emotional, psychological, and spiritual aspects, a person's journey that invariably includes dreams and longings, hopes and disappointments, happiness and suffering. For the immigrant, it is a life of cultural border encounters and crossings, some physical, most not. National borders are met and crossed in the act of migration, of course, but do not, in and of themselves, reveal the borders of interiority that represent a person's life or, by extension, a people-group's identity. The poet Alberto Ríos speaks to this reality and tension for the immigrant: "The border is a big, neat, clean, clear black line on a map that does not exist." And, unlike encounters of physical borders that appear as thresholds, walls, gates, bridges, official documents of proof of identity that might gain a rite (and right) of passage, "The border used to be an actual place, but now, it is the act of a thousand imaginations."[1]

This chapter addresses aspects of geophysical borders and their encounters, given the transatlantic character of the emigration of 1.3 million Swedes between 1840 and 1930, but primarily explores the nongeographic encounters that are cultural and personal by nature, a window as well into the experiences of the larger group. In this, the border is a way of seeing inwardly and outwardly rather than a physical place. Rich in detail and the intersection of multiple borders, the life of each immigrant represents a singular story, where the places they inhabit shape the person they are. Various approaches may illumine aspects of the interiority of the immigrant's experience, as physical boundaries are crossed, homelands displaced and discovered, identities hyphenated and negotiated—the subjectively journeyed tensions, even paradoxes, of external and internal borders in dialectical relationship, the interplay of roots and routes. The markers along the way, both secular and religious, alter the internal landscapes of place and home, demonstrating how migrants were part of constructing an idea about a Swedish–American borderland through their migrations and experiences. What are rites of passage in negotiating such borders of interiority, a forward motion in time and space? What is the integrative power of memory? How might the narratives of immigrants be distilled in their most elemental form, which demands a necessary filling in and fleshing out of detail and meaning? They leave as *emigrants* with a past and arrive as *immigrants* with a past *and* a future yet to unfold.[2] These questions for reflection are explored through a theoretical framework incorporating the concepts of liminality and topogeny, illustrated by two empirical examples of Swedish immigrant lives.

Liminality and the Swedish Immigrant

> The immigrated Swedish Americans are like a people of their own, separated from their fathers, separated from their children, and not so little misunderstood and rejected by both—a transitional people, who come into conflict, now with the one side, now with the other, and not too seldom with itself—a people that forms a bridge between the old and the new, and which is therefore so tramped upon.[3]

Written in 1912, these words by Johan Person, editor of the Minneapolis newspaper *Svenska Amerikanska Posten,* addressed the introspective longing for home, an immigrant trait—at least for a moment in time—of recollecting childhood place and family. While "home" has become a multilayered reality through migration, regarding the Swedish homeland, "Its geographic location lies in the heart."[4] Many immigrants spoke of "a divided heart" as they negotiated the emotional, psychological, and religious borders over time, not just physical places in time, connecting the past to the future but always taking place in the present. Memory and nostalgia were important aids to reading life's new landscape, participating in a manuscript that put them in the story.[5]

Liminality relates directly to borderlands. The two terms may be considered to overlap, with broader theories of liminality beneficial to understanding the interiority of immigrant experience. Immigrants, in the long process of uprooting and transplanting, encountered and crossed borders through thresholds described symbolically as a door, a gate, a crossroad, a bridge. They were "threshold people"—Person's "transitional people"—on the margins experiencing degrees of ambiguity, disorientation, and erosion of identity. And *borderlands* often became the restrictive *bordered lands* of doors closed, gates shut, bridges blocked, and walls erected, hopes and opportunities dashed. For many there was the irony of passing the Statue of Liberty only to navigate the labyrinth beyond the multiple gates of Ellis Island with its many, all-too-often unscrupulous, gatekeepers. It is estimated that one in six immigrants were detained there, usually overnight, but sometimes for days or weeks, and many (about a quarter-million), which often included family separations, were sent back to their country of origin as "undesirable aliens."[6]

A concept embodying stages and rites of passage, liminality was pioneered in the early twentieth century by French anthropologist and folklorist Arnold van Gennep, whose three stages may be applied to the interiority of immigrant experience, as well as to the more formal rites (secular or sacred) that resolve and recognize the spatial and temporal transitions of the individual or group.[7] The first stage is *separation,* where there is detachment from a stable, intrinsic cultural condition. The second is *liminal* or *marginal,* an ambiguous central stage where few or no attributes of the past survive intact, and new ones have not yet been acquired. This is where the threshold, the border, is experienced not merely in an extrinsic occasional moment but over time. And finally, the third stage is *aggregation* or *disambiguation,* an achievement of a stable condition in which the past and present coexist amicably. The first stage, therefore, is preliminal and the final one postliminal. In this, the immigrant may also be described by other terms—wayfarer, pilgrim, pioneer, sojourner, alien, exile, vagabond—where none fit the whole of experience.

In a pathbreaking study, *The Marginal Man,* sociologist Everett Stonequist depicts the one who has lost something of his former self and has not yet acquired a new or stable self.[8] In van Gennep's stages there is, nevertheless, the continuity of the whole in each individual story. This correlates with Victor Turner's refinement of van Gennep, namely, that *liminoid* (rather than *liminal*) is a preferable term because it leaves an open future of possibilities and outcomes in lived experience, options where personal crises are not necessarily resolved in any formal way.[9]

In her analysis of the huge global Italian diaspora of migration, Donna Gabaccia asks the suggestive question, "Is Everywhere Nowhere?"[10] American literary writer David James Duncan argues that a place is, by definition, a somewhere that is not going anywhere. For the migrant, places that have been home for a long time, and therefore intrinsic to personal identity, cease to be places and become increasingly extrinsic to experience. At worst, it is a kind of death; at best, a reintegration and rebirth. Duncan calls this "The Non Sense of Place."[11] The experience of feeling oddly at home, and yet profoundly out of place, is a limbo of liminality—or, as Nicholas Royle describes, "a particular comingling of the familiar and unfamiliar." With application to many immigrants, he notes that they are comfortable with the familiar (the homeland) and comfortable with the wholly unfamiliar (the place they have not yet arrived) as exotic, abstract, and outside themselves. When the two are combined in lived experience, however, they begin to feel unstable, with the result being the "experience of oneself *as* a foreign body."[12] The border becomes a barrier, not just a liminal line with a foot on each side, a stumbling search in the fog to discern boundaries and location, and the borderland of home increasingly a shadowland, landscapes carried in absentia. Alberto Ríos calls this hyphenation of the person "an equation in search of an equals sign."

An example voicing the experiences of many immigrants was Arthur Landfors, who portrayed unresolved longings in his 1950 poem "Fosterlandet" (My homeland), which parallels van Gennep's stages in its three stanzas:[13]

I remember what he said, the steamboat agent who sold the ticket,
How one would forget, when one came out in the world's swirl among
other

> people, new surroundings, where life roared at a faster rhythm and where the future waited.
>
> How one would forget, forget the small, narrow places at home, forget old friends for new, get sucked into the whirlpool, be a world citizen.
> A world citizen!
>
> Maybe some of us can become that, but most never will.
> We build ourselves homes.

The second stanza speaks of the daily existence of many native-born Swedish Americans, learning a new language of speech and life: *We never become at home here, never ourselves truly at home. We become citizens, we cast our votes in the elections, yet we remain always strangers.* This is a liminoid poem of being "betwixt and between" (Turner's description), which does not reach disambiguation in the third stanza but sustains in lament the marginalization of the second stage. Where is home? Where is nation? Where are *my* people? In this instance, not in Swedish America:

> My homeland!
> It is a coast with bare cliffs, where the sea rushes in, it is a smiling archipelago,
> where shadows play among islands. It is the field where the rye grows and the
> meadow where heather blossoms. It is the valley walk where the river runs and
> the mountains the sun goes down behind. It is the plain where wheat ripens
> and the marshes where the cloudberries grow.
> This is my homeland.
> And now I know that the steamboat agent who sold the ticket didn't tell the truth.

As extensive studies of Swedish-American life have documented, however, many immigrants did experience the journey through external and internal liminalities in a far more positive manner, seizing opportunities of employment, finding new homes in Swedish-American communities and neighborhoods, and daily navigating the borderlands as challenges to be met and crossed successfully—though often idealized, naive, or in denial of how long it might take. Because so many were young and single upon arrival, most had expectations of a long and flourishing future—if not for themselves, at least for their descendants. Swedish-American churches, fraternal orders, businesses, educational institutions, cultural traditions, and language persistence created avenues of participation, employment, and an emergent class of grassroots leaders to articulate and help interpret the immigrant experience. A prolific and pervasive social and religious ethnic press—local, regional, and national—provided the news of Swedish America, promoting its expanding institutionally complete life through reporting, articles, editorials, illustrations, and advertising. Especially important for liminal experience was current news from the provinces of Sweden that had been home; many subscribed to Swedish newspapers or read them in their local library. Equally important, the letters and correspondence sent back and forth, whether personally or officially, crossed both a transnational postal border and those of inner personal landscapes.[14]

While bumping against all sorts of borders, for a time—the so-called heyday of Swedish America until the 1920s—these aspects of community life collectively and constructively embodied a permeable *bordered land,* providing a secure sense of physical, psychological, and religious boundaries. It was said that for many immigrants from rural agrarian backgrounds it was far less a dislocation to find work and forge new lives in the enclaves of Swedish America than to move to cosmopolitan cities such as Stockholm or Gothenburg and find lodging and employment. This became reality for many, but not for all—those who remained unhappy and unsettled, disconnected outwardly and inwardly. They perhaps returned to Sweden or came back and forth more than once.

Topogeny and Border Narratives

Immigrant narratives are inherently teleological, that is, moving with a sense of direction that is purposeful in its quest of destination and fulfillment. Ideally, it progresses through van Gennep's stages from potentiality to actuality in existence—in philosophical terms, an entelechy not entirely demonstrable by empirical methods, which represents an exercise toward integrated wholeness. It depicts the most profound inner life of the person recounted in narrative forms, oral or written. This relates well to borderland studies because it is so particular and yet universal within each biographical narrative of migration; it exposes the ambiguities of the migrant experience, easily disguised by transcending, stereotypical interpretations.

Topogeny refers to the practice where the recitation of an ordered sequence of place-names forms the basic anatomical structure. It is storytelling at its most spare and lists a "thin" outline of location that allows for a "thick" narrative to embody substance, nuance, and meaning.[15] Keith Basso, a linguistic anthropologist, has applied this in his study of indigenous groups. In *Wisdom Sits in Places,* toponyms are mnemonic pegs that over time—even many generations—construct narratives and form identities. Stories take place, and places do not exist in isolation, but along well-worn trails journeyed by many with stories to tell.[16] As a genre, it may be contrasted with Western Euro-American linear written accounts because it perpetuates living oral traditions that carry through an integration of memory of the past into the present. Topogeny allows for the free rein of imagination to remain faithful to a familiar narrative but be freshly compelling, even transforming, each time it is told. It relies on inflection, intonation, and mood, the nonverbal body language of the storyteller. Those hearing for the first time may be drawn in and learn through their own imaginations; experienced listeners recognize and anticipate each place-name to the story and know its direction, the origin and destination of the narrative journey. The storyteller "relives and retells" a mental landscape with a subjectivity that may connect with an individual's interior life, including the affections. Over multiple retellings, it also allows for information to become knowledge and then wisdom. Toponyms have a border-like quality, the lists of place-names that express the externalization of memories.

As a theoretical framework, topogeny may be applied to immigrant stories told in different ways to different audiences. It may be in the genres of written memoir, biography, or oral history; in each form, a succession of place-names serves the same purpose of structural mnemonic pegs on which to hang the narrative. An example from twentieth-century literature serves to illustrate the role topogeny plays in personal narrative structure. Stephen Dedalus is James Joyce's alter ego in *Portrait of the Artist as a Young Man*. He is a sympathetic figure, young and homesick, struggling with a geography assignment. In his effort to find his rightful place in the universe, he writes in the flyleaf of his lesson book, "himself, his name, and where he was."

> Stephen Dedalus
> Class of Elements
> Clongowes Wood College
> Sallins
> County Kildare
> Ireland
> Europe
> The World
> The Universe

On the opposite page, he wrote: "Stephen Dedalus is my name, Ireland is my nation, Clongowes is my dwelling place, and heaven my expectation." What follows is his ongoing drama of place and displacement, and the toponyms are a grounding strategy for his life's story.[17]

Every biography of a Swedish immigrant is structured directly or indirectly around toponyms, place-names that denote an interior life, as well as the objective geographic border crossings and places of dwelling. Some wrote memoirs; others were important enough in their community to have been studied and written about in biographies; many have become known and remembered through genealogy and the writing of family histories for descendants. Most stories, however, have never been told and may well be irrecoverable. Hundreds of thousands of Swedish immigrants were relegated in short order to obscurity, unless family narratives perpetuated a memory of their stories. Some immigrants were more mobile than others in their border wanderings, and because of these layered migrations, topogeny forms and enhances the essential structure of the narrative.

Two Case Studies of Commonality and Difference

Written memoirs or autobiographies are nonexistent for most migrants. The documentary evidence of their lives beyond genealogy may be fragmentary, a few letters or jottings here and there, augmented by stories remembered and repeated by descendants. For a more select number of immigrants, their lives are well known to various degrees, even in the absence of their personal papers or self-conscious recorded recollection. The brief examples that follow demonstrate unfolding toponyms in the absence of personal primary resources, as well as the central role of religious conviction as a cohering force of identity in the migrant experience.

First, the following list of toponyms describes what may be fleshed out from an ordinary and invisible identity, in this case from oral storytelling through three generations of family and a few scattered surviving scraps of paper:

> AXEL ANDERSON: Hökelund, Kila, Värmland, SWEDEN; Minneapolis, Hennepin County, Badger, Roseau County, Minnesota, UNITED STATES OF AMERICA; Dried Meat Creek, Daysland, Alberta, CANADA; Turner Farm, Lake Minnetonka, Camden, Minneapolis, Hennepin County, Minnesota, UNITED STATES OF AMERICA.

Axel Anderson was born in 1865, the fifth of nine surviving children, at Hökelund in the parish of Kila in the province of Värmland, Sweden. His father, Anders Nilsson, who owned the farm that had been in his wife's family since the 1780s, was a village councilman and director of the school board. The family was caught up in the pietistic religious and folk renewal movements of nineteenth-century Sweden and became free church people without leaving the Church of Sweden—then a tense, disputed borderland of belonging as religious diversity and a demand for official toleration grew. In this familial and communal setting, Axel experienced conversion—a religious border crossing of interiority experienced by tens of thousands at the time. When his father died in 1879 at the age of sixty, young Axel—one of seven boys, and not the oldest—labored on nearby farms with only limited prospects in an overpopulated rural area.

Photograph of Axel Anderson, circa 1890. Author's collection.

Not quite twenty-two, Axel chose to emigrate in the summer of 1887, following compulsory military service (which he cut short and left secretly without the necessary papers from his home parish), to meet a friend in Minneapolis. Ship and train fare amounted to fifty dollars. For the next decade, he lived in boardinghouses in several neighborhoods, working as an unskilled day-laborer—six days a week, ten hours a day, for a dollar a day. He dug graves, worked in construction. Applying the one skill he brought with him to a rapidly expanding urban area (good with horses), his most secure work was as a chauffeur to wealthy families. Like many single Scandinavian men, during the 1890s Axel was drawn in winter to the northwoods of Minnesota, in his case in remote Roseau County on the Canadian border, to work as a lumberjack. Axel was a teamster, hauling felled logs over iced roads with sleighs pulled by large draft horses. It was commonly said that while Roseau was not the end of the world, one could see it from there. His existence was transient and essentially homeless.[18]

Axel most likely would have remained a bachelor, as did three of his four younger brothers who emigrated later, were it not for his closest friend—a man named Erickson—being killed in a sawmill accident. His life and border crossings then changed dramatically. Axel had known Erickson's fiancée, Hildur Lidholm, an immigrant domestic working as a nanny for the wealthy Brackett family in Minneapolis. Not well acquainted, they nevertheless became engaged when he visited Minneapolis at Christmas 1904. A frustrated farmer, he immediately headed to Alberta, Canada, to search for his 160-acre homestead, which he eventually located on Dried Meat Creek near Daysland, southeast of Edmonton, land newly opened to settlement by the Crown.[19] It was through letters, a few extant, that Hildur (thirteen years younger) and Axel got to know each other better and their love blossomed. He cleared land with oxen, built a sod house, and in April 1906 Hildur took the train to Canada with her widowed mother to get married in Wetaskiwin. Soon after, Axel built a four-hundred-square-foot primitive cabin, where between 1908 and 1912 four children were added to the family. In 1913, because of Hildur's frail health and the altitude, the family moved back to the familiar environs of Minneapolis. In old age, their pioneer memories of Canada were the fondest.

Axel could not have continued farming anyway, because in 1915 at age fifty his dominant arm was amputated, a radical measure at that time to save his life from melanoma. The family remained quite poor, living in the Camden neighborhood of North Minneapolis. Neighbors and the nearby Mission Covenant church came to their assistance, making it possible to sell eggs and milk. Axel eventually found work as a deliveryman (walking or by streetcar) and then as a freight-elevator operator at the Bureau of Engraving in Minneapolis. He lived a simple life with Hildur and their four surviving sons. One died in 1926, but the others were upwardly mobile and became bankers, fulfilling hopes of their parents and providing security in old age. Axel's topogeny was long (but not necessarily atypical), to which a seemingly unremarkable story through life is attached, until his death in 1952 at age eighty-six. He never returned to Sweden to visit, nor could he have afforded the journey. He stayed in touch with his relatives in Värmland and some correspondence has survived.

For example, while logging during the winter of 1892, he wrote from Badger near the Canadian border to his older sister Matilda in Hökelund, expressing liminal limbo: "I am here in this wilderness, entirely alone. Have been for the past 5 years or so. I have none of my relatives or childhood friends, or a trusted friend from the past to associate with, to talk to about what is new, or the past. As one would say, a person has this need, as all humans do. But, Sister dear, do not be troubled for my situation. I am not, myself, anxious about my future. I stated that I have been alone for the past five years. Not exactly alone. Here are many people of many Nationalities, races, and tongues. I will tell you that I am gripped by a real longing to go back home and see my relatives in Sweden."[20]

Axel never wrote much, but in his hand—written in Roseau County in early 1902—he recorded his innermost thoughts after receiving the news of his mother's death at Hökelund:

> During our childhood days, we recall how we played and ran among the rocks and bushes. But now, we are like young fledglings who have flown from the nest; still we think about, and speak often of our dear home, the happy Eden of our youth. It calls to mind the innocent childhood games and dreams, by the home's quiet "shoreline," where father and mother gave

their dear ones faithful and tender care . . . not a day goes by but those who left it still return there in their thoughts, even though they perhaps live in a far distant land.

To think about a good and happy home, plus reminding oneself of your childhood with its joyous delights, is like wandering on a path that brings with it both freshness and pleasure. On both sides of the home there quietly grows the fragrant lilies at the feet of the evergreen tree. The nightingales of memory seem to sing so beautifully that it sounds like heavenly music to one's heart. How eagerly one would like to join in the Poet's words, while one's deepest feelings are vibrating:

How delightful it is to grow up
in the quiet peace of our home;
To read and study our lessons
while gently surrounded by love;
Now is the happy time,
but as for me, it is already past.
I must be facing life's battles,
standing on my own two feet.

So many memories awaken
that I never had realized before;
I had gone with my mind closed tightly
to things within the portals of home.
Yes, when one is far away—and awakens
like Jacob with his staff,
Oh, how many advantages we miss
that our childhood home did give.[21]

Axel would live another fifty years, with marriage and children in his future, no longer a lonely bachelor. This essay and poem, typical of the thresholds of interiority described by other immigrants, was nevertheless unique to his own experience, both inwardly and in the many geographic borders he had already crossed, with more yet to come. Deeply religious, Axel wrote and spoke about a spiritual bridge over the borderlands that separated him from loved ones at home, frequently quoting

Swedish bishop Esias Tegnér: "Let us meet often on the bridge of remembrance." Over his sixty-five years in North America, Axel appears in the end to have navigated well the liminalities of Arnold van Gennep's stages, where past and present and future came to coexist amicably and—for his singular story—all the many borderlands of home may be said to have merged into one. Axel's long journey of a "divided heart" was ultimately mediated by the constant anchor of his religious experience.

Fredrik Franson, in contrast to Axel Anderson, was a multilingual entrepreneurial religious leader and peripatetic missionary about whose life and influence much has been recounted. Although he wrote a few books and pamphlets, translated at the time into several languages, personal papers and correspondence are nonexistent, though descriptive reports of his activities in religious periodicals are extensive. Axel certainly fell into the realm of Franson's religious influence about the urgency of faith and no doubt heard him speak at mass evangelistic missionary meetings in Minneapolis. They shared religious experiences in both Sweden and America—one man invisibly ordinary and private, the other publicly visible in an extraordinary way with a huge global and admiring following.

Until well into the nineteenth century, religion in Sweden had been circumscribed by a clearly delineated border, namely, the Lutheranism of the Church of Sweden, which had been made compulsory in both church and state since the Reformation of the sixteenth century until religious toleration became officially granted to dissenters in 1858 with the revocation of the 1726 Edict Against Conventicles. Many established boundaries were tested and redefined as new denominations emerged with transatlantic influences and counterparts: Baptist, Methodist, Episcopalian, Mission Covenant, Free, Adventist, Presbyterian, Holiness Pentecostal—along with sects like the utopian Eric Jansonists and Mormons. The religious borders of interiority could be far more confusing as many immigrants, through various conversions and turn of convictions, moved through several experiential stages, qualified by American influences. These groups could also represent the place-names of a person's religious topogeny.[22] Axel found a lifelong home in the Swedish Mission Covenant, a bridge between the old and the new lands; a congregation had been begun in 1882 in his childhood home in Kila, five years prior to his emigration.

Franson, however, disdained these distinctions and, in fact, came to see organized denominations as sinful. True Christians were united only in a heavenly, not earthly, existence.

The religious and geographic toponyms of Fredrik Franson are too long to list sequentially here; mapped out, they serve as mnemonic pegs to the complex and activist life of a popular revivalist and depict innumerable border crossings.[23] Born in Nora, Västmanland, Sweden, in 1852, Franson emigrated to the United States with his widowed mother and stepfather to Lindsborg, Kansas, in 1869 and moved shortly thereafter to Estina, Nebraska, where, gravely ill with malaria in 1872, he was converted and became a Baptist through the influence of his sister. He soon began working as an itinerant evangelist in the Midwest, until he encountered Dwight L. Moody, probably during late 1875 or early 1876 at campaigns in New York and Philadelphia. Franson followed Moody back to Chicago, participated in a great revival at the end of the year, and joined Moody's congregation. He learned the methods of revivalist preaching and applied them not only to the swelling tide of Swedish immigrants in America, but also in a pan-Scandinavian way among Norwegians and Danes. His primary influences were Anglo-American: pragmatic evangelism and the dispensationalism of John Nelson Darby (the Irish founder of the Plymouth Brethren) in antidenominationalism and premillenarian eschatology. He promoted international cooperation, became suspicious and severed all ties with denominations and institutions, yet supported individual congregations. He became known as Moody's "Swedish Disciple."

In 1879–80, Franson served as a missionary among Scandinavian Mormons in Utah, where he joined the efforts of American Presbyterian missionaries and agencies. Turning toward a more promising harvest, he led a successful prophetic conference in Chicago in 1881, the reputation of which spread throughout Sweden prior to his first return visit later that year. This began Franson's international wanderlust that would last more than a quarter century. A latter-day St. Francis, small and wiry with dark hair and penetrating eyes, he traveled without money, carrying only a satchel with Bible, umbrella, and little more than the clothes he wore. Franson claimed that he visited more than half the cities, towns, and villages in Sweden proclaiming his blend of Darby's any-moment

Second Coming and secret Rapture (which he predicted would occur in 1897), Mary Baker Eddy's Christian Scientism, and Holiness perfectionism. As his popularity grew, opposition from Swedish authorities intensified and he was for a time banned from public meetings. At one such confrontation, Franson produced his American citizenship papers and said in English: "If anyone causes me injury, he will have to reckon with fifty million American citizens who are behind this paper." The assertion of religious freedom, accompanied by his calm presence, the strange tongue, and the mysterious document left the people in awe.[24]

Franson then traveled to Norway and Denmark—where he would have his greatest success through the years—as well as to Finland, Germany, France, Switzerland, Italy, and Russia. He returned to Sweden in 1889 and was back in Chicago the following year. He organized the Scandinavian Alliance Mission in Minneapolis in 1891 and traveled to organize a branch in Sweden in 1892. From 1894 to his death in 1908, apart from a visit to the United States and numerous sojourns in Scandinavia, Franson circumnavigated the globe, organizing mission work in India, China, New Zealand, Australia, Japan, Korea, Burma, Turkey, the Middle East, South Africa, and several countries in South America—finally returning to the United States through Mexico to Idaho Springs, Colorado, where on August 2, 1908, he died at the age of fifty-six, "worn out by his incessant labours in service for the Master."[25] When asked if he wanted medical help, Franson's last words echoed Mary Baker Eddy: "No, God is my doctor."[26] His funeral was in Colon, Nebraska, where his brother August lived, with burial in Estina, perhaps the nearest place he knew to home.

In pondering the impact of these popular nineteenth-century religious movements, Harvard historian Arthur Schlesinger Sr. said that it is "the history of nobodies who became somebodies."[27] Franson was a nobody who became a somebody, though, of course, not everybody's somebody. He was hardly typical in the dizzying borderlands he quickly passed through. He surely spoke of his core spiritual identity, but his formal religious identities were constantly in flux and ill-defined. As a migrant, did he even have a physical sense of home, a place in time? Did he wrestle with liminality or ever achieve van Gennep's third stage of aggregation? He never wrote about this and it seemed not to matter. Confident that the world would soon end, perhaps he was too busy for such interiority. His motto: "Forward Until Upward."[28] Unlike Axel Anderson, a nobody who remained a nobody and who finally found home in marriage at the age of forty, Franson was homeless his entire adult life, never marrying and childless, crisscrossing the world and passing through multiple borders, never inhabiting any "place"—though his last will and testament, dated March 19, 1902, began: "I, Fredrik Franson, of the town of Chicago."[29]

Franson's out-of-the-ordinary life and work had enormous influence on the borderlands of other immigrants, especially the young and recently arrived. His religious convictions, derived from his own experiences but incessantly proclaimed publicly, drew others into the interiority of threshold encounters: conversions, convictions, and callings. Through the Scandinavian Alliance Mission, countless young immigrants heeded Franson's "Macedonian Call" and soon left the United States with little or no preparation for the "foreign fields" of his global organized mission activity, preaching the urgency of an imminent Second Coming. Transnational borders became global dotted lines on personal maps; cultural, religious, and linguistic boundaries were confronted and crossed; many apocalyptic idealists returned to North America, often disillusioned and culturally confused; and others lived out the remainder of their lives in remote regions of the world.

The descriptive biographical accounts of Axel Anderson and Fredrik Franson test, as well as demonstrate, the results of an empirical application to the theoretical framework of liminality and topogeny. By extension to others inhabiting the borderlands of Swedish America, every immigrant story embodies a distinct journey across the spectrum of liminality with degrees of movement from separation to disambiguation, thus revealing borders encountered physically or negotiated internally through time. No two are alike, yet they collectively deepen understanding of the larger group experience. Moreover, the mnemonic pegs of place-names provide an essential anatomy to the trajectory of individual migrant journeys and their telling. The old and new homelands—powerful absences coexisting as powerful presences—signify physical, emotional, psychological, and (for many) religious dimensions of lived encounters. They are consequences of migration, interiority, and notions of home.

Notes

1. Alberto Ríos, "The Border: A Double Sonnet," in *A Small Story about the Sky* (Port Townsend, Wash.: Copper Canyon Press, 2015): https://poets.org/poem/border-double-sonnet.

2. Cf. Roger Waldinger, *The Cross-Border Connection: Immigrants, Emigrants, and Their Homelands* (Cambridge: Harvard University Press, 2015); Roger Waldinger and Nancy Green, eds., *A Century of Transnationalism: Immigrants and Their Homeland Connections* (Urbana: University of Illinois Press, 2016).

3. Quoted in H. Arnold Barton, *A Folk Divided: Homeland Swedes and Swedish Americans, 1840–1940* (Carbondale: Southern Illinois University Press, 1994), 226. Barton addressed the process of assimilation and change as "conversion" in "From Swede to Swedish American: The Conversion Theme in the Literature of Swedish America," in *The Old Country and the New: Essays on Swedes and America* (Carbondale: Southern Illinois University Press, 2007), 106–15.

4. Barton, *A Folk Divided,* 226. Cf. Harald Runblom, ed., *Migrants and the Homeland: Images, Symbols, and Reality* (Uppsala: Uppsala Multiethnic Papers 44, 2000).

5. Dorothy Burton Skårdal noted that three-quarters of all Scandinavian-American literature dealt with nostalgia, home, and pilgrimage (*The Divided Heart: Scandinavian Immigrant Experience through Literary Sources* [Lincoln: University of Nebraska Press, 1974]).

6. For the history of Ellis Island, see Ann Novotny, *Strangers at the Door: Ellis Island, Castle Garden, and the Great Migration to America* (New York: Bantam Books, 1974); Thomas M. Pitkin, *Keepers of the Gate: A History of Ellis Island* (New York: New York University Press, 1975). Cf. Philip J. Anderson, "In the Snare of Uncle Sam: Carl Johan Nyvall's 'A True Story of My Experience and Treatment at My Landing on Ellis Island,' 1901," in *Scandinavians in Old and New Lands: Essays in Honor of H. Arnold Barton,* ed. Philip J. Anderson, Dag Blanck, and Byron J. Nordstrom (Chicago: Swedish-American Historical Society, 2004), 221–36.

7. Arnold van Gennep, *The Rites of Passage,* trans. Monika B. Vizedom and Gabrielle L. Caffee (Hove, England: Psychology Press, 1977), 21. This was first published in Paris in 1909 as *Les rites de passage.* Cf. Paul Elmen, "Immigrant Rites of Passage," in H. Arnold Barton, ed., *Ancient Folk in a New Land: Essays in Honor of Nils William Olsson,* a special number of the *Swedish-American Historical Quarterly* 35, no. 3 (1984): 309–15.

8. Everett Stonequist, *The Marginal Man: A Study in Personality and Culture Conflict* (New York: Charles Scribner's Sons, 1937). The concept "marginal man" was coined by Stonequist's mentor at the University of Chicago, Robert E. Park.

9. Victor W. Turner, *The Ritual Process: Structure and Anti-Structure* (New York: Penguin, 1969), 95.

10. Donna R. Gabaccia, "Is Everywhere Nowhere? Nomads, Nations, and the Immigrant Paradigm of United States History," *Journal of American History* 86, no. 3 (1999): 1115ff.

11. David James Duncan, *My Story as Told by Water* (San Francisco: Sierra Club Books, 2001), 49.

12. Quoted in Robert Moor, *On Trails: An Exploration* (New York: Simon & Schuster, 2016), 283. The experience of liminality is explored by Boey Kim Cheng in *Between Stations* (Artarmon, Australia: Giramondo Publishing, 2009). Cf. Boey Kim Cheng, "Home Is Elsewhere: Reflections of a Returnee," in *Hearth: A Global Conversation on Community, Identity, and Place,* ed. Annick Smith and Susan O'Connor (Minneapolis: Milkweed Editions, 2018), 117–28.

13. In Alan Swanson, *Literature and the Immigrant Community: The Case of Arthur Landfors* (Carbondale: Southern Illinois University Press, 1990), 51f.

14. See, for example, Philip J. Anderson and Dag Blanck, eds., *Swedish-American Life in Chicago: Cultural and Urban Aspects of an Immigrant People, 1850–1930* (Urbana: University of Illinois Press, 1992); Anita Olson Gustafson, *Swedish Chicago: The Shaping of an Immigrant Community, 1880–1920* (DeKalb: Northern Illinois University Press, 2018); Philip J. Anderson and Dag Blanck, eds., *Swedes in the Twin Cities: Immigrant Life and Minnesota's Urban Frontier* (St. Paul: Minnesota Historical Society Press, 2011); H. Arnold Barton, ed., *Letters from the Promised Land: Swedes in America, 1840–1914* (Minneapolis: University of Minnesota Press, 1975).

15. Cf. Clifford Geertz, "Thick Description: Towards an Interpretive Theory of Culture," in *The Interpretation of Cultures: Selected Essays* (New York: Basic Books, 1973), 3–30.

16. Keith H. Basso, *Wisdom Sits in Places: Landscape and Language among the Western Apache* (Albuquerque: University of New Mexico Press, 1996).

17. James Joyce, *A Portrait of the Artist as a Young Man,* Introduction and notes by Jacqueline Belanger (Hertfordshire, UK: Wordsworth Editions, 2001), 9f.

18. For an insightful description and analysis of Minneapolis during this period, especially the lives of single male laborers and living conditions, see Annette Atkins, "At Home in the Heart of the City," *Minnesota History* 58 (2003): 186–204. Her nuanced observations about "homelessness" expose the subjectivity of this label and serve as a caution against assumed generalization. Many boardinghouse residents objected to the term as prejudicial; it was also a basis for justifying the need for urban-renewal projects (300ff.).

19. In 1905, this area of Alberta was just beginning to be settled and towns formed. Scandinavians were arriving in greater numbers, railroads were being built, and pioneer life on this fertile land was remote and harsh. Axel may well have been influenced by the aggressive recruiting of the Swedish-American agent for the Dominion based in the Twin Cities, C. O. Swanson. See Elinor Barr, *Swedes*

in Canada: Invisible Immigrants (Toronto: University of Toronto Press, 2015). Axel wrote to Hildur from Wetaskiwin on February 25, 1905: "Have been out in the wilderness about sixty-five miles looking for a homestead, as you know was my intention. . . . How did I like the wild country? Well, Hildur dear, in some respects I did like it, in others I did not. I traveled over a lot of land in those two weeks, I tell you. Many miles a day, sometimes on foot, sometimes on horseback, sometimes in a sleigh. And I have seen most all kinds of people and most all kinds of animals" (manuscript, in possession of the author; Axel Anderson is author's father's father).

20. Axel Anderson to Matilda Svensson, n.d. [1892], trans. S. C. Albert Anderson. A ten-page letter, the first two pages are missing. Manuscript, in possession of the author.

21. Untitled manuscript, in possession of the author, trans. S. C. Albert Anderson. Later in life, Axel labeled it *Skrifvet i min lilla stuga i Roseau Co. 1902.* The poet remains anonymous.

22. The author has addressed borderland dimensions of Swedish-American religion elsewhere. See Philip J. Anderson, "The Lively Exchange of Religious Ideals between the United States and Sweden during the Nineteenth Century," in *American Religious Influences in Sweden,* ed. Scott E. Erickson (Uppsala: Tro & Tanke, 1996), 31–48; Philip J. Anderson, "From Compulsion to Persuasion: Voluntary Religion and the Swedish Immigrant Experience," *Swedish-American Historical Quarterly* 66, no. 1 (2015), 3–23.

23. Within a year of Franson's death, Josephine Princell published a lengthy biography, based on a variety of sources but no personal papers, thus an indication that there were none. Its twenty-six detailed chapters are structured solely around the toponyms of Franson's life (*Missionär Fredrik Fransons lif och verksamhet* [Chicago: Chicago-Bladet Publishing Co., 1909]). All subsequent biographical treatments have been organized similarly. For Franson in historical context, see especially David M. Gustafson, *D. L. Moody and Swedes: Shaping Evangelical Identity among Swedish Mission Friends, 1867–1899* (Linköping: Linköping University, 2008); and Edvard Paul Torjesen, "A Study of Fredrik Franson: The Development and Impact of His Ecclesiology, Missiology, and Worldwide Evangelism," PhD dissertation, International College, Los Angeles, 1984.

24. Quoted in George M. Stephenson, *The Religious Aspects of Swedish Immigration* (Minneapolis: University of Minnesota Press, 1931), 127.

25. Princell, *Missionär Fredrik Fransons lif och verksamhet,* 389.

26. Ibid., 353.

27. Quoted in Timothy L. Smith, *Revivalism and Social Reform: American Protestantism on the Eve of the Civil War* (Baltimore: Johns Hopkins University Press, 1980), 250.

28. In contrast, Franson's quite different acquaintance, David Nyvall (1863–1946), Mission Covenant leader and first president of North Park University,

wrote extensively over several decades on the issue of religious and ethnic identity, from which may be gleaned perceptive insights about "borderlands" experience and interiority. See Scott E. Erickson, *David Nyvall and the Shape of an Immigrant Church: Ethnic, Denominational, and Educational Priorities among Swedes in America* (Uppsala: Acta Universitatis Upsaliensis, 1996).

29. Princell, *Missionär Fredrik Fransons lif och verksamhet*, 392.

3

Imagining Borders and Heartland through Legend

Jennifer Eastman Attebery

The Swedish emigrants/immigrants crossed human-conceived borders to enter North America. They also found borders and borderlands to be powerful metaphors for expressing and interpreting their migration experiences. From a folklorist's point of view, metaphorical borders and borderlands are not just academic concepts but also are concepts of the groups that came to America—folk motifs shared informally to express and organize experience. The genre of folklore that most effectively distilled these concerns for the Swedish migrants was historical legend.

As folk concepts, borders and borderlands have strong roots in Europe, including Scandinavian culture. Thinking of areas of land as bordered and delimiting of cities, regions, and states and marking borders through interactions with the landscape and with competitors for resources emerges in Scandinavian folk narrative. Legends tell of the creation of boundaries through circumnavigating the landscape and the marking of boundaries with magically protected boundary stones. Boundaries that are disturbed can be haunted, then, by the ghosts of those who violated them, by moving boundary stones, for example.[1] As folklorists Reimund Kvideland and Henning K. Sehmsdorf note, "[o]wnership of land was the very basis of rural life,"[2] and hence these stories expressed important concerns about the accurate bounding of land. Also prominent in European lore, including that of Scandinavia, were encounters with hidden beings in the borderlands of summer farms and forests.[3] Protagonists are tested in these borderland zones and encounters within them, but story cycles also include the idea of helpful invisible folk figured as "good neighbors and friends."[4] When we look to the European sources for borderland concepts, borders and borderlands are lines and territories of negotiations between beings and mysterious or dangerous forces, holding potential benefits or harms.

Boundaries and border crossings were at the heart of the Swedish migration experience during the mid-nineteenth to early twentieth centuries. Swedish people who left their home parishes traveled across multiple boundaries—within Sweden from parish to parish and from rural landscape to city harbor; during the ocean passage from port to port across the North Sea, often by rail across northern England, and then across the Atlantic; from emigrant to immigrant status at Castle Garden or Ellis Island; and from rail stop to rail stop across eastern North America to the Midwest or West. At the end of these travels there was often a final city to rural transition that could include walking to a farm site. Once arrived, immigrants attempted to set up familiar boundaries but also continued to experience the shocks of cultural and environmental contacts that violated familiarity.

These migration experiences were distilled in folk narrative. Personal experience, related contemporaneous to an event, eventually became historical legend told and inscribed generations later. In these narratives, repeated motifs and other story patterns represent a transgenerational and culturally constructed sense of literal and metaphorical boundaries, border crossings, and borderland experiences. For this study, I take as my materials the local historical legends inspired by migration and community building that were shared among Swedish immigrants to the rural communities of the American Midwest and West.[5] Historical legends are stories about a people's past. While the term *legend* might signal untruth in everyday usage, in folkloristics the genre *legend* encompasses narratives told as true, or sometimes told in a state of suspended disbelief. Narrators and their audiences maintain an unspoken pact in their belief or quasi belief in the veracity of legends. For historical legend, this pact ordinarily constitutes quite earnest belief in the legend's truth about the community's past.

To say that historical legends are told as true, however, does not mean that the events related in legend can be corroborated. Rather, the truth of historical legend is, as folklorist Barre Toelken notes, "a cultural construct governed by values we share with others in our culture."[6] Toelken uses as an example the difficult-to-verify stories of Indians wanting to purchase golden-haired girls. From a folklorist's point of view (not a historian's), such narratives embody truths about "real cultural concerns [among the settler colonists, American and immigrant European, who moved into Indian land] about family identity, racial fears, sex roles, and social norms."[7]

Methods and Sources for This Study

To gather a wide swath of representative historical legends for comparative study, I use local histories, in which legends appear encapsulated within the text at moments when the writer breaks into storytelling. These volumes are written by local commemorative committees, often formed in response to a centennial or jubilee, or by an individual who by virtue of long residency and broad knowledge of a community and its people—rather than through academic training—has become a locally recognized history expert. More commonly than academic historians, local history writers break from the generalized discourse of historical narrative to focus on stories that they have heard or received from community members. In these passages, they slow down the pace of their text, narrowing the scope to focus on the actions of specific characters in a specific event and at a specific place. The slower pace and narrowed focus allow for description, action, dialogue, and characterization.

I take these storytelling passages as indicators of motifs and tableau scenes that have emerged in vernacular tradition and been inscribed in local histories because they resonate with meaning for the compilers and the community they represent. Although such narratives do vary over time, their motifs and tableau scenes are traditional narrative units with some continuity over generations. They are memorable handholds for storytellers and foci for the most strongly resonant community concerns. Thus, historical legends are doubly situated. Past narrators, those who originated the story, played a part in winnowing experience, but later tellers or inscribers of the narrative also play a part in continuing the use of core motifs and tableau scenes that represent a community consensus on the community's past.

Motifs are small, discrete story units repeated from narrative to narrative. They can include characters, actions, or objects that are distinctly recognizable. The helpful, Robin Hood–like western outlaw, for example, is a distinct character in legends across the Midwest and West.[8] Tableau scenes are strong central images combining motifs in memorable and meaningful ways and occurring at a peak moment in a narrative. The folklorist Larry Danielson identifies, for example, key descriptive passages in Midwestern historical legends about tornados, such as a character's being sucked up the chimney.[9] A tableau scene is so central to a legend that it can act similarly to catch-phrases, referencing the essence of a legend in conversations in which the narrative is not fully told. In formulating the idea of tableau scenes as a folk narrative component, Axel Olrik calls tableaux "sculptured situations" for their "power of being able to etch themselves in one's memory."[10]

In this study I draw on about two hundred legend texts from Midwestern and Western communities in which Swedish settlement was dominant, representing events spanning 1840–1920 that are related in historical legends inscribed at least a generation after the event. This body of folklore offers numerous texts in which borders and borderland crossings and encounters are highlighted. Through these we can see the migrants, having crossed many borders, attempting to anchor themselves in American localities. Broadly, these narratives fit within the categories of travel and transportation, acts of transplantation, and vulnerability in the new landscape. I make no claim, though, that all of these narratives are unique to the Swedish Americans. Among the store of narrative motifs and tableau scenes shared among Swedish Americans are several that are also shared outside of Swedish America as part of the metanarrative of the settler-colonial movement in which Swedish immigrants and their descendants were participants.

In this corpus, a few motifs and tableau scenes stand out as recurrent, marking experiences and concerns significant for this ethnic group and inscribing those experiences on the seemingly undifferentiated spaces into which they migrated. In the remainder of this essay I focus on three story patterns in which immigrants express their relationship to landscape borders and borderlands. Marking travel across the Atlantic and the shift from emigrant to immigrant status are stories of disembarkation at Castle

Garden, Ellis Island, or rail stops in the continental interior. Marking transplantation are stories of walking the land. Marking the immigrants' sense of vulnerability in their new landscape are stories of dramatic weather and landscape events.

These categories assuredly do not exhaust the many kinds of stories shared by Swedish Americans that feature borders and borderlands as those concepts can be variously defined. If we were to turn to the borders and borderlands of cultural contact, for example, we would find among the Swedish Americans a large body of narrative marking cultural contact with Indian tribes. The boundary of the domestic threshold is a motif in numerous stories featuring the tableau scene of an Indian or a group of Indians arriving at a farm and crossing the threshold apparently without warning. Sociologist Karen Hansen interprets these accounts as representing "a clash of cultural logics" surrounding visitation, hospitality, and generosity.[11] Certainly, an expanded study of the Swedish Americans' historical legends could examine this rich material in terms of borders and borderlands, but this present, briefer study will have to set aside the cultural contact narratives in favor of those stories that are more landscape-oriented.

Disembarkation Narratives

Disembarking upon reaching an American destination appears as a prominent tableau scene in historical legend. As recounted by later generations, these stories convey their ancestors' initial disorientation in their new environment and the beginning of a new national and ethnic identity. Marking this border crossing from sea voyage to American soil or from train passage to a town where they hoped to establish roots were story events hinging on language and cultural differences and physical, economic, and social preparedness.

Among the legends of Allen Erickson's family of Moorhead, Minnesota, for example, is the story of Erickson's father's arrival in Minneapolis:

> [M]y dad . . . remembered getting off the train at the Union Depot and walking down Washington Avenue and feeling like he didn't have a friend in the world and he didn't know what on earth he was going to do. Here he was

> in this strange new land he didn't know the language or anything. . . . [A]ll at once he heard some people speaking Swedish, and he said it was the sweetest sound he had ever heard in his life. And so he rushed over there and there were three fellows and he started talking to them and before they were through talking, they had lined him up a job working on the railroad.[12]

In disembarkation narratives like this the arrival point becomes a liminal zone. The immigrant is depicted as confused in new territory. Often this is dramatized through the immigrant's walking the streets of an unfamiliar town or city. Immigrants' degree of preparedness puts them at risk: they do not know English, they are easy prey for scams, they do not have enough currency for food, or those who intended to greet them are delayed. In an example from Hawley, Minnesota, a disembarking immigrant is depicted as having "five cents in his pocket. . . . he walked up and down the streets there. He didn't know just what to do. He didn't know anybody. He didn't know where to go and so he went into the store and he bought five cents worth of snuff for the five cents he had in his pocket." In this narrative the immigrant meets up with the narrator's father, who "staked him," that is, provided funds and a job.[13]

Because these stories are related by later generations in a rags-to-riches generic tradition, they end with recovery and survival.[14] They also open up space for humorously examining ethnic stereotypes. Spending one's last pennies on snuff evokes the masculine stereotype of the Swedish immigrant who highly values his *snus*—both acknowledging the stereotype and humorously critiquing Swedish culture. Similarly, a migratory narrative found as widely as Illinois, Wisconsin, Nebraska, Wyoming, and Texas uses the disembarkation tableau to examine the identity crisis assailing immigrants who in America encountered new bases for cultural difference. As related in Illinois, a black man made it a habit to meet unsuspecting Swedish immigrants disembarking at Galesburg, startling them by speaking fluent Swedish. In answer to their query whether he was Swedish, he replies, "Yes, but never mind. When you have been in this country as long as I have, you'll turn black, too!"[15]

The disembarking immigrant's vulnerabilities included gullibility in the midst of a culture not fully understood, yielding a subcategory of disembarkation narratives in which immigrants are scammed by confidence artists. An interestingly elaborate example appears in the repertoire of the descendants of Andrew Johnson, a tailor in Sweden who sold all his property and his business to emigrate. According to his descendant Albert P. Strom, who relates the story a century later, in 1868 Johnson arrived in New York City with two friends:

> [A] man who spoke Swedish convinced them to go to South Carolina instead of directly to Nebraska. . . . After working in South Carolina for a month, they asked for their wages, but received nothing. . . . They continued to work several more weeks, but still got no pay. By this time they decided they had been "taken in" and the sooner they left the better. By now a part of their travel funds were spent without getting any returns for their work in South Carolina. So they started out walking, picking up odd jobs where they could, until they had enough money to pay the rail fare to their destination.[16]

In Johnson's disembarkation story, his and his companions' vulnerability resulting from language and cultural differences places them in an extended period of liminality in which they have not yet fully stepped into an American existence. They are hence "taken in," positioned as green immigrants. It is a situation requiring that they literally and figuratively walk the landscape to redeem the situation.

With border crossing, immigrants risk the ambiguities present in a liminal state. Perhaps they gain something—a new hyphenated American identity along with an Anglicized name, as related in numerous family accounts about name changes—but there are also losses. In the most dramatic stories, personal losses are tragic, as if a sacrifice were required in order to cross into America. One such sacrifice is narrowly averted in a disembarkation narrative from Vernon E. Bergstrom's self-published 1989 compilation of newspaper columns about the history of localities in Minnesota:

> The Atlantic was calm, but midway across little Olaf came down with a good old fashioned case of the measles. His father, Gamnis Eric . . . anxiously asked the ship's captain for medical help. . . . Mindful of the dangers to the ship's passengers, the tough captain told Gamnis that no doctor was aboard. He sternly commanded: "throw the youngster overboard." However, the

> calloused captain had not fathomed the ingenuity of the Olsons. . . . Mother Margaret hid little Ole from the snooping captain, and when they docked in Ellis Island, Ole had almost recovered. The crafty little Swede pulled down his homemade stocking cap partly over his face—hiding the tell-tale blemishes on his boyish face. The immigration authorities were none the wiser. Mother Margaret's knitting was Ole's ticket to the "promised land."[17]

This motif of child sacrifice, represented in the imagined, averted tableau of casting a sick child into the Atlantic, has biblical connotations in Bergstrom's version, ending as it does with an arrival in a "promised land." Yet, Bergstrom signals to his readers that there will be a happy ending through the tone of his qualifiers—the disease being "good old fashioned," the captain "snooping," and the boy Ole a "crafty little Swede." *Ole* is a Scandinavian marker and a name used in America for representative Swedish male immigrants, giving this story of an averted tragedy a sense of more general applicability.[18] The child sacrifice motif appears fully realized in Thomas N. Holmquist's local history of the Smoky Valley, Kansas, in which he relates the story of a child left behind at Castle Garden, either because of cholera or in the keeping of an unreliable sitter; family versions vary, leaving the story open-ended.[19]

Transplantation Narratives

The narratives of extreme sacrifices upon disembarkation evoke ideas from Swedish legend in which it is dangerous and defining for land occupants and owners to be directly in contact with boundaries.[20] Through bodily contact and exertion, land is claimed, usually through walking or riding horses to set the boundaries of a property, bishopric, or realm.[21] In an example from Västergötland, Sweden, the custom was reportedly that

> new [land]owners have as much land as they could traverse within a given time. [A greedy person] wanted to have as much land as possible and ran around a huge piece of ground. He overexerted himself and fell down dead. That manor became bigger than [a bordering estate acquired by a less greedy and more prudent person] but it can never pass from father to son.[22]

This idea appears implicitly enacted in another category of legend tableaux in which immigrants walk the land. These narratives do not reference walking the bounds as a land custom—indeed, the custom did not apply in the American setting—but the idea nevertheless hovers over these stories as if through cultural reflex. In the American setting, these narratives still bear a relationship to land occupation but also serve new purposes. Those moving to the Midwest and West during the nineteenth century were engaged in land claims, but they also experienced "undifferentiated space." As noted by Lisa Gabbert and Paul Jordan-Smith, imagined places and spaces emerge through cultural practices, and thus "undifferentiated space may be transformed into identifiable and encoded place."[23] For the Swedish Americans, the very unsettling open spaces of the American Midwest and West could be controlled and resolved through narratives in which the land is bodily traversed.

Walking tableaux thus connote much more than their ordinary interpretation as representing how hard life was for the immigrants. They also represent how occupation is earned (evoking the Swedish legendary rationale), how America could thwart easy charting and occupation because of its apparent emptiness and unboundedness, and how the labor of charting and occupation could bring rewards or dangers. Consider, for example, this passage from C. J. Johnson's *History of the First Swedish Pioneers Who Settled Otter Creek Valley* (Iowa), in which walking a great distance to establish a land claim is emphasized:

> [A] . . . Wisconsin farmer decided to come out and see the rich soil in western Iowa. But instead of going to the railroad station and taking the train, he . . . decided to walk on foot from Wisconsin to western Iowa. So, taking food enough in a sack on his back, he started out on his journey and reached his destination in safety, but I leave it to any one to figure out how much the man saved on the trip.[24]

In his local history of Stanton, Iowa, Claus L. Anderson also emphasizes that many walked to the early railroad construction camp that would become the Stanton townsite: "Johannes Sellergren and Carl Anderson Vilgren walked all the way from Effingham, Ill., to see for themselves what inducements this project offered."[25]

The imagined vacancy of Midwestern and Western spaces appears in many walking narratives. In *A Kansan's Enterprise,* for example, a local history of Enterprise, Kansas, and its region, compiled by Ellen Welander Peterson, we find this narrative:

> C. W. always walked to and from work [at his shoe shop] daily. Some days he could not close shop until midnight. One dark night he was walking home late and got lost. He walked all night and as morning came he found he had been walking in a circle.[26]

The protagonist in this story is C. W. Peterson, whose farmstead was three miles southwest of Enterprise, but these are details we know only from other narratives. In this story, we have a space so undifferentiated that we receive no details—no streams, roads, flora or fauna, no sounds, no smells, no ups or downs of the landscape—just dark space through which Peterson walks in a circle without realizing it until morning. The sole demarcations of this space are the two points, his shoe shop and his home.

Walking journeys are narrative moments of risk or reward. For example, Albert Anderson's walk to Cinnebar Mine near Mt. Shasta, California, was marked by a scare: "One time he met a big bear, head on, going around a turn in the trail."[27] In another example, Jonas Peter Kallqvist "walked from his homestead to Ashland, [Nebraska] some 15 miles, for some supplies and dishes. It was a hard trip, and by the time he reached home he was exhausted, dropping his packages, breaking the dishes."[28] Or, the walk itself is disabling:

> The men would walk to Vermillion [South Dakota] for provisions. Sometimes, Mr. Sundstrom and youngest son, Oscar, would go to Sioux City with an oxen team and stoneboat to get supplies. On one trip, Oscar got a new pair of shoes, but his feet were too sore from the long walk to wear them for some time.[29]

Here, a price is paid for traversing the landscape, but this narrative also presents a common motif: the bearing of a heavy or awkward burden while walking the landscape, usually supplies. This motif appears in Carl Anderson's story of a Mrs. Nelson: "Mrs. Nelson was the doctor for the early settlers [in the Erhard, Minnesota, area]. One day she came back carrying a young calf over her shoulders, which was pay for nursing a man that had been sick for a period of time."[30]

If there is no price to the journey, there is a providential occurrence to mark it. A story told about carpenter Anders August Nygren by his grandson Carl marks a turn in an ordinary walk home:

> My father told me of prairie fires. . . . One in particular that started about ½ or ¾ mile south of the church and cemetery. The exact date is not known, but was probably in the early 1870's. Grandfather Nygren was walking home from Ashland with his carpenter's tools and got to the church in time to tear off some burning siding and save the building. The remains of the fire guards that were plowed around this building are still visible.[31]

Skilled in carpentry and even bearing his tools at the time, Nygren was the best person to be at the scene of the fire.

Encountering helpful objects while walking is another common motif. One of the early occupants at Lindsborg, Kansas, walked to Salina soon after having built a dugout. "Along the way he found an old spade. Delighted at his good fortune, he had a blacksmith named Swenson remake it into a hoe. With this crude tool the first sod was turned on the Hessler farm."[32] Often these objects are, like this spade-turned-hoe, essential to the process of successfully occupying the land.

Through walking narratives, immigrants emphasized the uncertainties of their lives, the distances of their new region, and their active presence on the land. They turned the undifferentiated spaces of the American Midwest and West into places with which they could directly identify. These narratives share with the disembarkation narratives the concept of a price for having traveled across boundaries or through liminal borderlands—moments of dramatic vulnerability.

Landscape Event Narratives

Vulnerabilities of the immigrants are at the core, too, of narratives in which dramatic landscape events—weather or plagues—are related. Folklorist Larry Danielson writes of tornado stories that they "are commonplace in contemporary oral tradition of the central United States" and often focused on "bizarre consequences of the storm" rather than tragedy.[33] Very common among the Swedish immigrant communities, these narratives are not exclusive to immigrant circumstances. However, for the immigrants we can see their motifs and tableau scenes as reflections on the newly adopted land.

We have seen in the walking narratives that the Midwestern and Western landscapes are often depicted as vacant. But in numerous narratives this blank canvas is suddenly disturbed by dust storms, thunderstorms, blizzards, wildfires, locust plagues, and other powerful events. For example, a cyclone descended upon the bridge across the Missouri River at Omaha, where watchman John Pearson was stationed in 1876:

> While watching the bridge from his little cabin at the Omaha end of the structure, one stormy night, about three o'clock in the morning, he saw to his horror one span of the bridge torn away by the wind, the same fitful gust tumbling him and his shelter down the high bank to the river's edge. With the lights at the other end of the bridge set clear for passage across, and knowing that an overland passenger train from the east would soon be due, John Pearson, with one of his legs seriously hurt in the fall, resolutely cast himself into the river and swam across in the darkness, flagging the train and thus saving many lives.[34]

These dramatic, unpredictable weather events place the characters at sudden risk and imperil all that they have built. Told from the point of view of descendants, the stories feature protagonists who are survivors through their resourcefulness and luck. For example, Fred Behrens is credited with a combination of luck and resourcefulness in surviving the blizzard of 1888 in Saunders County, Nebraska. The storm descended upon him in seconds, and he saved himself by following a fence, making a series of correct turns to reach safety. "The blizzard had been cheated of one victim."[35]

Plagues of insects, too, are depicted as unexpected and vast. A locust infestation of 1875 is described in a story from the Halland Settlement (Stanton) of Iowa:

> Suddenly out of that clear sky something came tumbling earthward. People hurried outdoors to find the cause of the break in the serenity of the day. To their consternation grasshoppers were coming down like rain out of

> the sky. . . . For three days the terrible scourge of hoppers held sway and then when the destruction was complete and only the black earth remained these sinister destroyers, their work complete, took wing and left the land to dismay and despair.[36]

As with tornados, not only were these insect events seen as disastrous, but they also focused on the kinds of bizarre consequences noted by Danielson. In an account of Minnesotans raising "homestead tobacco," on neighboring farmsteads, farmer Larson's tobacco patch was eaten to the ground by grasshoppers while farmer Johnson's were left untouched. Johnson generously shared his crop.[37]

The historical legends told by immigrants and inscribed in their descendants' local histories did important cultural work for the Swedish Americans. Through this expressive form, they narrated the vulnerabilities inherent in migration. Imagining the Midwestern prairies and landings at Castle Garden as liminal spaces, they dramatized in tableaux of physical contact and exertion how vulnerabilities could be overcome and rewards achieved. Their stories of disembarkation, walking, and dramatic weather and landscape events were both backward and forward looking. They were inflected with meanings from Old World sources—connotations such as the biblical theme of providence and Swedish-specific ideas about land, occupation, and the dangers of change in status and identity when crossing boundaries. But these ideas were also inscribed onto New World spaces through narrative motifs and tableaux adapted to new realities of American landscape and climate. Through this double focus, legend motifs and tableaux made sense of the migration experience. For the Swedish Americans, legend telling was a key means for imagining the move across boundaries and borderlands to become rooted in North America. Their direct, lived experience of border crossing became a source for reshaping their traditional, metaphorical borders and borderlands.

Notes

1. Reimund Kvideland and Henning K. Sehmsdorf, eds., *Scandinavian Folk Belief and Legend* (Minneapolis: University of Minnesota Press, 1988), 118–21, 331–35.

2. Ibid., 118.

3. Ibid., 214–38.

4. Ibid., 222.

5. In an expanded study one could also include the legends of urban Swedish immigrants, as suggested, for example, in the more urban-centric work of Linda Dégh, "Approaches to Folklore Research among Immigrant Groups," *Journal of American Folklore* 79, no. 314 (1966): 551–56, and "Two Old World Narrators in Urban Setting," in *Kontakte und Grenzen,* ed. Hans-Friedrich Foltin (Göttingen: Schwartz, 1969), 71–86; and Roy Swanson, "A Swedish Immigrant Folk Figure: Ola Värmlänning," *Minnesota History* 29, no. 2 (1948): 105–13.

6. Barre Toelken, "Folklore and Reality in the American West," in *Sense of Place: American Regional Cultures,* ed. Barbara Allen and Thomas J. Schlereth (Lexington: University Press of Kentucky, 1990), 16.

7. Ibid., 20.

8. See Graham Seal, *The Outlaw Legend: A Cultural Tradition in Britain, America and Australia* (Cambridge: Cambridge University Press, 1996).

9. Larry Danielson, "Tornado Stories in the Breadbasket: Weather and Regional Identity," in Allen and Schlereth, *Sense of Place,* 36–37.

10. Axel Olrik, "Epic Laws of Folk Narrative," in *The Study of Folklore,* ed. Alan Dundes, trans. Jeanne P. Steager from the original German publication of 1909 (Englewood Cliffs, N.J.: Prentice-Hall, 1965), 138.

11. Karen V. Hansen, *Encounter on the Great Plains: Scandinavian Settlers and the Dispossession of Dakota Indians, 1890–1930.* (Oxford: Oxford University Press, 2013), 29.

12. Gerald D. Anderson, *Prairie Voices: An Oral History of Scandinavian Americans in the Upper Midwest* (n.pl.: n.pub., 2014), 92–93. Erickson's account, related in the 1970s, looks back to family events of the early twentieth century.

13. Ibid., 97.

14. Probably the most famous American rags-to-riches example appears in Benjamin Franklin's *Autobiography,* in which he depicts himself arriving in Philadelphia unemployed and walking the streets with barely enough money to buy rolls.

15. Esther Palm Gayman, *Tock Sa Mecka: Swedish Pioneer Life on the Prairie Experienced by the Palm Family* (Galesburg, Ill.: Log City Books, 1978), 38. The migratory narrative also appears in Axel Eric Nelson's manuscript autobiography, M942, Denver Public Library, page 35 (a Wyoming example). It has been identified by Larry E. Scott, *The Swedish Texans* (San Antonio: University of Texas Institute of Texan Cultures, 1990), 103; Folke Hedblom, *Svensk-Amerika berättar* (Malmö: Gidlunds, 1982), 107–8 (an example set in Nebraska); James P. Leary (heard from Wisconsin Finns), personal correspondence, February 22, 2019; and Adam Hjorthén, *Cross-Border Commemorations: Celebrating Swedish Settlement in America* (Amherst: University of Massachusetts Press, 2018), Kindle ed. loc 2668 (told by Prince Bertil, Duke of Halland, at Rockford, Illinois, in 1948).

16. Albert P. Strom, ed., *Swedish Pioneers in Saunders County, Nebraska.* (n.pl.: n.pub., 1972), 47–48.

17. Vernon E. Bergstrom, *Home Folks* (Minneapolis: n.pub., 1989), 96.

18. See James P. Leary, *So Ole Says to Lena: Folk Humor of the Upper Midwest* (Madison: University of Wisconsin Press, 2001); Ann-Charlotte Harvey's study of the Ole Olson character, "Performing Ethnicity: The Role of Swedish Theatre in the Twin Cities," in *Swedes in the Twin Cities,* ed. Philip J. Anderson and Dag Blanck (Minnesota Historical Society Press, 2001), 166–68.

19. Thomas N. Holmquist, *Pioneer Cross: Swedish Settlements along the Smoky Hill Bluffs* (n.pl.: Hearth Publishing, 1994), 64.

20. Kvideland and Sehmsdorf, *Scandinavian Folk Belief and Legend,* 118–21.

21. Ibid., 332–35.

22. Ibid., 334.

23. Lisa Gabbert and Paul Jordan-Smith, "Space, Place, Emergence," *Western Folklore* 66, nos. 3/4 (2007): 222.

24. C. J. Johnson, *History of the First Swedish Pioneers Who Settled Otter Creek Valley, Situated in Otter Creek and Stockholm Townships, Crawford County, Wheeler Township, in Sac County, and Hayes Township in Ida County, Iowa, Now Known as Kiron, and Community, from 1867 to Present Time, 1915* (Denison, Iowa: Denison Review, 1915), 22.

25. Claus L. Anderson, *Gracious Bounty: The Story of Stanton, the Halland Settlement* (Stanton, Iowa: Stanton Viking, 1952), 18.

26. Ellen Welander Peterson, *A Kansan's Enterprise* (Enterprise, Kans.: Enterprise Baptist Church, 1957), 213.

27. Alberta Anderson Finke, *In Their Own Words: A Swedish Emigrant Story* (La Grange, Calif.: Southern Mines Press, 1990), 108.

28. *Mead Centennial 1877–1977* (Centennial Book Committee, Mead, Nebraska, ca. 1977), 74.

29. Centennial Book Committee, ed., *Beresford 1884–1984* ([Beresford, S.Dak.]: Dwayne Straw and Doug Hustrilid, 1983), 408.

30. Anderson, *Prairie Voices,* 116.

31. Strom, *Swedish Pioneers in Saunders County, Nebraska,* 30.

32. Holmquist, *Pioneer Cross,* 60.

33. Danielson, "Tornado Stories in the Breadbasket," 29, 32.

34. Dale L. Lund and Reuben T. Swanson, eds., *Swedish Omaha—Past and Present: Biographical Sketches of Swedish-Americans in the Omaha Area Gathered in 1933, 1935 and 1991* (Omaha, Neb.: Swedish Cultural Committee, 1991), 6.

35. *Mead Centennial 1877–1977,* 55.

36. Anderson, *Gracious Bounty,* 50.

37. Anderson, *Prairie Voices,* 114–15.

4

A Musical Borderland

How Jazz in Sweden Became Domesticated, 1920–1960

Ulf Jonas Björk

In 1921, a Swedish musician sounded the alarm bell about a new kind of popular music emanating from America. Comparing jazz to "a terrible infectious disease," Hjalmar Meissner called on his countrymen to "establish facilities for quarantine and delousing" to ensure that it did not reach Swedish soil.[1] Thirty-four years later, an activist in the Swedish movement for adult education wanted educational institutions to promote jazz. According to Bengt Melin, the music offered a way to engage teenagers in discussion about social issues and also served as an introduction to modern literature.[2] As the two texts suggest, the perception of jazz changed greatly in Sweden between the 1920s and the 1950s, and the purpose of this essay is to discuss that change, how this particular genre of American popular music went from being the alien menace of Meissner's warning to the essential and valuable component of natural culture of Melin's appeal. As will be seen, it was a change that entailed creating a borderland where jazz emerged as a melding of influences from two cultures. It also involved musicians traveling between the two countries, Americans touring Sweden and Swedes finding success in the United States.[3] Finally, it was a matter of downplaying the music's American, and specifically African American, roots.

The sources for the study are articles in newspapers, magazines, and trade journals. No assumption is made that these texts broadly represented Swedish public opinion. On the contrary, the large and enthusiastic audiences that attended dances and concerts from the 1920s on suggest that the opinion that many Swedes had of the new American musical import was greatly at odds with the negative attitude of journalists, particularly those assigned the task of covering culture and the arts.[4] It was, nonetheless, those journalists who, in the arts pages of their newspapers, reflected on the changing nature of jazz and on its place in Swedish society.

Before discussing the elevation of jazz to near high-art status, it is necessary to address the issue of how jazz was defined. As several historians have stressed, the definition changed over time, from referring primarily to a new dance style in the early 1920s to encompassing a wide range of musical styles that intended primarily to be listened to thirty years later. What did not change, however, was the understanding that the music had originated in America and the issue of where it belonged in the lives of Swedes.[5]

Jazz Comes to Sweden: Invasive Disease or Amusing Fad?

Modern historians claim that the term "jazz" first appeared in Sweden around 1919, and when the magazine *Orkesterjournalen*, which was started to promote jazz, provided its readers with a lighthearted history of the genre in 1936, it began its account "sometime around the end of the war."[6] An early and significant interest in the genre was taken by Ernst Rolf, a towering figure in the world of Swedish musical revues. Rolf included an "Original Jazzband from USA" in one of his productions in 1919, although only one of the band's members was an American.[7] The following year, some of the band members appeared once again, this time conducted by Rolf's main rival as a review producer, Karl Gerhard. Judging from newspaper advertisements for entertainment, however, jazz did not become a fad in Stockholm until 1921–22. In September 1921, two Stockholm restaurants offered dancing to the accompaniment of jazz orchestras; by the following April, their number had doubled.[8]

In retrospect, Hjalmar Meissner's warning, appearing in a trade magazine in early September 1921, has often been seen as having attracted a great deal of attention, but, in reality, only two of the ten or so dailies in the Swedish capital at the time took any notice of the article. Both of those newspapers reprinted extensive excerpts and added brief comments of their own, with *Nya Dagligt Allehanda* musing that jazz was a continental phenomenon that might soon reach Sweden, and *Svenska*

Pris 25 öre

ORKESTER Journalen

tidskrift för modern dansmusik

ÅRG. 4 • N:o 3 • MARS 1936

Utgivare: NORDISKA MUSIKFÖRLAGET • STOCKHOLM

DUKE ELLINGTON

Läs Herbert Sandbergs recension av "Reminiscing" *å sid. 18*

OrkesterJournalen, founded in 1933 to promote jazz, was an important forum for highlighting both American and Swedish musicians. Courtesy of JAZZ/ OrkesterJournalen.

Dagbladet jokingly praising Meissner for sacrificing his summer to research "the fascinating tones of jazz in Monte Carlo and elsewhere."[9]

Even as jazz began to take hold of Stockholm as fall 1921 wore on, the city's newspapers continued to view the new cultural import with diffidence. *Svenska Dagbladet* admitted in November that Meissner had been proven right, as Stockholm by then had "become thoroughly infected with the dancing germ and its most modern species, jazz." Although the paper thus repeated Meissner's disease analogy, it shared none of his concern, pronouncing the new kind of music as "melodious" and marveling at the skills of the musicians who performed it. Even as some organizations began to echo Meissner's concern in early 1922, the Stockholm press seemed to doubt that jazz posed any real danger. For example, a YMCA lecture about the dangers of jazz in April attracted the attention of only two papers, both of which doubted that the audience for the event, mainly elderly women, would fall prey to the lures of the new music.[10]

Only one newspaper, the conservative *Stockholms Dagblad,* seemed clearly worried about the new American import. In March 1922, the paper devoted an extensive article to the new musical genre. "The jazz bug is ravaging the capital with intensity," the paper declared, claiming that everyone, "from the bored idlers of high society to the idle moths of the demimonde, from the stiff bureaucrats in the government ministry to the middle-aged wife of the businessman, staff officers and young athletes, all are there, seized by the madness imported from the continent." In what would become a frequent theme of connecting jazz to race, the author of the article noted the music's African American roots, claiming that jazz had been composed by borrowing impulses from "the Negro neighborhoods of Boston or New York." Being nothing but "pots-and-pans music," jazz had caused a "madness" that had conquered America and then crossed the Atlantic to Europe, "where the horrors of war had made the soil fertile." Dancing jazz may look ridiculous, but there were serious aspects, according to *Stockholms Dagblad,* which cited critics to the effect that jazz aroused "erotic chase sensations" and had already caused "more than one family tragedy." A German doctor was even comparing the modern American import to the dancing madness following the Black Death, warning that the unrestricted pursuit of pleasure would lead to increases in sexually transmitted diseases and teenage pregnancy.

Still, *Stockholms Dagblad* saw a ray of hope in the fact that "the epidemic" seemed to be on the wane, as campaigns against jazz had been started in both America and France.[11]

Jazz Takes Hold: American Visits and Swedish Interest

Fervent as *Stockholms Dagblad*'s hopes that jazz was a waning phenomenon may have been, the genre continued to grow in popularity in Sweden as the 1920s wore on. One sign was that the Stockholm-based weekly magazine *Våra Nöjen,* launched in 1925, from the start treated jazz as an established entertainment genre in the capital and lauded it for rejuvenating "our ancient cultural organism."[12] A major impetus for the popularity of jazz was that American orchestras began appearing in Stockholm in the mid-1920s. Although Americans had occasionally appeared among the foreign musicians playing in Sweden in the early 1920s, the appearance of Sam Wooding and his ten-man band as part of the Chocolate Kiddies "Negro review" in August and September 1925 marked the first time that an entire orchestra from the United States played in Sweden. *Våra Nöjen* noted two thousand in attendance and found Wooding's performance "astounding, phenomenal, enchanting," a sentiment shared by much of the daily press, judging from the Bertil Lyttkens's compilation of newspaper coverage.[13]

Moreover, Americans were not the only ones playing jazz in Sweden. The captions for the photographs that accompanied *Orkesterjournalen*'s historical causerie about the early days of jazz suggested a thriving jazz community in Stockholm from the mid-1920s, a community where Swedish and foreign performers collaborated. It thus appeared that a borderland was already taking shape, and when *Orkesterjournalen* looked back at the 1920s in the following decade, it declared that "a Swede had no reason to be ashamed" of what his country had contributed, as it held up well in an international perspective.[14]

Appreciating and Defending Jazz

On the eve of Wooding's performances in Stockholm, *Svenska Dagbladet* published one of the first Swedish newspaper articles that discussed jazz in a dispassionate manner. Its author was Moses Pergament, the paper's music critic and a composer in his own right, and he began by noting that no popular dance had ever generated as much antipathy as jazz, a great deal of which had been fanned by the press. Pergament thought that many critics of the genre focused too much on "rumbling instrumentation" at the expense of the "humorous and often dazzling art" of the musicians.[15]

Svenska Dagbladet's reviewer also took care to make a distinction between the music played by blacks, who had originated jazz and had the rhythmic ability the music required, and jazz played by white Europeans, who lacked that ability because European classical music had not "developed the performer's sense of rhythm." While Pergament noted that the "absolutely new tonal effects and rhythmical features" of jazz had inspired European "creative musicians" such as Stravinsky, Prokofiev, and Satie, he nonetheless considered it a genuinely American art form.[16]

The latter half of the 1920s also introduced a forum for those enjoying and defending jazz. That forum was *Radiolyssnaren*, a magazine aimed at the audience for Sweden's newly established national broadcasting service, Radiotjänst. A monopoly established with the British Broadcasting Corporation as a model, Radiotjänst was obligated to offer broad programming appealing to all segments of the listenership, and the inclusion of jazz in its offerings was an indication of how popular the genre was perceived to be. It was also, however, controversial, and *Våra Nöjen* noted early on that there had been complaints about "too much jazz" on the radio.[17]

Radiolyssnaren's debate about jazz was set off in one of the first issues when a letter to the editor demanded that the "musical monster" that the American music was should be purged from the schedules, as it was leading young people astray. In a subsequent issue, two letters came to the genre's defense, the first noting that jazz occupied a small share of the programming schedules and the second claiming that the music was not only popular but also "a unique pleasure for the ear." A slew of subsequent comments from other letter writers, along with dismissive notes from the magazine's editors, made it clear that jazz still faced a great deal of opposition, but the 1927 discussion in *Radiolyssnaren* marked one of the first occasions when jazz supporters in Sweden spoke up for themselves and their music.[18]

How American Is Jazz?

Even as jazz continued to grow in popularity and increasingly was played by Swedish musicians, both its supporters and its detractors tended to stress its connection to the United States. That many journalists still considered it alien was evident from press reaction to the first Swedish appearance of Louis Armstrong in the fall of 1933, which produced a slew of negative and racially tinged reviews focusing on Armstrong's looks and singing style that likened the trumpet player to a monkey and linked his musical genre to African jungles.[19] Even *Orkesterjournalen*, started by the music publisher Nordiska Musikförlaget in 1933 explicitly to promote jazz and serve as a forum for the genre's supporters, tended to focus on U.S. musicians in its coverage.[20]

As newspapers started to treat jazz in a somewhat more sympathetic manner in the mid-1930s, they too saw it primarily as an American import, and they also began regarding its African (and African American) roots as positive rather than negative. A 1935 article in *Stockholms-Tidningen/Stockholms Dagblad* contrasted the music of Louis Armstrong, "a dark and intoxicating drink from Africa," with the "sugary and sentimental" Swedish popular music.[21]

An article in *Dagens Nyheter* the same year appeared to approach the nationality of jazz from the perspective of the audience rather than the musicians. Lauding the music of Duke Ellington, Nils Hellström (later the founder of the magazine *Estrad*, a serious competitor for *Orkesterjournalen*, and the editor of the first book about jazz in Swedish, *Jazz: Historia–Teknik–Utövare*) hinted that Europeans understood Ellington's genius better than most Americans (although that generalization did not extend to the musician's fellow African Americans).[22]

Is Jazz Culture—or Still a Menace?

Hellström's suggestion that Europeans, by virtue of their greater appreciation of culture, were better suited to appreciate jazz than (white) Americans would surface again in the 1940s and 1950s, and it also foreshadowed discussions in the 1940s of where this new and popular music fit into the hierarchy of musical genres. To some writers, jazz could be useful by serving as a springboard. When Kajsa Rootzén, the music critic at *Svenska Dagbladet,* discussed a survey of readers' interest in classical music in 1942, she cited one respondent who claimed that it was "through jazz that I learned to appreciate classical music, and at the same time I deepened my interest in the Negroid kind of music." To Rootzén, that comment, from a "true lover of music," was evidence that "the youthful interest in jazz and swing music should not necessarily be seen as an impediment to the development of good taste, as it instead can lay the foundation for a greater appreciation of the arts." Thus jazz was not yet "high" music, but enjoying it was no longer seen as precluding appreciation of classical European works.[23] As a panelist debating whether jazz was a "cultural menace" put it in 1944, those who enjoyed jazz would eventually "long for art that provides greater satisfaction."[24]

The 1944 panel debate had asked participants to respond to whether jazz was a cultural menace, a seemingly outdated approach given the broad popularity of the genre in Sweden by the 1940s and the increasing respect afforded to it in the press. Just how out of date the assumption that jazz was a threat was became evident two years after the panel when Erik Walles, a Stockholm schoolteacher, published a book titled *Jazzen anfaller* (Jazz attacks). Reviving arguments from forty years earlier, Walles claimed that jazz music produced "an ecstatic condition that brings about a strong sensual sensation, to be compared to the sensations of opium and cocaine." Echoing Hjalmar Meissner, Walles called jazz "a plague germ that has come to us from across the Atlantic."[25]

In contrast to Meissner's attack, which had received little press notice in 1921, Walles's diatribe was given extensive newspaper attention, almost all of it negative. Even *Stockholms-Tidningen,* which had been largely objective in its review of *Jazzen anfaller,* followed up the review with an article with comments by various prominent personalities that began by claiming that the defenders of jazz had appeared "on a broad front" to denounce Walles's book. As evidence, the paper offered answers by a composer, a high-school principal, two opera singers, a symphony conductor, an author, and the leader of a jazz band, all of whom disagreed with Walles and saw some or even a great deal of merit in jazz.[26] (In addition, *Stockholms-Tidningen* suggested that the racial arguments that permeated Walles's book should be considered against his past as an official of the Swedish Nazi party.) Other newspapers were equally skeptical. While the reviewer in the Social Democratic *Morgon-Tidningen* seemed ambivalent about the influences of jazz, he thought Walles's knowledge of the topic of *Jazzen anfaller* was so limited that it made the author's suppositions faulty and his perspective intolerant. In *Svenska Dagbladet,* music critic Kajsa Rootzén sounded similar themes, accusing Walles of a profound lack of knowledge not only of jazz but of musical history in general.[27]

Making Jazz Swedish

As was evident from *Stockholms-Tidningen*'s decision to solicit public response to *Jazzen anfaller,* jazz had by the 1940s become a cultural element whose presence was taken for granted in Sweden and whose supporters had ready access to the press. As the 1950s began, articles about jazz tended to focus less on the music's adverse effects than on what status to afford it and what its relationship was to Sweden. Whereas debates a decade earlier had pitted the American import against classical music, a debate that began in 1954 in the Communist paper *Ny Dag* centered on to what extent it was Swedish rather than foreign.

The *Ny Dag* debate began when Molly Åsbrink, a classically trained singer, characterized Swedish jazz as "borrowed" music that suffered from a serious shortcoming: it was impossible for Swedes and other white Europeans to play jazz the way it was intended or, for that matter, to dance to it. Swedes could no more "reproduce the folk music of the American Negroes" than "a Negro, a Chinese man or a Frenchman" could sing a Swedish folk song properly.[28]

Defenders of jazz responded to Åsbrink's criticism, particularly as it applied to the foreign nature of the genre. Jazz writer Matts Rying claimed that jazz by the 1950s had a long-standing place in the lives of Swedes, particularly younger ones, although he thought that jazz as played in Sweden could remove some of its foreign origin to become more Swedish in character: instead of slavishly following each new fad from America and writing lyrics in English, Swedish musicians should seek to develop jazz of genuine Swedish character.[29]

Per-Åke Nordbeck, a well-known Gothenburg jazz pianist, suggested that jazz was indeed Swedish music by virtue of its popularity with audiences and musicians:

> [W]e jazz musicians feel to the greatest extent that jazz is our music. Our generation has grown up with it. Thus, it is natural to us, despite its American origins—and the classic composers were not Swedes, either.[30]

To some engaged in the debate over the nature of jazz, making the genre more Swedish entailed moving it out of the sphere of popular culture. Writing in *Stockholms-Tidningen* in 1955, Lennart Reimers, a music teacher, thought that the development of what he called "progressive" jazz was not broadly popular (as opposed to the Dixieland music that most Swedish fans were "chained" to) but had artistic qualities necessitating transferring it to venues traditionally reserved for classical music, such as radio broadcasts and concerts.[31]

As Reimers's argument suggested, the elevation of jazz to a musical form of cultural value was connected to separating it from its foreign—that is American—context, reviving Nils Hellström's 1935 claim that the genre was better understood in Europe than in the United States. Author Lasse Renberg claimed in *Aftontidningen* in 1956 that white Americans had treated the genre with condescension or ignored it outright, in spite of its being "the only independent cultural contribution of the United States." It was, instead, the Europeans who had "discovered jazz an expressive form of art."[32] Europe's interest in jazz had, in turn, produced "a small but growing group of European jazz musicians who could give their American colleagues a run for their money," Renberg claimed. Among these, much to the author's satisfaction, were Swedes such as saxophone player Lars Gullin, whose work had been lauded not only at home but in America itself.[33] Gullin's success was evidence, according to Renberg, that jazz was becoming less of an American art form:

> A European can never experience or create jazz in the same original, simultaneously intense and relaxed way that an American, and particularly a colored American, can. But because the peculiar rhythmic pulse of jazz attracts people in the same way in different parts of the world, the

> European ought to be able to express, in his own fashion, something important through jazz.[34]

Jimmy Nyström, jazz critic at *Norrländska Social-Demokraten,* thought jazz was finding ever more fertile ground in Sweden, as "[o]ur Swedish musicians have gained a more knowledgeable and more interested audience and are, therefore, able to play the music they want to a higher degree than before."[35]

That European musicians were producing worthwhile jazz was acknowledged across the Atlantic as well. Jazz overseas, noted a 1956 *New York Times* review of recent records, had changed from "passive listening to active playing." Although the reviewer considered much of European jazz "derivative, patterned on the work of Americans or American groups," he nonetheless had praise for "a spate of talented musicians" from Sweden, including Gullin. A year earlier, the trade journal *Billboard* had praised Gullin as "facile, dexterous, inventive" and "exciting."[36] (As recent histories of jazz in Sweden have noted, the attention paid to Swedish musicians in America was at least in part owing to a concerted effort of the Swedish record company Metronome to promote its records in the U.S. market.)[37]

Conclusion: Creating a Borderland

Like Renberg, composer and pianist Carl-Olof Anderberg also saw flagging interest in jazz in the United States while the music was thriving in Europe, but that posed challenges, he told the readers of *Kvälls-Posten* in 1958:

> For the European jazz musician there is a problem to be solved, a truly hard nut to crack. We are talking about assimilating the idiom of jazz. Pure imitation of American jazz is a disaster . . . Personally, I do not think that jazz reaches its full potential if it is not assimilated in a positive direction. To give it full artistic currency, the European jazz musician must try, with all the means at his disposal, to translate the American jazz idiom into a European musical language, mix the two tongues, and eventually crystallize his own "brogue" with a clearly European character.[38]

The way to do that, according to Anderberg, was to draw on the European musical heritage, "one of the greatest cultural treasures in world history," to construct a "modern rhythmic music with contributions from important accents within North American jazz."[39]

Anderberg's path to a European (and Swedish) form of jazz suggests a musical borderland where American and Swedish influences were blended to create a new type of music. It was nurtured by U.S. jazz artists who by the 1950s had left their homeland and its waning interest in their genre and found a more welcome reception in Europe. According to Nyström, American "star musicians" touring in Europe had told him that they no longer could earn a living in the United States and were relocating to Europe. Without attributing the exodus to a lack of American interest, the *New York Times* noted in 1963 that "American jazz musicians in residence have become common in Sweden, Denmark, The Netherlands, Germany, Switzerland and Italy."[40] One of these expatriates was saxophonist Stan Getz, who toured Sweden with a Swedish band in the early 1950s and lived there later in the decade.[41] In live performances and recording sessions, Getz and his Swedish colleagues created physical borderland spaces where jazz emerged as a collaborative effort between Swedes and Americans.

The creation of a borderland also entailed building on American roots to create something distinctively Swedish. Jazz historian Stuart Nicholson coined a term for the form of "localized jazz" that developed in Sweden in the 1950s: the "Nordic Tone." Nicholson traced it back to the incorporation of Swedish folk songs in the 1920s and 1930s, and he stressed its international appeal by noting that one of those songs, *Ack Wärmeland, du sköna,* had been played by U.S. musicians Stan Getz and Miles Davis. According to Nicholson, the Nordic Tone found one of its most brilliant expressions in pianist Jan Johansson's album *Jazz på svenska* (Jazz in Swedish), released in 1964. Johansson, it should be noted, had played frequently with Getz in the late 1950s.[42]

Gaining acknowledgment abroad and searching for uniquely Swedish qualities when exploring a genre originating in America were important components in the creation of a borderland. So was establishing a sense of boundaries. As noted, the "progressive" jazz championed by Lennart Reimers should guide Swedes away from the overly commercialized

Dixieland music that emanated from the United States, and jazz also became a weapon when a new popular-music genre from America reached Sweden in the late 1950s: rock 'n' roll. Alarmed that teenagers had been "in ecstasy" during a 1958 concert in Stockholm, arts-pages journalists in the Swedish press wasted no time condemning the new import. To one of them, the poet and critic Lennart Odlander, rock 'n' roll, this "weed in the musical garden," had to be countered with "useful things" for young Swedes to be interested in, such as "intellectual" jazz.[43]

Notes

1. Hjalmar Meissner, "Varning för jazz!" *Scenen* 7, no. 13 (September 1, 1921): 200.

2. Bengt Melin, "Är jazz musik?" *Dala-Demokraten,* October 22, 1955, 4.

3. Histories of jazz in Sweden have stressed the success enjoyed by Swedish musicians in the United States and the cooperation between Swedes and Americans in Sweden. See, for instance, Jan Bruér, "Guldår och krisår: Svensk jazz under 1950- och 60-talen," *Studier i musikvetenskap* 17 (Stockholm: Svenskt visarkiv, 2007), 180–81; Göran Jonsson, *Frihetens blå toner: En berättelse om jazzen i Sverige* (Stockholm: Carlssons, 2018), 52–63, 77–80.

4. Bertil Lyttkens, *Svart och vitt: Utländska jazzbesök 1895–1939 i svensk press* (Stockholm: Svenskt visarkiv, 1998), 62; Göran Nylöf, "Jazz som kulturchock och generationskonflikt i mellankrigstidens Sverige," in Lyttkens, *Svart och vitt,* 12, 18.

5. For changing definitions, see Dan Malmström, *Härligt, härligt men farligt, farligt: Populärmusiken i Sverige under 1900-talet* (Stockholm: Natur och kultur, 1996), 71; Johan Fornäs, *Moderna människor: Folkhemmet och jazzen* (Stockholm: Norstedts, 2004), 13; Olle Sjögren, "'Det är tidens melodi': Från jazzrytm till swingscen," in *Från flygdröm till swingscen: Ungdom och modernitet på 1930-talet,* ed. Matz Franzén (Lund: Arkiv, 1998), 292.

6. Whispe Ring, pseud., "Det var en gång, när ordet razzia nämndes i samband med danssalonger: Ett kåseri om jazzens barndom i Sverige," *Orkesterjournalen,* December 1936, 8; Fornäs, *Moderna människor,* 20; Malmström, *Härligt, härligt men farligt, farligt,* 7.

7. Erik Kjellberg, *Svensk Jazzhistoria: En översikt* (Stockholm: P. A. Nordstedt & Söners förlag, 1985), 19.

8. Advertisements, *Dagens Nyheter* (hereafter, *DN*), September 11, 1921, 12; April 5, 1922, 12; advertisement, *Svenska Dagbladet* (hereafter, *SvD*), May 1, 1920, 12.

9. "Varning för jazz," *SvD,* September 9, 1921, 8; "Jazzen, en farsot," *Nya Dagligt Allehanda* (hereafter, *NDA*), September 12, 1921, 9. On Meissner, see Fornäs, *Moderna människor,* 21; Fornäs's characterization of Meissner's article as the

start of a "moral panic" over jazz seems a little exaggerated; judging from earlier contributions of Meissner to *Scenen,* he tended to write in an agitated style possibly intended to amuse readers. See Hjalmar Meissner, "Några tankar om Stockholms nöjesliv, I," *Scenen* 6, no. 17 (November 1, 1920): 270.

10. "Shimmy, jazz och Orfeus—ingenting för själen," *NDA,* April 1, 1922; "Shimmy och jazz på K.F.U.M. i går: Protestresolution," *DN,* April 1, 1922, 9; Kaifas, pseud., "Stockholm dansar," *SvD Söndagsbilaga,* November 6, 1921, 3.

11. "I jazzraseriets tecken: Stockholmarna angripna av modedansens bacill," *Stockholms Dagblad* (hereafter *SD*), March 12, 1922, 3.

12. "Riche spurtar," *Våra Nöjen* 34 (1925); see also Ingemar, pseud., "Svenskar på Cecil," *Våra Nöjen* 43 (1925): 6; D'occasion, pseud., "Jazz och juridik," *Våra Nöjen* 41 (1926): 29; Bengt Bering, "Jazzens lov," *Våra Nöjen* 26 (1926): 14.

13. "Negerglädje med många ljuspunkter på Cirkusteatern," *Våra Nöjen* 3 (1925): 13; Lyttkens, *Svart och vitt,* 32–34.

14. Ring, "Det var en gång, när ordet razzia nämndes i samband med danssalonger," 8.

15. Moses Pergament, "Jazzen," *SvD,* August 15, 1925, 8.

16. Ibid.

17. "Låtar och olåtar i veckans radio," *Våra Nöjen* 44 (1926): 21.

18. The debate in *Radiolyssnaren* lasted for thirty-two issues, from March to November 1927: "'Vox humana' svarar 'Vox celeste'" and "'Kvalitetsjazz' contra 'gamla låtar,'" *Radiolyssnaren* 6 (1927): 34; "Kultur—radio—jazz!" *Radiolyssnaren* 4 (1927): 41.

19. Lyttkens, *Svart och vitt,* 63–66.

20. "Varför jazzmusiken missförstås," *Orkesterjournalen,* July 1938, 14–15; on the publication's significance, see Kjellberg, *Svensk jazzhistoria,* 45.

21. Billy Boy, pseud., "Afrikas röst," *Stockholms-Tidningen (hereafter, ST)/SD,* April 21, 1935, 12; both the headline and the story itself played down the American nationality of the musicians it discussed.

22. Nils Hellström, "Niggerkung erövrar världen," *DN,* April 7, 1935, appendix, 4, 13; the odd headline ran contrary to the entire tone of Hellström's piece and was in all likelihood the newspaper's choice; although not as loaded as its English counterpart, the Swedish word *nigger* was still derogatory, and coupling it with *king* conjured up the chieftain of a primitive tribe rather than the article's sophisticated musician, who was praised by Europe's cultural elite. On Hellström, see Olle Sjögren, "'Det är tidens melodi': Från jazzmyt till swingscen och ungdomsfilm," in *Från flygdröm till swingscen: Ungdom och modernitet på 1930-talet,* ed. Mats Franzén (Lund: Arkiv, 1998), 305. On the Swedish reception of Ellington, see Olle Edström, *Duke Ellington och jazz i Sverige* (Stockholm: Carlssons, 2015).

23. Kajsa Rootzén, "Smak för musik," *SvD,* October 14, 1942, 11.

24. Jadwiga, pseud., "Är jazzen kulturfara?" *SvD,* August 23, 1944, 9.

25. "Stockholmslärare gör skarp bokattack: Jazz 'pestbacill, pöbeluppfostrande musik,'" *ST,* January 27, 1946, 13.

26. "Svenska 'busvalsen' värre än jazz, 'Walles vet inte vad han talar om,'" *ST,* January 28, 1946, 5.

27. Kajsa Rootzén, "Musikspalten," *SvD,* March 17, 1946, 8; F. H. T., "Två böcker om jazz," *Morgon-Tidningen,* February 16, 1946, 11.

28. Molly Åsbrink, "Är dansmusiken likförgiftad?" *Ny Dag,* April 22, 1954, 3.

29. "Gammal folkmusik skulle verka ny bland dagens ungdomar," *Ny Dag,* May 6, 1954, 3.

30. "'Klanka inte på jazzen—all god musik bör vårdas,'" *Ny Dag,* May 18, 1954, 3.

31. Lennart Reimers, "Jazzens dilemma," *ST,* November 22, 1955, 4.

32. Lasse Renberg, "Européerna först att upptäcka jazzen," *Aftontidningen* (hereafter *AT*), October 14, 1956, 2.

33. Lasse Renberg, "Européerna började spela jazz redan på 20-talet," *AT,* October 17, 1956, 2. On the success of Gulin and other Swedish musicians at the time, see Fornäs, *Moderna människor,* 30; Kjellberg, *Svensk jazzhistoria,* 123–25, 130, 143–49.

34. Lasse Renberg, "Europeisk jazz," *AT,* October 19, 1956, 20.

35. Jimmy Nyström, "Jazzens miljö," *Norrländska Social-Demokraten,* August 24, 1957, 4.

36. "Spotlight on Albums," *Billboard,* May 5, 1955, 84; John S. Wilson, "American Jazz Wins Overseas Audience," *New York Times,* March 18, 1956, 16.

37. Bruér, "Guldår och krisår," 180; Mischa van Kan, "Swingin' Swedes: The Transnational Exchange of Swedish Jazz in the U.S." (PhD diss., University of Gothenburg, 2016), 86–91.

38. Carl-Olof Anderberg, "Europa och Jazzen," *Kvälls-Posten,* May 28, 1958, 4.

39. Ibid., "Europa och Jazzen."

40. John S. Wilson, "Jazz Disks—a Two-Way Exchange," *New York Times,* September 8, 1963, 30; Nyström, "Jazzens miljö."

41. Stuart Nicholson, *Jazz and Culture in a Global Age* (Boston: Northeastern University Press, 2014), 132, 140.

42. Ibid., 132–33, 140–41.

43. Lennart Odlander, "Handsken är kastad," *Västernorrlands Allehanda,* April 19, 1958, 2; Begg, pseud., "Vi diskuterar idag: Rock-gala och extas," *Kvällsposten,* March 13, 1958, 2.

5

Ancestral Relations

The Twentieth-Century Making of Swedish-American Genealogy

Adam Hjorthén

In his seminal book from 1994, historian H. Arnold Barton described the process of Swedish emigration to North America as the history of "a folk divided." This had partly been the result of the mass migration, which brought over a million Swedes to North America in the late-nineteenth and early-twentieth century, but it was also a consequence of how homeland Swedes and Swedish Americans came to relate to each other over time. Barton's conclusion was informed by the observation that culture and religion had developed differently on both sides of the Atlantic.[1] While Barton focused on the mass migration as a process of separation, recent scholarship on transnational migration has emphasized how it also is a history of connections. As sociologist Roger Waldinger points out, "connectivity between sending and receiving societies is cause *and* effect of international migration."[2] The emigrants remained connected to the old homeland through travel, communication, and the exchange of capital, ideas, and material objects. Another area of connectivity is through experiences and memories, a mnemonic borderland made and lived across the Atlantic, that have been significant in the period after the mass migration. A particularly vibrant practice through which memories of the migration have been stimulated is Swedish-American genealogy.

The practice of researching emigrants who relocated from Sweden to the United States is today a popular pastime. For an individual starting the genealogical endeavor, there is a trove of handbooks specifically devoted to Swedish-American ancestry.[3] There are journal columns, Web sites, and social-media forums where one can post queries and get instant feedback. It is possible to solicit help from professional genealogists or contact one of several institutions on either side of the Atlantic who work specifically with Swedish-American genealogy for research advice. With most common genealogical sources available through online databases such as FamilySearch.com, Ancestry.com, ArkivDigital.se, or the Digital Research Room of the Swedish National Archives, there is today less need to visit a physical archive. The explosive growth of genetic genealogy, with U.S.-based DNA companies providing direct-to-consumer businesses to international markets, has added yet another avenue through which Swedes and Americans are able to create transatlantic ancestral relations.[4] Although by all means a practice that still demands significant skills and knowledge, it has never before been less difficult and less time-consuming to research family history. This essay investigates genealogy at a time when it was a more arduous undertaking, focusing on the period prior to the advancements of digital technologies and genetic genealogy. It examines how the field of Swedish-American genealogy came into being, focusing on the period from the 1920s to the 1980s.

Memories of the migration were, of course, nurtured already during the ongoing mass migration in the nineteenth and early-twentieth century. The first-generation immigrants stayed in touch with their families and relatives in Sweden through the frequent exchange of "America letters," and many harbored a nostalgic bond to the people, traditions, and places of their youth.[5] Organizations such as the Society for the Preservation of Swedish Culture Abroad and the Vasa Order of America worked, in different ways, with the maintenance of these memories, promoting sustained relations between Swedish Americans and Swedes based on the preservation of language, culture, and heritage.[6] This kind of remembrance is what Jan Assmann has called communicative memories, based on individual experiences and "everyday communications" with a "limited temporal horizon." As the first generation of immigrants, and eventually also their children, passed away, memories of the migration and of the transatlantic ancestral connections were increasingly maintained through other means. In Assmann's terms, this constituted a shift from communicative memory to cultural memory, set at a "distance from the everyday" and "maintained through cultural formation (texts, rites, monuments) and institutional communication (recitation, practice, observance)."[7] The primary means through which these cultural memories have been sustained is genealogy.

In this essay, I study the cultural formations and institutional communications of genealogy by looking at how media and infrastructures have affected the ways that genealogy is practiced, the set of actors engaged, and the meanings that the practice has been charged with. The role of media systems—constituted, for example, by letters, index cards, microfilm, and computers—does not simply reflect contents of social and cultural practices. Rather, they function as "mediators" that "transform, translate, distort and modify the meaning or the elements they are supposed to carry."[8] The development and introduction of new technologies have led to the emergence of new actors engaged in genealogy. The reason that this study concludes before the 1990s is the vast changes to the genealogical landscape brought on by the Internet.[9] In the remainder of the study, I will investigate how and why these processes unfolded in the realm of Swedish–American relations. Focusing on four thematical case studies, I demonstrate how people with widely varying, yet surprisingly compatible, interests have worked to create the means for the making of transatlantic relations grounded in ancestry.

Intermediaries and the LDS Church

The history of how genealogy developed into a popular pursuit is, in many ways, the history of how records and sources were made increasingly accessible to a broader public, through remediation and institutional centralization. But transatlantic genealogy was practiced long before these developments picked up speed in the mid-twentieth century. The community that most actively engaged in Swedish-American genealogy in the early 1900s were members of the Church of Jesus Christ of Latter-day Saints (LDS). Although Utah and Idaho had a considerably smaller Swedish-American population than the Midwest, they did have a substantial first- and second-generation Swedish-American community. By 1900, Swedes constituted the third-largest ethnic group in Utah, the majority of whom belonged to the LDS church.[10]

The Mormon ancestral interest was, and is, grounded in religious doctrine. In simplified terms, it stems from the belief that family is eternal, and that through genealogy it is possible to find deceased relatives and posthumously baptize them into the community of the church. However, this "mission to the dead" was difficult because most Mormons had European ancestry.[11] Because of the lack of a substantial genealogical infrastructure and accessible sources, it required either extensive (and expensive) traveling or someone who could do the work on demand. For decades beginning in the 1920s, the latter role in Sweden was filled by the Ella Heckscher Genealogical Bureau, founded in Uppsala in 1918.[12]

Ella Heckscher was the foremost genealogist in early-twentieth-century Sweden working with the LDS church. Born into a Jewish family in Stockholm in 1882, she left a noticeable mark on the general history of genealogy in Sweden. She was the genealogist at the Swedish Institute for Racial Biology in 1922–24, cofounded the Swedish Genealogical Society in 1933, and published the influential handbook *Sex kapitel om släktforskning* (Six chapters on genealogy) in 1939; its seventh edition appeared in 1970.[13] Heckscher directed the Genealogical Bureau until 1949 when the business was split between one of her employees, Ludolf Häusler, a Jewish refugee from Germany, and Henning Aschan, her associate in Lund. Heckscher died in 1964, and Häusler directed the remaining part of the bureau until his own death in 1979.[14]

The bureau was one of the first to take advantage of the generational shift in the Swedish-American community, constituting a step toward the transformation of the migration into cultural memory. During its six decades, the bureau conducted genealogy in a rather consistent manner. Its primary method of work was to search church records at the Regional State Archives and to write letters to local parish offices around the country. The regional archives in Sweden were relatively new by the 1920s. The first location had been established in Vadstena in 1899. By 1930, archives had opened in Uppsala, Lund, Visby, Gothenburg, Östersund, and Härnösand. These centers were responsible for the records of the regional agencies of the Swedish state—including that of the Lutheran state church. The church books were, and still are, the central source of genealogy in Sweden, as they contain biographical information about all persons born, baptized, married, and deceased, dating back to the seventeenth century. While church books previously had been kept in the local parishes where they were produced, the older records were transferred to a regional depository. The Genealogical Bureau had assistants at most regional archives. The inquiries that reached the bureau's office in Uppsala were relayed to these assistants, who sent the results back to Uppsala, where they were compiled on family group sheets and distributed to clients.[15]

Heckscher's bureau had initially catered to a Swedish market, but already by the mid-1920s it was Americans who constituted the majority of its clients.[16] Capitalizing on this interest, Heckscher in 1923 appointed an employee to distribute brochures about the bureau to passengers onboard the Swedish American Line's ship *Kungsholm.* The intention was to stimulate interest "in research on the family's history in the old homeland."[17] Soon, it dawned on Heckscher that the American interest primarily stemmed from one particular state. In a letter to her brother, the famous economist Eli Heckscher, Ella wrote in November 1924 that she was flying "on the wings of reputation over Utah."[18] The bureau's standing was aided by the Genealogical Society of Utah—organized by the LDS church—through the *Utah Genealogical and Historical Magazine.* In January 1928, the journal published a laudatory article about Heckscher, encouraging its readers to contact her to trace genealogy in Sweden.[19]

Heckscher made one visit to the United States during her lifetime. In the spring of 1938, she visited New York, Chicago, Minneapolis, San Francisco, and Salt Lake City to give lectures on the methods of doing genealogical research in Sweden.[20] Parts of her 1939 book were based on these lectures, which had been previously printed in the *Magazine.*[21] Heckscher had conflicted feelings about Mormons. She felt distant from their religious zeal and had difficulties accepting the notion that she was "sent by God to help them" in their genealogical-missionary endeavor.[22] But she also admired the way Mormons valued ancestry and the great interest they took in genealogical research.[23] She followed the work of the Genealogical Society of Utah closely and, in a personal letter to her brother, claimed to "steal . . . expressions" from the society when she corresponded with U.S. clients.[24] Although it remains unclear to what extent Heckscher was influenced by the Mormons' practices of genealogy, her research did have an effect on the ancestral knowledge among U.S. Mormons, as her research eventually became the foundation for published family histories.[25]

At a time when Swedish-American genealogy was limited to the infrastructure of the Swedish regional archives, the Genealogical Bureau became a link through which Mormons in the United States more easily could engage in the practice. To Heckscher's surprise, her services were in considerable demand. Leading up to the Second World War, memories of ancestral relations grounded in the Swedish mass migration were largely a religiously driven search for unity, with individual genealogists functioning as the primary facilitators.

Migrant Indexes and Circulation of Knowledge

The importance of intermediaries began to decrease after the Second World War with the creation of new resources for genealogical research. Several of these initiatives emerged in the 1950s, most notably the Emigrant Study Circle in the village of Långasjö in Småland, established in 1959, and the Emigrant Register in Karlstad, founded in 1960. These were heritage projects initiated by branches of the local heritage movement. Their goal was to make inventories of everyone who had emigrated to America from their respective communities, researching records in both Sweden and in the United States.[26] The aim of the Karlstad register was to "map the individual destinies of the emigrants" and to "connect the emigrant descendants with their father's homeland." They did so by creating a card index of people who had emigrated from the province of Värmland, and collecting addresses of first- and second-generation Swedish Americans in the United States. By the late 1960s, the index encompassed more than a hundred thousand individuals.[27]

There was a notion, shared by local activists and scholars, that these projects were important to those in Sweden who had emigrant relatives and to the ancestors of emigrants in America, but that they also were valuable to academic research. This interest was, in other words, not existential—connected to an individual or collective search for identity and belonging—but aimed at the production of knowledge.[28] Prominent scholars of social history cooperated with the groups in Långasjö and Karlstad and publicly hailed the national significance of their work. This included Birgitta Odén at Lund University and Sten Carlsson and Sune Åkerman of the major Emigration Research Program at Uppsala University, which engaged more than thirty scholars between 1962 and 1976.[29] The significance of the Långasjö and Karlstad projects lay in their mass of information; they were attempts at compiling information about a selected population in its totality. While these collective grassroots initiatives took place in Sweden, there were individuals doing similar work in the United States.

The most well-known Swedish-American genealogist of the postwar period was Nils William Olsson. Born in Seattle in 1909 by Swedish migrant parents and partly raised in Sweden, Olsson came to live a life shaped by his Atlantic crossings. After studies at North Park College in Chicago, Olsson went to graduate school at the University of Chicago where he received a PhD in Scandinavian languages in 1949. He had served as military attaché in Stockholm during the Second World War and continued in the 1950s to work in the U.S. Foreign Service stationed in Scandinavia. Parallel to this work, he was nurturing his deep-seated interest in Swedish history and heritage.[30]

In 1958, Olsson became the editor of a standing column on genealogy in the *Swedish Pioneer Historical Quarterly,* the journal of the Swedish Pioneer Historical Society founded in Chicago in 1949. The column claimed to tap into the "highly personal" dimension of the migration.[31] In the following decades, the section provided help to genealogists from Sweden and the United States with specific research inquires, probing the genealogical expertise of both the journal readers and Olsson himself. It was a common forum where genealogists in both countries could circulate ideas, methods, and knowledge. For the first time, Swedish-American genealogy had moved in the direction of decentralization.

Already during his stint in the Foreign Service, Olsson had started to travel to archives around the United States and Sweden to systematically collect information about emigrants. By 1957, he had reportedly created an index of six thousand people drawn from passenger lists of the early migration.[32] His research was published in 1967 as *Swedish Passenger Arrivals in New York 1820–1850,* a volume with information on four thousand individuals described by a reviewer as "an invaluable source material" and "a new gold mine" for genealogists.[33] From the 1940s until his death in 2007, at age ninety-seven, Olsson amassed an extensive private archive and library. Unlike Ella Heckscher, who traveled to archives to find answers to genealogical questions, Olsson created his own collection, which he regularly put to use in answering genealogical queries in the *Swedish Pioneer Historical Quarterly.*[34]

Olsson continued to publish the *Quarterly* column until 1980. The following year, he founded the *Swedish American Genealogist (SAG).* Its editorial board came from both sides of the Atlantic and included Sten Carlsson and Carl-Erik Johansson, a genealogist at the LDS church who in 1972 had published a popular handbook on Swedish-American genealogy.[35] *SAG* featured articles on family history and practical research advice, carried a forum for genealogical queries, and provided readers with extensive excerpted lists of biographical migrant data.

The initiatives of local heritage associations and enthusiastic individuals in the 1950s and 1960s laid the foundation for popular expansion of genealogy. Genealogists working on the mass migration could now be in conversation with one another. To the benefit of both genealogists and social-historical scholarship, it enabled a circulation of methodological and empirical knowledge that served to calcify the notion that memories of the migration were a culturally shared phenomenon.

Traveling as Practice and Performance

Nils William Olsson's practice of traveling far and wide to locate, copy, and excerpt resources was paralleled by a movement to elevate traveling as a central aspect of genealogy.[36] The culture of genealogical traveling dovetailed with the postwar expansion of commercial air traffic and the growth of the tourism industry. Until the early 1990s, with the deregulation of air traffic in the United States in 1978 and in Sweden in 1992, it was considerably more affordable to make the Atlantic crossing on a charter flight arranged by an organization or travel bureau.[37] From the 1960s to the 1980s, such charter tours were arranged by groups and associations in both Sweden and the United States.[38]

During a visit to Stockholm, Olsson had on several occasions been "called upon by harried officials of various libraries, archives and administration offices of that city, for help in guiding Americans."[39] As a response to this observed need, Olsson in 1962 published the article "Tracing Your Swedish Ancestry" in the *Quarterly.* It was aimed at prospective U.S. travelers to Sweden, informing them of the need to begin their research into their family in America, describing what records to study in Sweden, which institutions to contact, and what archives to visit. A year later, the article was republished as an illustrated booklet by the Swedish Ministry for Foreign Affairs.[40] This effort was part of a "tourism propaganda campaign" financed since 1951 by the Swedish government and directed by the Swedish Tourism Traffic Association (STTF), funded jointly by the state government and the tourism industry.[41]

The public–private interest in genealogy and tourism reached a climax in 1966 when STTF launched a public-relations campaign called Homecoming Year.[42] It was "dedicated to all those men and women of Swedish descent . . . now residing in other lands." The idea was to increase tourism to Sweden by specifically targeting Swedish Americans and inviting them to visit "the place from which he or his forefathers originated." To fulfill this aspiration, the association advised prospective travelers to order a copy of Olsson's booklet and offered to arrange genealogical research through two professional genealogists in Sweden—one of whom was Ludolf Häusler of the Genealogical Bureau.[43]

While the STTF set out to facilitate genealogy by proxy, following the model adopted by Heckscher, other initiatives were aimed at facilitating the mobility of genealogists. In 1969, Nils William Olsson had also started to arrange genealogical workshops in Sweden, titled "Finding Your Roots in Sweden," where Americans traveled around the country to visit heritage sites and archives.[44] In 1991, he shifted the location to Salt Lake City and made the workshops a yearly occurrence. Participants spent a full week at the downtown Family History Library listening to lectures by invited speakers and by Olsson himself on Swedish sources, language, and history. The bulk of the time, however, was spent in the LDS church facilities doing individual research.[45]

The reason for the workshop's relocation to Utah was the massive microfilming program of the LDS church. First started in 1938, the Mormon microfilming had rapidly expanded after 1945, both in the United States and abroad. In 1948, the church struck a major deal with the National Archives of Sweden to microfilm all Swedish church records. The church paid for the microfilming of the church books, the negatives of the films were sent to Salt Lake City, and a "free" positive copy was deposited at the National Archives in Stockholm.[46] When the project ended in 1964, Sweden was the most well-represented foreign country in the church's microfilm collection, sporting close to sixty thousand rolls of film, or slightly more than 13 percent of the total holdings.[47] By the late 1960s, the extensive remediation of sources had made Salt Lake City the world's primary center for genealogical research.

The connection of blood to place, exemplified in the notion of homecoming, constituted what cultural geographer Catherine Nash has called an "embodied inheritance."[48] Knowledge and memories of the migration had previously traveled through textual communication. Beginning in the 1960s, the efforts of the Swedish government and the tourism industry in cooperation with professional genealogists served to assert traveling as a natural aspect of Swedish–American ancestral relations.

Institutionalizing Research and Continued Remediation

The first institution outside Utah that specifically worked to support Swedish-American genealogy was established in Växjö in southern Sweden in 1965. The idea of creating an institute for emigration research was launched by the liberal politician Gunnar Helén, who recently had been appointed governor of Kronoberg County. The idea quickly found support among local politicians, the regional business and tourism industry, the universities of Uppsala and Lund, the Swedish National Archives, and the National Library of Sweden. Together, they founded the Swedish Emigrant Institute (SEI), since 1968 located in the House of Emigrants in Växjö.[49] The director of the SEI became Ulf Beijbom, a PhD student of Sten Carlsson in Uppsala. Beijbom would serve as the institute's director until his retirement in 2002.

The institute's board decided that the primary aim of the SEI was to become a resource and service institute for academic scholarship.[50] As a consequence of this focus, their first priority was to build a substantial archival collection. Its centerpiece became the microfilming of ministerial records and minute books of Swedish-American churches.[51] As part of his doctoral dissertation research on the late-nineteenth-century Swedish immigration to Chicago, Beijbom had spent time in Illinois in 1963. While there, he visited an old Augustana Synod church and was presented with the records of the congregation.[52] According to Beijbom, these records provided individual data that—together with U.S. censuses—constituted "the primary demographic and social sources" about Swedes in America.[53] Inspired by the work of the LDS church, Beijbom and the SEI board decided to embark on a major project to microfilm these sources to preserve them for posterity and to make them more easily available for research.[54]

The LDS church had, in fact, offered to pay for and perform the microfilming, but the offer was turned down because of opposition from some Swedish-American congregations that did not accept the Mormon practice of posthumous baptism.[55] Instead, Beijbom turned to the influential Wallenberg Foundation in Sweden, which granted the SEI repeated funding to ensure the project's continuation until 1978. The SEI hired Lennart Setterdahl—a forty-year-old Swede who had immigrated to the United States in the late 1950s—as its "field archivist." Using a portable microfilm camera transported in the trunk of his car, Setterdahl crisscrossed the continent to photograph church books. Following the same formula as the Mormons, one copy of each microfilm roll was sent to Växjö and another was deposited with the local church.[56]

The church records initially had been intended for academic scholarship, but it soon became clear that they primarily served as a central resource for genealogists.[57] The number of genealogists visiting the House of Emigrants increased steadily beginning in the early 1970s.[58] In the following decades, the institute acquired additional resources by purchasing microfilms of passport journals, census reports, and Swedish church records, and by excerpting and creating indexes of biographical data. In 1994, Beijbom claimed—quite rightly, if one considers Sweden—that the SEI had "become *the place* where Swedish Americans search for their 'unknown family' and their roots."[59] This was the result of the resources centered at the SEI, but also of the close collaborations with the regional tourism industry, which played an important promotional role during the institute's early years.[60]

The first nationally oriented institution in the United States working explicitly in the field was the Swenson Swedish Immigration Research

The reading room of the Swedish Emigrant Institute (SEI) in Växjö, Sweden, opened in 1968 and gave institute staff, volunteers, and the public access to its print and microfilm resources. Courtesy of the Swedish Emigrant Institute, Växjö, Sweden.

Center (SSIRC), established in 1981 at Augustana College in Rock Island, Illinois. The SSIRC was assigned a dual mission: to promote academic scholarship, and to enable genealogical research. As part of this latter focus, in 1982–84 the center supported the continued microfilming of the Swedish-American church records. Through an exchange with the SEI, the SSIRC secured a full set of copies of the old microfilms, thus creating two collections on either side of the Atlantic.[61]

However, the contents of the records do not belong to the SEI or the SSIRC. They are the property of the churches where they were produced. As a result of church mergers, they are today owned by the Evangelical Lutheran Church in America (ELCA). A few years ago, the ELCA, together with the SEI and the SSIRC, struck a deal with Ancestry.com, which has paid for the digitization of the original microfilm rolls.[62] The microfilms originally made by Lennart Setterdahl and funded by a Swedish foundation are now available for all to use in digital rendition through a billion-dollar company based in Utah.

The Making of Ancestral Relations

Knowledge about Swedish-American ancestry is not naturally given. It has turned from a communicative to a cultural memory through the development of new forms of media, technology, and infrastructures that over the course of the twentieth century changed the landscape of genealogy. The development of Swedish-American genealogy is connected to the infrastructure that has facilitated it: the work of professional genealogists, associations, journals, and archives. This infrastructure, in turn, relied on the remediation of information, repackaging it as indexes or reconfiguring it through microfilming. This remediation continued through rapidly evolving computerization. The 1980s introduction of desktop computers facilitated the creation of massive digital indexes, and the 1990s growth of the World Wide Web made it possible to access digital scans of original sources through online databases. With each technological invention, new actors have entered the field.

When Ella Heckscher facilitated genealogy in the interwar period, her work focused on providing Mormon clients with an ancestry in Sweden. The migrant indexes created in the 1950s and 1960s were different in that they sought to bridge the Atlantic, providing a resource that made it possible to trace the migrant's point of departure and, ideally, also the point of arrival. With the microfilming of Swedish-American church records, it became possible to move back and forth in time and space, tracing the migrants across the sea to their birthplace, or locating families in their new homeland. Because this knowledge had started to wane as a communicative memory, by the 1950s and 1960s it was increasingly undergirded as a cultural memory by genealogists, academic scholars, the Swedish government, and the tourism industry, stimulated by technological developments, political and commercial incentives, and religious interests. The changes were consequences of transatlantic connections that in turn served to produce knowledge about transatlantic connections.

As I have argued elsewhere, the notion that there exists an ancestral connection between Sweden and the United States is both popular and widespread.[63] This essay has explored some ways in which this notion of a mnemonic borderland was constructed during the twentieth century through cultural formations and institutional communications. The results of the study are contingent on a broad understanding of what genealogy is. Genealogy is most commonly considered an individual practice associated with a search for identity and belonging, and with deeply personal interests and feelings. The late-twentieth-century growth of genealogy has been described as "a process of democratization," with an emphasis on the agency of individual genealogists and their "democratic interest" in family history.[64] But genealogy is also an academic inquiry, a commercial market, a political tool, a technological practice, and a religious mandate. It is the hands-on research, where people pour over old documents at archives or through online databases, and it is the companies and institutions that produce and own those archives and databases. It is family reunions, but also the tourism industry that make those reunions possible. Neither the individual dimensions of genealogy nor the cultural memories produced through it could survive without these cultural and infrastructural aspects—especially in transatlantic settings.

The technologies, infrastructures, and actors analyzed here are relevant both for research on genealogy and for scholarship on Swedish–American relations. They highlight the important roles played by certain key agents and agencies in working to forward the culture and practice of genealogy. The image that emerges is that of a network of individuals whose connectedness was not primarily existential, but rather grounded in religious doctrine, in academic inquiries, or in political and commercial profits. Although their connections were instrumental, synchronized with their respective interests, they worked in, and effectively created, transatlantic borderlands of memories, informed by individual movements, that calcified histories of ancestral relations.

Notes

This work was supported by the Swedish Research Council under Grant number 2016–06769.

1. H. Arnold Barton, *A Folk Divided: Homeland Swedes and Swedish Americans, 1840–1940* (Carbondale: Southern Illinois University Press, 1994).

2. Roger Waldinger, *The Cross-Border Connection: Immigrants, Emigrants, and Their Homelands* (Cambridge: Harvard University Press, 2015), 5–6. On the history of Swedish emigration and return migration, see Harald Runblom and Hans Norman, eds., *From Sweden to America: A History of the Migration* (Minneapolis: University of Minnesota Press, 1976).

3. See, for example, Carl-Erik Johansson, *Cradled in Sweden: A Practical Guide to Genealogical Research in Swedish Records* (Logan, Utah: Everton Publishers, 1972); Per Clemensson and Kjell Andersson, *Emigrantforska! Steg för steg* (Stockholm: LT, 1996); Per Clemensson and Kjell Andersson, *Your Swedish Roots: A Step by Step Handbook* (Provo, Utah: Ancestry, 2004); Ted Rosvall and Anna-Lena Hultman, *Emigrantforskning* (Solna: Sveriges släktforskarförbund, 2012); Ted Rosvall and Anna-Lena Hultman, *Emigrantforska på nätet* (Stockholm: Sveriges släktforskarförbund, 2017).

4. For an overview of genetic genealogy, see Catherine Nash, *Genetic Geographies: The Trouble with Ancestry* (Minneapolis: University of Minnesota Press, 2015); Julia Creet, *The Genealogical Sublime* (Amherst: University of Massachusetts Press, 2020).

5. Jennifer Eastman Attebery, *Up in the Rocky Mountains: Writing the Swedish Immigrant Experience* (Minneapolis: University of Minnesota Press, 2007), 87–110; Dorothy Burton Skårdal, *The Divided Heart: Scandinavian Immigrant Experience through Literary Sources* (Lincoln: University of Nebraska Press, 1974).

6. Barton, *A Folk Divided*, 265–82.

7. Jan Assmann, "Collective Memory and Cultural Identity," trans. John Czaplicka, *New German Critique* 65 (spring/summer 1995): 126–27, 129. On immigrant generations and ethnic belonging, see Peter Kivisto and Dag Blanck, eds., *American Immigrants and Their Generations: Studies and Commentaries on the Hansen Thesis after Fifty Years* (Urbana: University of Illinois Press, 1990).

8. Bruno Latour, *Reassembling the Social: An Introduction to Actor-Network-Theory* (Oxford: Oxford University Press, 2005), 39. For a historical overview of the social and technological systems of media, see Asa Briggs and Peter Burke, *A Social History of the Media: From Gutenberg to the Internet*, 3d ed. (Cambridge: Polity Press, 2009).

9. Kevin Meethan, "Remaking Time and Space: The Internet, Digital Archives and Genealogy," in *Geography and Genealogy: Locating Personal Pasts*, ed. Dallen J. Timothy and Jeanne Kay Guelke (Aldershot: Ashgate, 2008), 99–114; Jerome De Groot, "Ancestry.com and the Evolving Nature of Historical Information Companies," *Public Historian* 42, no. 1 (February 2020): 8–28.

10. Frederick C. Luebke, *European Immigrants in the American West: Community Histories* (Albuquerque: University of New Mexico Press, 1998), xi–xii, xv.

11. Douglas J. Davies, *An Introduction to Mormonism* (Cambridge: Cambridge University Press, 2010), 236–39; Donald Harman Akenson, *Some Family:*

The Mormons and How Humanity Keeps Track of Itself (Montreal: McGill-Queen's University Press, 2007), 50–70.

12. Adam Hjorthén, "Genealogy from a Distance: The Media of Correspondence and the Mormon Church, 1910–45," *Historical Research* (January 10, 2021): https://doi.org/10.1093/hisres/htaa034.

13. Kerstin Thörn, "Att söka sin plats: En berättelse om Ella Heckscher," in *Obemärkta: Det dagliga livets idéer,* ed. Ronny Ambjörnsson and Sverker Sörlin (Stockholm: Carlssons, 1995), 59–87. See also Ella Heckscher, *Sex kapitel om släktforskning* (Stockholm: Albert Bonners, 1939); the latest edition appeared as *Släktforskning: Kort handledning för amatörer* (Stockholm: Albert Bonniers, 1970).

14. Lars-Göran Johansson, December 10, 1986, Finding Aid to Ella Heckschers Genealogiska Byrå, Swedish Emigrant Institute, Växjö.

15. These observations are based on studies of Ludolf Häusler genealogiska samling, ULA/10183, at the Regional State Archives in Uppsala, and the available records of Ella Heckchers genealogiska byrå at the Swedish Emigrant Institute in Växjö.

16. Beställningsbok 1919–1934, D3, vol. 1, Diverse förteckningar, Ludolf Häuslers genealogiska samling, 10183, the Regional State Archives in Uppsala.

17. "Amerikasvenskarna och släktforskningen: Ett samtal med chefen för genealogiska byrån i Uppsala," *Vecko-Journalen,* no. 26 (1923).

18. Ella Heckscher to Eli Heckscher, November 23, 1924, vol. 2, series 63, Brev från Ella Heckscher, Eli Heckschers efterlämnade papper, L 67, National Library of Sweden (hereafter EHP).

19. Clara J. Fagergren, "Ella Heckscher and Her Work," *Utah Genealogical and Historical Magazine* 19, no. 1 (January 1928): 9–10.

20. "Föredrag om släktforskning," *Svenska Amerikanska Posten,* April 6, 1938; Reinhold Ahléen, "Fröken Ella Heckscher från Uppsala vår allra nyaste sverigegäst," *Vestkusten,* March 17, 1938; "Svenskamerika," *Vestkusten,* March 10, 1938.

21. Ella Heckscher, "Genealogical Sources in Sweden," *Utah Genealogical and Historical Magazine* 29, no. 3 (July 1938): 97–110.

22. Ella Heckscher to Eli Heckscher, April 1, 1938, EHP.

23. "I stamträdets skugga," *Dagens Nyheter,* February 3, 1924.

24. Ella Heckscher to Eli Heckscher, September 6, 1932, EHP.

25. See, for example, the Bluth Family archives online at www.bluth.info, and Della A. Belnap, *"Our Bluth Family": 1570 to 1975* (Ogden, Utah: By the author, 1975).

26. John Johansson et al., *En smålandssocken emigrerar: En bok om emigrationen till Amerika från Långasjö socken i Kronobergs län* (Växjö: Långasjö emigrantcirkel, 1967).

27. Herman Norling, "Kom med oss!," *Emigranten* [Bryggan/The Bridge], no. 1 (1969): 1; "Värmländska emigranter på kort," *Dagens Nyheter,* February 25, 1963.

28. On the existential dimensions of genealogy, see Eviatar Zerubavel, *Ancestors and Relatives: Genealogy, Identity, and Community* (Oxford: Oxford University Press, 2012); Jackie Hogan, *Roots Quest: Inside America's Genealogy Boom* (Lanham, Md.: Rowman and Littlefield, 2019).

29. Sture Lindmark, "Emigrationsforskning i dag," *Svenska Dagbladet*, September 21, 1967; John Johansson, "Inledning," in *En Smålandssocken emigrerar*, 13; and Sune Åkerman, "Emigrantregistret och universitetet," *Emigranten* [Bryggan/The Bridge], no. 1 (1969): 15. On the Uppsala project, see Harald Runblom, "A Brief History of a Research Project," in *From Sweden to America: A History of the Migration*, ed. Harald Runblom and Hans Norman (Minneapolis: University of Minnesota Press, 1976), 11–18. On the interest of social historians in genealogical research, see Robert M. Taylor and Ralph J. Crandall, "Historians and Genealogists: An Emerging Community of Interest," in *Generations and Change: Genealogical Perspectives on Social History*, ed. Robert M. Taylor and Ralph J. Crandall (Macon, Ga.: Mercer, 1985), 17–26.

30. Chris Olsson, "Nils William Olsson, 11 June 1909–20 March 2007," *Swedish-American Historical Quarterly* 58, no. 2 (April 2007): 67–69.

31. Nils William Olsson, "Personal Pioneer History: Notes and Queries," *Swedish Pioneer Historical Quarterly* 9, no. 1 (January 1958): 24.

32. "USA-diplomat och forskare har 6 000 kort om emigranter," *Svenska Dagbladet*, January 11, 1957.

33. Nils William Olsson, *Swedish Passenger Arrivals in New York, 1820–1850* (Stockholm: Norstedts, 1967); Gunnar Qvist, "4000 utvandrare spårade," *Dagens Nyheter*, August 27, 1968.

34. "Rötterna till USA:s historia," *Dagens Nyheter*, April 13, 1949.

35. *Swedish American Genealogist* 1, no. 1 (March 1981); Johansson, *Cradled in Sweden*.

36. See, for example, Paul Basu, *Highland Homecomings: Genealogy and Heritage Tourism in the Scottish Diaspora* (London: Routledge, 2007); Carla Almeida Santos and Grace Yan, "Genealogical Tourism: A Phenomenological Examination," *Journal of Travel Research* 49, no. 1 (2010): 56–67.

37. Eric G. E. Zuelow, *A History of Modern Tourism* (London: Palgrave, 2016), 149–64; Mats Berglund, *Avregleringen av inrikesflyget* (Stockholm: Konkurrensverkets rapportserie, no. 1, 1996), 12–21.

38. As an example, the Långasjö study circle went on a U.S. tour in 1962, the Emigrant Register in Karlstad and the Swedish Emigrant Institute in Växjö organized several tours to the United States, and the Swedish-American Historical Society sponsored tours to Sweden. See Arnold Alfredsson, *I utvandrarnas spår: Långasjö emigrantcirkels Amerika-resa 9–29 juni 1962; Brev hem från resedeltagaren Arnold Alfredsson* (Växjö: Växjöbladet, 1962); "Släktresa New York–Göteborg," *Bryggan/The Bridge* 3, no. 4 (1971): 128; "I utvandrarnas spår: Rundresa i Mellanvästerns svenskbygder med Emigrantinstitutet, Smålandsposten och SJ Resebyrå,"

1973, vol. 3, Ö1, Emigrantinstitutets institutionsarkiv, Svenska Emigrantinstitutet, Växjö (hereafter SEI); Nils William Olsson, "The Pioneer Charter Flights 1960," *Swedish Pioneer Historical Quarterly* 11, no. 4 (October 1960): 172–74.

39. Olsson, "Personal Pioneer History," 24.

40. Nils William Olsson, "Tracing Your Swedish Ancestry," *Swedish Pioneer Historical Quarterly* 13, no. 4 (October 1962): 160–74; Nils William Olsson, *Tracing Your Swedish Ancestry* (Stockholm: Royal Ministry for Foreign Affairs, 1963). Olsson's booklet substituted the shorter pamphlet *Finding Your Forefathers: Some Hints for Americans of Swedish Origin* (Stockholm: Royal Ministry for Foreign Affairs, 1957).

41. Hans-Erik Olson, *Staten, turismen och rekreationen: Producenter och konsumenter i kampen om makten; En inledande studie* (Stockholm: Stockholms universitet, Framtidspolitiska studier, no. 2, 1987), 6–7, 13–14.

42. Adam Hjorthén, "Old World Homecomings: Campaigns of Ancestral Tourism and Cultural Diplomacy, 1945–66," *Journal of Contemporary History* (April 7, 2021): https://doi.org/10.1177/0022009420986841.

43. Brochure, "Welcome to Sweden," Homecoming Year, 1966, 31/51, Svenska turisstrafikförbundets arkiv, Swedish National Archives, Arninge.

44. "Announcing a Heritage and Genealogical Tour of Scandinavia, March, 1979," F6, Loose folders, Nils William Olsson Papers, Swenson Swedish Immigration Research Center, Rock Island, Illinois (hereafter NWO).

45. See *SAG* Workshop programs in Jill Seaholm's Vertical Files (uncataloged), Swenson Swedish Immigration Research Center, Rock Island, Illinois.

46. James B. Allen, Jessie L. Embry, and Kahlile B. Mehr, *Hearts Turned to the Fathers: A History of the Genealogical Society of Utah, 1894–1994* (Provo, Utah: Brigham Young University Studies, 1995), 213–64; Matts Lindström, *Drömmar om det minsta: Microfilm, överflöd och brist, 1900–1970* (Lund: Mediehistoriskt arkiv, 2017), 121–51.

47. "Microfilms of the Genealogical Society, as of January 1, 1967," F10, series I, subseries II:IV, NWO.

48. Catherine Nash, *Of Irish Descent: Origin Stories, Genealogy, and the Politics of Belonging* (Syracuse, N.Y.: Syracuse University Press, 2008), 70.

49. Minutes, Styrelsen för Emigrantinstitutet, June 15, 1966, vol. 1, AI, SEI.

50. Birgitta Odén, Ulf Beijbom, and Håkan Berggren, "PM angående Emigrantinstitutets arbete," attachment to Minutes, Stiftelsen Emigrantinstitutet, September 9, 1966, vol. 1, A1, SEI.

51. This included the Augustana Lutheran, Mission Covenant, Evangelical Free, Swedish Methodist, and Baptist churches.

52. Ulf Beijbom, *Oförglömligt: Ett liv i emigrationsforskningens tjänst* (Stockholm: Carlssons, 2014), 30–128.

53. Ulf Beijbom, "Emigrantinstitutet 10 år: En presentation av verksamhet och utställningar av Ulf Beijbom," vol. 1, 18–19, Ö1, SEI.

54. Emigrantinstitutet, Verksamheten 1966, vol. 1, 12 Ö1, SEI.

55. Hugh Kirkendall to American Swedish Institute, May 21, 1968, Mikrofilmsprojektet, vol. 1, FVb, SEI.

56. "Giant Microfilm Project in North America Finished," *EI Information* 4, no. 1 (1979): vol. 2, Ö1, SEI.

57. Sten Almqvist to Lennart Setterdahl, March 14, 1975, "Korrespondens med Lennart och Lilly Settedahl," vol. 7, FVb, SEI.

58. Emigrantinstitutet, Verksamheten 1973, vol. 1, Ö1, SEI.

59. Ulf Beijbom, "The Swedish Emigrant Institute and the Documentation of the Transatlantic Era," n.d. (ca. 1994), vol. 7, 8, Ö1, SEI.

60. Brochures, Homecoming Days 1968, in F4, vol. 12, Fi, and vol. 3, ÖI, SEI.

61. "In Search of Roots at the Swenson Center," *Swenson Center News* 1, no. 1 (1986): 4–6; Joel W. Lundeen, "Memorandum of Agreement," n.d., F18, Box 2, Series 1, SSIRC Archives, Swenson Swedish Immigration Research Center, Rock Island, Illinois.

62. "Swedish-American and Swedish-Canadian Church Records Now Online," May 8, 2018, Augustana College, https://www.augustana.edu/.

63. Adam Hjorthén, *Cross-Border Commemorations: Celebrating Swedish Settlement in America* (Amherst: University of Massachusetts Press, 2018), 143–51, 171–74; Adam Hjorthén, "Swedishness by Blood: Transatlantic Genealogy on Twenty-First Century Television," in *The Dynamics and Contexts of Cultural Transfers: An Anthology,* ed. Anna Williams and Margaretha Fahlgren (Uppsala: Uppsala universitet, Avdelningen för litteratursocologi, 2017), 129–47.

64. François Weil, *Family Trees: A History of Genealogy in America* (Cambridge: Harvard University Press, 2013), 181, 184. See also a similar argument about Sweden in Lennart Börnfors, *Anor i folkupplaga: Släktforskning som folkrörelse* (Lund: Landsarkivet i Lund, 2001).

6

Academics on the Move

The Nature and Significance of a Swedish–American Intellectual Borderland

Dag Blanck

In 2007, the Swedish author Per Wästberg published the second volume of his memoirs. It begins with an intense arrival to New York in the fall of 1953, which the author calls his "rite of initiation to the New World." New York was not, however, Wästberg's final destination. When his week in the city was over, he boarded a train for Boston. He was on his way to enroll as a student at Harvard University. Wästberg spent two happy years at Harvard and graduated with a B.A. in 1955. He describes his years at Harvard with great joy, where he found educational opportunities that no Swedish university could offer. Widener Library made him euphoric and Harvard seemed to be an "oasis of balance and tolerance where all kinds of endeavors and ideas were tried." His two years in Cambridge, he concludes, were "the most fruitful in my life."[1]

Wästberg is one example of the many Swedes who have come to American universities and colleges to study and do research. In fact, since the end of World War II the United States has become a dominant point of reference for Swedish academic life. During the nineteenth century, Swedish academic and intellectual life was oriented toward Germany, with lively patterns of exchange. Beginning after World War I, this orientation shifted toward the Anglo-Saxon world, with the United States as the dominant country after 1945. Swedish historian Johan Östling has shown how the end of World War II and the realization of the Nazi atrocities among Swedish intellectuals led to a collapse in the intellectual relations between

Sweden and Germany,[2] and the intellectual historian Svante Nordin talks of the "ideas of 1945" as a label for the major cultural and intellectual reorientation that postwar Sweden underwent, away from Germany toward the United Kingdom and, more important, the United States.[3]

This essay seeks to provide an analysis of Swedish–American scholarly contacts and the creation of an intellectual borderland between the two countries through which individuals and ideas have flowed back and forth. It is a borderland of close proximity between Sweden and the United States. It is a borderland where the relations have been asymmetrical, with the United States as the dominating part, and most of the flows have gone from the United States to Sweden. A few examples of the reverse movement exist, but will not be discussed here.

The academic migrations are central and include individuals who travel from Sweden, spend time in the United States, and then return to Sweden. Through these individuals a set of ideas reached Sweden, where they left important imprints. The experiences from both countries have together shaped a special set of social Swedish–American connections, or, to use Roger Waldinger's term, "a zone of intersocietal convergence, linking 'here' and 'there.'"[4]

The American Academy and Sweden

The United States is the leading destination for international students. In 2016 it ranked as the most popular destination, receiving 4.1 million students or 28 percent of all internationally mobile students. Two-thirds of the students come from Asia, while the 91,000 Europeans make up 9 percent.[5] The 4,700 Swedes make up a small share of these students,[6] but from a Swedish perspective the United States is the most popular destination, a position which the country has had for many decades. The number of Swedish students in American universities grew rapidly after World War II. By the mid-1950s, several actors in the field had been established. From the late 1910s, two foundations had dominated the traffic of scholars from Sweden to the United States (and back), namely, the American-Scandinavian Foundation, established in New York in 1911, and the Sweden-America Foundation, established in Stockholm in 1919. The Sweden-America Foundation was funded primarily by Swedish industry, and its leadership also included leading academics.[7] As Andreas Melldahl has shown, the foundation looked to the interest of the nation, and its program reflected the needs, real or perceived, of Sweden at the time. Since 1919, some three thousand fellows have been selected, the great majority since 1945.[8]

The initial impetus for these programs of Swedish–American academic exchange was to bring graduate students to the United States. During the decades after World War II, the foundation also started an extensive undergraduate program in cooperation with the Institute of International Education in New York, which made it possible for young Swedes, usually in their first year of university study, to spend a year as an undergraduate in an American college or university. In fact, the undergraduate program rapidly became more popular than the original graduate fellowship and in the 1950s and 1960s, the undergraduate scheme at times attracted twice as many Swedes. One estimate of the number of undergraduate fellowships from the foundation puts the number at about 3,600. Other institutions played an increasingly important role from the 1950s. They include the Fulbright commission, which was established in Sweden in 1952, and the Rockefeller Foundation. The link between the Rockefeller Foundation and Sweden goes back to the 1920s and 1930s. Between 1917 and 1955 the Rockefeller Foundation awarded 157 fellowships to Swedes.[9]

There are many reasons for this Swedish interest in studying in the United States. The strength, quality, and openness of the American academy have attracted students and scholars from all over the world, especially after World War II. The sheer size and the availability of resources are also important factors. Swedish anthropologist Ulf Hannerz, himself a part of the transatlantic exchange of knowledge, has talked about an American "scholarly industry, not likely to be matched in any other national academia," which has "left significant imprints on many visiting Swedes."[10] The Nobel Prize Laureate in Economics Bertil Ohlin echoed similar sentiments when he reflected about his years in the American universities in the 1920s, saying that "the American universities are strongholds for education and research in a sense that a European hardly can imagine before he visits them."[11] Another economist writing about the situation fifty years later concluded that "the lavishness and splendor of

American universities are almost staggering in comparison with continental or Scandinavian institutions."[12]

In addition, different American institutions for educational exchange, private and public, have been important in attracting students to the United States. According to historian Richard Pells, the Fulbright program should be seen in a political light and was from the beginning "entangled in the tentacles of the State Department." It became a part of the American cultural Cold War. The Smith–Mundt Act from 1948 had authorized the federal government to use its educational, information, and propaganda resources in the Cold War and the Fulbright program became a "reluctant participant."[13] Discussions at the board meeting of the Swedish Fulbright Commission in the 1950s also show that members were aware of the academic competition from the Soviet Union and saw the fellowships awarded as a way of minimizing Soviet influences in Swedish academic circles.[14]

As Andreas Melldahl has shown in an analysis of the graduate and postgraduate fellowships from the Sweden-America Foundation, there was a steady increase in the number of students, especially after World War II. Of the total number of fellowships, some 16 percent were granted before 1950 and 50 percent since 1980.[15] Examining the different fields of study, it is clear that technology has played a central role. It was the largest category until 1960, and has remained relatively strong. The social sciences were also important early on and constitute the second-largest category before World War II. The changes during the twentieth century can be seen in the interplay between technology, the social sciences, and the natural sciences. Before World War II, technology and social sciences dominated over natural sciences. After the war, the natural sciences and social sciences expanded greatly.

Some numbers will illustrate this.[16] When the work of the foundation resumed after World War II, dominant categories among the fellows were technology, with close to 40 percent of the awards, followed by the social sciences (19 percent) and the natural sciences (11 percent). By the 1970s, the positions had begun to shift and the social sciences now dominated (39 percent), followed by technology (21 percent), and the natural sciences (20 percent). During the last quarter of the twentieth century, the natural sciences became even stronger, establishing themselves in second place

(24 percent), behind the social sciences (37 percent) but ahead of technology (14 percent). Subjects such as biology and biochemistry account for a substantial part of the increase among the natural sciences, and by the beginning of the twenty-first century the increasingly interdisciplinary life sciences seem particularly important.

Other fields of study were always smaller. Less than 10 percent of the awards were in the humanities and the arts before World War II, but since the mid-1960s the share has increased to about 12–13 percent. Agriculture has been an even smaller area of study, although it should be noted that it played a relatively more important role during the first two decades of the foundation's history. The shifts between disciplines illustrate the changing natures of both Sweden and the United States in the twentieth century, toward both industrial and knowledge-based economies and societies. As noted earlier, the foundation often sought to act in the national interest, supporting perceived Swedish needs.

A Swedish–American Academic Borderland

How did these academic peregrinations create a Swedish–American borderland? The first level is that of the individual travelers. Through them both direct contacts and mental proximities were established, and once they had crossed and recrossed the Atlantic, they made an impact in Sweden. The effects were both professional and personal, but, once in place, the academic borderland created new links, both academic and nonacademic. The academic dimension of Swedish–American relations has thus resulted in significant and long-lasting relations between the two countries.

A few studies have focused on these consequences. Upon returning from a year in the United States, one Swedish scholar observed that "America does change people . . . but in ways so subtle that it is hard to describe," an attitude that is probably common among many returnees.[17] In a study by Franklin Scott from the mid-1950s, a majority of Swedes coming back from American universities considered themselves to have benefited from their time in America, both personally and professionally. Most of the students claimed that they had gained a broader outlook on the world, that they perceived Sweden in a new light, and that they had matured as individuals. Some answers also suggest that the American experience proved professionally advantageous, especially in the fields of technology, natural science, and business. Students in the humanities, on the other hand, seem to have had a more difficult time getting concrete career results out of their American experience.[18]

The attraction of the United States as both a place of study and a place of employment is also clear in a survey from the late 1960s of Swedish natural scientists and engineers who had left Sweden, many as a consequence of an initial academic migration. At the time, they had permanent positions in U.S. universities and they indicated that the greater opportunities for continued research and permanent employment were the dominant motivations behind their move to the United States.[19]

An examination of 108 Swedish Fulbright graduate student scholarship winners in the 1960s confirms the impression that those Swedes who had spent a period of time studying in the United States also pursued successful careers in Sweden upon their return. In 1977, about 40 percent of them had permanent academic positions in an institution of higher learning, 5 percent as full professors, around 20 percent occupied managerial positions in private industry, and 20 percent were found in the higher echelons of the civil service.[20]

For those who went back, returning to Swedish academic life was not always easy, at least not in the cohort from the 1950s. The older established professors who returned were, according to Scott, greeted with "mild curiosity" and some increased prestige. It was rather the younger returnees, those of the "docent class" whose careers lay ahead of them, who were watched for "tendencies of Americanization" and evidence of useful learning by those who had stayed at home. "In conservative Uppsala they meet more suspicion than in Lund or in the urban universities of Stockholm and Gothenburg." Those in the humanities and the social sciences found themselves in more uncertain positions than those in the natural sciences, where they enjoyed the advantage of the prestige that American universities had in the latter field. All these younger scholars, Scott concludes, had gone abroad "on coveted fellowships," and it was from them that the future professors would be chosen.[21]

The fellowship winners not only spoke of professional success, but also claimed that their private lives and personal outlooks were changed by America—examples given include increased self-confidence and a more international perspective. They saw both Sweden and the United States in a new light. These personal effects may be particularly strong among the many undergraduate students from the 1950s on. One such student from 1951 maintained that his year in the United States had "changed my entire view of Europe and America." It had been the best educational experience, "getting to know people from all parts of the world," and an opportunity to modify one's views of Sweden. Another student from the same year maintained that as he looked back, "hardly any phase in my life has given me more lasting impressions or impulses to further activities."[22]

Individuals in the Borderland

Gunnar and Alva Myrdal are two examples of Swedish academic migrants who became a part of their country's political elite and for whom the United States was of great importance. They served as cabinet ministers in Social Democratic governments, each received a Nobel Prize—Gunnar in economics, Alva in peace—and played a significant role in Swedish political and intellectual post–World War II life. Their first visit to the United States was in 1929–30 as Rockefeller fellows, where Gunnar studied sociology, more specifically "American methodology in Economics and the Social Sciences," while his wife focused on "Social Psychology of Children in the U.S.A."[23] They made many contacts with leading scholars in the social sciences, including Robert and Helen Lynd at Columbia University and W. F. Ogburn and Ernst W. Burgess in Chicago.[24] They became good friends with the economist Dorothy Swaine Thomas and sociologist W. I. Thomas, whose joint book *The Child in America* provided Alva and Gunnar with inspiration.[25]

Historian Walter Jackson has called their year in the United States a "turning point" in their lives.[26] They returned in 1938 when Gunnar became the director of the Carnegie Foundation project on American race relations, and would come back many times to the United States during the rest of their lives. The vital American academic milieus were of decisive importance. To Alva the first encounter with American research was "amazingly productive" and she made a list of fourteen research projects in social psychology and writes that she was "dizzy with the joy of discovery."[27]

Alva Myrdal devoted significant attention to progressive American educational practices and social policies throughout the 1930s. Imprints of these ideas can be found in her book *Stadsbarn* (Urban children) from 1935, in the Myrdals jointly published *Kris i befolkningsfrågan* (Crisis in the population question) in 1936, and in her school Socialpolitiska seminariet from 1936 with courses in family and child psychology as well as parenthood.[28] In *Kontakt med Amerika* (Contact with America) from 1941, another coauthored and very successful book, the Myrdals presented their views of the United States to a Swedish audience, during the height of World War II. It gives a highly positive account of the United States, and the Myrdals argued that Sweden had a great deal to learn from the United States, writing that "[i]t is a matter of life and death for our nation that we receive new and powerful impulses from American education."[29] The chapter devoted to education, where Alva most likely was the main author, presents American progressive education in very bright colors, calling the United States a laboratory for the future of education. They found the democratic ideals and the civic education that American pupils received particularly attractive and underscored the much broader social background of American students in higher education. They concluded that American schools ought to serve as an incentive for Sweden to improve its own.[30]

Much of what the Myrdals found so attractive in American education was connected to the progressive education movement associated with John Dewey. In a typical way, the Myrdals emphasize the significance of the ideological starting points in Dewey to clearly state the kind of society that child rearing and education would result in. For them, Dewey's motto "Education for a changing world" became central, and education a primary tool to create a democratic society.[31] The Myrdals also had direct experiences of progressive education. When the family moved to the United States in 1938, their son attended Lincoln Elementary School at Teachers' College at Columbia University, which was a center for the progressive movement and where its new educational methods were used.[32]

The Swedish government school commission that was created after World War II to reform the Swedish schools was also clearly influenced by the United States. Johan Östling argues that it was the United States that provided its intellectual inspiration and points to the central role that Alva Myrdal played in the commission.[33] In 1943 and 1944 she was a frequent contributor on educational topics in the Social Democratic newspaper *Aftontidningen*. In 1944 she penned the educational part "Ett skolprogram" (A program for schools) of the Social Democratic Women's policy platform, in which the first point was "the elimination of the division into different levels" in the Swedish schools, and "the creation of one compulsory school for all students."[34] To Myrdal, the school reforms were fundamentally about democracy, where American experiences of a comprehensive school and modern educational methods contributed to the creation of democratic individuals.[35] The final report of the school commission also shows these influences. Its starting point is "a democratization of Swedish schools,"[36] and it includes a number of proposals with American roots, such as the emphasis on practical and useful knowledge, citizen education (*medborgerlig fostran*), and an interest in psychological tests. Many of these ideas are already included in the chapter on American education in *Kontakt med Amerika*.[37]

The Myrdals developed deep ties to and sympathies for American society in general. Even though they were critical of American race relations and the American war in Southeast Asia in the 1960s and 1970s, they still maintained hope in the United States. When they received the Peace Prize of the German Book Trade in 1970, Gunnar Myrdal commented that as a consequence of their American sojourns, the couple "identified deeply with the U.S." It was an experience that they "had not been able to entirely shed."[38]

Undergraduate students were another important part of the borderland. Here the context is different—the students were young, and for many their time at an American university or college went beyond the purely academic and significant in shaping their outlooks on life. They often developed close relationships and affiliations with American society that became of great significance, not least for the United States. One interesting case of a Swedish undergraduate experience is that of the former Swedish Prime Minister Olof Palme, who spent the academic year 1947–48 at Kenyon College in Gambier, Ohio. As a member of the Swedish cabinet and as prime minister from 1969, Palme was critical of the United States and its involvement in the wars in Southeast Asia in the 1960s and 1970s. The most controversial incident was without any doubt his comments after the U.S. bombings of Hanoi in December 1972. Palme compared them to other atrocities, often linked to specific places, such as Guernica, Sharpeville, Lidice, and Treblinka. His comparisons of the United States to Nazi Germany led to a diplomatic crisis between Sweden and the United States that lasted for almost two years.[39]

Palme was often accused of "anti-Americanism," a charge he always denied. According to his close collaborator Jan Eliasson, Palme was in fact fascinated by American politics and democracy and had an almost emotional relationship to the country, going back to his years as a student in the United States. It was because of these strong ties that his critique became so severe, Eliasson argues.[40] In his insightful biography of Olof Palme, Henrik Berggren underlines the significance of Palme's time in the United States for his political development and his close relationship to American society. The time at Kenyon College opened new

Olof Palme was an undergraduate student at Kenyon College in Ohio in 1947–48 and played on the soccer team wearing number 32. Courtesy of Greenslade Special Collections and Archives, Kenyon College, Gambier, Ohio.

perspectives and "became a decisive experience for the young Olof Palme, and shaped him as a politician and statesman," Berggren writes. He gained another way of looking at the world and, according to Berggren, it was this "American progressive liberalism" that influenced his basic outlook on life throughout the years."[41]

In June 1970, during the height of the Vietnam War, Palme returned to his alma mater to receive an honorary degree. His visit was controversial, with one hundred security officers present, and was criticized by some alumni, local newspapers, and demonstrators. The college president defended the honorary doctor, arguing that his view of the war in Vietnam resonated with the students, and pointed out that Palme's address to more than a thousand persons did not deal with the war but with the fundamental American theme of "freedom." During his visit, Palme also talked to smaller groups of students.[42] He was obviously pleased to be back at his alma mater, suggesting the enduring significance of his academic ties to the United States.

Olof Palme engaged with students during his return to Kenyon College in 1970, when he was awarded an honorary degree. Courtesy of Greenslade Special Collections and Archives, Kenyon College, Gambier, Ohio.

Many similar accounts have been told, and the more than three thousand undergraduate fellows sent out by the Sweden-America Foundation were no doubt fundamentally influenced by their American academic and cultural experience at a relatively young age. They were exposed to American "soft power," and to many their mental maps have throughout their lives come to feature the United States in a prominent position.

Institutional Effects in Sweden

The Swedish–American academic borderland also had institutional effects in Sweden, as a few examples from the social sciences and humanities will illustrate. The significance of an American sojourn for the discipline of sociology seems clear, as the trajectory of its development in Sweden was tied to the United States and American developments. Anna Larsson has argued that when the subject was established in Swedish universities after World War II, two international research traditions were identified, one more philosophical rooted on the European Continent, and one more empirical emanating from the United States. She shows how Swedish sociology became linked with the American traditions, emphasizing the role of individual movements in this process, as Swedish sociologists traveled to American universities and American sociologists came to Sweden.[43]

In 1977, the first professor of sociology in Sweden, Torgny Segerstedt at Uppsala University, confirmed this scholarly choice for his discipline. It became "obvious," Segerstedt observed, that we had "the American pattern in mind in describing our concept of modern sociology." During the 1950s and 1960s, "most of the younger Swedish sociologists" also "spent a term—often a year—at some American university."[44] In the late 1940s and early 1950s, for example, four sociologists from Lund, Uppsala, and Stockholm also received Rockefeller Foundation fellowships.[45]

American sociologists were also influential guests in Swedish academic contexts. George Lundberg of the University of Washington in Seattle became a key figure. His works were widely read, visited Sweden regularly, and received Swedish academic visitors.[46] In a telling remark, Sverker Sörlin observed there were some Swedish sociologists in the 1960s who "commuted between Uppsala and Stanford and Columbia" and that new

American books in the discipline had barely left the printing presses "before they were read by the shores of the Fyris River [in Uppsala]."[47]

American connections were strong in other social sciences as well. In education, Torsten Husén has noted that after 1945 a "pilgrimage" to the United States was a necessity.[48] Husén himself became a key figure in what Sörlin called the fast and quite linear transfer of social sciences from the United States to Sweden.[49] American business practices and studies also became important in Sweden, and were an area that was emphasized from the very beginning by the Sweden-America Foundation.[50] Similarly, when the subject of business administration was established in Swedish universities American patterns were of great significance. The first incumbent at Uppsala University, Sune Carlson, received his PhD at the University of Chicago in 1936, and said that "the experiences from Chicago . . . were put to use as we built the Department of Business Administration at Uppsala."[51] Lars Engwall, Elving Gunnarsson, and Eva Wallerstedt point to the shift from a German to an American orientation after World War II, in terms of both study trips and textbooks in Swedish business schools.[52]

The contact patterns in the humanities have been fewer. Two early examples from Uppsala University can be mentioned. In 1951, Gunnar Tideström, the recently appointed holder of a chair in literary studies, spent a semester at Princeton University on a grant from the Rockefeller Foundation with the intention of studying the new criticism in American literary scholarship. He seems to have been the first Swedish senior professor (chair holder) in literature to have spent an extensive period of time in the United States. In correspondence with the Rockefeller Foundation, he writes that he is "anxious to have direct contacts with outstanding writers and scholars . . . in the United States." Tideström was very pleased with his time at Princeton and other places, including Harvard, where he "met everyone in the field of literary criticism." The foundation too was positive toward Tideström's time in the United States, noting that he had "profited greatly by his stay" and that "he will be a much more dynamic and forceful person upon his return to Sweden."[53]

His colleagues at the time in Uppsala were not as impressed or interested in intellectual developments in the United States; one talked of an "epidemic of love to American 'structural analysis' that had reached

Sweden and become a negative factor."[54] Tideström notes in a letter from Princeton that he is looking forward to employing his experience from the United States in Uppsala, and that "some people expect . . . that I will act as a reformer."[55] His biographer concludes that he was influenced through his American journey, in particular by new pedagogical and interdisciplinary approaches he had encountered at Princeton and introduced in Uppsala.[56] The same year, the Rockefeller Foundation also awarded a fellowship to the leading Swedish historian Erik Lönnroth from Uppsala. He too spent a semester at Princeton, but also visited Harvard, Yale, and the Universities of Chicago and Wisconsin. The foundation notes Lönnroth's position in Swedish academic life, also with a European reputation, and that he had been instrumental in a national commission for the reform of Swedish higher education. The purpose of the Rockefeller grant was to allow him to increase his familiarity with American higher education.[57]

In literary studies the situation seems to have shifted during the last decades of the twentieth century. Bo G. Ekelund has shown that the scholarship emanating from the United States became increasingly important in Sweden from the 1980s on. Interestingly, a significant part of this body of work was non-American, often French, but it was through its English-language translations at American university presses and its use by American literary scholars that it reached a wider audience of Swedish literary scholars.[58] This also meant that the interest in spending time at American universities increased. Two notable examples include Sara Danius and Stefan Jonsson, who came to Duke University in the early 1990s as Sweden-America Foundation fellows and received their PhDs from Duke in 1997. Unlike their colleagues in Franklin Scott's study from the 1950s who often found themselves in uncertain academic situations, the academic migrants from the 1990s have had notable careers in Swedish humanities, Danius as professor at Stockholm University and as a member of the Swedish Academy, and Jonsson as professor at Linköping University.[59]

From the early twentieth century, the American academy has played an important role in Sweden, in particular during the decades after World War II. The many academic movements between Sweden and the United

States have created an intricate network of academic contacts between Sweden and the United States, linking together scholars, universities, and research institutes on both sides of the Atlantic. The contact patterns show an asymmetrical relationship between the two countries as the emerging American academic superpower has dominated.

Different types of interests have characterized the interactions. The Sweden-America Foundation was supported by private Swedish business, claiming to act in the national Swedish interest. American interests included private philanthropic foundations from the early part of the twentieth century, such as the Rockefeller Foundation, as well as government-funded and initiated institutions from the Cold War period, such as the Fulbright program.

The academic effects have been significant. Several Swedish academic fields have been profoundly influenced by the United States, primarily technology and the social and the natural sciences. The relative importance between the fields has shifted over time, reflecting both the needs of Swedish society and the strengths of the American academy. For many Swedish students and scholars, an academic peregrination to an American university, research center, or laboratory has been of great importance to their careers.

Even though there are many institutional and governmental aspects of the relationship, the individual movements in the academic borderland have been of central importance. This is true both for the individuals such as Alva Myrdal, Olof Palme, or Per Wästberg who each benefited in different ways from their time of study at American institutions of higher learning, and for the development of academic disciplines where, for example, persons such as George Lundberg or Sara Danius became important links in the Swedish–American academic borderland.

Swedish–American academic interactions must be seen as a part of the patterns of Swedish–American relations. Impulses from American educational practices played an important role for the reforms of the Swedish school systems during the 1950s and 1960s, often transmitted to Sweden through transatlantic academic channels. Swedish students and scholars were also exposed to and influenced by American society in general, often bringing back a special relationship with the United States that, even though they may have disagreed with specific American actions or decisions, created a long-lasting connection and orientation to the United States. In that sense, that nature of Swedish–American relations cannot be fully understood without the numerous transatlantic academic peregrinations.

Notes

1. Per Wästberg, *Vägarna till Afrika: En memoar* (Stockholm: Wahlström & Widstrand, 2007), 8, 15, 19.

2. Johan Östling, *Nazismens sensmoral: Svenska erfarenheter i andra världskrigets efterdyning* (Stockholm: Atlantis, 2008), 209–10.

3. Svante Nordin, "De efterkrigstida idéernas förridare avliden," *Dagens forskning,* March 31, 2003, 1; Svante Nordin, "Lyckat porträtt av en pionjär," *Svenska Dagbladet,* May 27, 2009.

4. Roger Waldinger, *The Cross-Border Connection: Immigrants, Emigrants, and Their Homelands* (Cambridge: Harvard University Press, 2015), 6.

5. *A World on the Move: Trends in Global Student Mobility* (New York: Institute of International Education, 2017), 4, 6, 8.

6. Sveriges Officiella Statistik, Statistiska Meddelanden, UF 20 SM 1803, "Universitet och högskolor: Internationell studentmobilitet i högskolan 2017/18" (Stockholm: Statistiska Centralbyrån, 2018), 126, https://www.scb.se.

7. Dag Blanck, "Traveling Scholars: Swedish Academic Travelers across the Atlantic in the 20th Century," in *American Foundations and the European Welfare States,* ed. Klaus Petersen, Michael Kuur Sørensen, and John Stewart (Odense: Syddansk universitetsforlag, 2013), 165–67.

8. Andreas Melldahl, *Västerled tur och retur: Utbildning och ekonomi; En ekonomhistorisk studie av Sverige-Amerika Stiftelsens stipendieverksamhet 1919–2006,* vol. 1 (Uppsala: Rapporter från forskningsgruppen för utbildnings- och kultursociologi, 2008), 42.

9. Blanck, "Traveling Scholars," 172; Olof Ljungström, *Ämnessprängarna: Karolinska Institutet och Rockefeller Foundation 1930–1945* (Solna: Karolinska Institutet University Press, 2010).

10. Ulf Hannerz, "American Culture: Creolized, Creolizing," in *American Culture: Creolized, Creolizing and Other Lectures from the NAAS Biennial Conference in Uppsala May 28–31, 1987,* ed. Erik Åsard (Uppsala: Swedish Institute for North American Studies, 1988), 24.

11. Bertil Ohlin, *Bertil Ohlins memoarer: Ung man blir politiker* (Stockholm: Bonniers, 1972), 87.

12. Göran Ohlin, "Economics: The Interchange of Ideas between Sweden and the United States," in *Partners in Progress: A Chapter in the American-Swedish*

Exchange of Knowledge, ed. Allan Kastrup and Nils William Olsson (Minneapolis: Swedish Council of America, 1977), 57.

13. Richard Pells, *Not Like Us: How Europeans Have Loved, Hated, and Transformed American Culture since World War II* (New York: Basic Books, 1997), 60–62.

14. Folder 2. Sweden, 1953–1959, Group III. Fulbright Program; Box 124, MS Collection 468, Bureau of Educational and Cultural Affairs Historical Collection (CU), Special Collections, University of Arkansas-Fayetteville.

15. Melldahl, *Västerled tur och retur,* 21.

16. The following two paragraphs are based on Melldahl, *Västerled tur och retur,* 32–36.

17. Franklin Scott, *The American Experience of Swedish Students: Retrospect and Aftermath* (Minneapolis: University of Minnesota Press, 1956), 96.

18. Ibid., 64–65.

19. Göran Friborg, "Motives and Qualifications of Scientists and Engineers Emigrated from Sweden to the USA," in *Brain Drain and Brain Gain of Sweden,* ed. Göran Friborg and Jan Annerstedt (Stockholm: Committee on Research Economics, 1972), 62.

20. See the register of Fulbright grantees in Swedish Fulbright Commission, *Alumni Directory 1953–1977* (Stockholm: Swedish Fulbright Commission, 1977).

21. Scott, *The American Experience of Swedish Students,* 91–92.

22. Sverige-Amerika Stiftelsen, *Årsberättelse 1952* (Stockholm: Sverige-Amerika Stiftelsen, 1952), 29.

23. Sweden, Humanities, Gunnar Myrdal, Record Group 10.2, Fellowship Recorder Cards, Rockefeller Foundation Collection, Rockefeller Archive Center, Tarrytown, N.Y. (RAC).

24. Jan Olof Nilsson, *Alva Myrdal: En virvel i den moderna strömmen* (Stockholm: Brutus Östlings Bokförlag Symposium, 1994), 138–43.

25. Brita Åkerman, *Alva Myrdal: Från storbarnkammare till fredspris* (Stockholm: Cordia, 1997), 26–27.

26. Walter Jackson, "Gunnar Myrdal: America's Swedish Tocqueville," *Swedish-American Historical Quarterly* 50, no. 4 (October 1999): 209.

27. Quoted after Sissela Bok, *Alva: Ett kvinnoliv* (Stockholm: Bonniers, 1987), 86.

28. Yvonne Hirdman, *Det tänkande hjärtat: Boken om Alva Myrdal* (Stockholm: Ordfront, 2006), 170–73.

29. Alva Myrdal and Gunnar Myrdal, *Kontakt med Amerika* (Stockholm: Bonniers, 1941), 30.

30. Ibid., 96–98.

31. Ibid., 108–13.

32. Bok, *Alva,* 129.

33. Östling, *Nazismens sensmoral,* 203.

34. Alva Myrdal, "Ett skolprogram," in *Vad vi vill* (Stockholm: Sveriges Socialdemokratiska kvinnoförbund, 1944), 9.

35. Myrdal and Myrdal, *Kontakt med Amerika,* 101; Alva Myrdal, "Anteckningar för ett tal om utbildning i USA, 6/8 1940," Personliga handlingar, Alva Myrdal, Alva och Gunnar Myrdals arkiv, Arbetarrörelsens arkiv (Swedish Labour Movement's Archives and Library), Huddinge; Alva Myrdal, "Bildningsstandarden efter kriget," *Aftontidningen,* October 20, 1943.

36. SOU 1948:27, *1946 års skolkommissions betänkande med förslag till riktlinjer för det svenska skolväsendets utveckling* (Stockholm: Ecklesiastikdepartementet, 1948), 1.

37. Myrdal and Myrdal, *Kontakt med Amerika,* chapter 4.

38. Quoted in Lars Lindskog, *Alva Myrdal: "Förnuftet måste segra"* (Stockholm: Sveriges Radios förlag, 1981), 20.

39. Leif Leifland, *Frostens år: Om USA:s diplomatiska utfrysning av Sverige* (Stockholm: Nerenius & Santérus, 1997), 212–13.

40. Jan Eliasson, "Olof Palme och utrikespolitiken," in *Politikern Olof Palme,* ed. Erik Åsard (Stockholm: Hjalmarson and Högberg, 2002), 171–72.

41. Henrik Berggren, *Underbara dagar framför oss: En biografi över Olof Palme* (Stockholm: Norstedts, 2010), 119.

42. Bill Mayr, "Remembering Olof Palme," *Kenyon College Alumni Bulletin* 34 (winter 2012), http://bulletin-archive.kenyon.edu/x3901.html.

43. Anna Larsson, *Det moderna samhällets vetenskap: Om etableringen av sociologi i Sverige 1930–1955* (Umeå: Umeå universitet, 2001), 104–8.

44. Torgny Segerstedt, "American and Swedish Sociology," in Kastrup and Olsson, *Partners in Progress,* 297–98, 304.

45. *Rockefeller Foundation Directory of Fellowship Awards for the Years 1917–50* (New York: Rockefeller Foundation, 1950); *The Rockefeller Foundation Directory of Fellowship Awards: Supplement for the Years 1951 . . . 1955* (New York: Rockefeller Foundation, 1956). The fellowship winners included Georg Karlsson, Uppsala, 1948–49; Bertil Pfannenstill, Lund, 1946–47; Edmund Dahlström, Stockholm, 1953–54; and Lennart Thörnqvist, Lund, 1945–55.

46. Larsson, *Det moderna samhällets vetenskap,* 87, 89, 105–6.

47. Sverker Sörlin, *De lärdas republik: Om vetenskapens internationella tendenser* (Malmö: Liber, 1994), 204.

48. Torsten Husén, "Psychology and Education: U.S.-Swedish Scholarly Contacts in Psychology and Education," in Kastrup and Olsson, *Partners in Progress,* 244.

49. Sörlin, *De lärdas republik,* 206.

50. Dag Blanck, *Sverige-Amerika Stiftelsen: De första sjuttio åren, 1919–1989* (Stockholm: Sverige-Amerika Stiftelsen, 1989), 31.

51. Sune Carlson, *Studier utan slut: Ekonomi, företag, människor* (Stockholm: Studieförbundet Näringsliv och samhälle, 1983), 71.

52. Lars Engwall, Elving Gunnarsson, and Eva Wallerstedt, *Europa et Taurus: Foreign Inspiration of Swedish Business Administration* (Uppsala: Företagsekonomiska institutionen vid Uppsala universitet, 1987).

53. Gunnar Tideström, October 4, 1950, May 2, 1951, and August 14, 1951, in Series 800, Box 8, Folder 91, Record group 1.2, Rockefeller Foundation Collection, RAC.

54. Quoted in Bengt Landgren, *Gunnar Tideström: Litteraturhistoriker och litteraturpedagog* (Stockholm: Atlantis, 2007), 231.

55. Quoted in ibid., 237.

56. Ibid., 241–44.

57. Erik Lönnroth, May 7, 1951, Series 800, Box 7, Folder 78, Record group 1.2, Rockefeller Foundation Collection, RAC.

58. Bo G. Ekelund, "The Citational Universe of Swedish Literary Scholarship: Transmitting and Reproducing an Unequal World in the Periphery," in *Rethinking Cultural Transfer and Transmission: Reflections and New Perspectives,* ed. Petra Broomans, Sandra von Voorst, and Karina Smits (Groningen: Barkhuis, 2012), 21–23.

59. See *Wikipedia,* "Sara Danius," last modified November 26, 2019, and "Stefan Jonsson (författare)," last modified October 15, 2019, https://sv.wikipedia.org. See also *Sverige-Amerika Stiftelsen 100 år, 1919–2019* (Stockholm: Trafiknostalgiska förlaget, 2019), 81, 86.

7

The Role of Design in a Swedish–American Landscape

Frida Rosenberg

The period from the 1930s to the 1960s is particularly important for understanding the role of design as an arena for cultural contacts between Sweden and the United States. It was a time when different strands within modernism took hold in two very different nations. Beginning in the 1920s, a major influx to urban areas created a housing need in Sweden. As the Social Democratic party sought social unity and allowed for various stakeholders to develop solutions for the future, institutional research on Swedish living conditions began in order to improve housing. It was comprehensive, affecting everything from flatware design to urbanization, such as the implementation of subway lines and the location of suburban communities. Around the world, this shift is known as the inception of the Swedish welfare state and its middle-way politics.

It should also be noted that by the mid-twentieth century consumerism had become the dominant narrative in both Sweden and the United States.[1] The United States led the development of consumer-oriented architecture such as supermarkets, motels, and drive-through banks. With its growing Fordist economy, American society adapted to the rules and conditions of the automobile.[2] This kind of urbanization brought Swedish experts, urban planners, and architects closer to America: the housing shortage, industrial expansion, and the issue of tackling infrastructural urbanization called for strategies related to family life and working conditions that knew no national borders.[3] Although different in many ways, the two nations shared an urgency for modernization.

In his seminal book on the emerging Swedish car society, Per Lundin notes that Sweden had the highest level of car ownership per capita in Europe in the 1950s.[4] According to Thomas P. Hughes, this era saw the second discovery of America as a technological landscape and one of the world's most productive countries, and the United States was seen as a role model for technical, material, and cultural advancements.[5] One way of spreading American interests was to provide economic support for European rebuilding efforts and to enable European companies, institutions, authorities, and foundations to send delegations to observe and be inspired by American practices. One such initiative was the Marshall Plan, which promoted European economic recovery and facilitated international exchange.[6] Technological advances also facilitated exchange, such as the direct air-traffic route between Sweden and the United States established in the late 1940s by the Scandinavian airline SAS. The airline gradually became a leading carrier in transatlantic travel, making contact and communications easier.[7]

This essay highlights how design and design ideas served as a vehicle for intensified relations between Sweden and the United States. Design will be discussed as a platform that deepened the relationship between the two countries and ultimately prompted design to take a new direction as a direct result of particular moments of interchange. In the following, drawing, design, and housing reflect how a new society is constructed and render visible a connection between Sweden and America. Design illustrates the borderlands concept by touching on how transnational exchanges took place in relation to modernism's mass housing developments, as well as on how the evolution of product design became a driver for cultural exchanges.

Two examples will be used. In the first, the focus is on the borderlands concept in relation to urban planning through Catherine Bauer, an important American public-housing advocate. Bauer persistently steered postwar social housing in the direction of community planning in America. This shows how design ideas traveled across the Atlantic despite the Swedish sociopolitical ideals built into urban form. I argue for the significance of individual networks and interchange between architects who sought a more human-centered architecture than modernism, which they perceived as categorically subdividing living units from inner-city workplaces in the planning of suburban environments. Tracing the origins and implementation of the 1937 Housing Act to how Catherine Bauer and her husband, the architect William Wurster, established an environmentalist approach to architecture sheds light on the importance of exchanges between Sweden and the United States along with other European nations. In focusing on these transnational exchanges, I argue that the direction and conceptualization of environmental design can be a result of Swedish–American borderlands. Through certain individuals reading social politics and its effects, environmental design emerged. The borderlands concept is useful because it provides for a conclusive understanding of the importance of transnational networks in developing welfare housing as well as environmental design. In addition, Swedish–American borderlands advanced the profession of industrial designers toward ergonomic design. Through the designers' three-dimensional perception and tools, such as drawing, the profession thrived in this era of consumerism, development of technical appliances, and advancement in the motor industry.

This essay also explores the formation of the industrial designer as a key figure in modern society. The appliance industry skyrocketed in the 1950s and epithets such as "design for production" and "design for the market" were credos to which most manufacturing industries had to subscribe. The industrial designer is thus a key figure, interpreting, visualizing, and communicating technical progress as well as style. As such, the industrial designer became instrumental in manufactured industrial products becoming desirable. Here, Sweden tended to align more with America and its vision for the future than with any other European country.

One could speak of a specific "advanced Americanization" in the postwar era, as Allan Kastrup did in his book *The Swedish Heritage in America.* Kastrup worked for the American Swedish News Exchange (ASNE), which was tasked with circulating Swedish news in the United States, as well as facilitating other kinds of exchanges between the countries. With this in mind, one could argue that his claim was biased, as advancing Swedish interests in the United States was in his interest. Nonetheless, his reasoning that this Americanization did not "have an American origin but owed more to the fact that Swedish living standards approached those of the United States, or that economic competition in Sweden was more reminiscent of America than of many other countries in Europe," has also been a subject of interest for other scholars.[8]

Welfare Housing

Catherine Bauer, born in 1905 in New Jersey, was a well-known advocate of public housing in the 1930–60s and remains a symbol of the exchange and dissemination of knowledge between Sweden and the United States. She attended Vassar College and Cornell University College of Architecture and instantly became a housing expert when she was appointed executive secretary for the Regional Planning Association of America (RPAA) in her late twenties.[9] In 1939, she began teaching at the University of California, Berkeley, in the Department of Social Welfare, where she soon was appointed professor. Her influence on issues of public housing is broad and multifaceted; her view that "social research could greatly improve architecture," for example, had a far-reaching impact on the architecture curriculum at the University of California, Berkeley.[10] While much of her experience centered on the American East Coast, she also undertook several extended journeys to study European housing and its development.

Bauer's interest in Sweden was rooted in housing policy as a central theme in the establishment of the Swedish welfare state.[11] In Sweden, measures toward sanitation and better homes for the masses led to the establishment of the government's Housing Commission in 1933.[12] Implementing higher technical standards in housing resulted in both the demolition and the renewal of old housing communities. Modernization of this kind became large-scale urban-planning projects; the National Housing Board and the National Board of Building and Planning were set up in order to put the political aims into practice.[13] Swedish housing policy thus not only sought to alleviate housing shortages, but also acted as a cyclical stabilizer and encouraged family formation. In other words, housing policies in Sweden were part of a larger pattern of social welfare, economic stability, demographics, and urbanization.[14]

Bauer received a grant from the Guggenheim Foundation to study housing in Europe in June 1930. While in Sweden, she met architect Uno Åhrén, who was part of the government's Housing Commission together with the Swedish scholar and politician Gunnar Myrdal. At the time, Åhrén was one of the leading theorists for and advocates of functionalism, and in 1932 he was nominated as city architect of Gothenburg. Bauer also made the acquaintance of Sven Markelius, a functionalist architect influenced by the Bauhaus school who later coauthored the functionalist manifesto *acceptera*. Markelius had a deep influence on city planning as Stockholm's city architect from 1944 to 1954.[15] Throughout the mid-twentieth century, Catherine Bauer and William Wurster maintained these and other friendships as part of a long-lasting community of architects and planners who developed planning theories via correspondence, travels, and exchanges.

Some of the conclusions Bauer drew from her first trip overseas were published in an article in *Fortune* magazine; she noted how successful interactions between municipal initiatives, social policy, and modern architecture benefited an entire community.[16] Bauer argued that there were important lessons to be learned in America from the way in which European neighborhoods integrated a variety of housing types, open spaces, and community facilities. One of her objectives was to raise consciousness about the error of emulating a model based on white, middle-class, single-family homes, as well as the risk of leaving housing and urban planning in the hands of investors who disregarded the relationship of housing to jobs and social services. At the time, the landowners and developers could profit from the strong support by the Federal Housing Administration (FHA). Bauer's insights into public-housing strategies were linked to her travels to Europe, but were also founded in her work as the executive secretary of the Regional Planning Association of America in 1931–33 and as an assistant to the humanist and environmentalist architect Clarence Stein from 1932 until 1934.[17]

Bauer's position on instrumentally linking environmental design with the social sciences was formulated in her book *Modern Housing*, published in 1934.[18] The book, which documented government housing programs in Europe, gave her a platform, and after it was published she became the executive director of the new Labor Housing Conference (LHC) and toured the United States for two years seeking to convince the American Federation of Labor leaders to support her position on housing.[19] Bauer came to play an important role as a policy maker and housing advocate

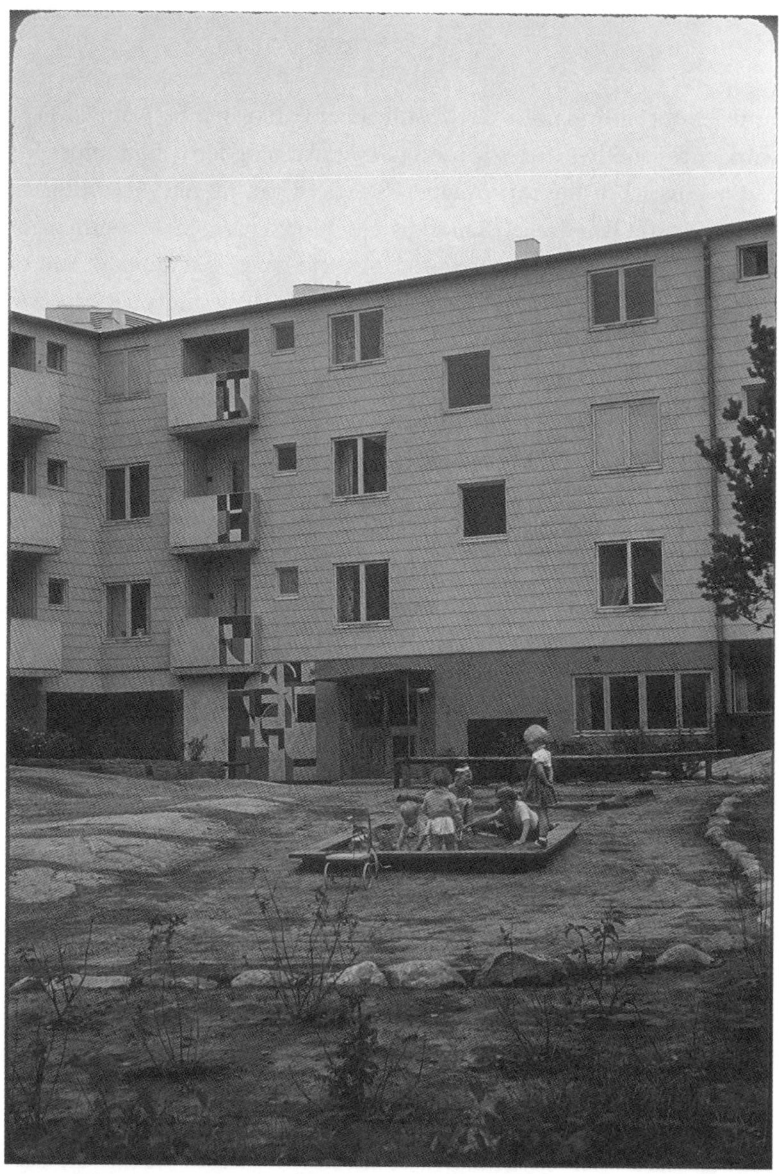

This photograph of the newly built housing project at Hjorthagen by Kooperativa förbundets arkitektkontor (KF) was taken by Catherine Bauer during her visit to Sweden in 1936. KF was Sweden's cooperative movement's main architectural office contributing to developing the welfare state. As the largest architectural office in Scandinavia, KF also influenced many of the period's key architects, who often worked in the organization for a few years. Courtesy of the Catherine Bauer Wurster Papers, The Bancroft Library, University of California, Berkeley.

in the 1930s and 1940s.[20] Her insistence that housing be planned near workplaces and her tireless promotion of planning for communities led to the passage of the 1937 Wagner–Steagall Housing Act. According to author Kristin E. Larsen, "[Bauer] had promoted passage of a permanent program that located housing near jobs and facilitated development of the complete community. Her significant advocacy and policymaking skills led to passage of the 1937 Wagner–Steagall Housing Act that August. The act connected slum clearance with new development, provided low interest loans for up to 90 percent of project cost amortized over a sixty-year period, offered capital and operating grants to maintain low rents, and set cost limitations for projects."[21] The low-interest loans built into the subsidies and regulation of new housing developments in the United States were in fact similar to the means by which the Swedish welfare politics had encouraged suburban development outside Stockholm in Sweden.

Bauer and Wurster visited Scandinavia again in 1937, this time with a focus on works by Danish architect Kay Fisker, Swedish architect Gunnar Asplund, and Finnish architect Alvar Aalto. During this trip, Wurster and Bauer became close friends with Aino and Alvar Aalto.[22] Aalto was renowned for his use and sensibility when it came to materials. Architectural historian Kenneth Frampton argues that Aalto's material sensibility "helped to assure the social accessibility of his architecture" and made it "more acceptable to the man on the street than any other modernist."[23] The Swedish interpretation of sensibility to nature, material, and scale was later known as New Empiricism. Older still, however, was the Swedish modernist agenda—so-called *funkis*—whose origins were more human-centered than the International Style that followed in America. Aalto and many other architects such as Steen Eiler Rasmussen, Kay Fisker, and Gunnar Asplund shared this social-design ethos, from which a concern for humans in their environment-centered approach to design emerged, related to material use, layout of volumes in relation to the landscape, and light condition present in the architecture.[24] Much later, looking over the architectural production of William Wurster's practice, one can also detect a particular interest in the relationship between architecture and landscape.[25]

The Bauer–Wurster relationships with architects and planners in Sweden, Finland, and Denmark and the resulting transnational exchanges lasted a long time and played an important role in the formulation of an environmental approach to design.[26] There are clear traces in Bauer and Wurster's archives, in diverse correspondence, travel reports, and photographs, of early attempts to express environmentalism as a field. When Bauer joined the Department of City and Regional Planning at UC Berkeley, she gained important leverage as an academic.[27] In 1950—while Bauer's husband was department chair—the departments for Landscape, Planning, and Architecture merged to become the College of Environmental Design. In those first formative years, from 1950 until 1959, Bauer established a curriculum for architects that laid the groundwork for social issues to become an essential part of the architecture design field.[28]

Streamline Design and the Cutaway Drawing

Streamline design emerged as a new design and technology trend in the United States between the First and Second World Wars. Streamlining translated scientific knowledge about air resistance into overdimensioned, stylized expressionism used on all manner of appliances and tools. Ideologically, the vulgar and voluptuous shapes of the trend embraced a colorful and flamboyant cultural shift from the Great Depression of the 1930s and articulated the power of technical accomplishments in the industrial production of vehicles. It has been argued that as a trend, streamline was American industrial design's most important contribution to twentieth-century design.[29] Three frontline figures included Raymond Loewy, who designed locomotives for the Pennsylvania Railroad and was called the father of streamline design by *Time* magazine; Norman Bel Geddes, who drew spectacular ocean liners, airplanes, and cars; and Henry Dreyfuss, who designed many commercial products and created a notation system for ergonomics.

In Sweden, a skilled draftsman by the name of Sixten Sason noted the streamline design trend and brought it to both the look and function of motorcycles. His drawings appeared in the magazines *Motornyheterna* and *Motor Nytt* in the 1930s.[30] The Swedish industrial designers Ralph Lysell and Alvar Lenning also produced so-called cutaway drawings—technical drawings where some of the surface elements of the object being rendered are removed to show what is hidden beneath. The Swedish term for such a drawing was *röntgenteckning*—X-ray drawing. Originally used industrially, cutaway drawings soon became fashionable outside of the industry.

Cutaway drawings emphasized the interrelation of diverse aspects of design such as technical development, product performance, form, and communication. The cutaway drawing expressed the essential details of mechanization while also depicting a future of speed.[31] A parallel can be drawn to attempts being made around the same time by architecture critic Sigfried Giedion, a Swiss-born architecture historian, to map a new society in which art, science, and technology merged and within which science was an integral part of Western culture. Giedion, whose work has exerted an enormous influence on the history of modern architecture, carefully researched the origins of mechanization via everyday products with an emphasis on rationality. He discussed modernization in his *Space, Time, and Architecture* (1941) and *Mechanization Takes Command* (1948), aligning himself with Frederick Taylor's argument for rationalization optimizing the product at the other end of the production line, which brought about Taylorism; the scientific management of work flows.[32] More important, Giedion put forward an understanding of cross-disciplinary developments allowing technology to be informed by culture and vice versa.[33]

Adrian Forty's *Objects of Desire* extensively discusses the transmission of ideas through objects. The book covers design over two centuries and argues that design is related to and shaped by economics and ideology. Forty emphasizes the interrelation of industrial design and production technologies, but he does not ascribe to the industrial designer any capacity to significantly impact production. But the designer and his/her tools of a drawing, such as the cutaway drawing, projected how a design should be assembled and what mechanical parts it contained. In this regard, the industrial designer had an impact on production. This was in fact the way in which a delegation from Atlas Copco first understood the concept of industrial design in 1955. Atlas Copco, which primarily produced compressors, tools for rock drilling, spray guns, and other handheld tools using pneumatic air, had joined a European delegation to visit construction offices and their departments for research, experiments, and

Staden och problemen med den ökande bilismen intresserade Sason. Här ett förslag, från 1936, till cirkulärt parkeringshus. Original i familjens ägo.

The cutaway drawing successfully describes several dimensions of an object. This illustration by Sixten Sason from 1936 shows a circular parking garage and comments on issues of an emerging car society. Courtesy of the Sixten Sason family.

production in the United States. The European delegation was financed by the European Recovery Plan (better known as the Marshall Plan).

Appliance Design—Ergonomic Design

The six-week tour in October 1955 was arranged by the Organization of European Economic Cooperation (OEEC), which helped distribute the funds from the European Recovery Plan. John R. Munck af Rosenschiöld, a civil engineer and the head of the Design and Research Compressor Department from Atlas Copco, was included among the Swedish representatives.[34] The costs were covered for most of the delegation, with the exception of participants from Sweden and Switzerland.[35] Munck and the other delegates were expecting to visit offices with an engineering focus, but because of a mistranslation of construction design as industrial design, the group's American hosts had instead coordinated a tour with attention to industrial design.[36]

In general, the delegation was impressed by the application of industrial design in the production process, as well as the role of the designers' skill in form finding and their design construction knowledge.[37] One of the younger delegates, the civil engineer Lars Bergman, concluded that "industrial designers in the United States take advantage of studying physiological and psychological aspects of humans, which affects the outcome of the product. These aspects are taken into account in the design process of, for example, how machines adapt to the body, how handles are easy to reach, and how instruments are made easy to read."[38] Bergman highlighted the role of industrial designers in American industry, especially in the automobile, airplane, aeronautics, and appliance industries—it was a design approach that took into account and integrated humans, machines, and the environment.

The European delegation's tour was one of the earliest direct encounters with *human engineering* and American industrial design for the Swedish delegation, and it included visits to industrial design departments and educational programs at Illinois Institute of Technology in Chicago and Massachusetts Institute of Technology in Boston.[39] The program had been put together by some of the era's best-known American industrial designers and not only brought the delegates to universities and construction offices, but also taught them about the American economy, state administration, and American living standards. The group traveled around the East Coast and the Midwest, visiting consulting businesses that collaborated on construction of products; this was still a particularly American practice, not yet widespread in Europe.[40] Two years later, John Munck and Svenska Slöjdföreningen (The Swedish Society of Industrial Design) coarranged a conference on the topic of industrial design at Tekniska Museet (the Swedish Museum of Technology).[41]

John Munck understood that it was important for Atlas Copco to incorporate what it had learned in the United States in order to increase sales. More focus was put on compressed air equipment for the industry, and designers, technicians, and engineers put great effort into realizing what became known as "ergonomically correct constructions."[42] Rune Zernell, who had been an industrial designer and a skilled draftsman at Volvo, was hired to develop a design department at Atlas Copco in 1956.[43] Zernell had collaborated with medical experts on the design of an ergonomically correct industrial handheld tool. In an interview, Zernell described the importance of an in-depth analysis of the appropriate anatomical grip through careful studies of weight distribution of the tool as well as studies of the operation of the command switch in relation to the hand.[44] Using clay models, plaster, and wood models, Zernell worked to shape a strict, neutral, and consistent form based on careful analysis of various elements.[45] Zernell felt that good design should impart a feeling of absolute necessity. As a designer, he was heavily influenced by the American designer Henry Dreyfuss, who was known for using measurements and studies of the human body to create ergonomically correct designs. According to design historian Lasse Brunnström, Rune Zernell bought Henry Dreyfuss's books on a visit to New York, and they were already worn from use upon his return to Sweden.[46] Zernell designed tools and machines that used compressed air, meaning that there was a great deal of vibration and shaking. One design solution utilized to eliminate a large degree of vibration was embossed or pressed plates in a curved shape that enhanced the ergonomic experience of the tool. The design was used in the handheld LBB33 screwdriver from 1960, which became a benchmark for Atlas Copco and set the standard for the company's subsequent production.

Clearly, industrial design as a field developed through active knowledge sharing, both as a result of the Marshall Plan and via institutional organizations that conducted field research overseas with the aim of advancing skills in particular industries. These research trips also benefited from the particularly expansive state of the Swedish economy in the 1950s and 1960s; the era has been dubbed "the record years" *(rekordåren)* because of the rate of industrial production and the increase in exports in this period. Most Swedish exports to the United States were machinery and equipment, vehicles, iron, steel, and pulp—these commodity groups accounted for nearly two-thirds of all export value.[47] The vast American continent with a high number of consumers became a significant export market for Swedish businesses.[48] A certain anxiety with regard to the development of common market and free trade following the establishment of the European Economic Community in 1957 was a motivating factor when it came to maintaining good relations with the United States—next to West Germany and the UK, the United States was among Sweden's most important trade partners.[49]

Highlighting design as a vehicle for relations across the Atlantic from the 1930s to the 1960s reveals how various international exchanges carried the design professions forward. The cutaway drawing traces the evolution of design in relation to technical advancements in the motor industry. Automobiles dictated urbanization in different ways in both Sweden and the United States, and they also affected the design professions more broadly—even the appearance of drawings. In an interview for the Atlas Copco internal magazine *Tryckluft* in 1958, a draftsman explains drawing techniques: Using perspective drawings in technology is quite old, he says. The breakthrough and use of drawings visualizing technical objects in a perspective view took place during the Second World War. The uneducated crowds that entered into the production industries at that time were unable to read the construction drawings, which inhibited production. As a result of the difficulty in reading and understanding complicated construction drawings, the solution was to describe construction through perspectives instead. In the United States, this technique developed rapidly. For example, says the Atlas Copco draftsman, when the American car factories introduced new models, production declined instantly. The workers needed more time to study the new drawings. Changing to perspective drawings significantly improved the time loss when introducing serial production of a new model. Later, discovering the value of perspectives have made them useful also as a tool in dialogue during construction, in design presentations as well as for commercials.[50]

To the editor's question, When is the cutaway sketch most useful? the draftsman responded that such drawing is most useful when "technical information is essential."[51] However, exploded axonometric drawings are becoming more and more useful in order to illustrate listings of the company's spare parts. The exploded axonometric drawing, which is a perspective drawing where all the parts are laid out in a sequence, in order to communicate how parts are mounted, serves two purposes: first, laymen are able to recognize the parts; second, this drawing serves as installation instructions when a machine has been taken apart for adjustment.[52]

The tools of the designer, from drawing to object, are by nature visual communication. While the requirements of the cutaway drawing communicated technical aspects of the product and assembling instructions, this kind of drawing technique transferred ideas about management of industrial production as well as the value of marketing strategies for products. This explains the nature of the design process—from drawing to a useful tool in the 1950s—in order to express how the mutual interest for adaption of industrial design products to the human body, and the use of the tool in the industry gave shape to a Swedish–American landscape in which designers took a direction toward developing the field of ergonomic design. The emergence of ergonomic design in Sweden reveals that it cannot be discussed without acknowledging its dependence on a Swedish–American borderland. Designers and architects both expressively visualized a new future and could act as a link between nations.

Catherine Bauer's knowledge and persistent activism pushing for the formulation of the 1937 Housing Act fostered the transfer of ideas between the two nations, not least through visits several years later, as in 1939, when she was particularly interested in Kungliga Socialstyrelsen (The National Board of Health and Welfare) and Hyresgästernas sparkasse- och byggnadsförening (The Savings and Construction Association of the Tenants, HSB).[53] Catherine Bauer's connections to architects mentioned earlier, but also an array of governmental figures in Sweden and other Scandinavian countries, promoted the development of an environmentalist approach to architecture with particular interest in social and economic factors in the San Francisco Bay Area, of which Bauer and her husband were part.[54]

The example of Catherine Bauer and how her familiarity with urban development in Europe influenced housing policy in the United States illustrates the importance of considering the sociopolitical exchanges between the two countries in the age of modernism. Architectural historians such as Gwendolyn Wright and Dolores Hayden, who effectively mapped housing, urban, and suburban development in the United States, have also explored gender issues related to this, as well as the consequences of private stakeholders coordinating property development rather than the state, as in Sweden. Yet, charting historical traces of the problems with American urban development has left the borderlands concept and its effects out of focus. Even studies such as David Popenoe's meticulous investigation of Vällingby in Sweden and Levittown, Pennsylvania, a suburb of Philadelphia, treats the study as a comparison. Vällingby, which was a built urban format called the ABC City (*arbete* = work, *bostad* = housing, *centrum* = commercial center) in suburban Stockholm was at the time praised for its urban plan and for respecting sociological behavior. Both suburbs developed out of similar circumstances, yet with different outcomes in the urban plan. Levittown consists of "sprawling" single family low-density housing, which became the characteristic suburban development in the United States. Even though this book is an enormous contribution in its empirical research and an understanding of how the two nations dealt with urban housing problems, the comparative analysis is a cross-national study. Adding and using the borderland concept for such a study can deepen the knowledge about influences, strategies, and construction processes contextualizing the architecture. Developing systematic discussions ahead on the effects related to the transfer of knowledge between Sweden and the United States regarding urbanization, housing, and suburban environments will further clarify how useful the concept of Swedish–American borderlands can be for our understanding of these processes.

Notes

1. See Joan Ockman, "Architecture and the Consumer Paradigm in the Mid-Twentieth Century," in *Swedish Modernism: Architecture, Consumption and the Welfare State,* ed. Helena Mattsson and Sven-Ove Wallenstein (London: Black Dog Publishing, 2010).

2. See, for example, Per Lundin, *Bilsamhället: Ideologi, expertis och regelskapande i efterkrigstidens Sverige* (Stockholm: Stockholmia, 2008); and Peter Hall, ed., *Rekordåren: En epok i svenskt bostadsbyggande* (Karlskrona: Boverket, 1999).

3. Later studies confirm the interest in analyzing similarities and differences in the development of the urban environment. See, for example, David Popenoe, *The Suburban Environment: Sweden and the United States* (Chicago: University of Chicago Press, 1977). In the 1940s, housing was considered a question of architecture and not only an urban and political strategy. See Talbot F. Hamlin, "Housing Is Architecture," *Pencil Points* (February 1939): 81–97.

4. Lundin, *Bilsamhället,* 21.

5. See Thomas P. Hughes, *American Genesis: A History of the American Genius for Invention* (New York: Penguin, 1999), 295–97.

6. There is an extensive literature on the Marshall Plan. See, for example, William F. Sanford, *The Marshall Plan: Origins and Implementation* (Washington, D.C.: U.S. Department of State, Bureau of Public Affairs, Office of Public Communication, Editorial Division, 1987); Charles L. Mee, *The Marshall Plan: The Launching of the Pax Americana* (New York: Simon and Schuster, 1984); Michael J. Hogan, *America, Britain, and the Reconstruction of Western Europe, 1947–1952* (Cambridge: Cambridge University Press, 1987). A number of articles deal with industrial design and American promotion programs. See Greg Castillo, "Domesticating the Cold War: Household Consumption as Propaganda in Marshall Plan Germany," *Journal of Contemporary History* 40, no. 2 (April 2005): 261–88.

7. See Anders Buraas, *Fly over Fly: Historien om SAS* (Oslo: Gyldendal, 1972).

8. Allan Kastrup, *The Swedish Heritage in America: The Swedish Element in America and American-Swedish Relations in Their Historical Perspective* (Minneapolis: Swedish Council of America, 1975), 7. On the topic of Americanization of Sweden, see Rolf Lundén and Erik Åsard, eds., *Networks of Americanization: Aspects of the American Influence in Sweden* (Uppsala: Acta Universitatis Upsaliensis, 1992), and Erik Åsard, ed., *Det blågula stjärnbaneret: USA:s närvaro och inflytande i Sverige* (Stockholm: Carlsson, 2016). Why Sweden remained close to America despite increasing criticism in the postwar era has been described by Dag Blanck, "Television, Education, and the Vietnam War: Sweden and the United States during the Postwar Era," in *The Americanization of Europe: Culture, Diplomacy, and anti-Americanization after 1945,* ed. Alexander Stephan (New York: Berghahn Books, 2006).

9. H. Peter Oberlander and Eva Newburn, *Houser: The Life and Work of Catherine Bauer* (Vancouver: University of British Columbia Press, 1999), 69.

10. Waverly Lowell, Elizabeth Byrne, and Betsy Frederick-Rothwell, "Introduction," in *Design on the Edge: A Century of Teaching Architecture at the University of California, Berkeley, 1903–2003,* ed. Waverly Lowell, Elisabeth Byrne, and Betsy Fredrick-Rothwell (Berkeley: College of Environmental Design, University of California, 2009), 21.

11. Tord Strömberg, "Bostadspolitik en historisk parentes," in *Den nya bostadspolitiken,* ed. Anders Lindbom (Umeå: Bora, 2001), 27.

12. The government's Housing Commission (Bostadssociala utredningen) was a Swedish government committee (1933–47) that aimed to map Swedish conditions in housing in order to implement guidelines and housing policies.

13. See Yvonne Hirdman, *Att lägga livet till rätta: Studier i svensk folkhemspolitik* (Stockholm: Carlsson, 2000), 97–101, 176–92.

14. See Daniel Movilla Vega, ed., *99 Years of the Housing Question in Sweden* (Lund: Studentlitteratur, 2017), chapters 1–11 and especially chapter 8, and Bent Greve, ed., *The Routledge Handbook of the Welfare State* (London: Routledge, 2013), chapter 2.

15. Gunnar Asplund, *acceptera* (Stockholm: Tiden, 1931), and Eva Rudberg, *Sven Markelius: Arkitekt* (Stockholm: Arkitektur, 1989).

16. Catherine Bauer, "Prize Essay: Art in Industry," *Fortune,* no. 3 (May 1931): 94, 96, 98, 101–2, 104, 109–10.

17. Kristin E. Larsen, *Community Architect: The Life and Vision of Clarence S. Stein* (Ithaca, N.Y.: Cornell University Press, 2016), 28.

18. Catherine Bauer, *Modern Housing* (Boston: Houghton Mifflin, 1934 [reprint, Minneapolis: University of Minnesota Press, 2020]).

19. D. Bradford Hunt, "Was the 1937 U.S. Housing Act a Phyrric Victory?" *Journal of Planning History* 4, no. 3 (August 2005): 197.

20. Larsen, *Community Architect,* 48.

21. Ibid., 124–25. See also file://ug.kth.se/dfs/home/f/r/fridaro/appdata/xp.V2/Documents/Ht%202019%20%20housing/STATUTE-50-Pg888.pdf; accessed November 29, 2019.

22. Richard Peters, "W. W. Wurster," in Lowell, Byrne, and Fredrick-Rothwell, *Design on the Edge,* 63.

23. Presentation by Kenneth Frampton at Moderna Museet, Stockholm, Sweden, December 3, 2012.

24. Correspondence reveals a shared social ethos. See Environmental Design Archives, College of Environmental Design, University of California, Berkeley: Wurster, William and Catherine Bauer Papers, (2008–15), Box 11, Folder Steen Eiler Rasmussen: Steen Eiler Rasmussen, letter to Catherine and William Wurster, August 21, 1954; William Wurster, letter to Steen Eiler Rasmussen, December 9, 1955.

25. See Marc Trieb, ed. *Thomas Church Landscape Architect: Designing a Modern California Landscape* (San Francisco: William Stout Publishers, 2003), 93–101.

26. Frida Rosenberg, "Transatlantic Humanism: Correspondence between William Wurster and Scandinavian Architects," Paper presented at Architectural Elective Affinities: Correspondences, Transfers, Inter/Multidisciplinarity, EAHN / FAUUSP Conference, São Paulo, Brazil, March 20–23, 2013.

27. See Environmental Design Archives, College of Environmental Design, University of California, Berkeley: Wurster, William and Catherine Bauer Papers (2008–15), Box 12–17, which includes lantern slides of important built environments, statistics, etc., used for research and teaching; and Catherine Bauer Wurster Papers, Bancroft Library, University of California, Berkeley (BANC MSS 74/163c), Box 22–23, 28–29 on housing research.

28. Wurster radically changed the direction taken by the previous dean, Warren Perry, by, for example, hiring female faculty members. See Inge Horton "Young Ladies with T-Squares: Early Women in Architecture," in Lowell, Byrne, and Fredrick-Rothwell, *Design on the Edge,* 39.

29. Rune Monö, "Produktdesign för arbetslivet," in *Svensk industridesign: En 1900-talshistoria,* ed. Lasse Brunnström (Stockholm: Prisma, 2004), 280.

30. See, for example, *Svensk Motortidning,* no. 6 (1938): 11.

31. Siegfried Giedion, *Space, Time, and Architecture: The Growth of a New Tradition* (Cambridge: Harvard University Press, 1941). The book is based on a set of lectures at Harvard University by invitation of Walter Gropius and thus had a clear foundation in the Bauhaus pedagogy.

32. This was formulated in Sigfried Giedion, *Mechanization Takes Command: A Contribution to Anonymous History* (New York: Oxford University Press, 1948), which more than the earlier book focused on the presence of craft and the emergence of material culture.

33. This can be traced back to his mentor Henrich Wöfflin. See Arthur P. Molella, "Science Moderne: Sigfried Giedion's Space, Time and Architecture and Mechanization Takes Command," *Technology and Culture* 43, no. 2 (April 2002): 379.

34. John R. Munck af Rosenschiöld, "Studieresans bakgrund och mål," in *Försäljningsinriktad konstruktion: Kontaktkonferens den 6 december 1955* (Stockholm: Sveriges mekaniska verkstäders förbund, 1956), 6.

35. There were twenty-six participants representing ten different countries: Sweden (4), Norway (3), Denmark (4), Holland (3), Belgium (3), France (3), Germany (2), Switzerland (2), Italy (1), Portugal (1) (ibid.).

36. Monö, "Produktdesign för arbetslivet," 302.

37. A detailed report from this visit published by Sveriges Mekanförbund (trade organization for ferrous metals manufacturing, mechanical and electronic engineering) included reflections from the four Swedish representatives. See

Försäljningsinriktad konstruktion. The travel report was also turned into one of the first books on industrial design. See *Industrial Design in the United States: Project Nr. 278* (Paris: European Productivity Agency of the Organization for European Economic Co-operation, 1959).

38. Lars Bergman, "Industrial designs funktion och betydelse i USA," in Sveriges Mekanförbund, *Försäljningsinriktad konstruktion.* Tekniskt Meddelande Ko 3, Kontaktkonferens den 6 december 1955 (Stockholm, 1956), 17; and "Hjälpmedel för ett säkrare och jämlikare liv," in *Svensk industridesign: En 1900-talshistoria,* ed. Lasse Brunnström (Stockholm: Prisma, 2004), 303.

39. Monö, "Produktdesign för arbetslivet," 302–3.

40. Harald Alexandersson, "Utbildning av industrial designers i USA," in *Försäljningsinriktad konstruktion,* 13–16.

41. Monö, "Produktdesign för arbetslivet," 303.

42. *Atlas Copco: The First Hundred Years: 1873–1973* (Stockholm: Atlas Copco, 1981), 90.

43. John Munck probably took the initiative to hire Rune Zernell. See Lasse Brunnström, "Hjälpmedel för ett säkrare och jämlikare liv," in *Svensk industridesign: En 1900-talshistoria,* ed. Lasse Brunnström (Stockholm: Prisma, 2004), 303.

44. Monö, "Produktdesign för arbetslivet," 303.

45. Rune Zernell, "Vår Industridesigner ser på sin uppgift," *Tryckluft* 257 (July 1957): 6–7.

46. See Brunnström, *Svensk industridesign,* 305.

47. Riksarkivet, Arninge (The National Archives Arninge): Svensk-Amerikanska nyhetsbyrån och USA-kampanjen Meet Modern Sweden, (B:102), "Sveriges handel med USA, P.M. från Kungl. Kommerskollegium, Utrikes- och utredningsavdelningen, EK/D 12, 27.8.1965."

48. The United States was not only the largest producing country of office machinery equipment by far, with about 70 percent of global production, but also the largest single provision market. The Swedish company Facit's market share in the United States was less than 1 percent, but this share still accounted for almost 15 percent of the company's total exports. Any change in the market share in the United States would thus have major consequences for the company. See Niklas Stenlås, *Den inre kretsen: Den svenska ekonomiska elitens inflytande över partipolitik och opinionsbildning 1940–1949* (Lund: Arkiv, 1998), 27.

49. Vivek Arora and Athanasios Vamvakidis show the extent to which the economy of trading partners has an influence on a country's economic growth. See Vivek Arora and Athanasios Vamvakidis, "How Much Do Trading Partners Matter for Economic Growth?" in *IMF Staff Papers* 52, no. 1 (2005): 24–40.

50. Gustaf Boberg, "Sprängt, skuret och genomlyst," interview of Stig Nilson by Gustaf Boberg in *Tryckluft* 6 (1958): 19.

51. Ibid.

52. Ibid.

53. Catherine Bauer Wurster Papers, Bancroft Library, University of California, Berkeley, (BANC MSS 74/163c), Box 1, Folder 23 and Box 4, Folder 11.

54. See, for example, William Wurster, "Architecture Broadens Its Base," *Journal of the American Architect* (July 1948): 30–36.

PART II

Exchanges and Entanglements

8

Borderlands in Another World

How Sweden Envisioned New Sweden, circa 1638–1702

Charlotta Forss

The Swedish colony New Sweden was established along the banks of the Delaware River on North America's east coast in 1638. The colony was located south of the Dutch New Netherlands and with the English colony Virginia to the southwest. After only seventeen years, the Dutch forced the Swedish colonial authorities to abandon the area, although formerly Swedish subjects lived on under Dutch and (after 1664) English rule. In Sweden, the colonial enterprise evoked initial interest and hopes of overseas trading opportunities, although with the ebbing fortunes of the colony this interest diminished. Toward the end of the seventeenth century, Swedish attention was renewed and clergymen sent out to ensure the spiritual well-being of the remaining settlers, although the colonial project itself was never revived.[1]

New Sweden is a short history of Swedish colonial presence in America, yet the episode lends itself well to a discussion of Swedish–American borderlands. Earlier research has studied the social and cultural history of New Sweden and explored topics such as the material entanglements and daily lives of settlers and surrounding peoples.[2] The case exhibits many of the traits associated with early American borderlands, such as permeable territorial boundaries, complex power relations, interdependencies, and shifting loyalties between individuals and groups of people.[3] However, less well understood is how individual travelers and the Swedish authorities (in the colony as well as in Sweden) conceptualized New Sweden as a geographic space with affinity to, yet distant from, Sweden.

In the present study, I address this question, asking: How did people involved in the colonial enterprise in the seventeenth century conceptualize these borderlands? In what ways did the Swedish authorities and individual travelers conceive of New Sweden's place in the world? These are questions about access to geographic knowledge, in which knowledge is seen as shaped by political ambitions, practical constraints, and individual and collective experiences.[4]

The analysis begins with the Swedish colonial authorities' ambition to map the Delaware River Basin as a means to establish control over the territory and make it a part of Sweden. This is contrasted with a closer look at how Swedish authorities, and in particular the last governor, Johan Risingh, motivated Sweden's claim to the Delaware River while framing it as part of America. Finally, the study considers how a broader range of Swedish travelers who journeyed from Sweden to New Sweden during the seventeenth century conceptualized the geographic location of New Sweden in relation to their personal experiences. What emerges are conceptualizations of Swedish–American borderlands, yet these conceptualizations were neither stable nor unitary. Rather, the borderlands could expand or contract depending on political contexts as well as personal experiences. From the early days of Swedish colonial rule, the colonial authorities as well as individual travelers conceptualized New Sweden as a place and related it to other geographic and political entities. I argue that to make use of the full potentiality of the borderlands concept, we need to pay attention to the range of historical conceptualizations of geographic distance and affinity by the people involved in the borderlands.

Mapping the Borderlands

Sweden in the seventeenth century was an expansionist state, striving to enlarge its territorial expanse and its political and economic sphere of influence. Most efforts were directed toward the lands around the Baltic Sea, yet, not least through the encouragements of Dutch merchants (who already had experience of overseas trade and saw a possibility for economic gain outside of the control of the Dutch trading enterprises), several initiatives to establish Swedish colonies and trading companies were made in the first half of the seventeenth century. New Sweden was one result of these expansionist ambitions. Twelve ships were sent from Sweden during the period of colonial rule, 1638–55, and the colony consisted of a few hundred settlers at its height. The settlements and fortifications centered on present-day Wilmington, Delaware, and primarily the western banks of the Delaware River.[5]

The Swedes were relative latecomers in their attempt to gain a foothold in North America. It is no surprise, then, that they soon felt beleaguered. Writing home to Sweden, Governor Johan Printz, who led the colony from 1642 until 1653, repeatedly expressed concerns about the security of the colony. He informed his superiors that the Dutch and English colonizers wanted to oust the Swedes. He also had concerns about the intentions of the Algonquin-speaking Lenni-Lenape living nearby and the Iroquois-speaking Susquehannocks, with whom the Swedes traded.[6] New Sweden was under multiple threats. What could be done about the situation?

Part of the answer, as conceived by Printz and embraced by the authorities in Sweden, was to map the colony. Printz claimed that it was "of greatest importance" to make maps and to fortify the colony if the state wanted to protect its possessions.[7] Printz's appeal did not fall on deaf ears. When a new colonial administration was sent to New Sweden in 1654, the new governor, Johan Risingh, immediately organized a survey of the settlements to send back with the returning ship.[8] Risingh was also accompanied to New Sweden by Per Lindeström, a fortifications officer and mapmaker. Lindeström was only twenty-two years old when he was sent on the voyage to New Sweden, but he had studied mathematics, mapmaking, and fortification at Uppsala University.[9] As part of his commission to New Sweden, he made maps of the colony and plans of new plots and fortifications around Fort Christina, including the earliest preserved map of the Delaware River.

Governor Printz's demand and the subsequent investment by the Swedish crown to map the colony indicate an awareness of the power of maps and provide insight into how the actors involved conceived of the colony and its place in the world. Historian Gunlög Fur has noted that there were significant similarities in the Swedish colonial ambitions toward the Sami people in northern Sweden and the Native Americans living along

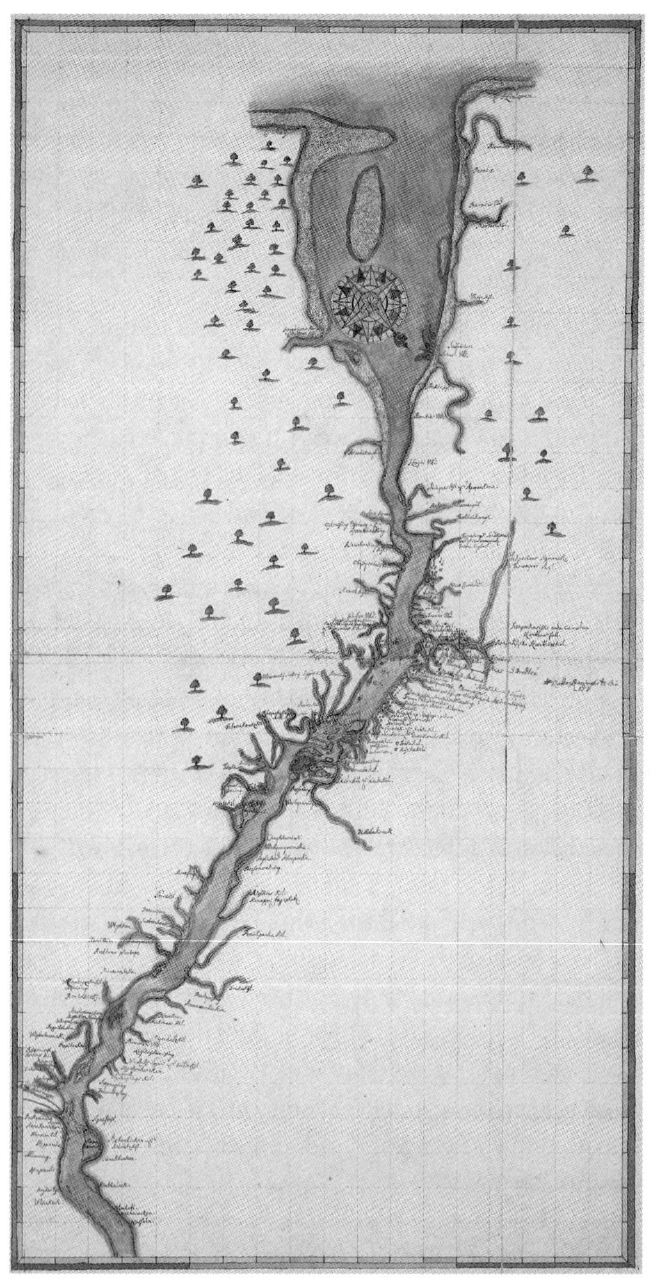

Map by surveyor Per Lindeström of the Delaware River and the Swedish Colony. From Per Lindeström, *En kort relation ok beskrifning öfwer Nya Sweriges situation ok beskaffenhet* (Stockholm: Royal Library, Rål. Fol 201).

the Delaware River.[10] Likewise, there were similarities in how the Swedish state related to the territory of New Sweden. In both northern Sweden and New Sweden, the state was only in partial control of the land, and in both places there were early attempts to make maps of the territories so as to increase control.[11]

An important driving force behind European mapping endeavors in the early modern period was a wish to delineate territory and thereby claim it.[12] That most maps of New Sweden were lost or survive only in later copies has most likely obscured the intent behind their making, as has the fact that the colony was lost only a year after Lindeström made his initial maps and fortification plans. However, there were parallel mapping projects in the surrounding colonies, such as John White's maps of the early English settlements.[13]

In Sweden, the newly set-up Land Survey Agency made systematic cartographic surveys of the realm.[14] Per Lindeström was not employed by this agency, yet he received a similar training to that of the surveyors, and the maps he produced should be seen as part of this larger early modern move to document the holdings of the state. It is clear that while New Sweden was different from other parts of early modern Sweden in its status as a colony, the authorities also envisioned New Sweden as a Swedish territory that should and could be mapped to exert control.

It is worth noting that this ambition to control the land did not result in maps with clearly delimitated borders. As historian Peter Sahlins noted, establishing permanent boundaries between states was a long and tenuous process.[15] In the case of early America, the demarcation of boundaries was made more difficult by a lack of knowledge about the land. Lindeström's geographic knowledge came primarily from explorations on the river, as evidenced from both his maps and textual descriptions that are written from the point of view of someone traveling by boat.[16] Another example of this is seen in John Smith's 1612 map of Virginia that marks the extent of Smith's firsthand explorations with symbols on the map.[17]

To be able to gain information about land farther away, as well as to be able to interpret even land that was close by, mapmakers such as Smith and Lindeström relied heavily on others who had been in the area longer, not least on Native American informers. Places such as the Dutch "Blommers

Kijl" and Algonquin "Naamans Kijl" on Lindeström's earliest map indicate the presence of other groups of people, and how Lindeström got information for his map.[18] As noted by Joan Rennie Short, European colonizers were dependent on their Native American neighbors for information.[19] Simply put, the Swedish colonizers were not alone when conceptualizing the geography of New Sweden.

Partly as a result, naming places became a question of claiming authority. In a letter to Governor Printz in 1643, the Swedish nobleman Per Brahe urged that "All rivers and streams as well as herbs and woods [should] be called with old Swedish names; abolish all expressions from the Dutch which now seem to be somewhat ingrained."[20] Following the same principle, Governor Risingh changed the name of the Dutch Fort Casimir to Swedish Fort Helga Trefaldighet. He noted that this was done so as "all Dutch names to exclude."[21]

Many of the Dutch and Algonquin names did disappear from the Swedish maps over time. Lindeström made several maps in the 1690s and these include fewer Lenape names.[22] This trend is even stronger on the maps of the armchair traveler Thomas Campanius Holm, a Stockholm printer who also worked at the Stockholm Office of Antiquities. Campanius Holm compiled and published a description of New Sweden in 1702 that included maps based on Lindeström's earliest map, but with decidedly fewer non-Swedish place-names.[23] In these cases, it is likely that the detailed information was deemed less important over time. Other maps of the area consciously excluded Swedish place-names. For instance, the Amsterdam bookseller Arnold Colom's map from 1656—made just after the Dutch takeover—shows the Delaware River as wholly incorporated in New Netherlands and with no Swedish settlements or place-names visible.[24] Among the Europeans who made maps of the region, the French, who had no immediate claims on the Delaware River, were those who most clearly marked it out as a Swedish possession.[25] However, changes in naming practices most likely also resulted from more mundane needs of communicating in the multilingual environment of the borderlands. Thus, it is not surprising that Swedish names disappeared from later maps.[26] The maps of New Sweden show the results of both attempts to control the land and the more practical aspects of living in and mapping borderlands.

Land, Lost and Claimed

Parallel to the attempts to map the colony, the authorities in New Sweden were involved in a debate about what right they had to the territory. Indeed, there was an ongoing disagreement in early America as to who was the rightful owner and user of the land. This was a question of differing legal traditions between Native Americans and Europeans, exacerbated by the potential future profits that the newcomers foresaw that the land might yield.[27] New Sweden's colonial administration—and especially its last governor, Johan Risingh—tried to frame the arguments in a way that would benefit Swedish claims. In so doing, they also vocalized ideas about what kind of land New Sweden was. Interestingly, these discussions brought forward a different conception of borderlands than the mapping had. Whereas the maps emphasized New Sweden as a part of Sweden, the debate about the right to the land constructed New Sweden not so much as a part of Sweden as of America.

The English and Dutch argued that they had a claim to the Delaware River because they had discovered it before the Swedes, but Risingh was adamant that "discovery" was not a valid argument. He told a visiting English envoy in 1654 that "[d]iscovery alone cannot give any secure right to the aforementioned New Sweden, which is shown by the example of the Spanish, who have discovered and sailed along all of the American seacoasts."[28] The Spanish who—according to Risingh—had first sailed the coasts of North America had no possessions in the area now. Consequently, neither could the English have any claim to this region on the basis of discovery. This argument was repeated to the Dutch, albeit now Risingh emphasized that the Spanish *and* the English had been in the area before the Dutch.

In this debate, Risingh conceptualized a large extent of land as one coherent entity—what we today call North America. In the words of historian Eviatar Zerubavel, Risingh was here involved in the "mental discovery" of America.[29] For the Swedish claim, it made sense to emphasize that the Spanish had discovered all of America rather than conceding that the English or Dutch had sailed the Delaware River before the Swedes. It is noteworthy that the discovery under discussion was really a question of "European discovery" because Risingh did not take into account the fact that the Lenape or Susquehannocks had discovered the land before the Europeans.

But Native American claims to the land became important to Risingh in the next stage of his argumentation. Having concluded that the Spanish had discovered America, he emphasized that this did not give them any rights to the land. Instead, he argued that the Swedes had stronger claims to the land than either the Spanish, English, or Dutch because the Swedes had bought the land from the Lenape, who were the "rightful owners."[30]

As Fur notes, the Lenape had different ideas about landownership than the Europeans. To the Lenape, it was not enough to purchase the land once. Instead, the land needed to be used, preferably for trade, and through this a purchase was reconfirmed.[31] The Europeans were well aware of these conditions, but they adhered to them only partially. In this case, the Swedes were in no position to oust the Lenape from the Delaware River. However, in relation to the Dutch and English claimants, their having bought land from the Lenape was an asset.

All through this debate, the Swedish side drew on ideas from contemporary discussions about European rights to extra-European sea and land. Risingh rejected the Treaty of Tordesillas of 1494, which had divided the extra-European world into a Spanish and a Portuguese sphere, and instead emphasized possession as a basis of ownership.[32] While Sweden was still in control of the Delaware River, this argument provided a strong claim to the area. After the loss of the colony in 1655, it was presumably less effective, although there were still Swedish and Finnish settlers in the area.

Arguably, the Swedish position on the Delaware River was never very strong. This, however, does not make the authorities' attempts to claim the area less interesting. On the contrary, Risingh's argumentation gives a fascinating example of an attempt to try to shape ideas about geopolitics to fit one party's particular interests. In relation to the other European colonial powers, this meant placing New Sweden in the context of a larger debate about Europeans' rights to extra-European land.[33] In this context, it made sense to emphasize that New Sweden was located on a larger American continent that had been discovered by the Spanish.

Far Away and a Difficult Journey

With a touch of melodrama, Governor Johan Printz wrote to Stockholm that "I look at myself at least a hundred times a day in this mirror, God knows with what doubts, for I sit here alone and [there are] hardly thirty men, of all who are here, upon whom I can rely."[34] This call for help is an example of how individuals in their roles as administrators as well as private persons emphasized that Sweden was far away from New Sweden.[35] Geography is not only a question about political arguments. Instead, place is experienced by people and conceptualized in close relation to experience. New Sweden was understood by authorities set on mapping the colony as a part of Sweden, yet it was also felt—by those same actors, as well as by others—to be far away.

The journey from Sweden to New Sweden took several months and was a passage full of hardships. Not least, crossing the Atlantic meant sailing out of sight of land for a significant period of time, and to be at the mercy of a temperamental sea. This experience was a recurring theme for authors writing about their journeys to New Sweden, and it was invariably about overcoming hardships. For instance, Lindeström wrote that the people were so sick during the crossing that "a person, even if she had a heart of stone, must still have felt grief and anxiety over this miserable situation."[36]

Similarly emotional language is seen in the letters home written by Swedish clergymen who were sent to the formerly Swedish colony at the turn of the eighteenth century. For example, Erik Björk, who was sent to New Sweden as one of three clergymen in 1697, wrote that "our hope of seeing the West Indian Swedish people was almost lost."[37] Others chose to convey the experiences of a difficult journey by leaving out, rather than including, their complaints. Björk's cotraveler, the young clergyman Anders Rudman, emphatically concluded in a letter that "To talk much about this sea journey would be too much and seems almost unnecessary, since each and every one can think what one has to endure during such travels."[38] Both the emphatic descriptions of Lindeström and Björk and Rudman's short comment convey the impression that crossing the Atlantic was a difficult experience. In these descriptions, the authors used a trope that was well established in early modern European travel writing.[39] The arduous nature of the journey became proof of the traveler's courage, yet, at the same time, the mode of description acerbated this sense of distance. In the accounts of a difficult crossing of the Atlantic, the first and last stages of the journey appear distant from each other, both literally and metaphorically separated by an ocean.

As an underlying theme, the difficult journey to New Sweden went hand in hand with parallel discussions about Sweden and New Sweden being located in two different worlds. The accounts describing journeys to New Sweden noted the newness of the geographic region where the colony was located. For instance, Campanius Holm stated at the beginning of his compilation of travel narratives:

> All the earth's round globe, consisting of water and earth, is by the erudite and the describers of the earth divided into the old and the new world. The old world is that in which we live, and includes Europe which is in the north, Asia east, and Africa southward, the new world is called America, and it is located towards the west.[40]

As Risingh had done in the discussion about discovery and the rights to land, Campanius Holm chose to frame his account of New Sweden with much larger geographic concepts. As we have seen, it was well established that America was associated with "discovery" and "newness" in this period.[41] However, this was not only a trope in administrative or scholarly works on geography, but a theme in the accounts of travelers' journeys. Thus, Björk described that upon arriving, he and his fellow travelers experienced what it was like "with the Old World's feet to step on the so-called New World's earth."[42] Passages like this emphasized the separateness of the destination from the place of departure, and connected it to the theme of a New and an Old World.

Björk's comment about his Old World's feet on the New World's earth also evokes a sense of a wonderous place, promising and hitherto unexplored. This theme is mirrored in one of the maps of New Sweden that the armchair traveler Campanius Holm made. While Lindeström had marked out a place called Cape Paradise ("Paradis Udd") on his earliest map of the colony without further comments, Campanius chose to make more of this curiously named promontory on his rendition of the map.[43]

Next to "Cape Paradise," Campanius Holm added a depiction of a wall of fire. To the early modern viewer, that would have been a familiar representation of earthly Paradise.[44] Scholars had long debated the location of Paradise. It was considered to be far away and inaccessible to humans, but there were different theories about its actual location. In addition to those who suggested places in Asia and Africa, Christopher Columbus had proposed that Paradise was located in South America.[45] Campanius Holm added to this debate by suggesting that Paradise was to be found in New Sweden.

Campanius Holm's Paradise was more allegorical than real. Historian Alessandro Scafi notes that the location of Paradise as a place in actual geography was largely abandoned by the sixteenth century. Paradise's location instead became an issue of antiquarian interpretation concerning what place-names in the present corresponded to biblical history and the location of Paradise in the past.[46] In light of this, Campanius Holm's image of Paradise should not be interpreted as a depiction of actual geography. Most likely, he included it as an embellishment and as a means to emphasize that New Sweden was a land of riches and promises, far away yet pleasant and full of wonders. Sweden had lost New Sweden as a colony, but Campanius Holm was part of a group that promoted a continued Swedish interest in the former possession.

Accounts stemming from both the early days of the colony and the late seventeenth century described New Sweden as a place far away from Sweden, and examples of emotional language appear throughout the period. Did the character of the emotional language change over time? Given the incomplete preserved sources, this is a difficult question to answer, yet some hypotheses can be put forward. On the one hand, there seems to have been a change from frustration among the colonial administrators in the period of colonial rule to wonder and fascination in the accounts of Campanius Holm and the clergymen who were sent to the former colony in the later seventeenth century. The emotional outburst of Governor Printz about feeling beleaguered and far away from all support is decidedly different from the clergyman Björk's wonder at coming to the New World. On the other hand, the differences could have had more to do with the writers' respective situations in New Sweden at the time of writing than with a change in conceptualization over time. Indeed, Björk's colleague Anders Rudman called his position as pastor of the Gloria Dei Church in Pennsylvania "his American yoke" when writing home to ask his superiors to be relieved a few years later.[47] But regardless of whether there was an overall change over time or not, these emotional responses were clearly tied to a conceptualization of New Sweden as situated far away from Sweden.

Borderlands in Another World

New Sweden's place in the world was conceptualized in several different ways. The colony was understood to be part of the early modern conglomerate Swedish state, yet the colonial authorities and individual travelers also located New Sweden in America and on the other side of the world. These conceptualizations emphasized, respectively, the affinity of Sweden and New Sweden and the distance between these two places.

Although at first seemingly contradictory, the perceptions of affinity and distance were not mutually exclusive conceptions of New Sweden's place in the world. Instead, they are evidence of the situational and unstable nature of geographic frameworks. This is seen in the case of Governor Johan Printz, who, on the one hand, called for closer control of New Sweden as a Swedish territory, and, on the other hand, lamented that he was far away and not getting enough support. Geography is not a view from nowhere, nor is it solely a question of water and land or distance measured in miles or kilometers. Instead, the present analysis has highlighted how an understanding of New Sweden's place in the world was closely tied to the colonial administration's ambitions in America, as well as individuals' experiences of traveling to, living in, and imagining a borderlands in constant change.

Notes

1. See, for example, Magdalena Naum and Jonas M. Nordin, eds., *Scandinavian Colonialism and the Rise of Modernity: Small Time Agents in a Global Arena* (New York: Springer, 2013); Stellan Dahlgren and Hans Norman, *The Rise and Fall of New Sweden* (Uppsala: Almqvist and Wiksell, 1988); Amandus Johnson, *The Swedish Settlements on the Delaware, 1638–1664,* 2 vols. (Philadelphia: Swedish Colonial Society, 1911).

2. Gunlög Fur, Magdalena Naum, and Jonas M. Nordin, "Intersecting Worlds: New Sweden's Transatlantic Entanglements," *Journal of Transnational American Studies* 7, no. 1 (2016); Gunlög Fur, *A Nation of Women: Gender and Colonial Encounters among the Delaware Indians* (Philadelphia: University of Pennsylvania Press, 2009).

3. Lu Ann De Cunzo, "Borderland in the Middle: The Delaware Colony on the Atlantic Coast," in Naum and Nordin, *Scandinavian Colonialism and the Rise of Modernity.*

4. See Charlotta Forss, *The Old, the New, and the Unknown: The Continents and the Making of Geographical Knowledge in Seventeenth-Century Sweden* (Turku, Finland: Illoinen Tiede, 2018); Charles Withers, *Placing the Enlightenment: Thinking Geographically about the Age of Reason* (Chicago: University of Chicago Press, 2007).

5. Fredrik Ekengren, Magdalena Naum, and Ulla Isabel Zagal-Mach Wolfe, "Sweden in the Delaware Valley: Everyday Life and Material Culture in New Sweden," in Naum and Nordin, *Scandinavian Colonialism and the Rise of Modernity,* 171.

6. Johan Printz, "Printz to Brahe, April 12, 1643," in *The Instruction for Johan Printz, Governor of New Sweden,* ed. Amandus Johnson (Philadelphia: Swedish Colonial Society, 1930), 150.

7. Per Lindeström, *Geographia Americae eller Indiae Occindentalis Beskriffningh* (1691), Vänermuseet, Lidköping, fol. 30r. (hereafter *GA* Lidköping).

8. Johan Risingh to National Board of Trade, July 13, 1654, Riksarkivet, Stockholm, Handel och sjöfart (hereafter RA, H&S), vol. 194, 7.

9. Lindeström, *GA* Lidköping, fol. 28r.

10. Gunlög Fur, *Colonialism in the Margins: Cultural Encounters in New Sweden and Lapland* (Leiden: Brill, 2006).

11. For example, see Andreas Bureus, *Lapponia* (1611).

12. Richard Kagan and Benjamin Schmidt, "Maps and the Early Modern State: Official Cartography," in *The History of Cartography,* vol. 3, ed. David Woodward (Chicago: University of Chicago Press, 2007).

13. John White, *La Virgenia Pars,* British Library, London, 1906, 0509.1.2; See also Barbara Backus McCorkle, *New England in Early Printed Maps 1513–1800* (Providence, R.I.: John Carter Brown Library, 2001).

14. Maria Gussarsson Wijk, Mats Höglund, and Bo Lundström, *Med kartan i fokus: En vägledning till de civila och militära kartorna i Riksarkivet* (Stockholm: Riksarkivet, 2013); Mats Höglund, *Kampen om fredsmilen: Kartan som makt- och kontrollinstrument i 1655 års reduktion* (Uppsala: Sveriges lantbruksuniversitet, 2017).

15. Peter Sahlins, *Boundaries: The Making of France and Spain in the Pyrenees* (Berkeley: University of California Press, 1989).

16. Per Lindeström, *En Kort Relation ok beskrifning öfwer Nya Sweriges situation,* Kungliga biblioteket, Stockholm (hereafter KB), Rål. Fol. 201; Dahlgren and Norman, *The Rise and Fall of New Sweden,* 168–69, 234–35.

17. John Smith, "Virginia," in *A Map of Virginia: With a Description of the Countrey* (Oxford, 1612).

18. A. R. Dunlap, *Dutch and Swedish Place-Names in Delaware* (Newark: University of Delaware Press, 1956), 17; A. R. Dunlap, *Indian Place-Names in Delaware* (Wilmington: Archeological Society of Delaware, 1950), 29.

19. Joan Rennie Short, *Cartographic Encounters: Indigenous Peoples and the Exploration of the New World* (Chicago: University of Chicago Press, 2009).

20. Per Brahe, "Brahe to Printz, 9 November, 1643," in Johnson, *The Instruction for Johan Printz,* 156.

21. Johan Risingh, "En kort berättelse om Resan till Nya Sverige uti America," in Dahlgren and Norman, *The Rise and Fall of New Sweden,* 166.

22. Lindeström, *GA* Lidköping.

23. Thomas Campanius Holm, *Kort beskrifning om Provincien Nya Swerige* (Stockholm, 1702).

24. Arnold Colom, "Paascaarte van Nieu Nederlandt . . . 1656," in *Zee-atlas, ofte Water-Wereldt* (Amsterdam, [1658]).

25. For example, Jean Baptiste Louis Franquelin, *Carte de l'Amerique Septentrionnale* (1688).

26. Thomas Holme, *A Mapp of Ye Improved Part of Pensilvania in America* (London, [ca. 1687]). See Per Hallman, "Kartografi och kolonisering vid Delawareflodens mynning: En undersökning av kartografiska namn och deras utveckling i området som koloniserades som Nya Swerige 1638–1655," BA thesis, Stockholm University, 2016.

27. Fur, *Colonialism in the Margins,* 107.

28. Johan Risingh, "En kort berättelse," in Dahlgren and Norman, *The Rise and Fall of New Sweden,* 178.

29. Eviatar Zerubavel, *Terra Cognita: The Mental Discovery of America* (New Brunswick, N.J.: Transaction Publishers, 2003), 56.

30. Johan Risingh, *Een Beskrifning om Nova Suecia uthi America,* RA, H&S, 196.1, fol. 3r.

31. Fur, *Colonialism in the Margins,* 107.

32. See, for example, David Armitage, *The Ideological Origins of the British Empire* (Cambridge: Cambridge University Press, 2000).

33. Benjamin Schmidt, *Inventing Exoticism: Geography, Globalism, and Europe's Early Modern World* (Philadelphia: University of Pennsylvania Press, 2015).

34. Johan Printz, "Relation till dätt höghloflige West Indische Compagnie," in *Kolonien Nya Sveriges grundläggning 1637–1642,* ed. Clas Odhner (Stockholm: Norstedt, 1877), 31.

35. Fur, Naum, and Nordin, "Intersecting Worlds," 4.

36. Lindeström, *Resa till Nya Sverige,* ed. Alf Åberg (Stockholm: Natur och Kultur, 1962), 53.

37. Erik Björk to Carl Viström, October 29, 1697, KB, Enge. B.X.1.63, fol. 1r–1v.

38. Anders Rudman to Jacob Arrhenius [October 20, 1697], KB, Enge. B.X.1.63, fol. 1v.

39. Marie Louise Pratt, *Imperial Eyes: Travel Writing and Transculturation* (New York: Routledge, 2008), 20. See also Anders Rudman and Erik Björk to Carl Leyoncrona, October 30, 1697; Andreas Rudman and Erik Björk to K. M:t., March 22, 1698, RA, H&S, vol. 197.

40. Campanius Holm, *Kort beskrifning om Provincien Nya Swerige,* 1.

41. Anthony Grafton, *New Worlds, Ancient Texts: The Power of Tradition and the Shock of Discovery* (Cambridge: Belknap Press, 1992); Christine Johnson, *The German Discovery of the World* (Charlottesville: University of Virginia Press, 2008).

42. Erik Björk to Carl Viström, October 29, 1697, KB, Enge. B.X.1.63, fol. 4r–4v.

43. First published in Johannes Campanius, *Lutheri Catechismus, öfwersatt på american-virginiske språket,* ed. Thomas Campanius Holm (Stockholm, 1696).

44. Alessandro Scafi, *Maps of Paradise* (Chicago: University of Chicago Press, 2013), 44.

45. Ibid., 80.

46. Ibid., 100.

47. Anders Rudman to Olaus Swebilius and Cons. Eccl., June 16, 1702, KB Enge., B.X.1 63, fol. 1r.

9

Captain Jack's Whip and Borderlands of Swedish–Indigenous Encounters

Gunlög Fur

In 1874, a curious object entered the collections of the ethnographic department of the national zoological museum in Stockholm. It was described as a riding whip that had belonged to the Modoc leader Captain Jack (Kintpuash, circa 1837–1873), who had led the Modocs in a last desperate war against the onslaught of American settler expansion into their territory in the western United States. The Modoc War made headlines across the world, and reports of excessive force against defenseless prisoners of war led the daily *Dagens Nyheter* to comment in June 1873 that "it is a sad fact that everywhere, where a strong and civilized nation has the inclination for colonization, it ends with the extinction of the indigenous tribes."[1] The whip was a gift to the museum from August Berggren, a Swedish migrant who had traded with the Modocs and who later became the Swedish consul general in San Francisco, via Hugo Nisbeth, who was a Swedish journalist on a tour of the United States.[2]

In 2008, the whip was added to the permanent North American display at the Ethnographic Museum. I saw it there while on a visit to the museum to look for evidence of Swedish–American Indian interactions. It struck me as odd, as objects associated with named American Indians are rare in the ethnographic displays. Why had Captain Jack's (riding) whip ended up in Sweden? A few years later, the ongoing work to digitize newspapers made it possible to search terms such as "Modocs" and "Captain Jack" and a research assistant helped me turn up a surprising number of articles reporting on the war in Swedish nineteenth-century media. Digitization also made it possible to perform a search in Swedish-American printed papers. The disparate pieces of information, gathered serendipitously on the side as I was engaged in other projects, began to take shape as I imagined the whip's leather strands unravel and stretch across the Atlantic to bring together separate elements in a joint cultural landscape that structured understandings of American expansion, Swedish migration, American Indian resistance and dispossession, and Swedish self-understanding. The methodology for sketching this particular Swedish–American borderland thus has taken an unanticipated form while connecting to my larger interest in understanding immigrant and Indigenous relations in North America.[3] It is based on the museum collection, newspaper reporting, family magazine articles, and biographical information to trace the evolution from political news reporting to entertainment and curiosities exchanges, and migration experiences. The rhapsodic nature is therefore by design, the purpose being to connect the dots in a vast landscape of shared and mutually reinforcing, but also sometimes contradictory, elements that consigned the whip—and with it excised its painful history—to a glass case in a museum. It should be remembered, however, that one significant piece is conspicuously missing, and that is the perspective of Modoc people, past and present, on the gift of this object to a Swedish museum and on the relations and events that surrounded that donation.

The whip thus provides an entry point to an exploration of the circulation of knowledge, its reusable qualities on both sides of the Atlantic, and the distribution of power to authorize meaning and exchanges. Borderlands thinking as a way to investigate cross-border relations and ideological exchanges emphasizes border crossing, conceptual boundaries, margins and marginality, fluidity, and multiple identities. This serves well to rethink Scandinavian and Indigenous encounters and relations. The strength of the borderlands concept is in its capacity to expand thinking on territory and geography, loosening the shackles of conventional methodological nationalism on historical imagination. It sets up many centers of confluence, identifies multiple agents, and necessitates taking different loci of power and authority into consideration. The whip sweeps over, as it were, a Swedish–American borderland that is neither entirely separate from a lived Swedish-American experience, nor from Swedish politics and culture or American–Indigenous relations at the time. In fact, it links them in ways that raises questions only a few of which may be hinted at in this essay.

The Modoc War and Swedish Reporting

The conflict known as the Modoc War reached international media after the Modocs in November 1872 successfully fought back an attack from the United States Army on their settlement in the border country between California and Oregon. The Modocs under the leadership of Kintpuash, who the whites called Captain Jack, had left deplorable conditions and broken treaty provisions on a reservation they shared with the Klamaths and established a camp on the Lost River, which they considered the heart of their territory. American troops attempted to force the Modocs back onto the reservation, but despite overwhelming force and firepower they had to retreat with several casualties. The Modocs withdrew into an area known as the Lavabeds where volcanic ridges and labyrinths made troop movements extremely difficult and Indigenous familiarity with the terrain a superior asset. In the following months, the Modocs ably defended themselves against all attempts to oust them, despite mortar shelling and vastly more numerous enemy forces. Confident American troops walked to their deaths and shocked military leaders called for a truce. A peace conference held on April 11, 1873, ended in tragedy when Captain Jack and his fellow delegates, no doubt remembering a deceitful peace meeting to which they had been invited by settler militia a decade earlier, shot and killed the chief negotiator, General Edward S. Canby, and Methodist minister Eleazar Thomas. The Modocs fled back to their stronghold and held out until the end of May, when they capitulated, exhausted and hungry. Jack and three other leaders were sentenced to death and hanged on October 3, 1873, while remaining tribal members were forcibly relocated to Indian Territory.

The conflict itself was precipitated by the dramatic changes Modocs and their Indigenous neighbors had experienced in the preceding decades. Previous limited interactions with European fur traders altered rapidly as settlers poured into their country and Modocs were squeezed between Oregon settlements expanding southward and a northward push from the gold-mining ventures in California. The government negotiated a treaty with the Modocs and Klamaths in 1864 that stipulated that the two peoples should share a reservation in southern Oregon. However, the treaty was never ratified by Congress and the U.S. obligations were not met. Modocs soon decided to return to their original territory in Northern California. There they maintained an uneasy relationship with white settlers, and some of them (including Captain Jack) did day labor and odd jobs for local farmers and ranchers. But tension increased and the white settlers pressured the federal government to authorize a military removal of the Modocs back to the reservation.[4]

The war attracted wide attention in the U.S. media and internationally. In Sweden, the first mention of the Modoc–U.S. conflict appeared in *Aftonbladet* on April 21, 1873, in a listing of wire news from around the world. "The attack against the Modoc Indians began last Monday. After three days of battle the Indians' position in the Lavabeds was taken. The Indians were blasted and pursued by cavalry. The American troops lost 5 dead and 10 injuries; the Indians' losses are unknown. One chief perished." Somewhat contradictory news items during the following months in both *Aftonbladet* and *Dagens Nyheter* demonstrate the volatility of the situation and the difficulty of ascertaining what had actually transpired. Numbers of casualties varied and so did information regarding developments. News items were terse, revealing the horrors of war without embellishment: "The Modoc Indians have offered to surrender on condition that their lives would be spared. The commander of the U.S. troops, Davis, demanded unconditional surrender, otherwise he would have all Modoc Indians shot," reported *Dagens Nyheter* on May 23.[5]

On June 21, 1873, *Dagens Nyheter* published a longer background piece, "The Last Modoc Indians." The article was an attempt to explain the rationale of the Modocs and place it within a larger frame of American expansion. To do so, it turned to James Fenimore Cooper and what historian Robert Berkhofer has identified as a paradigmatic formula depicting noble savages disintegrating as a consequence of the pressures from advancing civilization, a development that inspired a sense of pity and nostalgia but was portrayed as inevitable.[6] Cooper's success in Sweden was monumental and his books were translated into Swedish already in the 1820s. Countless Swedish migrants and travelers employed "Cooper" as a shorthand for all their expectations on American Indians. The reference to Cooper in articles about the Modocs demonstrates how "Indians" were bundled together and presented as one entity that could be encapsulated by Cooper's representation of smart and cunning—yet ultimately doomed—warriors, orators, and trackers. The fact that Cooper's heroes and villains were locked in contests in the forests of the Northeast of the United States made little difference to the imagery, although it did make some commentators uneasy.[7]

The *Dagens Nyheter* article represents a significant shift in the reporting of the conflict, away from factual reportage to an analysis that enlisted a broader span of perceptions and biases regarding Indigenous–U.S. relations. It also demonstrated that Swedish commentators often lacked reliable information. "Captain Jack and his companions have already moved on to 'the happy hunting grounds,' which, according to these wild people's belief, exists in a different, better world," the article asserted (even though Kintpuash and the others still had three months to live). Along with them went the last remnants of the Modoc tribe, "once the most powerful and strongest in North America." Cooper's "Uncas" from *The Last of the Mohicans* was invoked as a likely reference for readers who had read about the plight of the Modocs and felt a twinge of sympathy for them. But, in contrast to Cooper's hero, the Modocs were not to be romanticized as they were guilty of guile and barbaric cruelty that justified harsh reprisals from the American forces. However, "one cannot deny that the comportment of the whites is not always conducive to impart among Indians respect for the words of their conquerors." Captain Jack and the Modocs had cause for grievance, the article stated. A few years earlier they

> had been invited to just such a conference as the one that recently cost general Canby his life. While they were negotiating peacefully, the whites suddenly attacked their guests and shot most of them to death. Such perfidy brings forth in the Indian's heart a fervent thirst for revenge, and this must sooner or later be quenched. Captain Jack, who escaped the cowardly bloodbath, therefore considered himself fulfilling a sacred duty to his murdered comrades when he took advantage of the first likely opportunity to commit a similar act.[8]

While ostensibly sympathetic to the plight of the Modocs, the newspaper nonetheless employed a whole stock of set notions that painted them as something other than a civilized people. References to "happy hunting grounds," "guile and barbaric cruelty," and "the last of the redskins" resonated with readers already familiar with a division of peoples according to their perceived level of civilization.

But Cooper also formed the initial point of reference for a much more forthright critique of Indigenous society. An illustrated article in the June 1873 edition of the monthly magazine *Ny Illustrerad Tidning,* which also purported to offer a background to the Modoc War, took a quite different stance. While Cooper's heroes fought against unlawful intruders, it argued, American society had now grown so large and all-encompassing that readers ought not to confuse the justified grievances in Cooper's novels with contemporary attacks by "raw and drunken robbers on peaceful and industrious citizens in an ordered society." As a consequence, Captain Jack and his followers had failed to enthuse even the "most sentimental among the civilized." The article describes, in both text and a greatly exaggerated image taken from *Frank Leslie's Illustrated News Paper,* the conflict region and the spectacular lava formations where the Modocs had made their standoff. The language of the article is both racist and dismissive when describing the aftermath of the shattered peace negotiations at which Captain Jack shot General Canby:

> "The great father in Washington" got angry and decided to exterminate the "vermin." Thus, the Modoc War began in earnest; an Indian tribe, "Warm Springs Indians," are the Americans' allies and scalp Modocs to their heart's delight. Insignificant as the war has been in terms of participating troop numbers as well as its political significance, it is only through the picturesque theater of war and the peculiarity of a final Indian war—"a vanishing period"—that this struggle for so long has managed to attract more general attention.[9]

The metaphors and mental concepts provided by Cooper's authorship thus worked both for and against the Modocs, but it did not allow for an identification with them.

The Whip Arrives: Commodifying American Indians

In late June 1874, the readers of *Aftonbladet* were treated to the salacious story of a donation to the ethnographic collections at the National Museum of Natural History of Captain Jack's "riding whip." By that time, regular readers of the newspaper would have been familiar with the events of the violent and tragic conflict. Now the article reminded readers that the Modocs were "one of the most powerful of the then existing Indian tribes" who, under the leadership of "its astute chief, Captain Jack," kept a considerable portion of the United States Army at bay in a war that ended when the tribe was subjugated and the chiefs executed. The Modoc War, it insisted, held interest not only because it demonstrated that "Indian acuity and cunning are not just a myth, as Captain Jack in both of these considerations fully measured up to the characters who Cooper sketched," but also because it was likely to be the last Indigenous attempt at revolt against the United States. The whip came from August Berggren, a Swedish migrant who had traveled to the far West on the Oregon Trail and had carried on a considerable trade with the Modocs and thus entered into "friendly connections with the famous chief," who had given Berggren "as a keepsake this riding whip of leather thongs made in the Indian way by his own hands, a terrible weapon just as useful on animals as on people." The whip was now donated to the museum via "a traveling compatriot" and accompanied by photographic portraits of Kintpuash (Jack) and his fellow chiefs, whose identities were vouched for by the American commander in the war.[10]

Already in the initial phrases of this article the story of the whip began to unravel at the seams and the threads stretch out in separate directions. Attentive readers had indeed followed the reporting from the war in various news media, but could hardly have gotten the impression that the Modocs were "one of the most powerful" American Indian nations. Nor was the Modoc War the last conflict over territory in the United States. On the contrary, only a few months later, newspapers reported about the extensive battles between the army and Indigenous nations on the southern Plains, in comparison to whom the Modocs "were just a small people who did not even count among the bravest of the Indian tribes."[11] The war certainly proved devastating to the Modocs and cost the United States

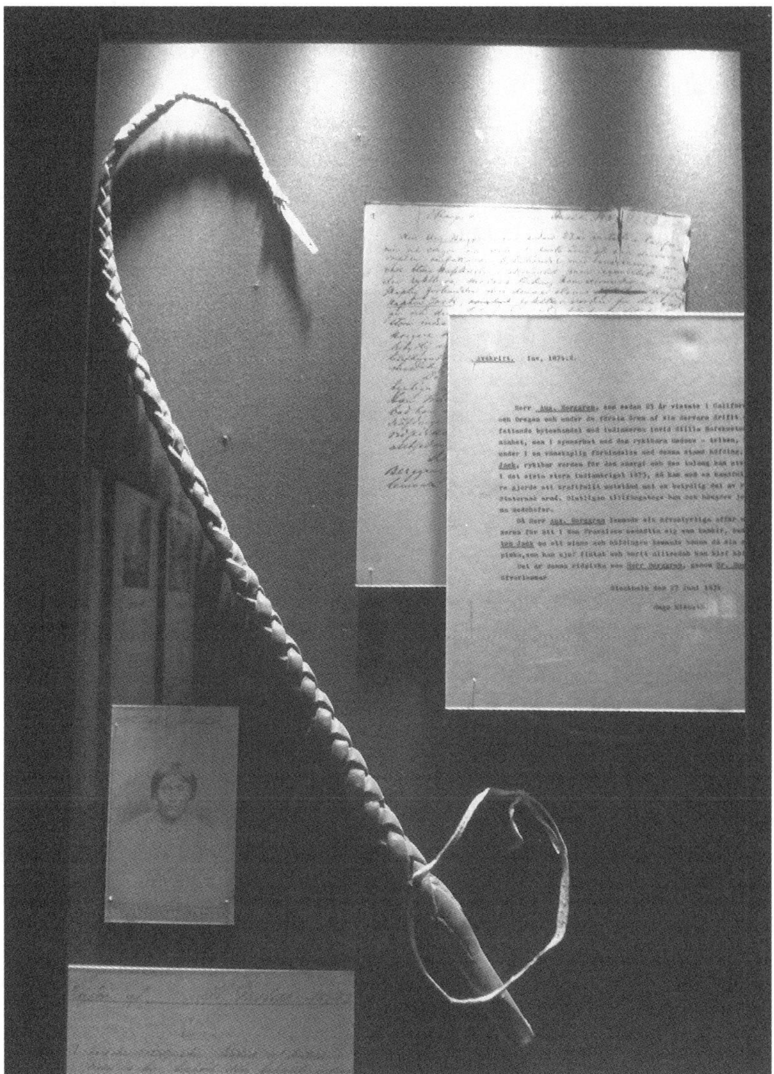

The whip of Modoc leader Captain Jack (Kintpuash, circa 1837–1873), displayed at the Ethnographic Museum in Stockholm and accompanied by a copy of the letter of donation and a photograph taken before the execution of Kintpuash.

a substantial amount in lives and money, but the article most likely exaggerated the might of the Modocs in the interest of raising the stakes in connection with the donation to the museum, just as it did when latching onto their unquestioned familiarity with James Fenimore Cooper's fictional portrayals of American Indians.

The object itself appeared to be shaped to fit the narrative. According to Martin Schultz, head curator of the American collection at the Swedish Ethnographic Museum where the whip is now housed, it is most likely not a riding whip but possibly a bullwhip. Nor is it likely that it was manufactured by Indigenous people. The braiding, leather, and stitching suggest that it is of Euro-American make. However, it is also likely that an Indigenous person had used the whip and added leather thongs at the grip and at the tip. Thus, the whip itself is a testament to the entwined relations in the borderland. From a white (probably) male leatherworker, it ended up in the possession of Kintpuash, perhaps as a tool he used when doing day labor for white farmers.[12]

Eight months after the execution of Kintpuash, the Modoc War had thus become consigned to an object placed on a shelf in a museum, and the uncertainties of reporting from a conflict zone were fixed in labels that determined that Jack was a criminal and August Berggren a friend of the Indians.

In his book *Remembering the Modoc War,* historian Boyd Cothran describes the macabre industry that arose around the imprisonment and eventual death sentence against the Modoc leaders. Physical reminders of Jack's and his compatriots' life, such as pieces of hair, hats, and moccasins, entered a market thirsting for the exotic and the exciting. The photographs in the Swedish museum collection all belong to the postcard-size souvenirs Louis H. Heller produced after visiting the Modocs in their jail cells. The authenticity of the photographic likenesses was guaranteed by the commanding officer, General Jefferson C. Davis, and they were sold for four dollars a dozen and easily available across the Northwest coast region. Cothran suggests that their popularity connected to the gruesome practice of trading in lynching photographs, common across the South, but also in the Northwest.[13]

A Swedish market for entertainment and objects connected to the exotic already existed, and the year after the Modoc War, the first group of Indigenous Americans toured southern Sweden. Three Pawnees—

Keh-wuk-oo-yah-kah (White Fox), Atta-kah-stah-kah (White or Gray Eagle), and Red Fox (whose name in Pawnee was not recorded in Swedish sources)—traveled the Nordic countries. Throngs of curious spectators in southern Sweden, Copenhagen in Denmark, and Christiania (Oslo) in Norway paid to see "real Indians." Sadly, White Fox succumbed to tuberculosis in the spring of 1875 and died at Sahlgrenska sjukhuset, the main hospital in the west coast city of Gothenburg. Red Fox and White Eagle demanded to take the body back to America to bury, but Swedish scientists wished to keep this specimen of "primitive physiology." The body was sent to Karolinska sjukhuset in Stockholm where Professor of Anatomy Gustaf von Düben performed an autopsy, after which the skin was removed from the body and fitted onto a gypsum cast of White Fox's torso. The skin was shown at Sweden's first anthropological exhibition in 1878.[14] This eerily echoed a brief item appearing in the Swedish-American newspaper *Nya Svenska Amerikanaren* in connection with the Modoc War. A "reliable rumor" had it that after execution, the heads of Captain Jack and his fellow resistance leader Schonchin would be cut off and preserved in alcohol and sent to a museum in Washington as trophies from the war. The paper suggested that it would be appropriate to send along the entire bodies for more effect.[15]

The collection and display of body parts constitute the appalling end of the spectrum of both scientific and entertainment interest in human difference and Indigenous peoples. But this market also offered Indigenous persons possibilities for a slim income as well as travel. Selling or exchanging objects that later made it into museum collections occurred out of necessity, desire, and in certain situations friendship.[16]

Race Wars and Swedish Innocence

Reporting on the war occurred, unsurprisingly, in a borderland of information, opinions, and emotions stretching from the scene of conflict across the United States and Swedish America and over to Sweden. Similar lines of reporting can be identified in both Swedish and Swedish-American newspapers. The large Swedish dailies, *Dagens Nyheter* and *Aftonbladet,* took the view most stringently voiced in Chicago-based *Gamla och Nya Hemlandet,* one of the first and most influential Swedish-language newspapers founded in 1855 and closely tied to the Augustana synod, which consistently argued that the Modocs had cause for dissatisfaction. So did liberal *Svenska Amerikanaren,* also published in Chicago, at the beginning of the conflict, but after the killing of Canby and Thomas the newspaper turned and offered descriptions of the Modocs that portrayed them as criminal and barbaric. Most clearly negative to the plight of the Modocs was *Nordstjernan,* founded in New York in 1872, whose language resembled that of *Ny Illustrerad Tidning.*[17] It is tempting to conclude that Swedish reporting only reflected internal U.S. debates about policies in relation to Indigenous opposition to expansion. However, it is more complex than that. Although there is evidence of communication between Swedish and Swedish-American news media, a comparison of dates of publication and content of various news stories in relation to the Modoc War does not indicate that Swedish newspapers just copied from their transatlantic counterparts. Instead, they took part in a joint field of reporting, perceptions, and interpretations regarding American Indigenous resistance to settler expansion.[18]

A recurrent strain in Swedish media stories reworks the message in a way specifically suited to the Swedish context. Despite deploring the murders at the peace commission, *Dagens Nyheter* strove to place the events in a larger framework and concluded:

> It is a lamentable fact that everywhere where a strong and civilized nation, which has a predisposition for colonization, forges ahead, it always ends in the extinction of the Indigenous tribes. Several governments in the United States have made attempts to get the Indians to settle in so called reservations—stretches of land, kept exclusively for Indians—and teach them to dig and plow, read and write. But unfortunately, the inclinations of the redskins have always been the same as those held by Ismael's ferocious descendants, whose hand was against every stranger, who met them. Seen from the other side, it appears that the Anglo-Saxon race has great difficulty in assimilating and amalgamating lower races, and as colonization now progresses with giant steps in *the far West,* the day may perhaps not be so distant when we may read the story of "the last redskin."[19]

While accepting the premise that Indigenous peoples may be doomed to disappear, the article apportioned some of the blame not only on inevitability but on the inability of the "Anglo-Saxon race" to "amalgamate" other races. A similar assertion, more strongly worded, appeared in Sweden's largest and most popular monthly journal, *Svenska Familj-Journalen,* in June 1873 describing the extinction of the Mandan tribe. It suggested that the tribe's unwillingness to adjust to "civilization" lay behind its disappearance, but blamed white people who "take everything without concerning themselves with either common human or judicial laws," and continued: "*Here is a race war, which never rests.* The Anglo-Saxons in America annihilate all other races, with whom they come in contact."[20] Ulf Jonas Björk notes that Swedish newspapers were dependent on German news agencies and that information regarding American events may reflect German views on British (Anglo-Saxon) colonial expansion at a time when Germany itself did not have any overseas colonies.[21]

I have argued that images of American Indians transmitted through the popular print media and in novels tailored to a young and bourgeois readership conveyed a discourse of innocence surrounding notions about migration and Indigenous dispossession that divorced expansive white settlement policies from American Indian removals. Maintaining that separation was possible because writers, readers, and migrants "managed to distance themselves from any active role in colonialism."[22] While often containing lurid details of spectacular violence, such notions in no way appeared connected to the horrors of war and ethnic cleansing. Such tropes of colonial innocence, intimately combined with what Susanne Zantop has defined as colonial fantasies, indeed appear to have suffused nation-building processes across transatlantic spaces. Boyd Cothran weaves a similar argument connecting how attention to the causes and consequences of the Modoc War served to validate the innocence of the American nation in the destruction of the continent's Indigenous societies "and imprinted the conflict with narratives of white victimhood and Indigenous criminality."[23]

It is in this context that it is relevant to read another series of articles appearing in Swedish newspapers in 1873–74 representing a shared conceptual landscape between Sweden and Swedish America that took on a specific meaning in Sweden. In September 1873, *Aftonbladet* ran an article titled "Minnen från de första svenska nybyggena i Norra Amerika" (Memories from the first Swedish settlements in America) that dealt with the history of New Sweden, the short-lived seventeenth-century Swedish colony along the Delaware River. The article was taken from the Swedish-American newpaper *Hemlandet* and written by its prominent editor, Johan A. Enander, one of the most influential ethnic leaders in Swedish America, who consistently strove to establish a specific Swedish-American history in the United States.[24] The article series began:

> What relationship did the first Swedish settlers in America have to the Indigenous people of the country? History offers an answer to that question, which is to the greatest credit to our nationality. It was not through cheating and deceit, nor through violence, that Swedes won their possession in this country. It was through honest purchase, through faithfully fulfilling agreements, that they acquired their ownership to "New Sweden." It was through a friendly and trustworthy demeanor that they won the friendship of the neighboring Indians and it was, finally, through Swedish persistence, through Swedish piety, that the first seeds of civilization were sown among the indigenes of the east. Had their successors continued the missionary endeavors of the Swedes in a similar spirit, many of the Indian tribes, who now have been exterminated through weapons of violence or from the "vices of education," may have become civilized and thus saved from ruin.[25]

This particular form of Swedish innocence in relationship to American Indians gained currency in the 1870s and has been ardently cultivated ever since. Enander published his articles inspired by the upcoming 1876 centennial and linked Swedish nineteenth-century migration to the United States and the New Sweden colony to establish a long-standing continuous Swedish presence on American soil.[26] A number of publications appeared in Sweden during the first years of the 1870s that retold the story of New Sweden and that, in very similar language, lauded the friendly relations between Indigenous owners of the land and the newcomers from Sweden. In Swedish folklorist Richard Bergström's portrayal of the colony, published in 1870 and then reprinted in several venues, this relationship took on "an almost touching beauty." The Swedes related to the peoples in the region "as people to people," trading fairly with them, teaching them and learning from them, and receiving them in their houses "as other guests."[27]

"Our ancestors' different manners of meeting the comparatively helpless sons of the wilderness" forms an encouraging story, Bergström asserts, "as in this memory, a memory of innocence, lies something wonderfully comforting in this age, when so much old guilt is repaid and perhaps new ones are amassed."[28] Such views were attractive on both sides of the Atlantic and have proved remarkably resilient over the years despite changing geopolitical realities and new scholarship.[29]

Concurrent Narratives in the Borderland

Swedish interest in news, fictional stories, and entertainment with a focus on Indigenous America appears to have taken off in the 1870s and then continued to grow in the following decades. Swedish emigration to North America rose sharply in the aftermath of an extensive famine, following failed harvests in 1867–69. Early accounts penned by visitors and settlers, such as Fredrika Bremer and Gustaf Unonius, drew up demarcation lines between civilization and Swedish settlements, on the one hand, and Indigenous wilderness, on the other. In 1868, Swedish newspapers reported with some frequency from the conflicts on the northern Plains, and they would follow with extensive coverage following the Battle of Little Big Horn in 1876.[30] Contacts between Sweden and Swedish America increased with letters crossing the Atlantic and print media sharing news and stories of settlement. By the 1870s, "Indian stories" were well established as sources of entertainment in Swedish magazines and dominated book publication aimed at young readers, leading to concern that these would "influence the young imagination in a harmful and excitable way."[31] In 1872–73, the popular monthly magazine *Svenska Familj-Journalen* introduced readers to what I have called the "Uncle Barkman cycle"—a series of adventure stories centered on the epic conflict between Indians and advancing settler communities.[32] Combined with actual displays of Indigenous Americans as "exotic" peoples, such as the tour by White Fox, Red Fox, and Gray Eagle, and in addition to the ubiquitous references to Cooper's work in newspaper articles, a conventional representation of "Indians" was firmly embedded in Swedish culture and consciousness by the end of the decade.

Captain Jack's riding whip reveals patterns that connected this fanciful and profoundly commercial image of "Indians" enfolded within an entertainment complex with political and scientific agendas and epistemologies. Hugo Nisbeth, who served as the conduit for the whip to the ethnographic collections, was a leading newspaper man and in 1872 he traveled to the United States as a correspondent for *Aftonbladet,* writing on American topics. Thus, it is more than likely he who penned the background articles regarding the Modoc War. In 1874, letters from his travels were published under the title *Två år i Amerika* (Two years in America). Nisbeth first encountered American Indians at Fort Kearny in South Dakota. "It was not without a cold chill down my spine that I approached the wigwams of the redskins. Bloody scalps, tomahawks, peace pipes, peace belts and war belts, etc. etc., with which Cooper's novels excite the imagination, danced helter-skelter in my head." However, reality contrasted sharply with imagination: "shortly we found ourselves surrounded by grinning and gaping squaws, and a gaggle of disgusting brats."[33] Nisbeth wrote encouragingly about emigration, and it is noteworthy that he clearly separated romance and disgust surrounding American Indian existence on the continent from migrant concerns. Writing in *Svenska Familj-Journalen* in 1874, his list of conditions that emigrants would meet contained not a word regarding Indigenous presence in the land.[34]

The whip's arrival at the Museum of Natural History thus occurred in a context of knowledge, representations, and images that circulated back and forth across the Atlantic, between the United States, Swedish America, and Sweden. At first glance, this might seem like a one-directional relationship, where images and ideas originating in the American context were adopted by Swedish journalists, intellectuals, and novelists and disseminated to a reading public via newspapers, magazines, entertainment venues, and museums. I argue that it was more complex than that, and that in fact this context constituted a borderland connecting the public on both sides of the Atlantic, and that it was created by a circulation of knowledge, representations, images, and objects. This space also allowed actors to utilize this circulation to develop or strengthen new nodes of authority, as well as to borrow from the borderland for more local purposes. But where were the Modocs in this? Was there space for Indigenous actors as well? The whip, in its enigmatic existence at the museum, indicates that this question is worth pursuing.

It is apparent that the conveyance of a whip belonging to Captain Jack occurred within a field of commercialization of images and representations. It is, of course, possible that the Modoc leader had become acquainted with a Swedish migrant and trader and had given him one of his whips as a memento, but the photographs that were added to the donation reveal how the collection itself derived its value from the speculative fascination with the Modoc War. Hugo Nisbeth added a note to the letter of donation: "Here follow the mentioned photographs, which ought to be suitable additions to Captain Jack's whip." The museum collection and the newspaper story connect the whip and the photographs, but the note suggests that they came into Nisbeth's hands at different times. Nisbeth must have acquired the photographs on his travels as a journalist in the United States and thought it appropriate to attach them to the gift of the whip with the notation that Jack and his fellow leaders were hanged for murder, adding to the collection a reminder of the spectacular violence attending the aftermath of the conflict. Thus, an American spectacle spread to Sweden and became adapted to a context in which migration played a major part. It made for an uneasy fit with reporting about conditions for emigrants and with an international debate with national twists regarding the justifications for colonialism and the "extinction" of Indigenous peoples.[35]

The museum donation wove together a mental territory that recognized certain specific forms of exclusion and inclusion. It blurred certain boundaries while upholding others; and while many of the characteristics of the narratives of Indigenous America mimicked those originating in the United States, other features shaped this into an essentially American–Swedish borderland, notably the stress on a particular legacy of friendship and democracy dating back to the New Sweden colony, which began to be cultivated at this time. The claim of friendship, which accompanied the gift of the whip, cannot be read as coincidental, but rather as lodged at the core of an emerging understanding of a Swedish role in America. What began as a disturbing piece of news reporting from a conflict zone, where nation building, migration, and dispossession clashed, ended in a display in a museum. Boyd Cothran argues that "memorials to settler colonial violence were key to the solidification of a public memory; they appropriated more than they represented the past, and in so doing, they became not merely evidence of power but a site for creating power in regimes of settler colonialism."[36] The donation, with its erroneous representation of the whip as an exotic Indigenous object connected to primitive violence, to which Nisbeth added execution memorabilia and a description of Captain Jack as a murderer, cut off the possibility of discussing the Modoc–U.S. conflict with social, political, and economic ramifications that also embroiled Swedish migration.

Notes

The author wishes to thank Adam Hjorthén, Martin Schultz, Linda Andersson Burnett, Cheewa James, and Boyd Cothran for aid and helpful suggestions. I regret that Cheewa James's book on Modoc history reached me too late to reference in this text, but I will do my best to do so as I continue this project.

1. "De sista Modoc-Indianerna," *Dagens Nyheter,* June 21, 1873. Unless noted, newspaper articles and items are not signed or titled.

2. The donation was reported in *Aftonbladet,* June 29, 1874, and *Dagens Nyheter,* June 30, 1874. Documentation of the gift is in the Swedish Ethnographic Museum collection database *Carlotta,* object 1874.02.0001, http://collections.smvk.se.

3. See Gunlög Fur, *Painting Culture, Painting Nature: Stephen Mopope, Oscar Jacobson, and the Development of Indian Art in Oklahoma* (Norman: University of Oklahoma Press, 2019); Gunlög Fur, "Colonial Fantasies: American Indians, Indigenous Peoples, and a Swedish *Discourse of Innocence,*" *National Identities* 18, no. 1 (2016): 11–33; Gunlög Fur, "Indians and Immigrants: Entangled Histories," *Journal of American Ethnic History* 33, no. 3 (2014): 55–76; Gunlög Fur, "Romantic Relations: Swedish Attitudes towards Indians during the Twentieth Century," *Swedish-American Historical Quarterly* 55, no. 3 (July 2004): 145–64.

4. Arrell Morgan Gibson, *The American Indian. Prehistory to the Present* (Lexington, Mass.: D. C. Heath and Company, 1980), 350–51, 417–18; Angie Debo, *A History of the Indians in the United States* (Norman and London: University of Oklahoma Press, 1970), 158–59, 260; Boyd Cothran, *Remembering the Modoc War: Redemptive Violence and the Making of American Innocence* (Chapel Hill: University of North Carolina Press, 2014), 15–18, 32–49.

5. *Aftonbladet,* April 21, 26, 1873; *Dagens Nyheter,* April 30, May 2, 23, and 26, 1873.

6. Robert F. Berkhofer, *The White Man's Indian. Images of the American Indian from Columbus to the Present* (New York: Vintage Books, 1978), 88, 91; Fur, "Colonial Fantasies," 18–19.

7. Fur, "Colonial Fantasies"; Ulf Jonas Björk, "Stories of America: The Rise of the 'Indian Book' in Sweden 1862–1895," *Scandinavian Studies* 75 (2003): 509–26; Fredrika Bremer, *America in the Fifties. Letters of Fredrika Bremer,* ed.

Adolph B. Benson (New York: American-Scandinavian Foundation, Oxford University Press, 1924), 10.

8. "De sista Modoc-Indianerna."

9. *Ny Illustrerad Tidning,* vol. 9, June 28, 1873, 201–2. On the exaggeration of the lavabeds region, see Cothran, *Remembering the Modoc War,* 165.

10. *Aftonbladet,* June 29, 1874.

11. *Aftonbladet,* August 7, 1874.

12. Oral communication from Martin Schultz, Swedish Ethnographic Museum, Stockholm, January 9, 2019.

13. Cothran, *Remembering the Modoc War,* 10–14.

14. Dan Jibréus, *White Fox' långa resa* (Stockholm: Fri Tanke förlag, 2013); Hjalmar Stolpe, "Den allmänna etnografiska utställningen II. Specialförteckning," *Tidskrift för antropologi och kulturhistoria* 3, no. 14 (1878): 1–192.

15. *Nya Svenska Amerikanaren,* October 25, 1873.

16. Cothran, *Remembering the Modoc War,* chapter 3; Philip J. Deloria, *Indians in Unexpected Places* (Lawrence: University Press of Kansas, 2004).

17. On Swedish-American newspapers, see Anna Williams, *Skribent i Svensk-Amerika: Jakob Bonggren, journalist och poet* (Uppsala: Avdelningen för litteratursociologi, 1991), 29–33. Williams discusses connections between Swedish-American newspapers and Swedish media. Although there were certainly contacts and exchanges, Swedish-American journalists, like Bonggren, expressed disappointment that there was not a greater interest in Sweden for news and cultural productions from Swedish America (48–54, 133–39).

18. See John M. Coward, *The Newspaper Indian: Native American Identities in the Press, 1820–90* (Urbana: University of Illinois Press, 1999).

19. *Dagens Nyheter,* June 21, 1873.

20. "En utdöd folkstam," *Svenska Familj-Journalen,* no. 6 (June 1873): 178, and no. 8 (August 1873), 232–34.

21. Ulf Jonas Björk, personal communication.

22. Fur, "Colonial Fantasies," 12.

23. Susanne Zantop, *Colonial Fantasies: Conquest, Family and Nation in Precolonial Germany, 1770–1870* (Durham, N.C.: Duke University Press, 1997), 7; Patricia Purtschert, Francesca Falk, and Barbara Lüthi, "Switzerland and 'Colonialism without Colonies': Reflections on the Status of Colonial Outsiders," *Interventions: International Journal of Postcolonial Studies* 18, no. 2 (2016): 1–17; Cothran, *Remembering the Modoc War,* 75; see also 78, 109, 139.

24. Dag Blanck, *Becoming Swedish American: The Construction of an Ethnic Identity in the Augustana Synod, 1860–1917* (Uppsala: Studia Historica Upsaliensia 182, 1997), 203–7; Birgitta Svensson, *Den omplanterade svenskheten: Kulturell självhävdelse och etnisk medvetenhet i den svensk-amerikanska kalendern Prärieblomman 1900–1913* (Gothenburg: Skrifter utgivna av Litteraturvetenskapliga institutionen, no. 27, 1994), 33–35.

25. "Minnen från de första svenska nybyggena i Norra Amerika," *Aftonbladet,* September 9, 1873. I have not been able to trace the original article in *Hemlandet.* However, it is mentioned and reviewed in *Den nya Svenska Amerikanaren* on June 21, 1873, and described as "a particularly worthy description of the relationship between our first emigrated countrymen to North America and the Indigenous people of the country. With praiseworthy discernment and not without a considerable amount of labor, the author has compiled the most important of the information occurring in major historical works about the first Swedes in America."

26. Blanck, *Becoming Swedish-American,* 188–90. The articles were later collected in a monograph titled *Förenta Staternas historia utarbetad för den svenska befolkningen i Amerika.*

27. Richard Bergström, *Svenska Bilder* (Stockholm: C. E. Fritze's Hofbokhandel, 1882), 68–69. First printed as "Nya Sverige: 1637–56" in *Svenska Familj-Journalen,* nos. 5–6 (1870), and reprinted in C. G. Starbäck, *Historiska Bilder* (Stockholm, 1871), and *Förr och Nu* (1871). Bergström's official biographer describes his folklorist scholarship (specifically on Swedish folk songs) as "critical and sober" and "free from poeticizing tendencies and desire to embellish." *Svenskt Biografiskt Lexikon,* https://sok.riksarkivet.se/Sbl/Presentation.aspx?id=18688.

28. Bergström, *Svenska Bilder,* 71.

29. See Adam Hjorthén, *Cross-Border Commemorations: Celebrating Swedish Settlement in America* (Amherst and Boston: University of Massachusetts Press, 2018). Ulf Jonas Björk finds that *Hemlandet*'s editorials (written by Johan A. Enander) supported its Republican leanings and frequently expressed criticism of government policies in relation to American Indians, but that a narrative of friendship with Indians—so frequent in Swedish commemorative writing—is all but absent in his editorials (personal communication).

30. It is striking that the most violent confrontation that involved American Indians and Scandinavian Americans, the Dakota War of 1862, received next to no reporting in Swedish newspapers or magazines and was not mentioned in emigrant literature. In contrast, *Hemlandet* reported heavily and extensively on the conflict. See Ulf Jonas Björk, "The Swedish Americans and the Sioux: How an Immigrant Group Viewed One Particular Indian Tribe," paper presented at Nordic Association for American Studies, 2007.

31. Björk, "Stories of America," 518.

32. Fur, "Colonial Fantasies."

33. Hugo Nisbeth, *Två år i Amerika* (Stockholm: Abr. Hirsch, 1874), 91–92.

34. Hugo Nisbeth, "Amerika ur emigrationssynpunkt," *Svenska Familj-Journalen* 13, no. 12 (1874): 366–67.

35. Nere A. Elfwing, "Äro Nord-Amerikas Indianer en af naturliga orsaker bortdöende stam?" *Ymer* (1879).

36. Cothran, *Remembering the Modoc War,* 164.

10

Double Life

American and Swedish Biographies of John Ericsson

Thomas J. Brown and Svea Larson

The most famous native of Sweden to live in the United States during the nineteenth century, John Ericsson personified for several constituencies the possibilities of cross-national exchange. Elected an honorary member of the Swedish Royal Academy of Sciences in 1847, eight years after he settled in New York City, he maintained a bilateral network of contacts in the fields of engineering and naval architecture well before the role of his ironclad warship *Monitor* in the 1862 battle of Hampton Roads propelled him to transatlantic fame. The spectacular repatriation of his remains after his death in 1889 prompted widespread reflection on engineers as prototypical modern figures. The burgeoning Swedish-American population of the late nineteenth century embraced him as a culture hero.[1]

The principal biographies of Ericsson published in the United States and Sweden during the early 1890s offered fresh interpretations of his contingent, creative mediation between political and social structures of his native land and the place where he spent most of his life. Neither author took a long-term interest in intersections between the two countries; neither sought to dramatize the international rise of professionalization or the experiences of immigrants. William Conant Church knew Ericsson well for more than twenty years before the octogenarian engineer asked the journalist to write an authorized life. Their relationship centered on the *Army and Navy Journal*, the weekly that Church founded in 1863 after brief service as a volunteer staff officer in the Union Army and would continue to edit for fifty-four years. From the outset Ericsson was among the prominent contributors, who also included Civil War commanders William T. Sherman and David G. Farragut, army reformer Emory Upton, and naval reformer Stephen B. Luce. Church started to learn about Sweden for his ambitious first book at the same time he also threw himself into the technical complexities of Ericsson's many inventions. Swedish biographer Claes Adelsköld similarly knew little of the United States beyond his interest in Ericsson. Born in 1824 into a family ennobled by Gustav III two generations earlier, Adelsköld worked as a civil engineer on railways and canals until his election to the First Chamber of the Riskdag in 1875. A prominent figure in aristocratic social circles, he was elected to the Royal Academy of Sciences in 1870 and became its president in 1891. Prior to his work on Ericsson he published travel accounts of journeys to Nordkap and Bornholm. He never visited America, and Church never visited Sweden.[2]

Although firmly rooted in their own countries, the two authors recognized Ericsson's entwining of the United States and Sweden as central to his legacy. Focused on the military contexts of Ericsson's personal identity and worldly achievement, Church highlighted his navigation of overlaps and parallels between the military organizations of the two countries. Ericsson's career pointed to the rewards of combining the best features of these social institutions. Adelsköld told Ericsson's story through the American trajectory of the self-made man, modified for Swedish readership. The immigrant's tale revealed a strategy for social mobility available at home. Both biographies envisioned their shared protagonist as the representative of a cultural borderland that invited further exploration.

Militarized Zone

Church stressed from his first pages that "John Ericsson was a Swede of Swedes," and over the subsequent two volumes he identified many ways in which Ericsson continued after permanent emigration at age twenty-three and arrival in the United States at age thirty-six to inhabit a biographical space between his birthplace and his eventual home.[3] The author nodded cautiously toward the racial theory that "the physical and intellectual vigor to which Greater Britain owes its glory is of Scandinavian origin" (1:1).[4] He ascribed to Ericsson character traits supposedly associated with Sweden, such as a fondness for flirtation; Church reported that "his native Swedish is said to lend itself to this form of expression more readily than any other European language, except the Spanish" (1:82). Church's principal interests were military, and he undertook the biography not merely as an act of friendship but as a record with lasting implications. His description of simultaneous Swedish and American identity was prescriptive. Ericsson embodied possibilities of intersection between the military formations of the two countries.

Church presented Ericsson as the product of Swedish military institutions that mirrored American experience. He regarded the engineer as a genius whose "comprehension of the science of motion was as intuitive as the perception of the harmonies of color with Raphael or those of musical expression with Beethoven" (1:21), but he emphasized that "fortune also favored him with exceptional opportunities for early training" (1:19). Those opportunities arose from family access to army and navy officers. Church detailed the instruction that the youthful Ericsson and his older brother Nils received from army and navy officers working on the Göta Canal, a project "military no less than commercial" that was conceived by Gustav (I) Vasa in the sixteenth century, promoted by Karl XII in the eighteenth century, and pushed to completion after Napoleon's marshal Jean-Baptiste Bernadotte took the Swedish throne as Karl XIV Johan (1:13). These apprenticeships and the Ericssons' subsequent acceptance as cadets in the Swedish Corps of Mechanical Engineers recalled the importance of the U.S. Army Corps of Engineers to the establishment of West Point and the proliferation of internal improvements projects in the early American republic.[5]

Church strengthened the thematic overlap by systematically underplaying the noble dominance of the Swedish military. Ericsson's decision to enter the army at the age of seventeen marked "a point in his career where two ways parted" (1:23) that offered a contrast between Nils and John. Nils, who did not join the army at this point, personified the aristocracy in this juxtaposition. He was "more fond of pleasure and society than his younger brother, less original and aggressive, and more disposed to follow the beaten track of conservatism" (1:23). The character sketch foreshadowed John's outrage at Nils's change of his surname to

Ericson upon elevation to the nobility (2:212). Church also presented Ericsson's enlistment as a defiance of his widowed mother and his highest Göta Canal patron, Count Baltzar von Platen. The author's version of the Royal Swedish Army was an American-style meritocracy rather than a calibration of social and martial rank.

Identification of Ericsson with the military extended to the most intimate aspects of life. The biographer reported that the young lieutenant did not marry his son's mother because "the laws of Sweden regulating the marriage of army officers were exacting" (1:32), although her superior social position was the real obstacle.[6] Church recognized that Ericsson prized his promotion to the rank of captain, a courtesy gesture that came after his migration to England, and used that title in social relations for the rest of his life (1:37–38). His coffin bore the name of his army regiment, "for with the service thus signified Ericsson's dearest recollections were associated" (2:324). In a survey of Ericsson's friendships, the author highlighted Swedish naval officer Axel Adlersparre, a nobleman by birth but "a rough, honest-hearted, and frank sailor" (2:237). Adlersparre had gained extensive experience on U.S. Navy vessels, including three years as a shipmate of Gustavus V. Fox, a crucial supporter of Ericsson's *Monitor* when Fox was assistant secretary of the navy during the Civil War. Church envisioned a martial fraternity of personal relationships and common sentimental attachments as well as professional expertise.

Ericsson's position within connected Swedish and American military cultures pointed toward a possible convergence in geopolitical thinking of the two nonaligned nations. Church endorsed Ericsson's view that Sweden's overriding security problem was the menace of Russian expansionism and that the gravest threat to the United States was the risk of European imperial dominance of the seas or intervention in the Western Hemisphere.[7] The biography championed armed preparedness as the solution to these dangers. The naval architect's goal "was to make the ocean such an uncomfortable place for the maritime bully, that a consensus of opinion would finally compel its recognition as neutral territory" (2:88). By developing a powerful defensive weapon, Ericsson became, in Church's judgment, "the prime minister of the tremendous forces shaping modern civilization" (2:313), and contributed as much as anyone "to realize the Christian ideal of a universal brotherhood, to formulate Tennyson's conception of 'the parliament of man, the federation of the world'" (2:257). Church drew the epigraph of his book from a letter in which Karl XIV Johan declared that "the virtuous man who faithfully fulfills his duties towards his native land has a right to recognition from his country. The philanthropist who devotes his light to the well-being of all humanity has the rights of a citizen throughout the world." The Swedish–American strategic junction was a militarized zone of peace.

Church's sympathetic portrait acknowledged that a dual life caused frustrations. By Ericsson's own reckoning, he came to think sixteen times faster in English than in Swedish (1:32). Despite the keen homeland interest in his inventions, he lacked the technical vocabulary to describe his work in his native language (2:280). Conversely, he did not establish some basic attachments after he settled in the United States. Church considered it "doubtful if he ever voted during the forty years of his American citizenship" (1:228). The New Yorker never visited Central Park and only saw the Brooklyn Bridge because his secretary took him there without notice while on a drive (2:309). This story of immigration did not focus on assimilation. Church noted that the pattern led to shortcomings in Ericsson's work. His deeply nostalgic identification with Sweden revealed a tendency to anchor in the past, and one of Church's challenges was to defend Ericsson's achievement in naval engineering despite the surge of enthusiasm for armored cruisers that had rendered monitors obsolete during the 1880s. At the same time, Ericsson's isolation from his immediate surroundings sometimes made him oblivious to market signals. Even in England many of his inventions were "more ingenious than profitable" (1:76), and toward the end of his life, "the habit of independence" prevented him from recognizing the usefulness of new methods (2:338).

The building of the USS *Monitor*, the centerpiece of Church's biography, represented the supreme synthesis of Ericsson's engagement with Sweden and America. The biography emphasized that the engineer had laid the foundations for the vessel not only in his training on the Göta Canal and in the army but more specifically through "observation of the behavior of raft-like structures in the storms sweeping over the Swedish lakes" (1:233, 262). He brought his lifelong interest in an armored, largely submerged vessel to maturity in a proposal that he sent via the Swedish consul in New York to Napoleon III for use against Russia during the

Crimean War, hoping to "cause the destruction of the fleets of the hereditary enemy of my native land" (1:241). He was therefore ready when Confederate attachment of iron plating to the salvaged USS *Merrimac* presented an emergency for the Union. Because Ericsson had worked out the idea of the *Monitor* on behalf of Sweden, he was able to realize his concept for the United States within the tight deadline that became fundamental to his success when the *Monitor* appeared in Hampton Roads on the day after the rechristened CSS *Virginia* sank the USS *Congress* and the USS *Cumberland* and left the USS *Minnesota* helplessly awaiting a final blow. Ericsson's youthful and ancestral memories of Sweden mingled with wartime patriotism and professional achievement in the United States.

This telling of the *Monitor* drama revealed Ericsson's dynamic, contingent negotiation of cross-national tendencies. His devotion to European ideals of systematic thought rather than American opportunism had shadowed his major project of the late antebellum period, an unsuccessful caloric engine. It was to a Swedish friend that he later grumbled that "I am an engineer and designer rather than an inventor. . . . Edison, in his ignorance, discovers or invents; Ericsson, acquainted with physical laws, constructs" (1:205). The pressures of the Civil War pushed him toward a more specific improvisation. Church quoted with approval the judgment of an expert on naval architecture that the *Monitor* was "peculiarly American" because so "admirably adapted to the special purpose which gave it birth" (1:264). In this instance, Swedish inspiration merged with American demand.

As Church confirmed in gleeful detail, acclaim for the *Monitor* made Ericsson the hero of two worlds. He became influential in naval planning in the United States and Sweden. The U.S. Navy made monitors (soon a generic term) the centerpiece of the fleet for the rest of the Civil War and in its aftermath. With Ericsson's encouragement and assistance, Sweden launched the HMS *John Ericsson* in 1865 and quickly added two more monitors. The American Academy of Arts and Sciences awarded him its Rumford Medal in 1862; Lund University recognized him with an honorary doctorate at the bicentennial of the institution in 1868. Stephen B. Luce, a founder of the U.S. Naval Institute, declared in a paper presented to the organization that the *Monitor* "exhibited in a singular manner the old

Norse element of the American Navy; Ericsson (Swedish, *son of Eric*) built her; Dahlgren (Swedish, *branch of a valley*) armed her; and Worden (Swedish, *worthy*) fought her."[8] The epic of Hampton Roads updated the tradition of Scandinavian sagas. "How the ancient skalds would have struck their wild harps in hearing such names in heroic verse!" Luce exclaimed. "How they would have written them in 'immortal runes'" (1:289).

Church's elaboration of his Swedish–American theme offered an alternative to a more obvious cross-national model of military development, American emulation of the British Navy. He noted that Ericsson had chosen his name for the *Monitor* to admonish Britain as well as France not to intervene in the Civil War, and he quoted Ericsson's claim that the vessel had accomplished this goal (1:254–55, 2:219). Ericsson's design differed radically from recent British ironclads, a contrast with political as well as military implications. Fox contended that the higher freeboard of the HMS *Warrior* represented a more hierarchical government than the unconventional, virtually submerged *Monitor*. "In a monarchy, a navy is part of the show that imposes upon the people," Fox wrote to Ericsson. "In a republic, it should be tolerated solely for its *fighting powers*" (2:63). For Church, bureaucracy was an even more ominous specter of convergent British and American military culture than monarchy. As David A. Mindell has observed, "the *Warrior* embodied state technology, the smart, thought-through solution of a secure officialdom."[9] The American parallels were the vessels designed by Ericsson's nemesis Benjamin F. Isherwood, chief of the U.S. Navy Bureau of Steam Engineering. Supportive as he was of the American military, the editor of the independent *Army and Navy Journal* would have enjoyed less influence in a more insular defense establishment. He gladly applauded his fellow freelance Ericsson for a creativity that both men found lacking in the British and American naval bureaucracies.

In Church's biography, Ericsson's amalgamation of Sweden and America was humorous, poignant, and sometimes disturbing. Like many intellectually ambitious biographers of the late nineteenth century, the author took his cue from the realist novel, and he did not hesitate to inform readers that Ericsson was "in every respect, a high-pressure engine" with an "ungovernable temper" and drank heavily until he was about fifty years old (1:85–86) or that his marriage was a failure and his relations with his illegitimate son were extraordinarily awkward (1:293–94, 2:213–19).[10] Most insistently, however, Church sought to tie his Swedish-American motif into a policy argument for a military culture that he hoped the United States would embrace. He read broadly about Sweden to offer a psychological study of a complex person but primarily to imagine a partly American and partly foreign domain that had produced one of the most meaningful successes of the Civil War.

Social Ladder

Adelsköld completed his biography in 1893, three years after publication of Church's work, and recognized the authorized life as the most comprehensive and reliable account because of its access to Ericsson's papers. But Adelsköld did not offer a translation of Church's book or an abridged paraphrase, as Swedish naval officer Oskar Stackelberg had presented his 1866 biography as an adaptation of P. C. Headley's *The Miner Boy and His Monitor* (1864), for which the wartime American writer also benefited from Ericsson's assistance.[11] Adelsköld borrowed Church's authority to reframe the Swedish-American hero's story for a Swedish audience. He, too, described a genius whose inventions would "rebuild the community and bring about revolutions of exchange between different peoples."[12] But the convergence he envisioned did not center on the military. Adelsköld instead told an American tale of social mobility in Sweden.

Although Adelsköld acknowledged Church's work on his second page and cited it frequently thereafter, he emphasized that his book also drew on Swedish sources. He saluted two recent profiles by well-known Swedish intellectuals, Otto Wilhelm Ålund's *John Ericsson: Några minnesblad* (1890) and Teofron Säve's *Minnesteckning öfver John Ericsson* (1890). More important, Adelsköld noted that he brought to bear the oral reminiscences of Count Adolf von Rosen, an important patron of Ericsson with whom Adelsköld had long been associated as a fellow aristocrat active in railway development. He did not bother to mention his even more informative friendship with Nils Ericson through their many years of collaboration in canal and railway projects. Adelsköld had never met Ericsson, but knowledgeable Swedish readers understood that the author could add considerably to Church's personal acquaintance and archival advantages.[13]

Adelsköld wrote his biography specifically for those knowledgeable readers. The work first appeared as an entry in the series of memorial profiles of members of the Royal Academy of Sciences, to which Adelsköld had delivered a eulogy in the presence of King Oscar II shortly after Ericsson's death. He had previously supplied a sketch of Nils Ericson for the Academy memorial series after the elder brother's death in 1870.[14] When he published his Ericsson biography in book form in 1894, the frontispiece was the medal of the engineer struck by the Academy for the April 1893 meeting to which Adelsköld presented his literary portrait. The medal, which featured a picture of the *Monitor* on the reverse, included an inscription reading "Swedish Royal Academy of Sciences to its most distinguished associate."[15]

The aristocrat's account of the Ericsson brothers' social background was crucial to his independent contribution to their story. Adelsköld's sketch of Nils identified the Ericssons' father as a miner at the time of their birth and indicated that their mother contributed to the household income by cooking for a workers' mess hall. This report may well have relied not only on Nils's reminiscences but also on Headley's *The Miner Boy and His Monitor,* an inspirational portrait for young readers that called John Ericsson the "miner-boy" and traced his rise from "obscurity." Adelsköld went on to claim that "the brothers Nils and John grew up in complete freedom, without obtaining any other instruction besides the scant teaching their mother could give in her spare time, and they could easily have become more neglected, if it weren't for the excellent Count von Platen, who put them to sensible work on the channel and brought them up at his own expense."[16] John Ericsson took offense at this characterization in an 1879 autobiographical letter to his son. He maintained that his father earned a sufficient income to support the family properly and played an important role in his son's education.

Adelsköld's biography of Ericsson dutifully reprinted the 1879 letter and praised the intelligence of both parents, but the aristocrat stood by his description of the family's social position. The future engineers, he wrote, descended from "an old mountain bunch, well aware of the family tree," comprised of "simple men known for morality, respect, honesty, and good natural sense" (5). He explained that his earlier error about Olof Ericsson's role in his sons' education resulted from a lack of information about

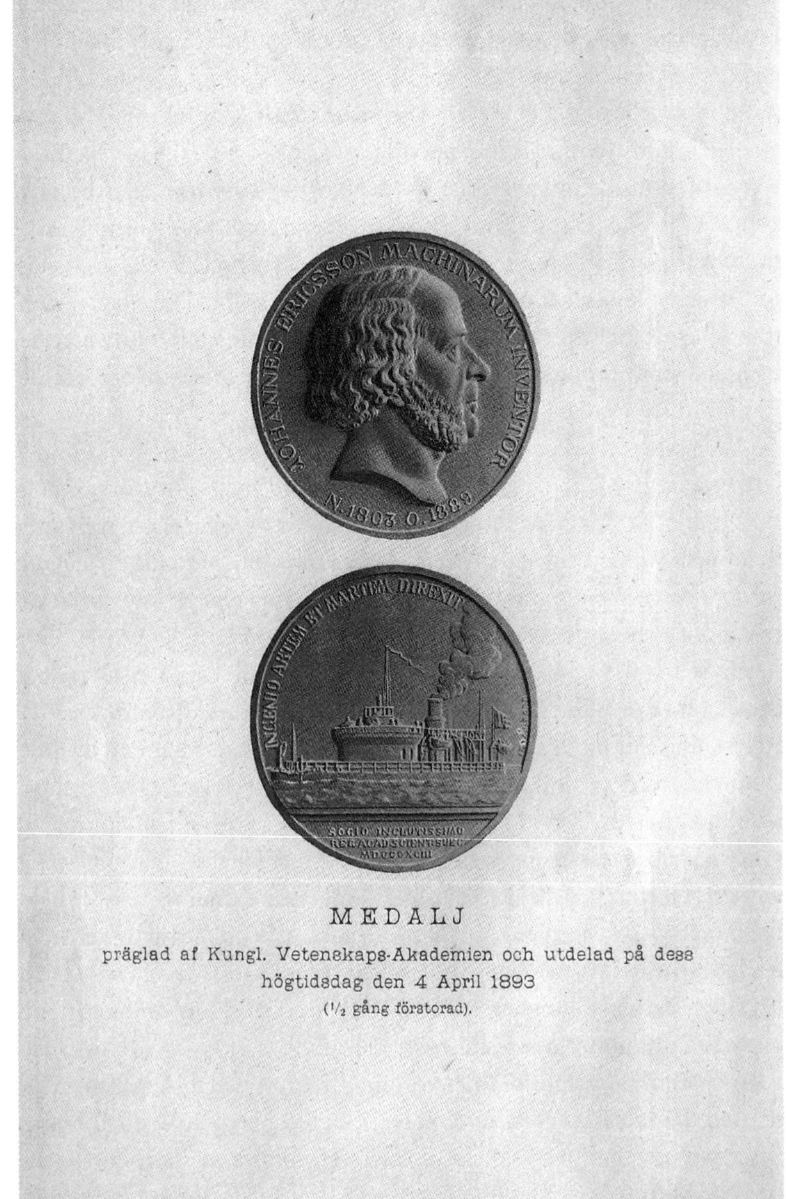

Frontispiece to Claes Adelsköld, *John Ericsson: Biografiska teckningar.* Courtesy of the Doe Memorial Library, University of California, Berkeley.

that specific point and from the author's eagerness "to clarify the formative days of the two outstanding brothers as self-made men" (11). To underscore that the self-made man was an American biographical paradigm, Adelsköld used the English-language coinage. His choice of terminology at this key point in the book, where the author found himself responding to his subject's criticism of Adelsköld's previous version of the story, stressed that the author applied an American arc to a Värmland childhood. For Adelsköld's saga of success, unlike Church's tale of military socialization, the similarities between the Ericsson brothers were fundamentally more important than the differences.

Adelsköld's plotline was part of a broader Swedish celebration of social mobility in the late nineteenth century. David Tjeder has found that "the American ideal of the self-made man" migrated to Sweden during the same decades that tens of thousands of Swedes migrated to the United States, often in search of economic opportunity. Benjamin Franklin, translated into Swedish since the late eighteenth century and recognized as a voice of political freedom, achieved fresh currency as an epitome of capitalist independence.[17] Financier, journalist, and politician André Oskar Wallenberg, the founder of Stockholms Enskilda Bank (now Skandinaviska Enskilda Banken, or SEB), became an early example of this cross-national modeling after he discovered Franklin's autobiography as a young Swedish naval officer on a merchant ship in Boston in the 1830s. Wallenberg frequently mentioned his admiration for the story of Franklin's ascent during his own remarkable expansion on a much more advantageous start in life.[18] Adelsköld and Wallenberg cooperated in First Chamber politics, and Adelsköld's daughter married Wallenberg's son in 1887. The parallel between the self-made inventors Ericsson and Franklin added a suggestive layer to Ericsson's antebellum election as a corresponding member of the Franklin Institute around the same time as his election to the Swedish Royal Academy of Sciences (124).

Adelsköld's description of the social ladder borrowed an American structure but featured Swedish steps. He highlighted the aristocratic patrons who opened a path for Ericsson. Unlike Church, he did not treat Ericsson's defiance of von Platen to enlist in the army as the instinct of a military man. A veteran of the Göta Artillery Regiment and the Värmlands Jäger Regiment, Adelsköld did not regard his subject as a personification of Swedish martial virtue. Ericsson's time as a soldier was a passionate young man's frolic in games, romance, and brotherhood. He lacked the requisite "subservience and respect for high command and authority" and willingness to become a "thoughtless machine" (28). For Adelsköld, von Platen's encouragement of Ericsson's engineering ambitions and discouragement of a military career showed that the paternalistic aristocrat knew Ericsson better than the young man knew himself.

Adelsköld also elaborated on the sponsorship of the royal family in an episode that Church did not mention. After his commanding officer submitted some of Ericsson's outstanding maps to Karl XIV Johan and the future Oscar I, the ensign quickly gained promotion and was thereafter in "the greatest favor with the great King and the Crown Prince." He continued to enjoy royal benefaction for years (28). Church in contrast described Ericsson as a "friend" of the Crown Prince in a tone that suggested a youthful camaraderie (37). Attention to the importance of royal backing recognized that the Swedish self-made man understood the hierarchical road to success.

Ericsson's most consistent patron in the biography was von Rosen, who "held much influence in vast social circles" (32). Drawing on personal conversations, Adelsköld added information unavailable in Church's work—for example, that von Rosen introduced Ericsson to English engineer John Braithwaite, the beginning of the partnership through which the young migrant began to make his reputation. Adelsköld stressed that von Rosen and Ericsson enjoyed a "heartfelt relationship" (239) and that the aristocrat often acted in a fatherly way toward his protégé even though they were only six years apart in age. On one occasion, while they were in England together, Ericsson declared that he would build ships that would "blow holes in the English wooden ships like children's toy weapons through cardboard." Von Rosen "smiled at what he thought to be a lot of lieutenant's boast" and replied, "Hush, my boy, you don't want to speak too loud or everyone in London will hear you and throw you in the Tower or Bedlam" (97).

Adelsköld's biographical portrait for the Royal Academy of Sciences did not share Church's literary ambitions to write a nonfiction counterpart to a realist novel. Adelsköld was considerably more discreet about Ericsson's engagement and the birth of his son, whom the author knew well through joint association with Nils Ericson and the railroad business. He barely mentioned Ericsson's wife but did cite an unpublished letter from John to Nils that suggested that the permanent separation may have had causes unknown to Church (56). In the American book, Ericsson's complicated personality and relationships reflected his unusual but important position as a link between two cultures. The Swedish biography, closer in design to Headley's variation on the rags-to-riches formula, offered an exemplary life. If Church took his epigraph from a letter of the Swedish king, Adelsköld took his English-language epigraph from Shakespeare: "He was a man take him for all in all / I shall not look upon his like again." Like Hamlet's father, Ericsson was a powerful ghost impelling current action.

Church and Adelsköld both shifted from writing books about Ericsson to promoting public monuments to Ericsson. Church urged the commissioning of a statue in New York, and he delivered orations at its unveiling in 1893 and replacement in 1903. Adelsköld was the driving force behind the dedication of memorials in Gothenburg in 1899 and Stockholm in 1901.[19] The parallel follow-up projects underscored the similarity between the two biographies. Eager to exalt Ericsson, the authors did not approach their shared subject from a lasting interest in connections between Sweden and America. In different ways, however, they made that theme central to the lives they wrote. Their stories of military structure and social mobility illustrate the power and multiplicity of narratives of cross-national exchange.

Notes

1. Dag Blanck, *The Creation of an Ethnic Identity: Being Swedish American in the Augustana Synod, 1860–1917* (Carbondale: Southern Illinois University Press, 2006), 177–78; Magnus Rodell, "Nationen och ingenjören: John Ericsson, medierna och publiken," in *Den mediala vetenskapen*, ed. Anders Ekström (Nora: Nya Doxa, 2004), 189–216; Eiko Tsuchida, "Science, Technology, and Swedish-American Identity: An Immigrant Acculturation in Chicago, 1890–1935," PhD thesis, University of Chicago, 2014, chapter 2.

2. The key sources on the two biographers are Donald Nevius Bigelow, *William Conant Church and* The Army and Navy Journal (New York: Columbia University

Press, 1952); and Claes Adelsköld, *Utdrag ur mitt dagsverks- och pro diverse-konto,* 4 vols. (Stockholm: Albert Bonniers, 1899–1901).

3. William Conant Church, *The Life of John Ericsson,* 2 vols. (London: Sampson, Low, Marston, Sarle, & Rivington, 1890), 1:3. Subsequent references to the biography are embedded parenthetically in the text.

4. Annette Kolodny, *In Search of First Contact: The Vikings of Vinland, the Peoples of the Dawnland, and the Anglo-American Anxiety of Discovery* (Durham, N.C.: Duke University Press, 2012), chaps. 3–4, traces this theory across the decades before the publication of Church's book.

5. Jon Scott Logel, *Designing Gotham: West Point Engineers and the Rise of Modern New York, 1817–1898* (Baton Rouge: Louisiana State University Press, 2016), is a recent treatment.

6. Olav Thulesius, *The Man Who Made the Monitor: A Biography of John Ericsson, Naval Engineer* (Jefferson, N.C.: McFarland and Co., 2007), 17.

7. Church's and Ericsson's assessments were widely shared. See Patrick Salmon, *Scandinavia and the Great Powers, 1890–1940* (Cambridge: Cambridge University Press, 1997), 27; Jay Sexton, *The Monroe Doctrine* (New York: Hill and Wang, 2011), 175–98.

8. John Worden, the commander of the *Monitor* at Hampton Roads, was the first president of the U.S. Naval Institute. John Dahlgren was chief of the U.S. Navy Bureau of Ordnance early in the Civil War and designer of the Dahlgren gun installed on the *Monitor.* The parenthetical translations are part of Luce's text as quoted by Church.

9. David A. Mindell, *Iron Coffin: War, Technology, and Experience aboard the USS Monitor,* expanded ed. (Baltimore: Johns Hopkins University Press, 2012), 12.

10. Scott E. Caspar, *Constructing American Lives: Biography and Culture in Nineteenth-Century America* (Chapel Hill: University of North Carolina Press, 1999), 303–18.

11. P. C. Headley, *The Miner Boy and His Monitor; or, the Career and Achievements of John Ericsson, the Engineer* (New York: William H. Appleton, 1864); Oskar Stackelberg, *John Ericsson och etthundra af hans uppfinningar* (Stockholm: P. A. Norstedt & Söner, 1866).

12. Claes Adelsköld, *John Ericsson: Biografiska teckningar* (Stockholm: P. A. Norstedt & Söner, 1894), 22. All translations by Svea Larson. Subsequent references to the biography are embedded parenthetically in the text.

13. Von Rosen and Ericson both figure prominently in Adelsköld, *Utdrag ur mitt dagsverks.*

14. Claes Adelsköld, "Nils Ericson, Friherre, Öfverste," in *Lefnadsteckningar öfver Kongl. Svenska Vetenskapsakademiens... ledamöter* (Stockholm: P.A. Norstedt & Söner, 1878–85), 2:63–87; Claes Adelsköld, "John Ericsson, Kapten och Civilingeniör," *Lefnadsteckningar öfver Kongl. Svenska Vetenskapsakademiens...*

ledamöter (Stockholm: P.A. Norstedt & Söner, 1886–94), 3:355–642; C. O. Troilus added a second tribute to Ericson: "Nils Ericson, Friherre, Öfverste," in *Lefnadsteckningar,* 3:221–79. Tore Frängsmyr, "Introduction: 250 Years of Science," in *Science in Sweden: The Royal Swedish Academy of Sciences, 1739–1989,* ed. Tore Frängsmyr (Canton, Mass.: Science History Publications, 1989), 6, notes the tradition of noble patronage of the Royal Academy.

15. "Medal of Ericsson," *American Journal of Numismatics* 29 (October 1894): 42.

16. Adelsköld, "Nils Ericson, Friherre, Öfverste," 63–64; Headley, *The Miner Boy and His Monitor,* 13, 33, 46.

17. David Tjeder, "When Character Became Capital: The Advent of the Self-Made Man in Sweden, 1850–1900," *Men and Masculinities* 5 (July 2002): 54, 64–65.

18. Göran B. Nilsson, *The Founder: André Oscar Wallenberg (1816–1886), Swedish Banker, Politician and Journalist,* trans. Michael F. Metcalf (Stockholm: Almqvist & Wiksell International, 2005), 33–34, 114, 237.

19. Thomas J. Brown and Svea Larson, "Swedish Migration, Naval Militarism, and Industrial Modernity: The John Ericsson Memorial in Washington, D.C.," *Winterthur Portfolio* 54 (summer/autumn 2020): 117–48.

11

Swedish-American Cookbooks

Linguistic Borderlands in Recipes

Angela Hoffman and Merja Kytö

In Swedish-American communities, multiple linguistic systems—that is, Swedish, English, and hybrid forms of the two languages—coexisted for many decades, from the latter portion of the 1800s through the mid-1900s and sometimes later, depending on the Swedish migration patterns in a given community.[1] In such immigrant communities, bilingual residents played an important role as linguistic intermediaries in translating words or expressions for the benefit of family members who were monolingual.[2] Bilingual residents also served as cultural intermediaries, explaining Swedish cultural practices to American-born persons. To serve as a cultural intermediary in an immigrant community involves making choices as to which language forms to use for naming cultural concepts. In the present study, we examine such vocabulary in the transmission of culinary culture across national borders and within a local neighborhood.

This essay examines dynamic patterns of bilingualism and language contact in immigrant communities.[3] The empirical portion of our investigation applies some of the central frameworks developed in historical sociolinguistics in order to understand language patterns in Swedish-American communities. We examine "specific purposes at a specific time in a specific historical context by people with a specific background."[4] Using material collected from the time period 1936 to 1996, we aim to identify the roles that Swedish-born women played in transmitting recipes across national borders to local American cookbooks, as well as the roles local cookbook committees performed in opening linguistic borders between Swedish and English. We present evidence that committee members were aware of the sociolinguistic tension that emerged when *fluid linguistic forms* were used as recipe names in cookbooks. Later we provide evidence that a complementary force, namely, the impetus to use *standardized language forms,* was also perceptible in Swedish-American cookbooks. We use microlevel studies to understand the wider sociolinguistic tensions relating to texts in circulation in Swedish-American immigrant communities.[5] We also situate the cookbooks in the timeline of books published for Swedish-American readers.

A Brief Historical Overview of Swedish-American Cookbooks

While religious texts were the first to be printed by Swedish-American publishers, cookbooks appeared in the title lists of such publishers already by the end of the nineteenth century.[6] In 1895, a bilingual Swedish-American culinary guide, *Svensk-amerikansk kokbok/Swedish-English Cookbook,* was published in Chicago by the Engberg-Holmberg Publishing House. Spanning nearly four hundred pages, the book presented recipes in a parallel language edition, enabling both Swedish- and English-speaking cooks to prepare a wide range of dishes from each other's traditions, namely, cooking practices with roots in Sweden and those associated with American tastes and styles of entertaining. Of special interest for our study of language patterns in Swedish-American cookbooks is that this publication visually separated Swedish and English in all portions of the book. For example, recipes in Swedish appeared on the left-hand side of each page, and English translations on the right.[7]

Swedish recipes were also conveyed to American households via the scores of cookbooks compiled and sold by Swedish-American churches and civic organizations.[8] The cookbooks, typically featuring several hundred recipes, spiral-bound, self-published and printed locally, represent the effort of many volunteers working in various capacities. Individual members of women's groups submitted cherished recipes to a cookbook committee, who in turn collated the submissions and worked with illustrators to design the decorative elements of the pages and covers. Many cookbooks in Swedish-American communities contain an introduction to the "Swedish" style of cooking represented in the recipes, offering clues to readers about the meaning of the printed recipes for family dinners and for entertaining guests in America. (With the use of quotation marks placed around the word *Swedish,* we signal a cultural link to Sweden rather than to the Swedish language.)

Recipe names in these Swedish-American cookbooks belong to the domestic sphere rather the official domain of language use; thus, the names of food dishes are drawn from everyday uses of language.[9] As will become apparent, some of the recipe names, lists of ingredients, and descriptions of cooking preparations in the self-published cookbooks have obvious links to cookbooks published in Sweden by Swedish publishing houses. Immigrants from Sweden living in Minneapolis who were experienced cooks presumably knew these books well, and some of these persons served as culinary couriers, thanks to their social network ties in the Swedish-American communities. Further, some of these cooks copied the recipes and sometimes lightly modified them before submitting them to cookbook committees. In turn, the local cookbooks then became a conduit that continued to transmit the Swedish culinary practices to the Swedish-American neighborhoods. As many Swedish-American culinary practices have been shaped by individuals who disseminated recipes through their social networks, we see reason to believe that Swedish food culture was not simply transported across the border to America as an amalgam of general ideas concerning traditional Swedish cooking, but were conveyed by some cooks to the cookbook committees with whom they had contacts. In a qualitative case study in the next section, we focus on a cook, a woman who was born in Sweden in the 1890s and migrated to Minneapolis in the 1920s, who gained recognition for her culinary knowledge. We also briefly mention another Swedish-born woman who migrated to the United States at the same time. Our analysis traces how cookbook committees acknowledged and showcased the culinary knowledge of these two women.

In the Footsteps of Emma Henell, Swedish Immigrant Cook

Our case study traces the stages of transmission of selected recipes attributed to an individual cook. We follow how the names of her recipes were anglicized and also how processes of language hybridization became symbolically linked to Swedish immigrant heritage.

One of the early cookbooks printed in Minneapolis to which we have access was compiled by volunteers affiliated with the American Swedish Institute: *Swedish Recipes Compiled by Ladies Auxiliary Swedish Institute Male Chorus 2601 Oakland Ave., Minneapolis, Minnesota,* printed in 1942. This title not only identifies the group that compiled the recipes but also the neighborhood in which the organization was located. Such detailed information signals how specifically local and "Swedish" the Ladies Auxiliary intended their publication to be. The cookbook contains 162 recipes printed on sixty-three pages. Fourteen of these recipes, approximately 9 percent of the total number of printed recipes, were attributed to Mrs. Axel Henell, that is, Emma Henell.[10] She also contributed the contents in the final portion of the cookbook titled "A Word about the Swedish Smorgasbord."[11]

Emma Justina Henell was born in Ljusdal, Sweden, in 1892 and married Axel Vilhelm Henell in 1918. The couple immigrated to St. Paul, Minnesota, in 1927, when Emma was thirty-five. Emma and Axel Henell became members of the Svithiod Lodge in 1934, a mutual aid society for Swedes living in the United States, and joined the local chapter Harmony Lodge in Minneapolis. According to the records of the lodge, Emma's employment was "Husarbete" (housework), and Axel's was "Machinist." Several decades later, in 1965, when the Henells were in their mid-seventies, they returned to Sweden.

Henell's recipes for Swedish dishes appear in each of the Minneapolis cookbooks we have located.[12] The extent of Henell's contributions to the 1942 cookbook, not the least with respect to her role in having contributed information on the Swedish *smörgåsbord* and a suggested menu, gives us reason to believe that she was respected for her knowledge of Swedish cooking. A *smörgåsbord,* in traditional Swedish culinary practice, includes, for example, a selection of appetizer-type dishes arranged on a buffet table. We trace the likely path of transmission of eight of the recipes attributed to her and printed in the 1942 cookbook. Some of the recipes correspond (sometimes word for word) to the names, lists of ingredients, and instructions for preparations as presented in recipes in *The Princesses' Cook Book,* written by Jenny Åkerström. Published in 1936 by the Albert Bonnier Publishing House in New York, Åkerström's book was the English-language version of Åkerström's authoritative culinary guide *Prinsessornas Kokbok: Husmanskost och helgdagsmat (The Princesses' Cookbook: Traditional Home Cooking and Holiday Dishes)* published by Bonniers in Stockholm, also in 1936. Åkerström's books were, of course, not the only major cookbooks published in Sweden in the first decades of the twentieth century.[13] Crucially, however, for our purposes of tracing the movement of recipe contents, we note that recipes in Åkerström's cookbooks closely match some of the recipes that were attributed to Henell. Åkerström was well known for her cooking school in Stockholm, which was reported to have been attended by a number of crown princesses, and we presume that Henell was eager to share with Minneapolis readers her knowledge of the recipes.[14]

We now focus in greater detail on Henell's recipes that also appear in Åkerström's books. The list presents a chronological view of such recipe names. In the left-hand column we list some recipe names in Åkerström's Swedish-language cookbook printed in 1936; in the middle column we present the corresponding recipe names in Åkerström's book that was published in the same year for an English-speaking audience; and in the right-hand column we include the recipe names for the same dishes as submitted by Henell. The names of the recipes as reproduced in the columns maintain some of the conventions as printed in the books.[15] In Åkerström's book in Swedish, an asterisk placed at the beginning of the recipe name indicates that the recipe was a particularly popular dish among the pupils in her cooking school. Another convention used to a certain extent in both editions by Åkerström is that a recipe name (in line 1) is accompanied by additional information about the dish (in line 2). In some cases, the information in line 2 indicates the number of servings, known as *portioner* in Swedish, abbreviated as *port.*, whereas other recipe names include an additional name for the dish. The convention of presenting an additional name for a dish is particularly interesting for our study, as we note that, to some extent, Henell continued following the practice, and the second names she provided designated a name in Swedish. We believe that she was interested in communicating dual linguistic forms.

We use the correspondences made visible in these three columns to track how recipes moved from Stockholm to New York before continuing

Åkerström, *Prinsessornas kokbok* (Stockholm, 1936)	Åkerström, *The Princesses Cook Book* (New York, 1936)	*Swedish Recipes* (Minneapolis, 1942) [eight recipes attributed to Mrs. Axel Henell]
*Ansjovisrätt à la Irma (6 portioner)	Anchovies à la Irma (6 servings)	Anchovies a la Irma
Kokning av kräftor	To Cook Crayfish	To Cook Crawfish
Får i kål (6 portioner)	Lamb with Cabbage—*Får i Kål* (6 servings)	Lamb in Cabbage (Far i kal)
Kalops (6 portioner)	Collops (6 servings)	Collops (Kalops)
Svensk omelett (4–6 portioner)	Swedish Omelet (4–6 servings)	Swedish Omelette
Plättar (6 portioner)	Swedish Pancakes—*Plättar* (6 servings)	Swedish Pancakes (Plattar)
Enkel klimp till buljong (6 portioner)	Molded Dumplings (6 servings)	Molded Dumplings (Svensk Klimp)
*Solöga (Falsk kaviar)	False Caviar—*Solöga*	Ox Eye (False Caviar or Ox oga)

Names of recipes for corresponding dishes in three cookbooks. Asterisks are retained from the source materials.

the path to the Ladies Auxiliary in Minneapolis. The Swedish lexis, that is, the vocabulary, in the cookbook printed in Minneapolis does not contain instances of the Swedish orthographic characters *å, ä,* and *ö.* The absence of these characters is categorical in the cookbook, suggesting that the cookbook committee, the typist, and/or the printer of the book, rather than Henell and other recipe contributors, made a choice to disregard diacritics in Swedish lexis. We suspect that the orthographic choices were practical ones in that the typist/typesetter used an American typewriter without the Swedish characters.[16] The choice to bypass the diacritics must have applied to the content in the verso of the title page of the cookbook, as a table prayer in Swedish appears there without *å, ä,* and *ö.* The prayer text reads as follows, with our explanations in brackets: "I Jesu namn Till bords vi ga [= gå], Valsigna [= Välsigna] Gud Den mat vi fa [= få]. Amen." An English rendering of the prayer text accompanies the Swedish prayer: "In Jesus' name Our board [= table] is set, And may God bless The food we get. Amen." Later in the book, we observe that the word *Smörgåsbord* has been anglicized as *Smorgasbord.*[17]

Orthographic anglicization is evident in recipe names when the Swedish characters *å, ä,* and *ö* were substituted with *a* and *o.* One of the striking anglicisms in the rightmost column of our list is the rendering of the Swedish name of the recipe "Lamb in Cabbage" written as *(Far i kal).*[18] As the Swedish diacritics are absent, the name *(Far i kal)* is only notionally Swedish. This is because the orthography in Swedish for "lamb in cabbage" is *får* (lamb) *i* (in) *kål* (cabbage). The orthography of the notional Swedish creates what we call sociolinguistic tension. Persons who know Swedish will understand that *Far i kal* is a "Swedish" rendering, but they would reasonably ask, "What is *Far* (Father) doing in the recipe?" The recipe name only marginally retains its Swedish traces, but as mentioned these traces are notional and not the lexis that native speakers of Swedish would use. When *Får i kål* is recast as *Far i kal,* the change in orthography renders the words into hybrid forms that exist in liminal linguistic space, that is, an orthographic space that is neither Swedish nor English.[19] Readers who do not know or cannot guess what the Swedish words are would face a challenge in locating the words in a Swedish–English dictionary. When orthography does not correspond to one language, the naming patterns have open and fluid borders. In practical terms, the names designating recipes would not, of course, influence the taste of the dishes, but in symbolic terms, names do matter in the cookbooks. In some cases, the names signal a beyond-the-border quality that readers perhaps will find more attractive, exotic, and authentic.

The anglicization process influencing the recipe names that Henell submitted to the 1942 cookbook is not the only type of hybridization we identify in Swedish-American cookbooks. What follows is a categorization of some of the ways we find that recipe names in Swedish-American cookbooks have been rendered with patterns showing open boundaries between languages. Note that the ordinal numbers identifying the categories are not to be understood as necessarily a sequential process but as different types of anglicization.

The first categorization concerns orthographic anglicization. Recipe contributors submitted names of recipes in standard Swedish orthography but typists and/or typesetters replaced the Swedish vowels *å, ä,* and *ö* with *a* and *o* in the production process. Examples: *Kräm* (Swedish Grape Pudding) as *Kram*; *Gräddkaka* (Sour Cream Soufflé) as *Graddkaka*; *Bröd* (Bread) as *Brod*; *Herrgårdssås* as *Herrgardssas* (Swedish Salad Dressing). The same process has likely applied to the concept *smörgåsbord* having become *smorgasbord.*

Second, there are cases of putative misinterpretations of words, likely by typists and typesetters not familiar with Swedish words. Recipe contributors may have submitted recipes in handwritten forms that were misinterpreted or misread during the production of the cookbooks. Examples of some potential misreadings are *Talsh Ostkaka* for *Falsk ostkaka* (= false cheesecake) and *Smorgas Bordet* for *Smörgåsbord.*[20]

A third way of rendering recipe names is through adaptations to the orthography of compound words and phrases. Recipe contributors may have submitted Swedish recipe names in compound forms not corresponding to standard Swedish orthography. Examples: *Godakakor* (for *Goda kakor,* "Good Cookies"), *Druv och Ananas Sallad* (for *Druv och ananassallad,* "Grape and Pineapple Salad"), *Kryddråglimpa* (for *Kryddig råglimpa,* in which the English-language name is rendered as "Rye Bread with Seeds").[21] It may also be the case that the examples in this third category have involved lexical and/or stylistic innovations that emerged when the recipe contributors wanted to mark a special meaning.

The fourth categorization concerns combined lexis. Recipe contributors have sometimes purposefully altered other patterns in the naming of Swedish recipes. They may have actively created English-influenced versions of Swedish recipes. Examples of combined lexis in the *Var Så God* cookbook include *Swedish Smörgåsbord Rice, My Favorite Pepparkakor,* and *Hjorthornssalt Cookies.*[22]

The processes just described create lexical patterns corresponding neither to standard Swedish nor to English. Swedish-American recipe names exhibit traces of liminality when linguistic forms are suspended between the borders of two languages. Evidence of the first and second processes is visible in the early cookbooks (those published in 1942 and

1956) but virtually disappears in community cookbooks starting in the 1980s.[23] The third and fourth processes can be attributed to contact with English. Recipe names that are rendered in lexis from English and Swedish are mixed forms that preserve transitional borderlands.

Important clues that reveal how Swedish Americans viewed the hybrid and liminal language forms can be found in the introductions written by cookbook committees. In the cookbook published in 1980 by women affiliated with the American Swedish Institute, the committee members describe how they conceptualized their editorial work in producing the cookbook and the process by which they collated so-called heritage recipes from individuals.[24] The committee also explains that they purposefully preserved some nonstandard Swedish in the names of the recipes printed:

> As the cook book committee met to prepare the book, we asked ourselves what is a Heritage recipe? We agreed it could not be called 'heritage' unless it reflected the individuality of the person who sent it. It was important that it be identified with that person's name. It meant a minimum of editing, adhering as much as possible to the exact wording and method as was suggested in the recipe that was received. We did not want to lose this "touch." Very often, the title of the recipe reflected the phonetic rather than the correct Swedish spelling; or, the commonly used title in their neighborhood evolving from the influence of other ethnic groups. The original 'recipes' and 'know how' immigrated, unprinted, with the first member of the family to come to the new land as early as the late 19th century.[25]

The cookbook committee signals that the linguistic "touch" is different from the majority languages English and Swedish. Our interpretation of the committee's decision is that they preserved the borderlands visible in lexis and orthography when they consciously decided not to standardize the language forms. The committee thus preserved linguistic forms from the immigrant community and assigned such recipe names social meaning, namely, as being linked to "heritage."[26]

In the extract from the introduction to the cookbook, the committee emphasizes that the recipes are tied to the cooking know-how of the contributors and neighborhoods. Further, the committee signals that local meaning was a central concern. They explain that the transmission of the names of recipes came from the grass roots in that "the title of the recipe reflected the phonetic rather than the correct Swedish spelling; or, the commonly used title in their neighborhood evolving from the influence of other ethnic groups."[27] Examination of the recipe names in *Var Så God* reveals that the so-called phonetic spelling of Swedish words appears to be limited mostly to the composition of compound words in Swedish.

To explore further how immigrant lexis has become symbolic of heritage, we turn to Jeffrey Shandler's notion of postvernacular language and culture. Shandler's theoretical framework, based on investigations of the Yiddish language in, for example, Jewish American communities, helps account for how old language forms become treasured. In Shandler's framework, a *vernacular* language is one that is widely used in daily life, whereas a *postvernacular* language is one whose lexis increasingly carries symbolic value. Shandler explains how Yiddish, for *some* speakers in *certain* communities, has moved from being a widely used language to becoming mainly symbolic:

> What most distinguishes postvernacular Yiddish is its semiotic hierarchy; unlike vernacular language use, in the postvernacular mode the language's secondary, symbolic level of meaning is always privileged over its primary level. In other words, in postvernacular Yiddish the very fact that something is said (or written or sung) in Yiddish is at least as meaningful as the meaning of the words being uttered—if not more so.[28]

For many decades, the Swedish language in Minneapolis has been, and still is for many speakers, a *vernacular* language, in Shandler's sense, as it truly serves as a language used in daily life. For recipe contributors who emigrated from Sweden, such as Emma Henell, the Swedish language was indeed their vernacular. Yet, for others in the Swedish-American community—likely for those whose grandparents or great-grandparents had immigrated from Sweden to Minnesota—the Swedish language may have instead a *postvernacular* status in the sense that Swedish lexis carries symbolic value when English is the main language for such speakers in everyday interactions. We surmise that by 1980, at least some members of cookbook committees were embracing the symbolic value of "Swedish" recipe names. Shandler's conceptualization of postvernacular language and culture helps us understand the impetus for printing recipe names rendered in hybrid forms. In the same cookbooks, however, we see evidence that many other recipe names were expressed in standard Swedish. The cookbooks evince the dual forces of hybridization as well as language standardization in the use of Swedish lexis and orthography.

Lilly Lorénzen, Another Culinary and Linguistic Courier

Briefly, we turn to a recipe contributor who influenced language standardization processes in many ways: Lilly Lorénzen, who was born in Hakarp, Jönköping County in 1893 and emigrated to America in 1923, when she was thirty years old. She was known in Swedish-American networks in Minneapolis for her dedication as a teacher of the Swedish language at the University of Minnesota and at the American Swedish Institute, and for her enthusiasm in explaining Swedish cultural practices to Swedish Americans.[29] The 1980 *Var Så God* cookbook printed three recipes in her name: "Lilly Lorénzen's Smoked Whitefish Hor's d'oeuvre," "Lilly Lorénzen's Quiche Lorraine," and "Lilly Lorénzen's Cookies Mandelmusslor," all submitted by Bergith Atkinson.[30] Reproduced here is a scanned image of the cookie recipe, providing a glimpse of how the cookbook committee used the separate lines of the recipe names to indicate two separate dimensions for English and for Swedish (cf. Henell's two-line approach in

Lilly Lorénzen's Cookies
Mandelmusslor

1 c butter	2 c flour
½ c sugar	1 tsp almond extract
1 egg	

Cream butter and sugar. Add egg and sifted flour and extract. Work until thoroughly mixed. Chill the dough. Press dough the size of walnut into ungreased fluted forms. Bake at 350° for 10 to 15 min. Remove from forms when slightly cooled. Makes about three dozen cookies.

Bergith Atkinson

Recipe for "Lilly Lorénzen's Cookies," in her cookbook *Var Så God* (1980).

naming recipes). The first line of the recipe name showcases Lilly Lorénzen, the local Swede, while the second line identifies the kind of cookie recipe with the Swedish name *Mandelmusslor*, an almond-flavored sugar cookie. The layout of the recipe names creates spatial zones separating two visual fields. We also note that the recipe-naming patterns contain standard forms; none of the four naming patterns described in the categories in the preceding section are found here. The recipe shows fixed rather than fluid linguistic borders.

Later in the same cookbook, the committee chose to print extracts from Lorénzen's book *Of Swedish Ways*, extracts in which the cultural practices of "Swedish Lucia Day" and "Fettisdagsbullar" (Shrove Tuesday Buns) are described.[31]

Swedish-American Cookbooks: From Separate Language Zones to Borderlands

Contrasting with a practice in the 1890s, in which Swedish-American cookbooks were designed as parallel language editions, with Swedish- and English-language contents maintained in separate zones on the pages printed by Engberg-Holmberg, many later cookbooks were designed by local committees in part as a way to showcase the knowledge and individuality of cooks. In our analysis of the local cookbooks, we used the concept of borderlands as a heuristic tool to help us understand how individuals helped transmit "Swedish" culinary culture to local Swedish-American networks in a developing book market. We traced how Swedish-born Emma Henell submitted eight recipes from Åkerström's well-known books to a community cookbook. In doing so, Henell helped continue transmitting Swedish culinary practices to a Swedish-American network in Minneapolis. Our analysis of recipe names in the earlier period of Minneapolis cookbooks (1942) showed how linguistic borders between the Swedish and English languages were fluid, due to anglicization and other language hybridization patterns. We observed, for example, that the recipe name rendered as *Far i kal* (Lamb in Cabbage) was no longer strictly Swedish when the diacritics were removed; nor did the recipe name become English, and that it hovered in liminal linguistic space. We also located and categorized some additional linguistic phenomena evident in Swedish-American cookbooks, identifying ways that cookbook committees helped to create symbolic heritage. Some recipe contributors and cookbook committees actively created notion, using linguistic phenomena to signal that recipe names existed in a midway dimension, that is, in a liminal space. Even so, quite a few other recipe names for "Swedish" dishes have been rendered in standard Swedish. We briefly illustrated this movement toward standardized names of recipes by turning to some examples attributed to another Swedish cook, Lilly Lorénzen. The recipes submitted in her name gave us an opportunity to track patterns that were standard. In the recipes that were attributed to her, we see that the English and Swedish languages are kept separate, not only at the phrasal level, but also in the lines of the layout of the recipe name. To some extent, "Swedish" culinary culture in the 1980s is communicated in stabilized, standard Swedish, and Lorénzen's legacy was apparent.[32]

We observed that language hybridization and standardization are linguistic forces that have worked in different strengths in different situations. By applying the conceptual ideas of national and linguistic borderlands to our material, we gained insights concerning language forms: English and Swedish appear in recipe names, but in different combinations, to a great extent dependent upon the editorial choices of the volunteer cookbook committees and the practices of typists/typesetters. While our study has focused on linguistic patterns produced by these committees and some of the individual recipe contributors, in our historical sociolinguistic study we also need to remember that the language patterns in the local cookbooks were a part of the larger context of Swedish–American cultural relations. We know that culinary traditions from Sweden have been transplanted to American homes thanks to a great extent to the production of recipe books of varying kinds. Along with this process of transplantation, elements of the Swedish language have been adopted by American cooks and their families. Sometimes the Swedish language forms reveal signs of hybridization, displaying various patterns of anglicization in recipe names; elsewhere, the names appear in standard Swedish forms. Overall, the contribution of our study has been to highlight the linguistic aspects of the relations between Sweden and America in the domestic sphere and to uncover the pathways that some cherished recipe names have taken across national and textual borders.

Notes

1. Multigenerational bilingualism in Swedish-American communities is examined in Nils Hasselmo, *Amerikasvenska* (Stockholm: Esselte Studium, 1974); and Angela Hoffman (Karstadt), *Tracking Swedish-American English: A Longitudinal Study of Linguistic Variation and Identity* (Uppsala: Acta Universitatis Upsaliensis, 2003). For an introduction to intergenerational bilingualism and heritage languages, see Guadalupe Valdés, "Heritage Language Students: Profiles and Possibilities," in *Heritage Languages in America: Preserving a National Resource,* ed. Joy Kreeft Peyton, Donald A. Ranard, and Scott McGinnis (McHenry, Ill.: Center for Applied Linguistics, 2001), 37–77.

2. An analysis of how a young bilingual man served as a linguistic intermediary in correspondence to his elders living in Sweden is presented in Angela Hoffman and Merja Kytö, "Varying Social Roles and Networks on a Family Farm: Evidence from Swedish Immigrant Letters, 1880s to 1930s," *Journal of Historical Sociolinguistics* 5, no. 2 (October 2019), special issue on "Historical Heritage Language Ego-Documents: From Home, from Away, and from Below," ed. Joshua Brown, https://doi.org/10.1515/jhsl-2018-0031.

3. We thank the editors and an external reviewer for their insightful comments and suggestions. We are grateful to Renée Lund Danielson, Barbara Hoffman, Muriel Johnson, Bruce Karstadt, Gunilla Wallén, and Ulla Åkesson for helping us locate cookbooks. Renée Lund Danielson and Jill Seaholm helped us locate genealogical information on recipe contributors.

4. The quotation on the historical contextualization of linguistic patterning appears in Stephan Elspaß, "Between Linguistic Creativity and Formulaic Restriction: Cross-Linguistic Perspectives on Nineteenth-Century Lower Class Writers' Private Letters," in *Letter Writing in Late Modern Europe,* ed. Marina Dossena and Gabriella Del Lungo Camiciotti (Amsterdam: Benjamins, 2012), 47.

5. See especially Päivi Pahta, Minna Palander-Collin, Minna Nevala, and Arja Nurmi, "Language Practices in the Construction of Social Roles in Late Modern English," in *Social Roles and Language Practices in Late Modern English,* ed. Päivi Pahta, Minna Nevala, Arja Nurmi, and Minna Palander-Collin (Amsterdam: Benjamins, 2010), 1–27.

6. The history of the Chicago-based Engberg-Holmberg company can be found in Raymond Jarvi, "The Rise and Fall of the House of Engberg-Holmberg," in *Swedish-American Life in Chicago: Cultural and Urban Aspects of an Immigrant People, 1850–1930,* ed. Philip J. Anderson and Dag Blanck (Uppsala: Acta Universitatis Upsaliensis, 1991), 255–63.

7. Further details on the 1895 cookbook appear in Angela Hoffman and Merja Kytö, "The Linguistic Landscapes of Swedish Heritage Cookbooks in the American Midwest, 1895–2005," *Studia Neophilologica* 89, no. 2 (2017): 261–86.

8. We examined the following cookbooks in the present study: Elise Adelsköld, Sigrid Westfelt, and Ingeborg Zethelius, *Hemmets stora kokbok och rådgivare*

(Stockholm: Lars Hökerbergs Bokförlag, 1927); Jenny Åkerström, *Prinsessornas kokbok: Husmanskost och helgdagsmat* (Stockholm: Albert Bonniers förlag, 1936); Jenny Åkerström, *The Princesses' Cook Book: From the Original Swedish "Prinsessornas kokbok,"* trans. and ed. Gudrun Carlson (New York: Albert Bonnier Publishing House, 1936); Bethany Teachers' Wives, *Measure for Pleasure: Featuring Hyllnings Fest Smörgåsbord, Lindsborg, Kansas* (Lindsborg, Kans.: Bethany College, 1961); The Bethany Dames Club, *The New Measure for Pleasure* (Lindsborg, Kans.: Bethany College, 1970); Ladies Auxiliary, *Swedish Recipes Compiled by Ladies Auxiliary Swedish Institute Male Chorus 2601 Oakland Ave., Minneapolis, Minnesota* (Minneapolis: American Swedish Institute of Swedish Arts Literature and Science, 1942); Lilly Lorénzen, *Of Swedish Ways* (Minneapolis: Dillon Press, 1964); *Var Så God: Heritage and Favorite Recipes & Handbook of Swedish Traditions* (Minneapolis: American Swedish Institute, 1980, 1996); Kerstin Wenström, *Husmoderns kokbok: Det borgerliga hemmets kokbok,* new ed. (Stockholm: B. Wahlströms Bokförlag, 1932); Women's Club of the American Swedish Institute, *Swedish Recipes: Compiled by the Women's Club of the American Swedish Institute, Minneapolis, Minn.* (Minneapolis: Women's Club of American Swedish Institute, 1956). As the Minneapolis cookbook committees used capital letters in the phrase *Var Så God* in the main title of their cookbook, we retain their convention when referring to contents in the editions of the book. When we present names of recipes, we purposefully retain the spelling and the use of other patterns, such as the use of diacritics (or the absence of such) and spacing between words, as adopted by the cookbook committees.

9. In addition to Hoffman and Kytö, "The Linguistic Landscapes of Swedish Heritage Cookbooks in the American Midwest, 1895–2005," see Angela Hoffman and Merja Kytö, "Heritage Swedish, English, and Textual Space in Rural Communities of Practice," in *Selected Proceedings of the 8th Workshop on Immigrant Languages in the Americas (WILA 8),* ed. Jan Heegård Petersen and Karoline Kühl (Somerville, Mass.: Cascadilla Press, 2018), 44–54.

10. In some of these recipes, the woman's surname is spelled "Hennell," which we believe is a typographical error. We have not yet located Emma Henell's maiden name in genealogical databases.

11. Ladies Auxiliary, *Swedish Recipes,* 62–63.

12. Henell's *smörgåsbord* menus appear in each of the Minneapolis cookbooks we have located to date (*Swedish Recipes,* 1942, 1956; *Var Så God* 1980, 1996). Starting with the 1980 cookbook, cookbook committee members included a passage describing Henell's culinary knowledge; see *Var Så God* (1980), 223–24.

13. Other major cookbooks published in Sweden around the same time include Adelsköld, Westfelt, and Zethelius, *Hemmets stora kokbok och rådgivare,* and Wenström, *Husmoderns kokbok.*

14. The introductory pages of Åkerström's *Prinsessornas kokbok* and *The Princesses' Cook Book* feature the names of the princesses who attended her cooking school (Jenny Åkerströms Husmodersskola in Stockholm).

15. For the sake of readability in the figure, we chose not to retain the use of such conventions as numbered recipe names and boldface type (some of the conventions used in Åkerström's cookbooks) and the all-capital letters (a convention used in *Swedish Recipes* [1942]).

16. In one of the cookbooks we analyzed in Lindsborg, Kansas, the diacritics for the Swedish letters *å, ä,* and *ö* appear to have been added by hand in the production process. See Bethany Teachers' Wives, *Measure for Pleasure.*

17. Anglicization is also evident in the surnames of recipe contributors (e.g., *Hellstrom* for "Hellström" and *Sjoberg* for "Sjöberg"). We elected not to analyze the orthography of the surnames for the present study as we suspect that Swedish Americans had Americanized (or had been prompted by immigration officials to alter) the spelling of their family names when they immigrated.

18. We use double quotation marks (for example, "Lamb in Cabbage") to indicate the English renderings of the Swedish recipe names in the cookbooks.

19. Presentations of liminality may be found, e.g., in Bjørn Thomassen, "Liminality," in *Encyclopedia of Social Theory,* ed. Austin Harrington, Barbara L. Marshall, and Hans-Peter Müller (London: Routledge, 2006), 322–23; and Victor Witter Turner, *The Ritual Process: Structure and Anti-structure* (New Brunswick, N.J.: Aldine Transaction, 2008 [1969]).

20. The examples in this category come from the cookbooks *Measure for Pleasure* (1961 and 1970) and from *Swedish Recipes* (1956), 167. In our analysis of recipe names, we note that capitalization patterns in Swedish-American cookbooks diverge from patterns used in Swedish books. The scope of the present study does not permit a detailed presentation of the contrasts.

21. These examples appear in *Var Så God* (1980 and 1996).

22. Examples from *Var Så God* (1980), 147, 162, 170. *Smörgåsbord* is a "traditional Swedish buffet," *pepparkakor* are "gingerbread cookies," and *hjorthornssalt* is "baking ammonia."

23. Hoffman and Kytö, "The Linguistic Landscapes of Swedish Heritage Cookbooks in the American Midwest, 1895–2005."

24. *Var Så God* (1980 and 1996).

25. "Introduction," *Var Så God,* 1980 (n.p.). In this passage, quoted verbatim, we preserved the use by the cookbook committee of the quotation marks that alternate from double to single.

26. Cf. the concept *enregisterment.* Asif Agha, "The Social Life of a Cultural Value," *Language and Communication* 23 (2003): 231–73. See also Hoffman and Kytö, "The Linguistic Landscapes of Swedish Heritage Cookbooks in the American Midwest, 1895–2005."

27. In its introduction, the cookbook committee does not elaborate on which ethnic groups influenced the names of some of the other recipes printed. Some hints, however, as to the other ethnic groups they presumably were thinking about appear in such recipe names as "English Cucumber Pickles," "Finnish Fresh

Mushroom Salad," and "Speedy Danish Kringle" (*Var Så God* 1980 and 1996). For a discussion of sociolinguistic forces relating to noninstitutional, bottom-up phenomena, see Alexandra Jaffe, book review of *Speaking Pittsburghese: The Story of a Dialect* by Barbara Johnstone, *Journal of Sociolinguistics* 19, no. 4 (2015): 559–63.

28. Jeffrey Shandler, *Adventures in Yiddishland: Postvernacular Language and Culture* (Berkeley: University of California Press, 2006), 22.

29. Lorénzen published the book *Of Swedish Ways* in 1964. Information on the memorial scholarship established in her name may be found at "2019 Lilly Lorenzén Scholarship," American Swedish Institute, https://www.asimn.org (accessed October 11, 2019).

30. The recipes are found on pages 5, 65, and 174, respectively, and are quoted verbatim.

31. Extracts from Lorénzen's book are printed in *Var Så God* (1980), 229, 236.

32. We further examine the historical sociolinguistic influence of Lorénzen in Angela Hoffman and Merja Kytö, "*Of Swedish Ways* and (Sometimes) in Swedish Words" (in preparation).

12

A Postwar Italian Kitchen Shining in the Swedish–American Borderlands

Franco Minganti

Transatlantic Borderlands

This essay will address my family's move from a countryside periphery to the center of a small town in the context of the intersectional, virtual space that reverberated through the cultural and material triangulations between America, Sweden, and Italy—in a way, Europe—that took place in the postwar era of transatlantic relations. In fact, it will mainly discuss the iconic place of the kitchen table in that new apartment of ours as a paradigm of sorts. It will do so by juxtaposing different styles that characterize specific contexts of cultural display, scholarly discussion of primary sources, and openly subjective experiences.

When dealing with transatlantic borderlands, it should be pointed out that the critical discourse on global Americanization calls for complexity, articulate sophistication, difference, and specificity. And yet, what is materially processed is more often aligned on a binary order of things—Swedish–American relations, Italian–American connections, and so on, one nation after the other—even though, in times of turbulent technological reworkings, transatlantic cross-fertilizations triangulated, often eluded, and sometimes obliterated genealogies, ideas, and national branding.

In the European–American set of relations, a number of exchanges, both ideas and artifacts, developed along intricate routes, traveling back and forth across the Atlantic as well as across the borders between European countries, which would encourage flirting with notions of spatial imagination, such as Michel Foucault's "heterotopias"[1] or John Berger's or Henri Lefebvre's "trialectics of seeing"[2]—the triadic interplay of spatiality, historicality, and sociality. Thus, I would articulate my family's new kitchen of 1958, the shining postwar Italian kitchen of the title, as a kind of narrative *dispositif,* a chronotope (with Mikhail Bakhtin)[3] that might find an Italian place and raison d'être in the space of the Swedish-American borderlands, triangulating thirdspace otherness (with Edward W. Soja)[4] in turn with them.

Imola, 1958

It is necessary to open by providing a temporal-spatial frame intertwined with autobiographical references that shed some light on the "factional" setting of this narrative, exactly at the intersection where—on echoing anthropologist James Clifford—historically specific cultural and geographic relations become visible and certain stories can take place.[5]

The coordinates: the year, 1958; the place, Imola, my hometown, twenty miles east of Bologna, in the "red" region Emilia-Romagna. Actually, Imola is in neither Emilia nor Romagna; it is, ideally, the very hyphen in-between, an element that links and connects—a most classic site of hybridization and bastardization, and also, quite likely, a place in the mind, a soul state where borders often blur and easily collapse. My family lived in a tiny apartment in a small shared house in the outskirts of town, where you could still feel the adjoining countryside. In May of that year—I was six at the time—we moved to a flat on the fourth floor of a newly built condominium closer to the center and, by our taking an elevator for the first time, we suddenly turned *modern.*

In the postwar world, ideas of modernity circulated with new speed and efficacy, reconnecting nations and cultural horizons through narratives and policies on civilization and progress that took place in sociocultural norms and material practices, displayed in international events as well as in the everyday around the family kitchen. Italy was booming after the physical and moral ruins of World War II, quick to jump to the "forefront of European economic integration."[6] "Europe"—that is, the original Mercato Comune Europeo (MEC), soon to be named the European Economic Community (EEC)—was in the making, in both reality and symbols. The notes of Marc-Antoine Charpentier's *Te Deum* would open for the virtual, if participatory, space of the Eurovision: never did a term appear more appropriate to reference an idea, the project and projection of Europe. In 1958, my elementary-school class entered a competition to design the MEC logo and various celebratory stamps, while the Eurovision Song Contest, born two years earlier, was well on its way. That was the year of Domenico Modugno's "Volare" and of Sweden's first appearance in the competition. Actually, we were slowly preparing for my soon-to-be favorite TV program ever, the iconic *Giochi senza frontiere/Jeux sans frontières/Spielen ohne Grenzen,* which would be launched a few years later, in 1965.

Glimpses of United States and Sweden

In the context of Europe's makeover under the aegis of the Marshall Plan, Italy was hurriedly reinventing itself into a *modern* country.[7] The economic boom pushed more and more Italians to buy their own home, a new fact that both reaffirmed traditional values and witnessed Italy's determination to actively participate in a changing world. As history of design scholar Penny Sparke has commented, "linked to traditional values, in particular that of the family, and yet susceptible also to the pull of 'modernisation,' the postwar Italian home [served] both as an anchor with the past and as a means of demonstrating Italy's will and ability to become part of the twentieth century."[8] A lot was at stake, beyond individuals: already in 1946, Ernesto N. Rogers, the editor of *Domus,* Italy's most influential architecture and design magazine, had anticipated that "it [was] a question of forming a taste, a technique, a morality—all aspects of the same function. It [was] a question of building a society."[9]

America was all around and the instances of "Americanization" were vocal and in full view, but how did my own Italian-Swedish borderlands fare back then? How could one try and map out such a territory? Some of my own Italian Sweden came blurred from America, indeed from Hollywood: "divine" Garbo, "scandalous" Ingrid Bergman "*in Rossellini,*" "sex goddess" Anita Ekberg (soon to be directed to Hollywood-on-the-Tiber fame by Federico Fellini in *La dolce vita* in 1960), and maybe Ingmar Bergman, ready for an early landing on Italian TV. On the international infosphere, Dag Hammarskjöld, the secretary-general of the United Nations, if from New York, embodied civic Sweden, empowering neutrality and peace enforcing missions for a child's imagination, open to a progressive world. In everyday life, we would perform gymnastics in school on wall bars and ladders known as "*spalliera svedese*" and "*quadro svedese,*" respectively, ideally imitating Sweden, which, at least since the 1930s, had won a strong reputation in the field of physical education and "aesthetic gymnastics," highly praised by Italian doctors because it focused on the shaping of graceful movements. Somehow paired with this, there came the ethical functionality and aesthetic cleanliness of the "aesthetics of the Middle Way," "*medelvägens estetik*" in the words of art history scholar Jeff D. Werner, an approach of Swedish design "perceived as a temperate version of modern."[10] Then, on a peculiarly glocal level, there was motocross. Imola was Italy's pioneer capital of the discipline and the site of the Italian Grand Prix of the World Championship. Since 1955, Sten "Storken" Lundin and Bill Nilsson came to set a winning streak of seven years in a row: total domination. Thus, in 1958 Sweden was no longer a distant, mythical country: the Swedes were in Imola and I—a young fan—could see them in body and flesh, and the blue and yellow flag they sported appeared to me the most beautiful flag in the world, a sentiment that only wavered after Brazil won the soccer World Cup at the end of June, in and against Sweden.

Modern Kitchens

When it comes to kitchens, with British sociologist June Freeman it should be noted that "[t]here are few examples of international architectural modernism being embraced by the public in the way the concept of the fitted kitchen has been."[11] By focusing on a scenario that tells about the modern kitchen, with Museum of Modern Art curators Juliet Kinchin and Aidan O'Connor we could surmise that

> [t]he modern kitchen epitomizes and embodies its owner's lifestyle and relationship to consumer culture; it also retains its archetypal significance as the symbolic core of the home, the center around which the modern family revolves. It has come to articulate and at times actively challenge societal relationships to food, technology, the domestic role of women, and

> international politics. . . . Progressive architects in Europe and the United States designed increasingly compact, sparely furnished environments, often with unified kitchen-living spaces that took inspiration from modest rural interiors. Many were also involved in the ethnographic recording of such spaces, which were felt to embody national traditions and culture in a purer form than monumental architecture. . . . Whether conceived as a galley for food preparation or a collective facility outside the home, these variants of the New Kitchen shared an admiration for scientific reason and utopian aspirations for a more egalitarian society. Transformation of daily life at the level of the kitchen, it was argued, would be followed by behavioral change and improved social well-being.[12]

The hagiographies of the Marshall Plan idealized the storyline of the postwar American kitchen as an exported, technological archetype transferred unidirectionally across the Atlantic, and yet "the process [actually] involved modification, cross-fertilization, and hybridization."[13] Actually, not everyone in Europe accepted American models at face value, least of all Russia. For instance, one should sensibly refer to the well-known Cold War "Kitchen Debate" that took place on July 24, 1959, when Nikita Khrushchev and Vice President Richard Nixon had an animated feud in front of General Electric's lemon-yellow dream kitchen displayed at the American National Exhibition of the Moscow Fair. Yet, for the scope of a presentation that ideally posits 1958 as its end year, that instructive entr'acte in the USSR has been kept aside. American models were often contested and rejected; most of the time they were hybridized through local touches of pragmatic creativity. The specific cultural history of the modern kitchen tells a story of intense transatlantic, cross-fertilizing exchanges, circulations and triangulations, misunderstandings, ideological twists, appropriations, hazards, and raised bids. For instance, Europeans tended to minimize the American Tayloristic extremes that had established the foundations of the modern kitchen,[14] while Americans would erase the socialistic ideals that inspired, for one, Grete Schütte-Lihotzky's Frankfurt kitchen of 1926–27, "the mother of all modern kitchens." Europeans gave up their own histories of planning and design when reframing the modern kitchen as "American," while Americans would often reexport European ideas to Europe.[15]

Kitchens within and across Borders

In postwar Europe, the "fitted kitchen" was a winning concept. As June Freeman contends, it was characterized "by matching units and appliances built to standardized measurements compatible with the dimensions of the units. . . . [It] also [had] long worktops which [ran] continuously over a number of base units, and their walls [carried] rows of matching cupboard units also planned to maximise the use of space available."[16]

In early 1950s Germany, Poggenpohl started building such standardized kitchen units in series, while in other countries the debate was mostly derivative: for example, in England it focused on U.S. kitchen models and advertised indigenously produced kitchens as American-inspired.[17] Historian Jenny Lee writes that, while in most European countries in that decade kitchens remained something that the individual household designed, more and more standardized solutions became available. Referring to Freeman's study, she shows how German kitchen manufacturers had a great impact abroad, often appearing more innovative than the domestic manufacturers.[18]

In Italy, advertising agencies preferred to push the button on the "Americanness" of such a new modernity. Maristella Casciato, Getty Research Institute's Senior Curator of Architectural Collections, explains that "the first kitchen fixtures with standardized components manufactured for the Italian market were generically dubbed *cucina all'americana* [American-style kitchen]."[19] Such super-equipped live-in kitchens were advertised in American magazines, alas destined to remain an unattainable dream with Italian consumers. Of course, some of the most efficient public relations for such kitchens came directly from Hollywood movies: cultural critic Natalie Fullwood has emphasized that "[i]ndeed, *cucina all'americana* was used as a catch-all term to describe the modern, shiny, clean 'assembled kitchen' with vertically integrated units and multiple electrical appliances which many Italians first saw in Hollywood films."[20]

In the Swedish- and Italian-American borderlands, one should recall that Åke Ekelund and Yngve Steen, in their 1950 *Köket av i dag* (The kitchen of today), while trying to profile the average standards of the international kitchen issue, warned about the urgency of fair comparisons, particularly in reference to the American luxury kitchens especially designed for fairs, showrooms, or the glossy magazines of interior design, all units that were never mass-produced.[21] Italian-assembled kitchens of the 1950s tried to escape from American standards: after all, already in earlier decades there had been notable vernacular forays into modernization. For instance, in 1930, Piero Bottoni, one of Italy's leading architects, displayed the kitchen of *Casa Elettrica* at the IV Esposizione Internazionale delle Arti Decorative ed Industriali di Monza, the ancestor of the widely recognized Milan Triennale, offering a unique manifesto of Italian rationalism projected on the International Style backdrop.[22]

While in the prewar/postwar transition years academic and professional architecture had been proceeding almost everywhere in Europe by acknowledging international contributions,[23] in 1954 Augusto Magnaghi's kitchen design for Saffa was awarded the first Compasso d'Oro prize for its "stylistic independence from the omnipresent American model" and for "the morality of the modern taste characterizing its focus on purity of design and not on luxury," as the official motivation went.[24] In the 1950s, *Domus* and other popular magazines entertained the idea of explicitly containing the influence of an American imagination for the kitchen by emphasizing the parallel notions of revaluating an Italian way to kitchen design and looking for other solutions across Europe. On the one hand, in March 1954, in introducing his own kitchen project, architect Mario Tedeschi could remark that his was "an Italian kitchen, conceived to fulfill Italian needs. As such, somehow it counters the American kitchen that today looks like the most advanced concept in kitchen design."[25] On the other hand, the new gaze around Europe made space for the idea of *cucina svedese* (Swedish-style kitchen), which was hinted at and commercially communicated, while the Swedish approach was particularly honored. For instance, in July 1950, Swedish architect Lena Larsson introduced the social perspective of Swedish design to *Domus* readers, a topic Italians of the boom years were particularly sensitive to: "In order to fully understand today's production of furniture in Sweden, one must consider that for the most part it is aimed at manufacturing furniture that is simple, low-cost, and built in series. Production is linked, strictly and spontaneously, to the movement of development and social settlement that the country has been committed to for the last twenty years."[26]

Kitchen Tables

Now, if we return to my family's move of May 1958, through metonymic passages we might ideally travel from a house to a flat, from the new apartment to its new kitchen, and from it, ultimately, to its table, quite likely the real chronotope, the *dispositif* for a bit of cultural storytelling. If we zoom in on the kitchen table as the symbolic, if contested, essence of the modern kitchen, its presence appears problematic, or just symptomatic, in kitchen design. Most typically, American kitchens were large rooms on the ground floors of suburban houses, and would normally include a small service table, the likes of which Europeans had been witnessing in Hollywood films.[27] Such images were now intensified through the new popular imports of such television programs as *Leave It to Beaver,* the quintessential suburban TV series from 1957 that quickly became a hit also in Italy, which allowed a closer look at the materiality of everyday life in the United States.

Small European kitchens in popular housing told other stories, though. The 1926 Frankfurt kitchen had no dining table at all, the Pullman car being an inspiration; the 1933 Dutch Bruynzeel kitchen designed by Piet Zwart was basically a furnished wall offering a long, linear worktop, a design reelaborated for mass production in 1938. In Le Corbusier's 1946 Marseille project "L'Unité d'Habitation," Charlotte Perriand conceived the tiny working area of the kitchen as separated from a dining table, opening onto other living spaces, thus recuperating the centrality in the home that the kitchen had in the Middle Ages;[28] while the Swedish HFi, Hemmens forskningsinstitut (Home Research Institute),[29] accurately processed the table issue in its 1952 *Kök planering inredning* (Kitchen planning interior), insisting on offering a five-seat table with one side attached to the wall, in order to gain space for moving, a solution that Ikea has fostered since its inception.[30] In fact, the experts directed that the kitchen table should "be set in a delimited part of the kitchen . . . preferably next to a large enough window,"[31] so that those sitting at the table—the whole family and one to two guests, according to the counseling literature—would have a view.[32] Indeed, everyone's comfort—enough arm and leg space, fluid movements, ease of traffic around the table, and optimal visual field—was thought to be crucial for well-being in a delicate moment of societal and family life transformation.[33] Ulrika Torell, superintendent at the Department of Cultural History of Nordiska Museet, interestingly notes that, in retrospect, "the strong image of family cohesion, well-being, and community (at the kitchen table) of the 1950s and 1960s emerges as a last resort before traditional meal arrangements and family dinners would begin to dissolve and fragment. Perhaps it was emphasized and stressed so strongly just for that reason."[34]

In Italy, kitchen tables hardly appeared in advertising, likely for reasons connected with the mostly frontal photographic display, or because they were considered marginal or even optional, or else they were not "designed" enough into the projects.[35] Nevertheless, Italy's premodern subconscious worked differently and the centrality of the table in the room was quintessential to everyday life. Neither American nor Swedish kitchens could fulfill such a fundamental role in Emilia-Romagna, the land of *pasta sfoglia, tagliatelle,* and *tortellini.* The young Swedish housewife pictured by HFi in her efficient and aptly measured kitchen, while rolling dough for baking buns on a tiny space, has nothing to do with the *arzdora*

The 1958 kitchen table belonging to the author's mother in Imola, Italy. Photograph copyright Massimo Golfieri.

romagnola (the woman who presides over housekeeping matters) and her conspicuous rolling pin making tortellini on a huge board resting on the table top.

The manufacturers of the 1958 kitchen my mother used until she passed away in July 2020 at ninety-nine were a local boom company that went quickly out of business. Unfortunately, it has not been possible to trace their brand name, nor their corporate story; they must have worked just fine, though, oblivious to planned obsolescence, if their kitchen still looks gorgeous, shining like new, sixty years later. What made their design unique was concentrated in the details of the table: the Formica top hid the huge pastry board you had to just slide out and put on the table, and a suitable lodging was carved for the long rolling pin, with space for a smaller cutting board and a drawer.

If our kitchen table could speak, you would register a whole set of human activities performed around it. Consuming meals surely was the ideal, but grandma rolling the dough with her rolling pin to make pasta (we children often helping her out) or performing all the arrangements for cooking and storing away food preparations (eggs for future pastas, fruit jams, tomato preserves, pickled or fresh vegetables for the winter, homemade liquors), mother concocting her great desserts, father reading the paper (well, grandma too), mother writing notes for her lessons in school, the kids doing our homework or assembling fantasy objects with our Meccano (a British game for kids), grandma sewing, mother knitting, and everyone listening to the radio (we would have a TV set only later) or playing cards together and celebrating special occasions with *tombola* (our bingo), talking with occasional visitors or relatives, maybe sitting around sharing coffee or some social, recreational consumption of wine (visits never went without grandma offering a glass of the home brand)—such were among the hundreds of actions the kitchen table enabled because it was the absolute, if invisible, central *dispositif* in the theater of our kitchen. No table, no party.

Before the full boom of Italian revolutionary plastics, shiny, easily cleanable metal had won the war over wood in our kitchen, and yet the colorful Formica worktops had touched base with the ideal clean lines of white kitchen design that had merged with the new hygienic and sanitizing ethos symbolic of getting rid of the dirt and rubble of World War II.

The resulting narrative was one of manufacturing system and design culture able to interpret Italian kitchen dreams, maintaining concepts of assemblage and rationality, with a particular taste for quality materials and color, something Swedish designers either cast blame at or for which they were envious of their Italian colleagues.

Kitchen Evocations

What were we, my family and the emerging middle class, buying? American? Swedish? Modern? "*Cucina all'americana,*" "*cucina svedese,*" "*cucina componibile*" (modular or assembled or fitted kitchen) were the conceptual kitchen idiom at the time, definitions that often overlapped in everyday use, while mostly referring to the very same objects. The "American" collocation paid off particularly well, while in interior design the "Swedish" attribution was more and more often associated with furniture—like the essential design of bookshelves—that was simple, functional, modern, morally impeccable, intrinsically aesthetic.

Like "my own" Sweden, the United States was, indeed, a "*country-of-evocation,*"[36] whose essence was being built out of subtle, strategic campaigning that went beyond simple national branding. If the image of the American kitchen, in the words of Ruth Oldenziel, history of technology professor at Eindhoven University of Technology, had become "the standard icon of American modernity,"[37] Paolo Scrivano, associate professor of history of architecture at Milan's Polytechnic University, would assess that "dreams and fantasies about Americanization shaped our universe of abstract desires filled with visions that were both attractive and generic: the adjective 'American' came not only to refer to products imported from the United States but also to anything modern or progressive, contributing to a redefinition of citizenship from the public to the private sphere."[38] Moreover, the material conditions of exports/imports and, generically, exchanges over the Atlantic complicated the picture: direct imports did not work smoothly and more often American companies would license Italian manufacturers. At times, the latter just imported American technology with the help of some Marshall Plan support, so that they could soon bend American technological standards to local requirements. The modified clones were simpler, and definitely more functional to Italians, as well as much less expensive than their overseas models.[39]

Italian manufacturers—sometimes entrepreneurs who traveled (across both the Atlantic and European borders), explored, connected, and became important mediators of sorts—involved young designers starting joint efforts that would soon favor the boom of Italian international design. These developments reinforced the self-reassuring common assumption that Italians were great craftsmen-artists, more creative artisans and designers than reliable industrial producers.

Going for *Modern*

How much of America and how much of Sweden was there in my Italian kitchen? Whatever the amount was in 1958, it quickly faded away. Those cultural markers were soon metabolized, put into parentheses, and taken for granted: in this specific realm, the national brand evaporated. In both Italy and Sweden, it felt kind of necessary to tone down the often-bombastic boast of American "superiority" in every field. Italian designers bloomed and plastic would soon become the surging symbol of Italy's "petrochemical revolution" that would play such an important role in the country's economic boom.[40]

On June 15, 1961, a symptomatic moment took place on Italy's television screens. *Campanile Sera* was a very popular program, a pioneering vehicle of the actual concoction of the identity of postwar Italians. It was hosted by Mike Bongiorno, the Italian American, iconic testimonial of the United States on early Italian TV, soon to be ironically celebrated in "Fenomenologia di Mike Bongiorno," a groundbreaking essay by Umberto Eco originally published in 1961.[41] In it, two cities from different regions parochially competed in various fields, and in one segment, modeled after the American show *The Price Is Right,* two families from each city tried to guess the price of common objects.[42] In this episode, a new, modern kitchen was introduced and Bongiorno would marvel while illustrating a "supermodern" kitchen "entirely made of laminated plastics."

This signaled the closing of an era, the suspension of the continuous (re)positioning at the crossroads of material exchanges and cultural negotiations: from the dream image to the real (imported) thing, to copies and clones just "passing" for either "Swedish" or "American," Italians just settled for *modern*. The traces of such triangulations may be doomed to fade, and yet they are facts left open for further cultural archaeological campaigns. Kitchens were kitchens, and interior designers and advertising agencies had started out, yet again, for other (communication) frontiers. But those would be other borderlands . . .

Notes

1. Michel Foucault, "Of Other Spaces," *Diacritics* 16 (Spring 1986): 22–27.

2. Henri Lefebvre, *The Production of Space* (Oxford and Cambridge, Mass.: Blackwell, 1991), 42.

3. Mikhail Bakhtin, "Forms of Time and of the Chronotope in the Novel," in *The Dialogic Imagination* (Austin: University of Texas Press, 1981).

4. Edward W. Soja, *Thirdspace: Journeys to Los Angeles and Other Real-and-Imagined Places* (Malden, Mass.: Blackwell Publishing, 1996).

5. James Clifford, *Routes: Travel and Translation in the Late Twentieth Century* (Cambridge: Harvard University Press, 1997), 11.

6. Paul Ginsborg, *A History of Contemporary Italy: Society and Politics 1943–1988* (London: Penguin Books, 1990), 213.

7. Victoria De Grazia, *Irresistible Empire: America's Advance through Twentieth-Century Europe* (Cambridge: Belknap Press of Harvard University Press), 2005, Position 4438/7884 (Kindle Edition).

8. Penny Sparke, "'A Home for Everybody?' Design, Ideology and the Culture of the Home in Italy, 1945–72," in *Culture and Conflict in Postwar Italy*, ed. Zygmund G. Baranski and Robert Lumley (London: Macmillan, 1990), 225.

9. Ibid., 227.

10. Jeff D. Werner, *Medelvägens estetik: Sverigebilder i USA*, 2 vols. (Hedemora: Gidlund, 2008), 2:387.

11. June Freeman, *The Making of the Modern Kitchen: A Cultural History* (Oxford: Berg, 2004), 50.

12. Juliet Kinchin with Aidan O'Connor, *Counter Space: Design and the Modern Kitchen* (New York: Museum of Modern Art, 2011), 5, 11.

13. Ruth Oldenziel, "Exporting the American Cold War Kitchen: Challenging Americanization, Technological Transfer, and Domestication," in *Cold War Kitchen: Americanization, Technology, and European Users*, ed. Ruth Oldenziel and Karin Zachmann (Cambridge: MIT Press, 2009), 316.

14. The American Christine Frederick, a columnist of the *Ladies' Home Journal*, pioneered the application of Tayloristic concerns in the project of more functional homes, particularly for women, and published her studies as *The New*

Housekeeping: Efficiency Studies in Home Management (1913), a book that was extremely influential all over Europe.

15. For a definition of "*cucina all'americana,*" see Francesca Balena Arista, "Cucina all'americana," in *Cucine & Ultracorpi,* ed. Germano Celant (Milan: Electa/Triennale Design Museum, 2015), 263.

16. Freeman, *The Making of the Modern Kitchen,* 56.

17. Ibid., 46.

18. Jenny Lee, "Det moderna köksrummets historia," in *Köket: Rum för drömmar, ideal och vardagsliv under det långa 1900-talet,* ed. Ulrika Torell, Jenny Lee, and Roger Qvarsell (Stockholm: Nordiska Museets Förlag, 2018), 49.

19. Maristella Casciato, "Between Craftmanship and Design: Italy at Work," in *La arquitectura norteamericana, motor y espejo de la arquitectura española en el arranque de la modernidad (1940–1965),* ed. José Manuel Pozo Municio and Javier Martínez González (Pamplona: T6 Ediciones, 2006), 9–10.

20. Natalie Fullwood, "Recipe for Change: Kitchens in Comedy, Italian Style," in *Cinema, Gender, and Everyday Space: Comedy, Italian Style* (New York: Palgrave Macmillan, 2015), 167.

21. Åke Ekelund and Yngve Steen, *Köket av i dag* (Stockholm: Utgiven av Hem i Sverige, 1950). The authors thus concluded: "[T]he Swedish kitchen standard is considerably higher than in any other country, America included. It may sound like boasting, but it is a fact in terms of material quality, equipment, and planning" (143; my translation).

22. Giacomo Polin, *La Casa Elettrica di Figini e Pollini, 1930* (Rome: Officina Edizioni, 1982).

23. A classic study such as Siegfried Stratemann's *Grundrisslehre: Die Stockwerkswohnung* (Berlin: Verlag des Druckhauses Tempelhof, 1941/1951) is amply echoed in a popular project planning manual such as Enrico A. Griffini's *Costruzione razionale della casa* (Milan: Hoepli, 1931/1948), which compares the Frankfurt kitchen to "typical" American kitchens. While a well-known architecture treatise of 1954, Pasquale Carbonara's *Architettura pratica: Volume primo; Composizione degli edifici* (Turin: Unione Tipografico-Editrice Torinese, 1954/1976), would review state-of-the-art kitchen design by offering, among others, sketches and illustrations for the "normalized Swedish kitchen" and some graphic rendering of classic HFi (Hemmens forskningsinstitut) studies, drawn from the March 1947 issue of *L'Architecture d'aujourd'hui.*

24. Francesca Balena Arista, "Cucina componibile," in Celant, *Cucine & Ultracorpi,* 265.

25. Mario Tedeschi, "Una cucina italiana," *Domus* 292 (March 1954): 75–76; my translation.

26. Lena Larsson, "La Svezia produce in serie," *Domus* 248 (July 1950): 75; my translation. The INA-Casa project of 1949, *Piano Incremento Occupazione Operaia: Case per lavoratori,* likely the most consistent state-coordinated program of

public housing Italy has ever known, offered architects and builders numerous examples of virtuous planning to be followed, most of them from Scandinavian architecture and interior design (Matteo Verdelli, *Il piano INA-Casa,* academia.edu; visited January 8, 2019).

27. Nancy Carlisle and Melinda Talbot Nasardinov with Jennifer Pustz, *America's Kitchens* (Boston: Historic New England, 2008), 11.

28. Christian Dupavillon, *Éléments d'une architecture gourmande* (Paris: Monum, Éditions du patrimoine, 2002), 208–9.

29. HFi was launched in 1944, with the aim of studying and improving living standards, with a particular focus on women's working conditions in the home.

30. Orsi Husz and Karin Carlsson, "Kökskunskap: Svenska kök mellan social ingenjörskonst och global kommersialism," in Torell, Lee, and Qvarsell, *Köket,* 283.

31. Ulrika Torell, "Köksbordet: Mönster och möblering för vardag i hemmen," in Torell, Lee, and Qvarsell, *Köket,* 173; my translation.

32. Ekelund and Steen, *Köket av i dag,* 26.

33. Erik Berglund, *Bord för måltider och arbete i hemmet* (Stockholm: Seelig, 1957), 28–47.

34. Torell, "Köksbordet," 176; my translation.

35. Silvana Annichiarico, "Lustra, linda, disabitata: La messinscena della cucina nella pubblicità cartacea italiana," in Celant, *Cucine & Ultracorpi,* 97.

36. Werner, *Medelvägens estetik,* 384.

37. Oldenziel, "Exporting the American Cold War Technology," 315.

38. Paolo Scrivano, *Building Transatlantic Italy: Architectural Dialogues with Postwar America* (New York: Routledge, 2017), 174–75.

39. On Italy's new "industrial geographies," see Guido Crainz, *Storia del miracolo italiano: Culture, identità, trasformazioni fra anni cinquanta e sessanta* (Rome: Donzelli, 2005).

40. Marcello Colitti, "La Montecatini e la rivoluzione petrolchimica," in *ENI: Cronache dall'interno di un'azienda* (Milan: Egea, 2008).

41. Umberto Eco, "Fenomenologia di Mike Bongiorno" (1961), now in *Umberto Eco: Sulla televisione; Scritti 1956–2015* (Milan: La nave di Teseo, 2018), a collection of the scholar's essays on television edited by Gianfranco Marrone.

42. In this episode, Arona, Piedmont, in Italy's northwest, challenged Monfalcone, Friuli-Venezia Giulia, in the northeast.

13

Imaginary Borderlands

Ingmar Bergman's and Michelangelo Antonioni's Implicitly American Contact Zones

Maaret Koskinen

Even though film is by its very nature international, historically it has been defined nationally, along geopolitical borders. The process of globalization from the 1990s on, however, has prompted theoretical developments among film scholars, resulting in a revision of the concept of national cinema and traditional, nationally based film histories. To cite *World Cinemas: Transnational Perspectives,* if previously the assumption was that the export of European and U.S. cinema to the rest of the world, from the silent period onward, "inspired only derivative image cultures," this assumption has been replaced by "a dynamic model of cinematic exchange, where filmmakers around the world are known to have been in dialogue with one another's work, and other cultural and political exchanges." Borders, then, are seen to have been "always permeable, societies always hybrid, and international film history to have been key to the process of globalization."[1]

In this context, it could be noted that the term "transnational" in distinction to the term "international" "evolved from signaling the generalized permeability of borders to the current usage in which it has taken on, as well, what had been previously meant by the adjective 'international.'" That is, whereas "international" is "predicated on political systems in a latent relationship of parity," the prefix "trans" implies relations of unevenness and mobility, which gives it a relative openness to modalities of geopolitical forms, social relations, and relations in film history.[2]

In this essay. the hypothesis is that the concept of imaginary borderlands may contribute to the ongoing and growing research on transnational flows, permeable cross-border relations, and other cultural encounters in film culture, particularly if guided by piecemeal, contextualizing empirical studies. By now, such studies on a global level are virtually boundless, and research honed in on particularly Swedish–American cinematic relations is also growing. Here studies concerning transnational flows cover a wide field—Victor Sjöström/Victor Seastrom's Hollywood career, the Scandinavian colonies of silent era Hollywood, the American remake of Ingrid Bergman's Swedish "sexploitation" films and "Dirty Harries" in the Swedish welfare state and the cop genre, and the distribution of Swedish films in the Swedish-American diaspora in the 1920s and 1930s—not to mention Ingmar Bergman's international impact, or latter-day Swedish-American remakes, including Stockholm noir and Nordic Crime, in the wake of the global success of Stieg Larsson's *Millennium* novels and their female hero Lisbeth Salander.[3]

It goes without saying that such piecemeal transnational studies will continue in nuancing film history and film historiography—at least to the extent that the dominant part of this history has been written from the vantage point of grand narratives such as national cinema and canons based on individual auteurs. However, for all (or exactly because of) this research activity in new directions, little sustained scholarly attention has been paid to refining and updating the particularities of *art cinema* as a category. This is noted by the editors of *Global Art Cinema: New Theories and Histories,* who insist that it remains important to recognize "art cinema's geopolitics" as a sustaining concept in the larger field of global film studies.[4] This is the vantage point of this essay, in attempting to point toward how the seemingly entrenched boundaries of Swedish and/or "European" (art) cinema in relation to "American" cinema and culture might be regarded as crossed or traversed by the more permeable and thus more nuanced concept of borderlands.

Lucrative case studies in this regard are Swedish director and writer Ingmar Bergman (1918–2007) and the Italian director Michelangelo Antonioni (1912–2007), who, by a curious coincidence, died on the same day, July 30, 2007. More important is that these two often have been ushered together, for all their cultural, ideological, and other differences—all in the name of the theory of the auteur as individual genius. A telling example is Peter Cowie's book *Three Monographs: Michelangelo Antonioni, Ingmar Bergman, Alain Resnais.*[5]

The result of individual directors thus lumped together by their (implied) genius is that they at times have remained curiously separate, seemingly freed from worldly constraints such as conditions of production and other cultural discourses—as sovereign, creative fountainheads, as if able to gestate all by themselves. In addition, as Janet Staiger has noted, over the many decades that the auteur and its underpinning idea—the author as original source of (all) meaning—have been the focus of cinema studies, scholars often have had reason to recognize that authoring practices change over the course of individual lives and therefore are contradictory. Despite this, she notes, one of the most common features of authorship studies is seeking repetition, because it is mainly this that provides the illusion of coherence and the (apparent) guarantee of causality, pointing back to the individual author as sole or dominant source of meaning.[6]

This is certainly true of the major readings of both Bergman's and Antonioni's work, where not least repetition of themes has been emphasized over time. Similarly, when differences have been registered—for instance, in narrative style—these are more often than not explained by reference to biographical or other internal contexts. In short, by emphasizing the auteur approach in a narrowly individualistic manner, scholars have tended to lose sight of other relevant contexts, in particular certain historical and societal aspects. One such context is—ironically—the fact that the very notion of auteur is saturated with European/Swedish–American relations. This concept, originally coined by French film critics in the 1950s, soon became the ideal not only for the French New Wave filmmakers (e.g., Godard and Truffaut) but for the production policies of the newly established Swedish Film Institute in 1963 as well. Around the same time, the influential American critic Andrew Sarris imported and championed the notion in the United States, which in turn was instrumental in opening up the U.S. market for European films, not least by Antonioni and Bergman.[7]

Here some further contexts will be delineated, first in an overview of the reception of Bergman, and second with Antonioni employed as a transnational comparative sounding board. Thus, it goes without saying that this inquiry into the borderlands concept, including Swedish–American relations, will be performed in a (seemingly) oblique fashion, as it is done by way of employing an Italian director. However, this is exactly the point of this inquiry—to show to what extent dualistic poles of "Swedish" versus "Italian" are crossed by other factors, which inevitably blur the boundaries. One such factor is precisely the contemporary American influence, which in this context can be regarded as an intermediary of sorts, but a very influential one, which circulated between these two "European" agents in various ways and on a number of levels. In other words, this comparison will not limit itself to remaining within the borderlands of European cinema ("Sweden" and "Italy"), but will also bring in a wider transatlantic context through the borderlands concept. For instance, to what extent can these two auteurs, so often treated as deeply "European" art-film artists, also be regarded as contributing to crossing that "deep divide" between art house film and the popular that is still so prevalent in daily discourse, and even in received historiography?

Case Study: Ingmar Bergman

In the case of Ingmar Bergman, the concept of imaginary borderlands and transnational flows (on various scales) can be approached in a number of ways. When regarding the themes and ideas of his films, for which he was first noted internationally, not least for their brand of Lutheranism, one enters transnational territory almost by default. For while traditional scholarship has insisted on the religious motifs in Bergman's films as being an expression of some Swedish or northern exoticism, these motifs, by their very nature, transgress borders. The same can be said of the multitude of psychological, psychoanalytical, and philosophically oriented studies that followed in Bergman scholarship.[8]

It is particularly telling that Bergman's work from early on became the object for study in relation to some core issues in classical philosophy, such as time and memory—again themes and motifs that, in essence, are existential or universal. In this context, one should of course note that the phenomenon of time, in all its multidimensional facets, has since long (and before Bergman entered the stage) been regarded as one of the most important aspects, if not *the* most important media-specific component of the film medium as such. After all, film is, according to its own theorists and philosophers, considered to be among the foremost of time-phenomenologically based media. As Malin Wahlberg puts it, "the ephemeral and concrete work in cinema of mediated rhythm, stasis, and the existential impact of the film image as a trace of the past represent two overlapping concerns of image and time that have always appealed to filmmakers and film critics and that illuminate the phenomenological inheritance of existential phenomenology in classical film theory."[9]

Therefore, the moving image always also encompasses *the viewer's experience* of time in that it allows the viewer to experience a past in and through a continuously engendering now—indeed, as if film allows us to see time literally materialized before our very eyes. Arguably, then, one of the reasons that we as audiences constantly seem drawn to the (illusion of) real time offered by moving images may very well be that it allows us to retrieve the sense of absolute presence, and thus paradoxically regain "lost" time—that proverbial sand that constantly runs through our fingers and is diluted in memories of the past or expectations of the future.

Not surprisingly, philosopher Henri Bergson's concept *la durée*—the dynamic duration of time—has come to good use in Ingmar Bergman's case. Interesting in this regard is the French filmmaker Jean-Luc Godard, who in the 1950s was a staunch admirer of the "prolonged" moment in Bergman's films. "His films," Godard wrote, "are made more profound by splitting up time—in the manner of Proust but much more powerfully, as if Proust were multiplied by both Joyce and Rousseau all at once, resulting in a gigantic and enormous meditation based on one moment."[10] If that is indeed the case, then when watching Bergman's films, the audiences (again) find themselves in existential, "universal" borderlands.

A final example worth mentioning that illustrates Bergman's position in various scholarly interactions is the fact that his production encompasses several art forms and media—film, theater, television, and writing. For, as director/writer of about fifty features, director of more than one hundred plays, and author of a multitude of short stories, novels, and plays, Bergman's work has lent itself to a multitude of academic and interdisciplinary approaches. As Jörn Donner put it in his book on Bergman from the early 1960s, "No director has ever come to films with such a great reliance on literature."[11] True enough, since Bergman's work has long been studied under the umbrella concept of interarts or, with a more recent term, intermediality, which includes more modern media such as television.[12]

Everything that has been noted so far regarding Bergman can be found in the scholarship on Michelangelo Antonioni as well. Just to mention a few examples, there is the theme of time and his use of prolonged takes and silences. Art historian Angela Dalle Vache also points out how this tendency in Antonioni to "undo narrative development into *temps morts*, waiting and duration" turn some of his films into a kind of painterly still lifes.[13] A similar intermedial context is introduced by Antonioni's use of architecture and how this is conducive to interdisciplinary research, through the notion of space, cinematic as well as actual space. The fact is that space and architecture is one of the most studied aspects of Antonioni's films, in terms of both narrative and style.[14] Lucy Fischer shows how Barcelona's architecture is used as filmic mise-en-scène in Antonioni's film *Professione: Reporter* (The Passenger) from 1975.[15]

A Theoretical Aside: Intercultural Border Crossings, Cultural Adaptation, Contact Zones?

If the theoretical aim of intermediality is to loosen the borders between academic disciplines, it is safe to say that this encompasses cultural links across borders as well. In Bergman's case it includes bridging what, particularly in the United States, was—and still is—considered a popular medium (movies), on one hand, and serious "highbrow" arts (cinema), on the other, which by default enters into mental and/or cultural borderlands.

In this context, it may be relevant to introduce a related concept—the notion of "cultural adaptation." For if adaptation in the humanities traditionally has been reserved for the relations between individual works (for instance, close readings of the process "from novel to film"), recently the notion has been significantly expanded. As the editors of *Adaptation Studies: New Challenges, New Directions* note, there is in present-day adaptation studies clearly a "movement away from one-to-one relationships, that is *one* source (such as a novel) and *one* film," to an increased interest in investigating "the field 'between' source and adaptation"—that is, adaptation of material that cannot readily be identified with a single text.[16]

In an attempt at getting at what this area "in between" might be, the editors of *Impure Cinema: Intermedial and Intercultural Approaches to Film* argue that once one mentions various border crossings in adaptation and/or in intermediality, it is always necessary to add *intercultural* border crossings as well. Because, they argue, involving "cinema's interbreeding with other arts and media" inevitably also means involving its "ability to convey and promote cultural diversity," as "culture and cultural products are always the result of struggles, negotiations and productive intersections between different systems, practices and interests."[17]

In this context, it may be of use to introduce yet another related term—"contact zone." This term, originally proposed by Latin Americanist Mary Louise Pratt, has a postcolonial provenance and refers to "social spaces where cultures meet, clash, and grapple with each other, often in contexts of highly asymmetrical relations of power such as colonialism, slavery, or their aftermaths as they are lived out in many parts of the world today."[18] Her definition, however, has been remapped and expanded by transnational cinema theorists, who use the term for considering "the geopolitical scales of cinematic exchange to operate as contact zones" on various levels and multiple scales.[19] A recent example can be found in Gunnar Iversen, who in an analysis of the reception of a 1950s Norwegian travelogue film about a jungle in South America, references Pratt, defining the term "contact zone" as "a place where two cultures contact and inform each other," and "spaces of encounter, negotiation, domination but also sometimes reciprocal exchange."[20] The latter definition aligns with my usage, as it is not potentially acrimonious asymmetry that is my concern here but reciprocal exchanges over time and space.

Regarding Bergman's work in the context of intermediality, then, immediately offers more possible explanations for his international success than do arguments based on the mere putative "quality" of the individual works themselves. Thus, in the context of Swedish/Nordic/European and U.S. relations, for example, more factors and a larger map need to be considered. Some of these factors would include, just to take a few obvious examples, reception factors such as the general zeitgeist of the time;

the development of film studies as a discipline in the United States in the 1950s and 1960s; the importance of influential American critics such as Andrew Sarris, who championed Bergman's cause, and the concomitant reception of Bergman's films among the audiences at large, in the United States and elsewhere;[21] the importance of branding and distribution channels in the United States;[22] or, for that matter, the importance of commercially attractive actors. In the latter case, I myself have attempted to show the high degree to which actress Liv Ullmann functioned as a celebrity "auteur star" in the transatlantic success story of Bergman's films in the 1960s and 1970s.[23]

In short, while "Bergman borderlands" have often been studied within national or European frameworks, there is reason to believe that the picture is more fractured, and that processes and movements overall are more mixed and complex. Bergman scholar Birgitta Steene is onto such a more complex map when she notes that philosophical affinity alone does not explain Bergman's unique position and reception in America. Rather, she argues, one also has to add the extent to which certain pictorial references in Bergman's films have become emblematic over time (for instance, the chess game between the Knight and Death in *Det sjunde inseglet* [The Seventh Seal] from 1957), which then have been usurped or appropriated by popular (U.S.) culture—and thus, one could add, part of a cultural coinage circulating in (Western) culture at large. Or, as Steene puts it, Bergman's films came with "a cultural frame of reference that transcends the medium, the time, and the filmmaker's original intentions with the work. This is an example of how a cultural expression is assimilated by another culture as if it were a native product."[24]

It goes without saying that such cultural "imprints" and movements at large, which take place across time, in this case transatlantically, are extremely hard to pinpoint, let alone prove empirically, without extensive research. Interestingly, as this is written one such strand of research is under way that focuses on sociological oral history research on film audiences, framed by the dynamically burgeoning multidisciplinary research area of memory studies. Here film, media, and communication studies are regarded as among the prominent disciplines, given that "over the past century, collective memory has been crucially informed by mass media, including and perhaps especially audiovisual media like cinema."[25]

This is why, "over the past two decades, the relationship between cinema and memory has been the object of increasing academic attention, with growing interest in film and cinema as repositories for representing, shaping, (re)creating or indexing forms of individual and collective memory."[26]

From this perspective, it is not surprising that Ingmar Bergman's career, encompassing a production that spans sixty years, can be looked upon as one huge memory archive of sorts—one that can be tapped into by researching the audiences that literally grew up with the film medium, and for whom Bergman's films were a staple diet. One such study is Jono Van Belle's dissertation, in which she uses sociological and oral history methods in comparing the reception of Bergman's films among elderly audiences in Belgium and Sweden. By honing reception across time, as well as on geographically separate but historically compatible audiences, it is theorized that the individual director's agency is not the one decisive factor for his or her position in cinematic history (writing), but (re)contextualized across temporal and spatial parameters, with the potential of writing other histories, on both a national and international level.[27]

However, besides such empirically verifiable borderlands phenomena in film studies—indeed, in the humanities in general—more often than not there remain those elusive imaginary borderlands that are harder to verify, but which, exactly because of this, are all the more intriguing. Let us therefore, as a thought experiment, point toward a different type of Swedish–American relations, in which the concept of borderlands enables us to broaden the field by including phenomena and practitioners that normally have not been regarded as working in Swedish–American relations.

The Great Divide: A Different Type of Swedish–American Relations

Ingmar Bergman is traditionally considered "Swedish," while Michelangelo Antonioni is considered "Italian." How might these two directors fit into the notion of borderlands in a North American context, except through the traveling notion of the auteur? And how might such a proposal be helpful in shedding further light on their links, in ways that film research of European film has not already achieved? Well, perhaps precisely because these two directors seem so entrenched in their Europeanness versus the United States in line with conventional thinking, and what Arnold Huyssen famously has called "the great divide"—that is, on one hand, the American and the popular (e.g., mainstream movies), and, on the other hand, the European and the highbrow (e.g., art-house cinema).[28]

Therefore, let us first note that Antonioni made some of his most well-known films in an Anglo-American context. His classic *Blow-Up* (1966) famously caught "Swinging London" not only in and for European audiences but for young generations across the Atlantic as well. The same goes for *Zabriskie Point* (1970), shot in California and wholly produced in the United States by Metro-Goldwyn-Mayer, which dealt with college youth as well as "dropouts" and the Vietnam War generation. In terms of reception, then, Michelangelo was in the 1960s, and in the United States, considered an international director, and at the very least a filmmaker belonging to the Western Hemisphere. In addition, among scholars he is considered a filmmaker whose films circulated globally—just as his colleague Bergman's did. What was considered "Swedish" or "Italian" in this context, then, is not easily established.

Certain hard-core production issues regarding the putative differences between "art-house" film and "commercial" film should be mentioned in this context. On the occasion of the deaths of the two directors, for instance, noted film scholar David Bordwell published an article on his Web site titled "Bergman, Antonioni, and the Stubborn Stylists." He pointed out, first of all, that it is wise to assume that art-house auteurs at this time were no less commercial than their Hollywood counterparts simply because they were sustained by national film industries and supported by the international film trade.[29]

In addition, when comparing the two directors from a stylistic point of view, he noted that while "the rise of European art house auteurs in film culture of the 1950s and 1960s put the question of personal style on the agenda," scholars back then did not have many tools for analyzing stylistic differences. But this is possible in hindsight, he claimed, more specifically to discern how the development of lenses and colors was important for questions of style. Thus, Bergman and Antonioni both, broadly speaking, passed through the same arc of "deep-focus compositions" in the 1950s and early 1960s to telephoto flatness in later color films—just as, one could add, American film did.[30] In other words, Bordwell's analysis of the two directors is based in concrete technological issues, and thus in empirically verifiable industry practices, which soon became international practice across borders.

In this context, one could also note that both Bergman and Antonioni were treated as celebrities, and albeit auteur stars, stars nonetheless—yet another border across "art film" and "Hollywood movies."[31] Bergman and Michelangelo, then, were in a latter-day sense brand names whose products circulated internationally between nation-states, within Europe and transnationally, in a more complex fashion, across borders, including the United States. In sum, film culture works on several scales at once, as it moves from place to place and interacts with its surroundings while traveling, so that sometimes "national" or "art-house" film can even become another's subculture.

In the next section, I will suggest a few other contact zones between Bergman and Antonioni that seem to have worked transnationally across borders, not only within the various geographic scales of Europe but also transatlantically.

Modernity: Women, Sex, and the City

One such overarching contact zone is *modernity,* for within the universalist aspirations of both filmmakers, there is also a strong streak of the time-bound crises of what back in the day was called "modern man" or, better, modernity.[32] As we have seen, while Bergman was and is categorized as particularly "Swedish" or at least vaguely Nordic, his concerns in this regard, just as Antonioni's, seemed to have been everyone's contemporary property as well, across Western geographic borders.

Let us focus on three major concerns here, which characterize the films of both directors—sex, urbanity, and women, all of which come together in intricate ways, particularly in two films, Antonioni's *La Notte* (The Night, 1961) and Bergman's *Tystnaden* (The Silence, 1963). What is proposed here are relations that have been shaped by individuals who are connected culturally, in this case cinematic expression of modernity.

As for the first—sex—it was at the time an issue both in Western societies (e.g., the pill) and on cinema screens in the West. This was certainly the case in the American literary landscape and U.S. culture at the time, in which Bergman's film *Tystnaden* landed and became an object of concern for the American censorship authorities, who cut almost two minutes from the film. Interestingly, Bergman saw no reason to pick a fight, as this was his chance to break into the American market.[33] He agreed to a very timely interview with *Playboy* in 1964.[34] Although this magazine had done highly acclaimed interviews with a variety of personalities and intellectuals (among others, Martin Luther King Jr., Ayn Rand, Albert Schweitzer, Jean-Paul Sartre, Stanley Kubrick, and Malcolm X), thus priding itself for being in the avant-garde not only in terms of sexual mores but of ideas in general, it must have come as a virtual find that a European art-film auteur suddenly seemed right up their alley. As we shall see from a close reading of some chosen scenes from these two films, the issue of sex is also important in Antonioni's film.

The other major area for lucrative comparisons between the two directors' films is growing urbanity and the modern city. Indeed, the close link between film and the city is a reiterated truth of modernity. As noted in *The City and the Moving Image: Urban Projections,* "the city and the moving image have, from the very outset, remained inseparable constituents of the modern urban imaginary". If nothing else, there is, as this book's subtitle suggests, a decidedly scopic affinity between place/space and film, besides other shared properties such as technology and movement.[35] One such affinity is film and architecture, which at times is referred to as a symbiotic one, and even has given rise to the neologism *cine-tecture.*[36]

Space and architecture is one of the most studied aspects of Antonioni's films, and as we shall see from the close reading of some chosen scenes from the two mentioned films, the issue of the city is also important in Bergman's film.

But first, having mentioned this "sex and the city" aspect, there is (by default) the final link, or contact zone, if you will—women. The prominent and existentially sophisticated roles given to women protagonists are arguably the most striking similarity between the two directors—Monica Vitti and Jeanne Moreau in Antonioni's films, Ingrid Thulin and

Gunnel Lindblom in Bergman's. In this regard, there may even be some empirically verifiable links between the two. For instance, in a late interview from 2002, Bergman mentions Antonioni and suddenly saw reason to rate the films of his colleague: "He has made two masterpieces, the other films one can live without. One is *Blow-Up,* which I've seen many times, and the other is *The Night,* which is wonderful as well, but largely because of the young Jeanne Moreau." But then he adds: "In my collection I have a copy of *The Cry,* and hell it's boring. So devastatingly tedious . . . I never understood why Antonioni became so incredibly elevated. And his muse Monica Vitti I thought was just crap as an actress."[37] Here Bergman seems to downplay any relations between him and his contemporary colleague, yet admits to having seen his films—which may raise a suspicion that he was more influenced or inspired by Antonioni that he wanted to admit.

Another telling factor worth considering in this context is that while cities and modern cityscapes are proverbial in Antonioni's films, and particularly the location shots of Milan (then growing and full of construction sites) in *La Notte,* it should be noted that Bergman up to this point had hardly displayed any interest in the modern city at all. Rather the opposite—his landscapes were small towns (particularly in his early films) and nature, as famously in *Sommaren med Monika* (Summer with Monika, 1953), which more often than not blended into general backdrops (the notable exception being the empty streets in *Smultronstället* [Wild Strawberries], 1957). The city in *The Silence,* however, took center stage. It is telling that it was entirely built on the production company Svensk Filmindustri's grounds of Råsunda (the Swedish "Cincettà" of the time), at an inordinate cost.[38]

Let us anchor these general observations in a close reading of a select number of film scenes.

"Sex and the City": Cinema-Style

La Notte is at one level about a disintegrating marriage. Well into the film, we find Lidia (Jeanne Moreau) at a party at the publishing house of her husband Giovanni (Marcello Mastroianni), where his latest novel is being celebrated. But she decides to take off by herself, and here follows one of those lengthy urban walks, in prolonged, long takes, that are considered quintessential to Antonioni's style. What is particularly noticeable is the constant noise from the traffic and drilling from construction sites, as are a number of men who constantly glance at Lidia, and whose gaze she reciprocates. As her walk ends up in an unknown, derelict part of the city, those glances become increasingly threatening, and she is forced to flee.

Something very similar happens in *Tystnaden*. Here too we find Anna (Gunnel Lindblom) walking the streets of an unknown city, full of honking cars and the noise of construction drills. In her case too there is a vaguely threatening presence of men; in one lengthy take, she is seen walking the pavement in the wrong direction, against a veritable throng of men walking the other way. In both films, the streets are flooded with harsh sunshine and people are adorned with prominent black eyeshades, a concrete modernist thematization of looking and being looked at—the urbanized gaze of the twentieth century.

And then there is sex: the couple openly engaging in a sexual act at a cabaret that Anna visits. Here Bergman was spurred on by his own agenda of directing a conscious attack at the Swedish censorship authorities, but one can surmise that Antonioni's film helped him along in this effort, because in *La Notte* there is a curious scene that stands out from the rest of the film. It occurs at the very beginning, when Lidia and her husband visit an old writer friend at a hospital. Lidia leaves earlier, and it is at this point, when Giovanni is left to himself, that a young woman calls him into her room and attempts to seduce him. Although she is obviously mentally ill, he reciprocates and is on the verge of engaging fully sexually with her when some nurses happen to enter the room and immediately rush up and restrain the woman, while allowing Giovanni to calmly walk away without any questions asked.

This seems very odd today, but one can surmise that such a scene played into what John Orr has called the "estranged desire" between men and women in Antonioni's films.[39] But a similar estranged desire also characterizes sexual relations in Bergman's film. The couple's lovemaking at the cabaret theater is every bit as awkward as the contorted wrestling fight in the hospital room in Antonioni's film. It should be noted that in both films these encounters take place in public places, while at the same time being anonymous. As Anna tells the waiter that she picks up and sleeps with, "it's so good that we don't understand each other."

"Italy" meets "Sweden" through the American notion of "star." Two alienated women in the modern world: Jeanne Moreau in *La Notte* (The Night, 1961) and Ingrid Thulin with Gunnel Lindblom in *Tystnaden* (The Silence, 1963), copyright AB Svensk Filmindustri; photograph by Sven Nykvist).

In both films there are even similar audiovisual transitions from these sexual encounters to the scenes that follow. In *Tystnaden,* Anna, after having observed the couple, runs straight out to the city streets, which are full of noise and bustle, while Lidia and Giovanni leave the hospital in their car and the equally noisy and extremely chaotic traffic, which Antonioni lingers on, while husband and wife remain silent. In both films, then, there is a breakdown of language, engulfed by either silence or unintelligible noise—a dislocation in voice and image, in John Orr's terms. Are such parallels pure coincidence or can they be explained by a general inspiration of one over the other (against Bergman's vehement attempts at downplaying such a possible influence)? As I have attempted to show, there may be some support for the latter, based on comparative interpretation and close reading, and not least the fact that Antionioni's film came two years before Bergman's.

But should this not be the case—no actual, empirically verifiable "contacts"—then it may be more fruitful to frame any discernible contacts by the borderlands concept, mental or cultural. In this essay, various aspects of modernity were tested as one of many possible contextual links between Ingmar Bergman and Michelangelo Antonioni, in a close reading of their two films *Tystnaden* and *La Notte,* both with the view toward what at the time was taken as universalist notions of what it meant to be "modern man," and modern women, all against a backdrop of a generically Western urban landscape that transgressed borders.

I have also attempted to map some of the larger strands in the historical reception of Ingmar Bergman, while pointing toward how these might be nuanced in future research by furthering transnational and borderland concepts in film studies. If nothing else, such concepts will help open up sustained dualistic opposites (such as the putatively "popular" versus the "artistic," "USA" versus "Europe") and so, in their wake, pave the way for discerning links and contact zones in sometimes unexpected places.

In any case, it is safe to say that Ingmar Bergman and Michelangelo Antonioni were not only contemporary but were arguably also received in a borderlands geospace—the West, including Europe and the United States—conducive to what they had to offer.

Notes

1. Kathleen Newman, "Notes on Transnational Film Theory," in *World Cinemas: Transnational Perspectives,* ed. Natasa Durovicova and Kathleen E. Newman (London: Routledge, 2010), 4.

2. Natasa Durovicová, "Preface," in Durovicova and Newman, *World Cinemas,* ix–x.

3. See, for instance, Bo Florin, *Transition and Transformation: Victor Sjöström in Hollywood 1923–1930* (Amsterdam: Amsterdam University Press, 2013); Arne Lunde, *Nordic Exposures: Scandinavian Identities in Classical Hollywood Cinema* (Seattle: University of Washington Press, 2010); Elisabet Björklund and Mariah Larsson, eds., *Swedish Cinema and the Sexual Revolution: Critical Essays* (Jefferson, N.C.: McFarland and Company, 2016); Mariah Larsson, "Ingmar Bergman, Swedish Sexploitation and Early Swedish Porn," *Journal of Scandinavian Cinema* 5, no. 1 (2015); Tytti Soila, ed., *Stellar Encounters: Stardom in Popular European Cinema* (Eastleigh, UK: John Libbey Publishing, 2009); Michael Tapper, *Swedish Cops: From Sjöwall & Wahlöö to Stieg Larsson* (Chicago: Intellect Books, 2014); Ann-Kristin Wallengren, *Welcome Home Mr Swanson: Swedish Emigrants and Swedishness on Film* (Lund: Nordic Academic Press, 2014); Birgitta Steene, *Ingmar Bergman: A Reference Guide* (Amsterdam: Amsterdam University Press, 2005); Anna Westerståhl Stenport, "Nordic Remakes in Hollywood: Reconfiguring Originals and Copies," in *A Companion to Nordic Cinema,* ed. Mette Hjort and Ursula Lindqvist (Malden, Mass.: Wiley-Blackwell, 2016).

4. Rosalind Galt and Karl Schoonover, eds., *Global Art Cinema: New Theories and Histories* (Oxford: Oxford University Press, 2010), 5, 10.

5. Peter Cowie, *Three Monographs: Michelangelo Antonioni, Ingmar Bergman, Alain Resnais* (London: Tantivy Press, 1960).

6. Janet Staiger, "Authorship Approaches," in *Authorship and Film,* ed. David A. Gerstner and Janet Staiger (New York: Routledge, 2003), 30–31.

7. Andrew Sarris, "Notes on the Auteur Theory in 1962," in *Film Theory and Criticism: Introductory Readings,* ed. Leo Braudy and Marshall Cohen (New York: Oxford University Press, 1999 [1962]), 515–18.

8. See, for instance, Charles B. Ketcham, *The Influence of Existentialism on Ingmar Bergman: An Analysis of the Theological Ideas Shaping a Filmmaker's Art* (Lewiston, N.Y.: Edwin Mellen Press, 1986), and *Cinema, Philosophy, Bergman: On Film as Philosophy* (Oxford: Oxford University Press, 2009). For further sources on Bergman, see reference guides by Birgitta Steene, *Ingmar Bergman: A Reference Guide* (Amsterdam: Amsterdam University Press, 2005); and Erik Hedling, "Ingmar Bergman," in *Oxford Bibliographies in Cinema and Media Studies,* ed. Krin Gabbard (Oxford: Oxford University Press, 2017), DOI: 10.1093/OBO/9780199791286-0222.

9. Malin Wahlberg, *Documentary Time: Film and Phenomenology* (Minneapolis: University of Minnesota Press, 2008), xv.

10. Jean-Luc Godard, "Bergmanorama," in *Ingmar Bergman: An Artist's Journey: On Stage, on Screen, in Print,* ed. Roger W. Oliver (New York: Arcade, 1995 [1958]), 39.

11. Jörn Donner, *The Personal Vision of Ingmar Bergman* (Bloomington: Indiana University Press, 1974 [1962]), 153.

12. See Maaret Koskinen, ed., *Ingmar Bergman Revisited: Performance, Cinema and the Arts* (London: Wallflower Press, 2008); and Jan Holmberg and Anna Sofia Rossholm, "Screened Writing: Notes on Bergman's Hand," *Word & Image* 31, no. 4 (2015): 464, 465.

13. Angela Dalle Vache, *Cinema and Painting: How Art Is Used in Film* (London: Athlone, 1996), 50.

14. Seymour Chatman, *Antonioni, or, The Surface of the World* (Berkeley: University of California Press, 1985); and Carlo di Carlo and Giorgio Tinazzi, eds., *The Architecture of Vision: Writings and Interviews on Cinema* (Chicago: University of Chicago Press, 2007).

15. Lucy Fischer, *Cinema by Design: Art Nouveau, Modernism, and Film History* (New York: Columbia University Press, 2017).

16. Jørgen Bruhn, Anne Gjelsvik, and Eirik Frisvold Hanssen, "'There and Back Again': New Challenges and New Directions in Adaptation Studies," in *Adaptation Studies: New Challenges, New Directions,* ed. Jørgen Bruhn, Anne Gjelsvik, and Eirik Frisvold Hanssen (London: Bloomsbury, 2013), 8.

17. Lúcia Nagib and Anne Jerslev, eds., *Impure Cinema: Intermedial and Intercultural Approaches to Film* (London: I. B. Tauris, 2014), xix–xx, xxiv.

18. Mary Louise Pratt, "Arts of the Contact Zone," *Profession* (1991): 34.

19. Newman, "Notes on Transnational Film Theory," 9.

20. Gunnar Iversen, "In the Contact Zone: Transculturation in Per Høst's *The Forbidden Jungle,*" in *Small Country, Long Journeys. Norwegian Expedition Films,* ed. Eirik Frisvold Hanssen and Maria Fosheim Lund (Oslo: Nasjonalbiblioteket, 2017), 212.

21. See Linda Haverty Rugg, "Globalization and the Auteur," in *Transnational Cinema in a Global North: Nordic Cinema in Transition,* ed. Andrew Nestingen and Trevor G. Elkington (Detroit: Wayne State University Press, 2005); and Daniel Humphrey, *Queer Bergman: Sexuality, Gender and the European Art Cinema* (Austin: University of Texas Press, 2013).

22. Tino Balio, "Ingmar Bergman: The Brand," in *The Foreign Film Renaissance on American Screens 1946–1973* (Madison: University of Wisconsin Press, 2010).

23. Maaret Koskinen, "Reception, Circulation, Desire: Liv Ullmann and the Transnational Journeys of a Scandinavian Actress," *Journal of Transnational American Studies* 7, no. 1 (2016).

24. Birgitta Steene "'Manhattan Surrounded by Ingmar Bergman': The American Reception of a Swedish Filmmaker," in *Ingmar Bergman: An Artist's Journey;*

On Stage, On Screen, In Print, ed. Roger W. Oliver (New York: Arcade Publishing, 1995), 152–53.

25. Annette Kuhn, Daniel Biltereyst, and Philippe Meers, "Memories of Cinemagoing and Film Experience: An Introduction," *Memory Studies* 10, no. 1 (2017): 4.

26. Ibid., 1.

27. Jono Van Belle, "Scenes from an Audience. Memories, Affect, and Interpretative Strategies of Historical Film Audiences of Ingmar Bergman," PhD dissertation, Stockholm University/University of Ghent, 2019.

28. Andreas Huyssen, *After the Great Divide: Modernism, Mass Culture, Postmodernism* (Basingstoke and London: Macmillan, 1988).

29. David Bordwell, "Bergman, Antonioni, and the Stubborn Stylists" (posted August 11, 2007), http://www.davidbordwell.net/blog/?p=1139.

30. Ibid.

31. Maaret Koskinen, *Ingmar Bergman's* The Silence: *Pictures in the Typewriter, Writings on the Screen* (Seattle: University of Washington Press; Copenhagen: Museum Tusculanum Press, 2010), chapter 1.

32. Erik Hedling has anchored the notion of modernity in a specifically Swedish context. See "The Welfare State Depicted: Post-Utopian Landscapes in Ingmar Bergman's Films," in *Ingmar Bergman Revisited: Performance, Cinema and the Arts,* ed. Maaret Koskinen (London: Wallflower Press, 2008); and "Ingmar Bergman and Modernity: Some Contextual Remarks," in *Swedish Film: An Introduction and Reader,* ed. Mariah Larsson and Anders Marklund (Lund: Nordic Academic Press), 2010. John Orr in turn has used the concept in an exclusively European context in *The Demons of Modernity: Ingmar Bergman and European Art Cinema* (New York: Berghahn Books, 2014).

33. See Koskinen, *Ingmar Bergman's* The Silence, chapter 2, "Censorship Issues."

34. Cynthia Grenier, "Ingmar Bergman: A Candid Conversation with Sweden's One-Man New Wave of Cinematic Sorcery," *Playboy* 6 (1964).

35. Richard Koeck and Les Roberts, eds., *The City and the Moving Image: Urban Projections* (Houndmills, UK: Palgrave Macmillan, 2010), 1 and 8.

36. Ibid., 2.

37. Jan Aghed, "När Bergman går på bio," *Sydsvenska Dagbladet,* May 12, 2002 (my translation).

38. Koskinen, *Ingmar Bergman's* The Silence, 28.

39. John Orr, "Camus and Carné Transformed: Bergman's *The Silence* versus Antonioni's *The Passenger, filmint. (Film International)* 5, no. 3 (2007): 55.

14

Political Correctness in Sweden

A Borderland Conceptual History

Magnus Ullén

Perhaps no other concept has so drastically altered the nature of contemporary public debate as that of *political correctness,* or *PC* for short. The concept rose to public awareness in the early 1990s in relation to debates about higher education in the United States, but it very quickly spread to countries on the other side of the Atlantic, and has become the hub of debates about ethnicity, feminism, free speech, and democracy ever since. While the *phenomenon* of political correctness has been convincingly disclaimed as a myth, as a *term* the concept has nevertheless played an important role in public discourse over the last three decades.[1] In what follows, I will sketch how *PC phrases/terms* (here understood as the Swedish equivalent of "political [in]correctness," "politically [in]correct," or any variant thereof) were imported into a Swedish context from the United States. Conceptualizing this reception in borderland terms encourages us to stress the singularity of the local reception of the concept, while simultaneously highlighting how this reception in turn affected the American understanding of PC. Doing so may also be a first step toward understanding the broader transatlantic interchange on PC, because the swiftness with which the concept of PC took hold in Europe suggests that the Swedish reception of the term is part of a more general transatlantic transference.

In what follows I will heuristically divide the reception of PC terms in Sweden into an *introductory,* a *consolidating,* and an *activist* phase. As will be seen, PC was introduced as an American phenomenon and explicitly thematized as such in the first two phases, while in the third phase, a more radical conception of PC emerges. Informed by an internal tradition of skepticism to the Swedish Social Democrats, as well as by the neofascist theories of the Nouvelle Droite, this radicalized Swedish articulation of PC is eventually exported back to the United States. In the process, a number of, as it were, mediated borderlands—Web sites, publishing houses, radio channels, and so on—are created that become hubs of a Swedish-American articulation of the notion of PC, in which Sweden is often read as a metonym of Europe, which in turn is metaphorically seen as the soul of the United States. In effect, as we shall see, the very concept of PC emerges as a conceptual zone that lies "in the intersection of frontiers, borders, and boundaries": as a borderland urgently in need of further mapping.[2]

Introducing PC as a "New" Term

"Political correctness" was presented as a new coinage when reports about debates in American universities started to emerge in Swedish newspapers in the early 1990s, but the phrase has in fact been used in Sweden now and again for well over a hundred years, without any bias toward either the right or the left. It appears, for instance, in an 1894 article in the leading conservative daily in Sweden, *Svenska Dagbladet (SvD),* in which Queen Victoria of Great Britain is praised for her "complete political correctness, which has allowed her to always forgo her personal sympathies for the public good."[3] In fact, the expression "politically correct" and variants thereof are used sporadically, if infrequently, right up to the end of the 1980s in Sweden, but always indexically, that is, "in reference to a norm specific to the given case," without any preconception as to what kind of politics would count as "correct."[4] Talking about the Swedish State Church, for instance, an editorial in *Dagens Nyheter (DN)* states in 1955 that most likely, "this time too, silence and circumvention will be the politically correct course, according to a decades-old tradition." In 1982, there was a news item in *Aftonbladet* (October 6) reporting on a crayfish of two colors: "Its right side and right claw are clearly light blue, whereas its left half, politically correct, is of a color that [is] reddish-brown." As these usages confirm, PC was not a loaded concept at this time.

But then, before its adherents were presented as the new "thought police" on the cover of the December 1990 issue of *Newsweek,* PC was by and large an uncontroversial concept in the United States as well, often used as a playful mark of approval, not the least in relation to consumer choices. Thus, *Mother Jones* magazine carried ads for chairs that were declared to be "politically correct" (August/September 1985), while the *Washington Post* reported on "politically-correct coffee beans made by workers in Nicaragua" (December 27, 1987) and such "politically correct companies as Ben & Jerry's Ice Cream, Grand Street, Birkenstock sandals and Working Assets Visa card" (April 26, 1988). At the time, to the extent that PC phrases were used nonindexically, they were predominantly positively loaded.

This started to change within the academy, especially in the radical feminist circles that had been instrumental in establishing the term as a positively loaded concept in the first place. The modern understanding of PC as a form of censorious McCarthyism can in fact be tracked to the controversy around the ninth Scholar and the Feminist Conference, titled "Towards a Politics of Sexuality," held at the women's center at Barnard College on April 24, 1982. The questions raised included that "of whether there is such a thing as a 'politically correct' feminist sexuality," and provoked such protests from the antiporn camp (considered PC at the time), that a postconference petition published in several leading feminist journals accused their supposedly politically correct opponents of "McCarthyite tactics to silence other voices," marking the first time PC is charged with silencing free debate and causing direct harm to its opponents.[5] While this debate caused a rift within the feminist movement, it had limited impact on the rest of the academic community, but contributed to the dissemination of the term, and perhaps to kindling a slowly building sense of exasperation with the attitude associated with it. Notably, Richard Bernstein's short yet very influential *New York Times* article, "The Rising Hegemony of Political Correctness" (October 20, 1990) channels a critique of PC that was at the time largely internal to the left-wing academic scene, lifting several of its key characterizations of PC from papers at a Western Humanities Conference at the University of California, Berkeley.

One of the first persons to discuss the American debate about PC in Sweden was writer and critic Stefan Jonsson, who eventually became professor of ethnic studies at Linköping University. At the time, however, he was a doctoral student at the Program in Literature at Duke University, which enabled him to provide an on-site report of the PC debate virtually in real time. He published a series of articles in *DN,* Sweden's largest morning paper, in 1991, which he later developed into a book, *De andra: Amerikanska kulturkrig och europeisk rasism* (The others: American cultural wars and European racism), that was very widely read. In many ways, *De andra* marks the first mature work of postcolonial theory in Sweden, and as such the beginning of a critical debate that is still very much ongoing.

In two chapters, Jonsson provides an on-site report of the PC debate that was in full rage during his studies in the United States in 1990–92. The anti-PC movement, Jonsson is careful to explain, was not some spontaneous outburst of academics protesting the state of the arts, but a carefully orchestrated attack funded by conservative foundations.[6] Besides providing a background to the debate, he interviews literary theorists Stanley Fish and Barbara Herrnstein-Smith on the left, and lawyer Donald Horowitz and art critic Roger Kimball on the right, highlighting the importance of the notion of eternal values to the right in general and that of "aesthetic substance" to Kimball specifically. The interview with Kimball is especially instructive: Kimball defends the right of racists to speak their mind, so that we get a chance to critique their reasoning. Yet the second edition of Kimball's *Tenured Radicals,* Jonsson points out, makes plain that he is not willing to extend the courtesy offered to the tenured racist to the tenured radical. Multiculturalism, Kimball opines, poses a threat that needs to be dealt with differently: "A swamp yawns open before us, ready to devour everything. The best response to all this—and finally the only serious and effective response—is not to enter these murky waters in the first place. As Nietzsche observed, we do not refute a disease. We resist it."[7] PC, Jonsson concludes, amounts to a rhetorical strategy whereby conservative critics were able to dismiss those who challenged the status quo, without having to confront the arguments of their critics.

Jonsson provocatively ends his book on the American cultural wars by applying the lessons he has learned to the situation in Sweden, in which, he ventures, a new form of racism is on the rise. Racism, he contends, need not take the form of a doctrine of racial differences, but can be articulated in a variety of ways, and will exist as such "only for so long as it fills a political function."[8] Rather than speak of racism, Jonsson therefore suggests we speak of *the discourse of racism*. From such a view, racism is not an identity but a set of social practices, no longer necessarily tied to individuals' consciously held views, but more likely to appear in the form, for instance, of linguistic practices. Racism thus becomes an overdetermined phenomenon, a symptom of the political unconscious of society, making it much more difficult to pinpoint, yet much easier to symptomatically infer—much too easy, some of Jonsson's critics felt: one critic complained that Jonsson's "rubberband definition of racism" sets the stage for a "witch hunt" and allows "the actual racists to become invisible."[9]

For the most part, *De andra* was very well received. Given its critique of the concept of PC, one might thus think it would make Swedes wary of it, but this is not quite what happened. By framing his critique of what was happening in Sweden at the time in the terms he had picked up in the United States, Jonsson instead implicitly encouraged his critics to replicate the tactical maneuvers of the American debate, in effect transferring the debate wholesale to Sweden. In response to Jonsson's book, a number of prominent figures spoke up in defense of supposedly Western values in Sweden as well. The upshot of his "politically correct" critique of the Western canon, these critics held, is a situation in which "there will no longer be a culture left to defend, only a conflict-filled world where word stands against word, and every assertion of one's own living space automatically constitutes a threat to others."[10] Importantly, although most of these writers belong to the right, none of them held views that were particularly extreme, even by Swedish standards. Somewhat paradoxically, then, the concept of PC enters Swedish cultural discourse through a book that critiques it.

Although *De andra* highlighted the concept of PC, the concept hardly occurred at all in the reception of the book, suggesting that the term was still not widely in use in Sweden when the book was published in May 1993.[11] It had started to be introduced, however, particularly in *SvD*. Karin Henriksson, who at the time was the paper's cultural correspondent in the United States, reported from Washington, D.C., that the "abbreviation PC for political correctness appears in all reports about the atmosphere at U.S. universities" (March 18, 1991), before referring to Dinesh D'Souza's attack on PC in *Illiberal Education*. Ingmar Björkstén noted that President George Bush Sr., at the University of Michigan on May 4, 1991, accused the "political correctness" movement of conducting an Orwellian "crusade for civility [that] has soured into a cause of conflict and even censorship," but went on to observe that Bush's own administration condoned attempts to censor various forms of homoerotic art through exercising pressure on the National Endowment for the Arts (July 24, 1991). Henriksson used the concept in two more articles that year, one of which noted that an increasing number of "American schools are adopting curricula with a new ethnic content" (August 21, 1991), the other noting that PC was now part of the marketing strategies of Disney, as witness the independence and intelligence of Belle in *Beauty and the Beast* (December 19, 1991). Drawing upon John Taylor's cover story for the January 1991 issue of *New York* magazine, "Are You Politically Correct?," Stefan Jonsson used the term in one of the articles that predated his book (October 9, 1991). In addition, the concept was discussed on Swedish radio on May 8, 1992, when Susanna Roxman provided an account of the U.S. canon debate on *Obs! Kulturkvarten*; in the wake of Jonsson's book, it was also the topic of a forty-five-minute radio debate (April 6, 1993).

Early usages of PC terms in Sweden thus tended to articulate PC as a distinctively American phenomenon. But the phrase soon enough was unmoored from its American origins. In a trajectory echoing that of the United States, PC phrases were picked up by reviewers in Sweden: in 1993, the journalists using them most frequently at *SvD* were pop music reviewer Stefan Malmqvist (six articles) and columnist Kerstin Hallert (seven articles); a year later, PC phrases appeared as often in the entertainment section of *Aftonbladet* as in the paper's cultural pages.

Consolidation: Political Correctness "in Swedish"

At the same time that the concept of PC was finding its way into major dailies in Sweden and becoming part of everyday discourse it was also picked up in a variety of oppositional magazines, ranging from independent right-wing journals such as *Fri information* and the antisocialist *Contra* (founded in 1974), to openly Nazi publications such as *Nordland*.

PC terms were used in the former two from 1993 and 1994, respectively, while the latter journal explained in its second issue of 1995 that "The 'politically correct,' distorted view of man is disseminated through mass media on a daily basis, and is imprinted on susceptible youth in schools"; the term appears relatively frequently in the journal from thereon.

Despite the popularity of the term, it still lacked a clear ideological articulation. The 1998 arrival of the anthology *Politisk korrekthet på svenska* (Political correctness in Swedish), edited by Pierre Kullbom and Per Landin, can be seen in retrospect as an attempt to explore more systematically the ideological implications of PC in a Swedish setting. The editors, however, deny any such programmatic intentions, and truth to say, the collection bears all the traces of a hastily put together product. In the majority of the essays, the concept of PC is rather peripheral—in half it is not used at all, and it is central only in six. The fourteen male and four female contributors cover a range of subjects—feminism, Swedish daycare practices, ethics and religion, universities, "multicultural" television, censorship, journalism—yet quite often seem to be protesting against a very personal sense of having been silenced, or simply willfully misunderstood. Thus, editor Landin grumbles about having been misrepresented in Swedish media after having written a series of articles about the New Right in Germany. This circumstance gives the lie to the editors' introductory claim that "PC is not so much content as method, a way of putting the lid on the debate and silencing certain nonconformist truths," for it is of course very difficult to create a furor in public debate unless you have access to, and are allowed to express yourself in, that public debate, a circumstance pointed out in a review of the book.[12]

Only two contributions, by editor Pierre Kullbom and Jonas de Geer (the most controversial contributor to the anthology, often accused of anti-Semitism—de Geer joined the neo-Nazi Svenskarnas Parti in 2011), make a case for political correctness as an ideology in its own right. Interestingly, both cite Alexis de Tocqueville's description of American democracy as populist tyranny as an early case study in political correctness. Kullbom goes so far as to argue that, not unlike the project of modernity as such, America is "also a metaphysical entity, something that takes place *within us* and which in its narrow-minded inhuman functionality leads to spiritual decay and social desolation regardless of where we live."[13] A few reviewers found this line of reasoning suggestive, notably Carl Johan Ljungberg, closely associated with new liberal think tank Timbro in Sweden, and Per-Olof Bolander, who one year later launched the short-lived culturally conservative journal *Salt* with de Geer.[14] Most critics dismissed Kullbom's analysis as preposterous, and the overall reception of the book was negative, with *Göteborgs-Posten* going so far as to declare it "a rotten *[urusel]* book."[15] But a bad review is still a review, and the importance of a book is not necessarily dependent on its quality. In retrospect, the book seems a timely intervention: it was reviewed in every major Swedish newspaper and discussed in several radio programs, and thus most certainly stimulated interest in the concept at a time when usage of the concept in newspapers was apparently declining.

Indeed, it might well be that the volume with all its weaknesses made a better case for invoking PC as a rhetorical strategy for the right than it could have had it been a stronger book intellectually. As it stands, the anthology suggests that simply by presenting something as politically incorrect, what one had to say would acquire an aura of heroic resistance to the norm dictated by a tyrannical political correctness (a strategy

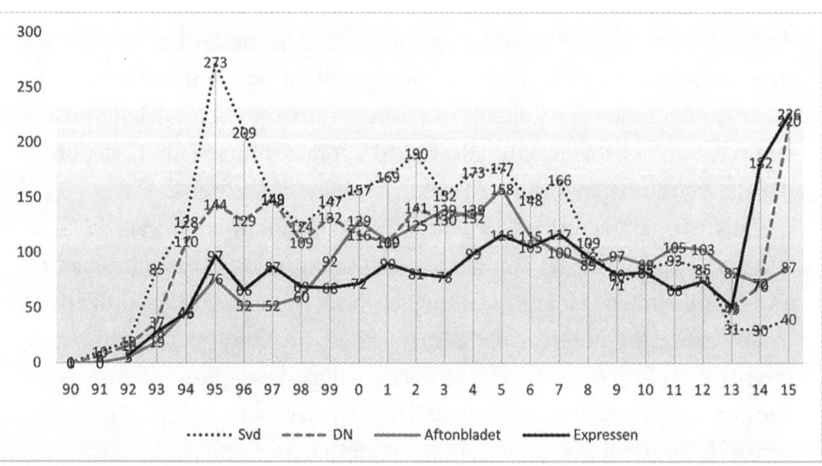

PC terms in Swedish newspapers, 1990–2015: the number of articles including PC terms in the four main national dailies in Sweden between 1990 and 2015. Source: Media Archive at the Royal Library.

continued by *Salt,* the second issue of which admonished its readers to purchase "the politically incorrect Christmas gift—one year with *Salt,*" for 250 Swedish crowns). It also presents political correctness as a concept pliable enough to encompass virtually any experience of not having been listened to, while nevertheless presenting cultural conservatism as the core value allowing PC to be fought. Most important, the anthology presented PC as a phenomenon worthy of serious attention, and even while it made no attempt to present a coherent definition of PC, its key conception of PC as a *method* for suppressing relevant critique nevertheless proved influential, not least because it lent an intellectual aura to a term that was on the verge of imploding under the weight of its various usages.

While Bolander was enthusiastic about Kullbom and Landin's anthology, he complained that it lacked a "deeper" understanding of the phenomenon it spoke about. Such a deeper understanding of the notion of PC was soon to emerge, however, most importantly in the form of the theories of French philosopher Alain de Benoist, founder of the Nouvelle Droite. In truth, the happenstance nature of *Politisk korrekthet på svenska* belied the extent to which it was already indebted to the French philosopher. An article Kullbom wrote in *SvD* (April 23, 1997) just a year prior to the publication of the anthology makes clear that the source of his anti-Americanism was in fact Benoist, whose "ethnopluralist" call for an alliance between Europe and Russia, Kullbom held, offered third-world countries an alternative to an "enforced American way of life." Landin, too, was impressed by Benoist. In one of his most controversial pieces on the German New Right, he wrote about the weekly *Junge Freiheit,* approvingly noting that it has rejected "the failed project of muliticulturalism" in preference for "ethnopluralism, which implies an acknowledgment of one's national heritage but without chauvinistic elements."[16]

This linkage to the Nouvelle Droite would become even more prominent in the succeeding discussion of PC in Sweden. This was, however, also affected by the fledgling counterjihad discourse emerging out of the paleoconservative camp spearheaded by Paul Weyrich, cofounder of several conservative think tanks, including the Heritage Foundation and the Free Congress Foundation, and by a Swedish white supremacy discourse keen on presenting itself as intellectually *comme il faut.*

Activism: PC and the Metapolitics of the New Right

The most genuinely Swedish attempt at providing a "deeper" view of PC was offered by John Järvenpää, former drummer in the white power band Dirlewanger.[17] Järvenpää, who enthusiastically reviewed Kullbom and Landin's anthology in *Borås Tidning* (March 7, 1999), went on to make a case for PC as a form of thought control in two self-published books. For Järvenpää, political correctness amounts to "uniformity, suppression of free opinion, and dichotomization" and ultimately leads to "calling into question the Swedish population, whiteness as such."[18] Järvenpää's understanding of PC thus bears clears traces of white supremacy discourse, but he also draws heavily on a notion long cherished in right-wing circles, namely, that Sweden is not fully democratic, but rather a soft-totalitarian state. Launched by British journalist Roland Huntford in 1971, the argument that "modern Sweden has fulfilled Huxley's specifications for the new totalitarianism" was eagerly developed by right-wing critics in Sweden, who proved especially receptive to Huntford's argument that television in Sweden was "turned into a political weapon" by Olof Palme.[19] Symptomatically, when PC was launched as an ideologically central concept in the journal of the neonationalist Sweden Democrats, *SD-kuriren,* in 1999, it was presented as the result of the policies of "Olof Palme, a person not anchored in reality, with a diabolical, albeit well-intended, vision."[20] Writing in *Salt,* the editor of the online neonationalist magazine *Blågula Frågor* argued similarly in 2000 that "Sweden is now increasingly approaching the totalitarian model of dictatorship" in which "the question of what is true and false" is replaced with what is "sanctioned from above, that is, what is politically correct."[21] The most immediate influence on Järvenpää, however, was Swedish-American social anthropologist Jonathan Friedman, according to whom PC is expressive of "a logic of association and a relation of power to be maintained by this logic," resembling the way fascism is seen as the product of the obliteration of free thought in Ionesco's 1959 play *Rhinoceros.*[22] Attempting to justify such conspiratorial understandings of PC, Järvenpää argues that "political correctness seems unusually powerful in Swedish society," where it is "woven into the structure of society, like a ghost made invisible and unconscious for the absolute majority of the people."[23] For Järvenpää, then, the concept of PC provides a strategic means to unveil the hegemony of the societal elites.

As such a means to challenge the status quo, the concept was systematically used by the informal "Network Against Political Correctness," the central force of which was the Web site called Politiskt Inkorrekt (2008–11). Purportedly autonomous, the Web site was in fact run by members of the Sweden Democrats and made no secret about its support of that party. Kent Ekeroth, the party's spokesperson for international issues at the time, clandestinely helped collect money for the site; he was also deeply involved in the counterjihad movement that gained momentum after 9/11, arranging for anti-Muslim writer Robert Spencer to speak for the Sweden Democrats in 2010, and keeping up contacts with the Gates of Vienna Web site that was an immediate influence on Norwegian terrorist Anders Behring Breivik.[24] When the Sweden Democrats were voted into parliament on September 26, 2010, the Network Against Political Correctness announced its suspension, having "achieved its first goal: to open the eyes of the Swedes sufficiently to achieve a desirable election outcome."[25]

The Network Against Political Correctness was not the first, nor, arguably, the most important, Internet platform for launching a more systematic critique of PC, however. In 2006, Daniel Friberg, a self-styled businessman who has been engaged in Swedish white supremacy groups since the mid-1990s, was instrumental in launching three important online projects that may well have inspired the Network Against Political Correctness: the blog portal Motpol, which quickly developed into a major conveyer of the identitarian (some would say neofascist) ideas of Benoist, Guillame Faye, and others; the Wikipedia clone Metapedia, which presents itself as "an alternative encyclopedia about culture, philosophy, science, and politics"; and finally, the online community Nordisk.nu.[26] Each of these projects can be seen as a step toward initiating a new form of radical nationalist activism, in which the concept of PC plays the role of the overarching ideology that must be resisted. Motpol was key in establishing an intellectual community for radical nationalists in Sweden (Järvenpää and de Geer both become contributors), and as such also steered radical right activism in a *metapolitical* direction, that is, "towards spreading certain ideas and values within a culture(s) which make up a 'world-view' *(Weltanschauung)*" to cite the definition of "Metapolitics" on the English-language Metapedia site. The goal of New Right metapolitics,

Friberg explains, is "to develop perspectives which undermine and tear down both the politically correct haze in which we find ourselves, as well as the baseless feelings of guilt and self-hatred, evident to any thinking person, which are weighing the peoples of Europe down."[27] The online encyclopedia itself is an example of such metapolitical work: first launched in Sweden, this virtual borderland "is today available in eighteen languages, even if the number of articles available in each language varies very much."[28] Nordisk.nu, finally, made it possible to reach a large international audience—according to Swedish Metapedia, by 2011, it had twenty thousand registered users.

In the 1990s, Friberg wrote articles for the neo-Nazi *Folktribunen* (1997–2002), where PC phrases were early on explicitly identified as a means to further a radical nationalist agenda. One of Friberg's colleagues, Lennart Berg, put together a manual instructing writers on how to give the impression that the journal's articles "convey the unfalsified truth about what goes on in the world" in an apparently unbiased manner. This called for a "slanting that was so sophisticated that it is not noticeable for an untrained eye," through choice of subjects and choice of words; enemies could be called things like "hostile to Swedes," "loyal to the regime," "politically correct," "traitor of the people," or "collaborator" while friends of the nationalist cause could be called "patriot," "critic of the regime," "politically incorrect," "dissident" or "oppositional."[29] These instructions were part of a deliberate effort among agents on the nationalist far right to package its racist ideology in a more acceptable form, and the concept of PC proved helpful to this end.

While much more extreme in their views than Kullbom and Landin, Berg and Friberg likewise found inspiration in the thinking of the Nouvelle Droite. Equally important, they quickly realized the advantages of looking beyond the borders of Sweden to advance their cause. Together with other leading Swedish neo-Nazis, they set up Nordiska förlaget (The Nordic Press) in 2001, translating books by David Duke, Kevin MacDonald, and Richard McCulloch into Swedish. Nine years later, this publishing venture transmuted into Arktos Press, which has since been instrumental in making the writings of European New Right writers available in English. Friberg has struck up close collaborations with several people on the American far right, most notably Richard Spencer, another Benoist enthusiast, who allegedly coined the phrase Alt-Right; together, they set up Altright.com, a joint Swedish/American-platform.[30] According to Spencer, "PC isn't just silly, and isn't even just 'egalitarian'; PC is anti-White and is directed at removing White people from positions of influence, at all levels," a statement that makes clear that he has adopted the radical understanding of PC promoted by Järvenpää.[31] Yet another example of a mediated Swedish–American borderland is Red Ice Radio, a Web-based radio channel run by Henrik Palmgren and Lana Lokteff, which, according to Swedish Metapedia, "analyzes the enforcement of the 'religions' of our time: political correctness, cultural Marxism, and multiculturalism."

While sites such as Motpol and Altright.com employ a vast register of concepts, that of PC remains especially important in that it has become entrenched in everyday language in a way that such terms as "cultural Marxism," "ethnopluralism," "metapolitics," or even "mass immigration" have not. The expression thus works somewhat like a linguistic Trojan horse, providing everyday language with a radical right inflection by posing as an everyday phenomenon that anyone can agree to object to. Central not just to radical nationalists, but to right-wing critics generally, the concept of PC constitutes, as it were, a linguistic borderland in which everyday and extremist discourse intermingles, in Sweden and in America alike. Much as Donald Trump repeatedly has declared that the problem with the United States is political correctness, at the blog-post *Det Goda Samhället* (The Good Society) owner Patrik Engellau—one of the main intellectual architects behind the neoliberalization of the Swedish state in the last two or three decades—claims that the "dominating ideology in Sweden today is the teaching of political correctness, PC-ism" *(PK-ismen),* which he habitually presents as an ideology in its own right.[32]

At the same time, the concept of PC has become an important locus for the somewhat paradoxical universalization of the nationalist agenda at the center of the alt-right movement, in the rhetoric of which the boundaries between America and Europe tend to dissolve. "Whites alone defined America as a European society and political order," Spencer claims in the Charlottesville Statement he had meant to deliver at the white supremacist demonstration in 2017, at which both Friberg and Christopher Dulny, former group leader of the Sweden Democrats in Stockholm, were present. While its emphasis is different, the statement shares with Breivik's *2083: A European Declaration of Independence* the virtual blending of America and Europe into one cultural entity. Implicitly suggested by the very title of the Norwegian compendium, Spencer makes this cultural identity explicit in declaring that "Europe is our common home, and our ancestors' bone and blood lie in its soil."[33] And just as Breivik's compendium presents Sweden as "the one Western nation where Political Correctness has reached the worst heights," in a panel discussion including Daniel Friberg and Jonas de Geer, Altright.com presents Sweden as "The World Capital of Cultural Marxism."[34] If PC once was introduced in Sweden as an American phenomenon, for some time now Sweden itself has thus been exported back into American political discourse as the very embodiment of this supposedly American invention, a reminder of just how complex are the relations between nations and ideas in this era of mediated borderlands.

Notes

1. For PC as myth, see John K. Wilson, *The Myth of Political Correctness: The Conservative Attack on Higher Education* (Durham, N.C.: Duke University Press, 1995).

2. John W. I. Lee and Michael North, "Introduction," in *Globalizing Borderlands Studies in Europe and North America* (Lincoln: University of Nebraska Press, 2016), 1–13, 2.

3. "Nutidens furstar," *SvD*, January 13, 1894. All translations of Swedish sources are my own.

4. Solveig Granath and Magnus Ullén, "'The Elevation of Sensitivity over Truth': *Political Correctness* and Related Phrases in the *Time* Magazine Corpus," *Applied Linguistics* 40, no. 2 (April 2019): 265–87, 273.

5. "Post-Conference Petition," *Off Our Backs* 12, no. 7 (1982): 26.

6. See also David Beers, "Behind the Hysteria: How the Right Invented PC Police," *Mother Jones* 16, no. 5 (1991): 34–35, 64–65.

7. Roger Kimball, *Tenured Radicals: How Politics Has Corrupted Our Higher Education* (New York: Harper, 1991), 204.

8. Stefan Jonsson, *De andra: Amerikanska kulturkrig och europeisk rasism* (Stockholm: Norstedts, 1993), 256.

9. Kay Glans, *SvD*, May 25, 1993.

10. Steve Sem-Sandberg, *SvD,* May 10, 1993. See also Mats Svegfors, *SvD,* May 14, 1993; Kay Glans, *SvD,* May 25 and August 1, 1993; Steve Sem-Sandberg, *SvD,* July 21, 1993; Mats Gellerfeldt, *Finanstidningen,* May 18 and 28, 1993; Jan Söderqvist, *Expressen,* May 10, June 3, and June 22, 1993; Knut Carlqvist, *Finanstidningen,* May 10, 1993; and Peter Luthersson, *SvD,* July 21, 1993.

11. Of the thirty-two reviews I have looked at, only three mention PC: Tuva Korsström, *Hufvudstadsbladet,* September 5, 1993; Steve Sem-Sandberg, *SvD,* May 10, 1993; Oscar Hemer, *Sydsvenska Dagbladet,* May 10, 1993, who questions Jonsson's unsubstantiated claim that PC was originally a self-ironic joke among leftists.

12. Magnus Schmauch, *Ariel* 4 (1998): 82–83. The quotation is from the preface of Pierre Kullbom and Per Landin, *Politisk korrekthet på svenska* (Stockholm: Symposion, 1998), 7.

13. Pierre Kullbom, "Den amerikanska livsstilen som politisk korrekthet," in Kullbom and Landin, *Politisk korrekthet på svenska,* 75.

14. See Carl Johan Ljungberg, *SAF tidningen Näringsliv* 22 (1998) and *Upsala Nya Tidning,* November 8, 1998; and Per-Olof Bolander, *SvD,* August 12, 1998.

15. Johan Dahlbäck, *Göteborgsposten,* August 16, 1998. Of the eighteen reviews I read, ten are clearly negative, while only four are clearly positive.

16. Per Landin, "En revolutionär nyhöger: Svärmar för nationen och fornstora dagar men ser sig inte som nazister," *DN,* November 1, 1996.

17. See "Heroes-bandet som försöker tvätta bort naziststämpeln," *Expo,* April 16, 2003.

18. John Järvenpää, *Politisk korrekthet: Likriktning, åsiktsförtryck och dikotomisering* (Gothenburg: Reson produktion, 2006), 160.

19. Roland Huntford, *The New Totalitarians* (London: Allen Lane, 1971), 348, 290. For the impact of Huntford's book in Sweden, see David Östlund, "Maskinmodernitet och dystopisk lycka: den sociala ingenjörskonstens Sverige, upplaga Huntford 1971," *Polhem: Teknikhistorik årsbok 2006–2007* (2009): 40–63.

20. Jimmy Windeskog, "Politik är inte att vilja: Varför kommer det liberalmarxistiska samhället aldrig att fungera?," *SD-kuriren* 35 (1999): 8–10.

21. Jan Milld, "Ny diktatur," *Samtidsmagasinet Salt* 7 (2001): 11.

22. Jonathan Friedman, "Rhinoceros 2," *Current Anthropology* 40, no. 5 (1999): 679–88, 688.

23. John Järvenpää, *Invandring och demokrati: Om politisk korrekthet i Sverige 1988–2001* (Gothenburg: Reson produktion, 2002), 10.

24. Gellert Tamas, *Det svenska hatet: En berättelse om vår tid* (Stockholm: Natur & kultur, 2016).

25. All Web sources cited in this essay were accessed on August 9, 2019.

26. See, for instance, Benjamin Teitelbaum, *Lions of the North: Sounds of the New Nordic Radical Nationalism* (New York: Oxford University Press, 2017), 47–51.

27. Daniel Friberg, "Metapolitics from the Right," undated [2017], https://www.altright.com.

28. Henrik Arnstad, "Ikea Fascism: Metapedia and the Internationalization of Swedish Generic Fascism," *Fascism: Journal of Comparative Fascist Studies* 4 (2015): 194–208, 196.

29. Lennart Berg, "Att skriva notiser till Folktribunen," cited after Mattias Wåg, "Nationell kulturkamp—från vit maktmusik till metapolitik," in *Det vita fältet: samtida forskning om högerextremism,* ed. Mats Deland, Fredrik Hertzberg, and Thomas Hvitfeldt (Uppsala: Swedish Science Press, 2010), 97–126, 103.

30. J. Lester Feder and Pierre Buet, "They Wanted to Be a Better Class of White Nationalists. They Claimed This Man as Their Father," BuzzFeed.News, December 27, 2017: https://www.buzzfeednews.com/.

31. Richard Spencer, "Cultural Appropriation," *Radix Journal,* November 22, 2015, https://radixjournal.com/.

32. Patrik Engellau, "PK-ismen," *Det goda samhället,* November 10, 2016, https://detgodasamhallet.com/.

33. Richard Spencer, "What It Means to Be Alt-Right," https://altright.com/. For a highly rewarding discussion of the rhetoric of the Swedish-American alt-right, see Karl Ekeman, "Solecism or Barbarism (Part 1): The Swedish Nationalist Milieu and a Cultural Struggle from the Right," *Public Seminar,* http://www.publicseminar.org.

34. Fjordman, "Jihad Destroys the Swedish Model," cited in Anders Behring Breivik, *2083: A European Declaration of Independence,* section 2.55; and "Sweden—the World Capital of Cultural Marxism," https://altright.com.

15

History and Heritage in Bishop Hill, Illinois

Preservation, Representation, and Tourism in a Swedish–American Borderland

Margaret E. Farrar and Adam Kaul

Bishop Hill, Illinois, one of dozens of towns originally founded in nineteenth-century America as experimental communal societies, understands itself to be a "Utopia on the Prairie." Once boasting a population as high as 1,500 in its heyday,[1] today Bishop Hill is a small village of approximately 125 permanent residents centered around a green town square with many brick buildings built before the American Civil War. Nestled in a pastoral farming landscape in rural western Illinois, it depends largely on a regional day-tripping tourist economy focused on the history of its founding and on numerous festivals that have been developed over the years. Bishop Hill has survived into the twenty-first century in part because it has the benefit of both striking architecture and a somewhat sensational origin story: a charismatic messianic leader establishes a communitarian sect with his followers from Sweden but is murdered only a few years later by an interloper in a romantic dispute. Its longevity is largely due to its status as a borderland: a place where an international Swedish diaspora can find both commonality in its history and traditions and innovation through the creation of a uniquely American tourist destination.

For us, the borderland is an active and dynamic concept. Anthropologist Renato Rosaldo describes borderlands "not as analytically empty transitional zones but as sites of creative cultural production."[2] As anthropologists, Edward M. Bruner and Rosaldo examine ethnographic contexts and conduct synchronic analyses in contemporary intercultural spaces. We follow their lead into the "busy intersections"[3] of the borderlands, although our analysis is also diachronic—across time. We see the porosity of what happened in the past (history) and how it is understood, interpreted, and reenacted in the present (heritage) as another aspect of this borderland worth exploring. In this essay, we draw on data from multiple methods we have employed since 2010, including archival research, ethnographic observation, interviews, and a visitors' survey, to examine the concept of Swedish-American borderlands through the ways in which history has been transformed into heritage at this site that plays such a key role in Swedish migration to North America. Our aim is to illustrate how heritage is claimed and reimagined to inform new identities—including Swedish-American identities—in twenty-first century America.

Historical Borderlands

In order to understand contemporary Bishop Hill and its status as a borderland, it is essential to understand why it was founded and how it has survived intact at all. In some ways, Bishop Hill's founding is commonplace by mid-nineteenth-century standards when more than a hundred different experimental utopian communities with a combined membership of more than one hundred thousand people were scattered across the American landscape.[4] Bishop Hill's particular flavor of utopianism was religious, a dissident offshoot of Swedish Lutheranism founded by lay preacher Eric Jansson. In the mid-nineteenth century, Lutheranism was the official religion of the Swedish state, but by that time dissatisfaction with and corruption within the church had led to a significant dissident movement, known as *läsare* (or lay readers), that emphasized learning about the Bible outside the confines of state doctrine. The *läsare* appealed to direct and divine inspiration for salvation.[5] Jansson's beliefs became even more radical than that, culminating in the assertion that the Bible was the only true religious text, meaning that even Luther's writings, for example, "'ought to be burnt.'"[6] This was not merely hyperbolic sermonizing; Jansson did, in fact, organize a number of book burnings of Lutheran hymnals, church tracts, and other sacred texts, including Luther's catechism. He also began to argue for his own divinity. His contentions were considered a threat to the state's religious interests, and he eventually landed in prison on several occasions, and then went into hiding in Norway. Understandably, perhaps, Jansson became a threat to the state's religious authority, and he eventually fled Sweden for the United States in 1846.[7]

Jansson's exodus from Sweden was not at all spontaneous or ill-considered. By the time he left the country, he had attracted literally thousands of followers, a few of them quite wealthy. He sent follower Olof Olson ahead to the United States on a scouting expedition to locate suitable land. He found it in what was later named Bishop Hill, Illinois (for Jansson's birthplace in Sweden, Biskopskulla), and the community pooled their resources and made the journey to their new world. More than 1,200 people ("Janssonists") arrived in Bishop Hill between 1846 and 1854, making it the first and one of the largest centers for Swedish settlement in the United States. In fact, migration researchers have referred to Bishop Hill as "the mother colony of Swedish America."[8]

The Janssonists thus established themselves in what was conceived more literally at the time as a "borderland" in the expanding American colonial project. Most people then (and later, many historians) would call it a "frontier," eliciting images of a hard border. In fact, of course, the more porous notion of a borderland is far more accurate. The Indigenous Meskwaki peoples (mislabeled first by the French as "les Renard" and later by English speakers as the Sac and Fox), for example, had only recently been removed from the area in the 1830s, but not completely.

The Janssonists quickly transformed their purchase into a fully functioning village and twelve thousand farmed acres, and initially at least one new construction project was completed each year.[9] Villagers lived, worked, and worshipped communally, sharing residences, resources, and common spaces. As the colony grew, it experienced a tension common to such experimental communities: between spiritual integrity and assimilation to the culture and values of the United States. Eventually, this tension manifested itself in a drawn-out dispute between Jansson and an "outsider" named John Root, who had married Jansson's cousin. Root attempted to kidnap the young woman away from Bishop Hill against her will. When the two men encountered each other at the local courthouse, Root shot Jansson, killing him on the spot.

Because of Jansson's belief in his own divinity, his followers naturally expected him to rise from the dead. They laid him out in the colony church and waited three days and three nights before finally burying him.[10] The colony survived this crisis, but by 1861 corruption in leadership and social pressures to assimilate, combined with the exodus of young men who left to fight in the Civil War, led to the colony's demise. A long and divisive dissolution took place over the next thirty years. By the early 1890s, Bishop Hill's population had diminished to around 330 citizens.[11] Nonetheless, the Swedish origins of the town remained central to its identity; for years the most powerful political group in the town was the people descended from the first colonists, known to this day by the community as The Descendants.

Bishop Hill's founding and subsequent decline in the nineteenth century is in some ways unique, but the narrative also seems to fit neatly into a broader history of European migration to North America, the conquest and settling of its people and land, and eventual assimilation into American society. It is a story of Swedes crossing the Atlantic, a grand oceanic border between two nations, two cultures. Setting aside the problematic simplicity of that common narrative, what we are far more interested in is not the transnational history of the migrant story, but the cultural borders created and re-created through heritage making over the following century. This is a much more metaphoric "borderland" between Swedishness and Americanness that developed through the misty lens of nostalgia in the twentieth and twenty-first centuries as Bishop Hill became, in the first instance, a site of historical preservation and representation, and second, a site for tourist consumption of the preserved and the sometimes (mis)represented past.

Framing History, Painting Heritage

Part of this larger and more metaphorical story of Bishop Hill as a Swedish–American borderland is a stunning collection of paintings of Bishop Hill by an amateur artist named Olof Krans created from memory starting in the late 1800s. Krans's work occupies a prominent place in Bishop Hill's understanding of itself and the way it presents itself to others; the Bishop Hill Museum in Illinois claims 106 of Krans's works, reproductions of which are featured prominently in the town's promotional materials.

Olof Krans's family moved from Sweden to Bishop Hill in 1850 when he was twelve. His career as an artist began in the mid-1890s. Today, Krans is celebrated for his "primitivist" style of portraiture and landscape paintings, and his work is now recognized as an important contribution to early American folk art. In a retrospective of Krans's work, art historian Esther Sparks describes how his first set of reminiscent paintings of the colony in 1896 were mostly met with praise, although some descendants from the original colony days had a series of questions about some of the details that he got wrong. "Such questions may be appropriate for the dedicated historian," she writes, but Olof Krans "painted what he remembered."[12] The fact is that Krans only began painting these portraits and scenes at the fiftieth anniversary of the founding of Bishop Hill, from memory and from his imagination derived from local folk histories. Thus, his paintings are not so much ethnographic depictions of colony life as they are impressions from his own—and others'—memories, leading to what Sparks describes as "undisguised nostalgia" in the work.[13] This also means that the public's contemporary nostalgia generated by Olof Krans's paintings is therefore two or three times removed from lived history. But while he painted scenes of life in the colony from memory many decades after its dissolution, it is interesting to note that he is often described matter-of-factly as a faithful "recorder of Bishop Hill Colonists and their lives."[14] One prominent folk art collector wrote, "Without Krans's portraits of these hardy settlers, we would know much less about this nineteenth century social experiment."[15] As such, viewers are led to believe that his paintings get us closer to an "authentic" version of the past, but this is debatable.

In Krans's work we find not just manufactured remembrances, but also buried and forgotten histories, and manufactured Swedish-American identities. One painting, *Helbom and the Indian,* is a visual folktale told from a settler's point of view. The image depicts the wild-eyed Swede Nils Helbom, dressed in a bearskin coat and hat, growling as he sidles next to a knife-wielding American Indian figure. There is potential for violence, and it is hard to say who looks more startled. *Helbom and the Indian* references a legend about the early days of the colony when, supposedly, bands of Native Americans still wandered the landscape. According to one version of the tale, reports about a group of Native people passing by Bishop Hill reached the residents, so a plan was devised. The villagers would send out the largest Swede they could find dressed in bearskins. Surely, they thought, the Natives would think Helbom was a real bear and would run for their lives.[16] Although it was originally intended to be a comical tale, it also highlights the colonists' naive and ethnocentric view of the displaced Native inhabitants. If these events ever really happened, and if the American Indians were scared of anything, it would have been this erratically behaved and strangely dressed Swede, but surely not because they thought he was an actual bear.

The legend, and Krans's painted version of the tale, say more about white immigrant stereotypes about the "primitive savages" that had been so recently displaced than it does about real American Indians. It is a visual history imagined from a white point of view, a glimpse of a lingering displacement, and the anxiety caused by a population of exotic "Others" recently removed but apparently not far or thoroughly enough. At the same time, it speaks volumes about the silencing of certain histories and the amplification of others in the process of making heritage, the remembering and forgetting required in the formation of identity.[17] Bishop Hill's heritage requires amnesia about Native *dis*placement, and the simultaneous nostalgia about white domestication of the American landscape emphasizes the taming of the wilderness, something anthropologist Catie Gressier, in a very different ethnographic context, has called a narrative of "white *em*placement" in the landscape.[18] Those twin forces of amnesia and nostalgia, of course, are what have allowed Bishop Hill to survive by commoditizing its history.

Preservation and (Re)Creation

Despite Olof Krans's artistic reminiscences, for many years the town's residents did not have any particular interest in preserving their history per se. Like many immigrant groups in the nineteenth and early twentieth centuries, Bishop Hill villagers concentrated on assimilation rather than memorialization, and in many ways sought to distance themselves from their storied past. Or, as one longtime Bishop Hill area resident told us,

"They weren't preservationists in the early years. They turned their back on Sweden and all things Swedish."[19] In fact, given the colorful history of the founding of the village, many residents fully embraced a general cultural Americanness over Swedish identities.

For example, the village baseball team—that great American pastime—became a key symbol of Bishop Hill identity early on. The placement of the baseball field is symbolic: the field was constructed on the site of a massive colony-era building called "Big Brick" that burned to the ground in 1928, where it sat adjacent to the original green town square. The field, then, might be a metonym for the assimilation process and much like a second town square, designed not for the needs of a nineteenth-century religious commune but for the needs of a twentieth-century American community.

Despite their best efforts at assimilation in the early twentieth century, though, the past never really became past in Bishop Hill. In fact, it was the colony's original commitment to communal living that made it rather difficult to change the physical structure of the village. When the colony was officially dissolved in 1861, a complicated set of rules governed the distribution of communal property: anyone who had belonged to the colony for five years or more was given a share of the property, with the value of that share determined by age. In the end, a total of 415 shareholders received various amounts of "land, livestock, right to occupy parts of the communal buildings, and personal property."[20] The result was dozens of owners for single plots of land and individual buildings.

In other words, the communal nature of the colony had the unintended consequence of ensuring historic preservation, as in subsequent years it was practically impossible to locate all of the owners for a single structure, let alone convince them to agree on what to do with it. For example, the Steeple Building, one of the largest and most impressive buildings in the village, had to be purchased from more than one hundred heirs, with thirty-eight "owners" for one room.[21] As a result, the buildings fell into disrepair over the years, but they stayed standing as they passed from one generation to another, and the fundamental integrity of the original colonists' vision remained intact.

Genuine interest in preserving the colony's history and legacy was only sparked at the occasion of the hundredth anniversary of the colony's founding. In 1946, the village donated its central park, the Colony Church, and a collection of Olof Krans paintings to the State of Illinois. The state named the village a State Historic Landmark and began restoring the Colony Church as a historic site. Since then, the residents of Bishop Hill, the government of Sweden, and the larger Swedish diaspora have increasingly sought to capitalize on the village's unique and colorful past by preserving, memorializing, and marketing it to outsiders. In 1984, the village was named to the National Registry of Historic Places. Now a National Historic Landmark District, Bishop Hill has managed to preserve all thirteen pre–Civil War buildings and has received state, federal, and international funding to support its conservation and promotion efforts. The integrity of the site makes it unique. As the nomination to the National Registry described it:

> The visual and physical flow the colonists would have experienced between the agricultural lands and the communal heart of the colony is present today. A typical view presents a loose weave of nineteenth century clapboard dwellings interspersed with coal and cob houses, weathered privies, perhaps a small barn, an edge of picket or board fence, a patch of garden . . . Although the pattern unravels at the edge of town, dissolving into fields, it is firmly fixed at the square in the solid regularity of the original colony structures . . . The hills are dotted with small farmsteads, many owned by descendants of the Colony, and some bearing strong marks of their Swedish vernacular origins. Thus, the proposed Landmark District exists in a landscape setting which not only evokes but bears extensive physical evidence of the historic past.[22]

Thus, despite the relatively short duration of the colony itself, Bishop Hill left an impressive and rather outsized cultural and architectural legacy in rural Illinois, a legacy that resisted "assimilation" in favor of something more interesting and more nuanced: a migration borderland where Swedishness and Americanness continue to intermingle in fascinating ways.

Swedish–American encounters in the Bishop Hill borderland are rather straightforward, facilitated through material spaces and active organizations created expressly for this purpose. In 1974, Bishop Hill became the designated home of the archives of the Vasa order, the Swedish-American fraternal organization. Dedicated to making available "records, documents, works of art, science, inventions and manufacture by persons of Swedish ancestry" and "promot[ing] public knowledge of an interest in the history of persons of Scandinavian and particularly Swedish ancestry," the archives regularly attracts international visitors, from amateur genealogists to accomplished scholars.[23]

In fact, as the "mother colony" of Swedish immigration, Bishop Hill is better known to most Swedes than it is to many Americans; it is mentioned, for example, in Swedish schoolbooks and it is featured as a "must see" destination for Swedes on popular tourism Web sites.[24] The village's centrality to the narrative of Swedish identity is reinforced by periodic visits by Swedish officials; the king and queen came to the village in 1996, and in 2016 Bishop Hill hosted the U.S. ambassador to Sweden. In Sweden, the Bishop Hill Society was founded "to spread interest in the history of the Bishop Hill colony that became central to the entire coming Swedish emigration to America and to promote contacts with our neighbor Bishop Hill in Illinois."[25] In fact, the original Bishop Hill (Jansson's birthplace, Bishopskulla, Sweden) boasts a museum dedicated to the U.S. colony, featuring pictures, court documents, research, newspapers, and books about the village, as well as an exhibit on Olof Krans. In both the Illinois village and the Swedish museum, Swedish-American identity is bound in and understood through the remembrance of and the (re)creation of a place. It is no wonder, then, that one resident of the U.S. site estimated that she sees several hundred Swedish visitors per season.

Even in these seemingly straightforward exchanges, though, "Swedish heritage" is constructed and contested. According to one recent Swedish immigrant to Bishop Hill, some of the traditions promoted in the village bear little resemblance to those practiced in Sweden. When we asked her whose heritage was being represented in this place, she responded:

> It was Swedish in the beginning, but it is American as well . . . It's *supposed* to be a Swedish heritage . . . They've changed it here. [The] Lucia [tradition] is really different over here . . . It's very unique over there [in Sweden] . . . most of the time companies close down because of Lucia . . .
>
> [During Lucia Nights in Bishop Hill] they have a goat [a person dressed in a goat costume] running around and scaring people. What is that? I've

> never seen that before in my whole life. [Laughs.] The tradition over here has changed a lot . . . I don't even know what kind of heritage it is.

Inventing a Destination

This ambiguity about "what kind of heritage" Bishop Hill represents is an indication that the interests of all of the stakeholders in Bishop Hill are not necessarily aligned. It is important to recognize that the village's desire to preserve or restore buildings and artifacts from the past has never simply been about the intrinsic value of maintaining a connection to its history or ties to the mother country. An organization called the Bishop Hill Heritage Association (often simply called "The Heritage" by locals) was formed in 1962 following the demolition of one of the original colony buildings, but the business of preservation in the village has always also been a *business*.[26] The vast majority of visitors to Bishop Hill

A sign near the entrance to Bishop Hill reads: "Just Ahead Historic Bishop Hill: This farm was the home of Mary Malmgren Olson first child born in Bishop Hill Colony 12–27–1846."

come not from Sweden but from other parts of Illinois, and the village needs to be responsive to their interests in order to survive.[27]

In places like Bishop Hill—where its status as a commercial center collapsed early on and where most farming has become a largely industrialized affair—historic preservation and the tourist dollars that follow are often seen as providing a solution to economic woes.[28] Even as early as 1968, The Heritage referred to tourism as a key vehicle for preservation and economic sustainability,[29] although fewer than ten thousand tourists a year were visiting the village at that time.[30] This was the same year that Olov Isaksson, the director of the Museum of National Antiquities in Stockholm, undertook a massive research project about Bishop Hill that resulted in a definitive book on the history of the colony period and a large exhibit at the museum.[31] Over the years, Isaksson was also central in raising substantial funds from the Swedish government to help preserve buildings in Bishop Hill.[32]

While the Swedish focus could be more purely about historical preservation, in Bishop Hill residents also had to make a living. They needed to monetize their assets. By the early 1970s, Bishop Hill was attracting around thirty thousand visitors a year; by the mid-1970s, this number had doubled, and the village had aspirations for greater numbers of visitors still. Certainly, by the time Bishop Hill was vying for a spot in the National Historic Landmark program in the 1980s, references to the economic importance of heritage tourism were plentiful. One particularly striking example can be found in an endorsement for the status: "[T]here can be no doubt about the potential value of Bishop Hill to our economically hard-pressed region. The significant contribution that Bishop Hill already provides in visitors and tourist dollars can only increase in the future. In fact, [we] cited Bishop Hill . . . as a prime example of how to develop and tap this area's tourism potential. The National Historic Landmark designation that Bishop Hill so richly deserves will certainly add to that potential."[33]

What are tourists looking for today when they visit a heritage tourist destination like Bishop Hill? For contemporary tourists, their motives reveal the sometimes surprising disconnect between history and heritage: while tourists often casually claim that they are interested in "history," what we discovered via a visitors' survey is that they are less interested in the particulars of the village's past (things such as "immigration history," "the Janssonist religion," or the nature of the "early communal society") than in their own contemporary experiences of the village—things such as "dining," "shopping," or "architecture." In fact, in the survey, "watching craftspeople work" was more important than "immigration history" or "the Janssonist religion" combined. Even "Swedish heritage," which ranks quite high on the list, might arguably indicate an interest in contemporary Swedish identity rather than a historical one. One resident summed up this distinction nicely:

> We've always had this kind of tightrope between people coming to shop and do commercial things, and people coming for the history . . . For the most part, I think we have walked it fairly well. But it seems since the recession . . .

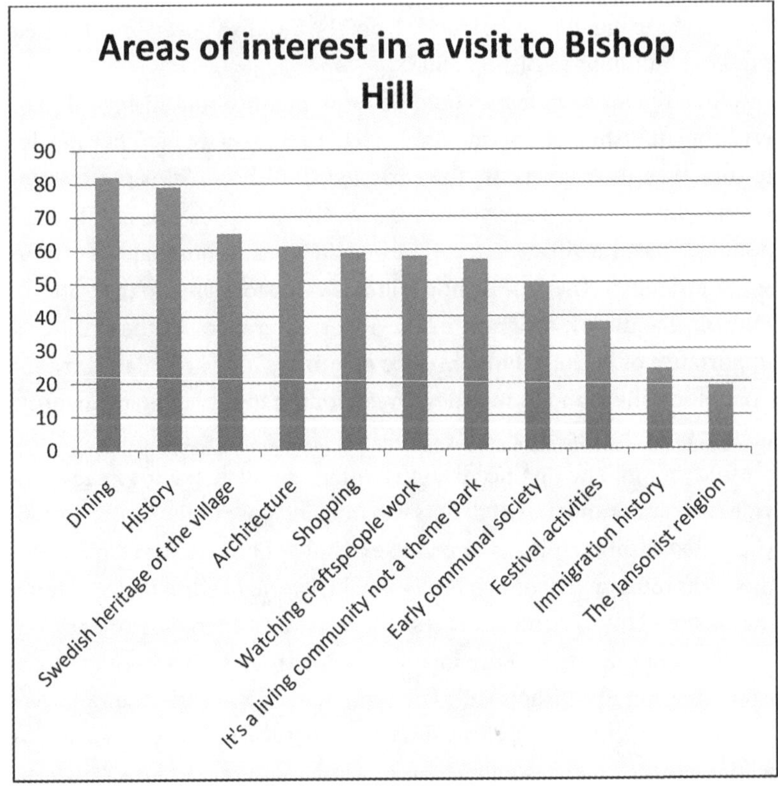

Results from Bishop Hill visitor experience survey, compiled by Adam Kaul in 2011–12.

> everything seems much more "come and shop and see our events." [Everything is] more event-driven in some ways.

In fact, local residents involved in the tourism industry know that focusing too much on history, even on its highly sanitized Swedish version, is a risky bet. As the manager of Bishop Hill's Web presence told us, a part of the community is "selling the Swedish story, but . . . ten years of answering e-mails, I know that people don't want to eat the lutefisk. [Some people] insist on calling [things] by their Swedish names . . . [but] it's like a club you don't belong to." In other words, historical accuracy and authenticity may actually make the place more exclusionary than it can afford to be.

This is not unique to Bishop Hill by any means. Heritage tourism elevates some things, some stories, and imbues them with an almost sacred aura, while other things are considered polluting. It has also been shown in many tourist contexts that visitors prefer verisimilitude over historical "authenticity," and in many ways this verisimilitude is regarded by the touring public as "more true."[34] One tourist compared her motives for visiting Bishop Hill with her experience of touring other heritage sites around the country:

> I always say to myself, "What was it like then? Here we are, standing here, this structure is still the same, but what did everything around it look like? What was going on around this place when [people] still lived there?" . . . sometimes you can catch that individual feeling, and that makes me feel emotionally charged.

This is a classic illustration of how the imagination filters and frames our experiences of a heritage site in powerful ways that are sometimes emotional and personal rather than strictly historical. Through our tourist gaze, we try to imagine the historical past by filtering out polluting aspects of both the past and the present. Consider this characterization of the landscape around Bishop Hill from the Henry County Tourism Bureau guidebook:

> While driving through Henry County back roads, you will see rich farmland with picturesque agricultural vistas that seem to stretch forever. The

> fertile farm ground and the promise of the good life drew early pioneers to settle Henry County. Dotting the scenery are small towns and villages telling the stories of the land . . . *A visit to Henry County will conjure thoughts of a simpler time.*[35]

One local resident who has had a hand in historic preservation work in the region used a similar phrase:

> You have people who are just interested in *the time period that Bishop Hill represents.* I mean, we represent 1850s rural Americana . . . and there are some people who are interested in that time period, *a simpler time* before the Civil War.[36]

So, today Bishop Hill might spark an imagined representation of "simpler times," but given what we know about Bishop Hill's past, it was anything but simple, including as it did religious extremism, a deadly cholera epidemic, and a hardscrabble existence in what was essentially a small communist enclave on the prairie. Not surprisingly, the actual history of Bishop Hill gets thoroughly sanitized in the tourist-friendly iteration. Communal economic models are transformed into hardy "frontier ethics" and the capitalist ingenuity of white immigrants. Religious extremism becomes "a quest for religious freedom." In other words, the story of Bishop Hill becomes more palatable and more quintessentially American in its retellings. In fact, several of our interviewees characterized it as such; as one stated, "It's not just a Swedish story, it's like the classic immigration story." Swedish signifiers (*tomte* dolls, *dala* horses, lutefisk) are seen as quirky and nostalgic rather than alien, menacing, or colonizing. This dominant version of the Bishop Hill narrative, then, has become "the story of the brave and determined Swedes who became brave and determined Americans."[37]

Porous History, Porous Borders

When we talk about Bishop Hill as a borderland, then, it is in multiple senses of that word. It owes its existence to transatlantic border crossings and the colonization of U.S. borderlands in the nineteenth century. Its character over time, like that of so many immigrant communities, has been created and re-created through the push and pull of identification and assimilation, and through the ways that its citizens had to navigate the boundaries of their identities in their everyday lives. It is a borderland, too, in the sense that it serves as a nodal point for Swedish–American cultural exchange. But it is also a borderland in a more nuanced sense. Given the fact that historic preservation is influenced by competing voices and interests, and given the fact that the products of that preservation (the colony buildings and the stories they tell) are "consumed" by a diverse set of actors (local day-trippers, Swedes following the immigrants' trail, and amateur genealogists), Bishop Hill is a borderland between history and heritage. As such, the preservation of Bishop Hill's buildings and traditions is not, in Peter Cannavò's phrase, "an exercise in geographic taxidermy,"[38] but rather an ongoing negotiation with the built environment, with history, with Swedish and American identities, and with contemporary social life in the village. This porosity makes Bishop Hill such an intriguing and vibrant place—a place that inspires thought about the intersection of memory and forgetting.

Notes

1. The exact figure is unclear. Some accounts, such as the 1984 application to nominate Bishop Hill for inclusion on the National Register of Historic Places prepared by Kathleen Lidfors, claim that once the population stabilized after its initial cholera outbreaks, it only reached between eight hundred and one thousand people (U.S. Department of the Interior, National Park Service, *National Register of Historic Places: Nomination Form for Bishop Hill Colony,* Form Number 10–306 [Washington, D.C.: U.S. Government Printing Office, 1984 (Bishop Hill: Bishop Hill Heritage Association)]; accessed September 30, 2014, BHHA archives).

2. Renato Rosaldo, *Culture and Truth: The Remaking of Social Analysis* (Boston: Beacon Press, 1989), 208.

3. Ibid., 194.

4. Mark Holloway, *Heavens on Earth: Utopian Communities in America 1680–1960,* 2d ed. (New York: Dover Publications, 1966), 18.

5. Linda O'Neill, *History, Memory, and Ethnic Identification: Rediscovering Community in Bishop Hill, Illinois* (DeKalb: LEPS Press, Northern Illinois University Press, 1996), 10; Janet Ruth White, "The Intersection of Culture and Architecture in Three Nineteenth-Century Utopian Communities: The Bethel Colony,

the Bishop Hill Colony, and the Oneida Community," dissertation, Cornell University, Architecture, 2001, 161.

6. White, "The Intersection of Culture and Architecture in Three Nineteenth-Century Utopian Communities," 165.

7. Ibid., 165–66.

8. Quoted in O'Neill, *History, Memory, and Ethnic Identification,* 9.

9. White, "The Intersection of Culture and Architecture in Three Nineteenth-Century Utopian Communities," 225.

10. Ibid., 175; O'Neill, *History, Memory, and Ethnic Identification,* 15.

11. O'Neill, *History, Memory, and Ethnic Identification,* 20. See also Michael A. Mikkelsen, *The Bishop Hill Colony: A Religious Communistic Settlement in Henry County, Illinois* (Baltimore: Johns Hopkins University Press, 1892).

12. Esther Sparks, "Olof Krans: The Artist," in *The Art of Olof Krans: A Prairie Vision,* ed. Martha Jane Downey et al. (Peoria, Ill.: Peoria Riverfront Museum, 2014), 37.

13. Ibid., 34.

14. Merle Glick, "Preface," in Downey et al., *The Art of Olof Krans,* 12.

15. Ibid.

16. Olov Isaksson, *Bishop Hill: A Utopia on the Prairie* (Stockholm: LT Publishing House, 1969), 124.

17. Margaret E. Farrar, "Amnesia, Nostalgia, and the Politics of Place Memory," *Political Research Quarterly* 64, no. 4 (2011): 723–35.

18. Catie Gressier, *At Home in the Okavango: White Batswana Narratives of Emplacement and Belonging* (New York: Berghahn Books, 2015).

19. See also Kate Horberg, "Bishop Hill: A Study of Community Identity," unpublished student research paper, Augustana College, Rock Island, Illinois, 2011.

20. White, "The Intersection of Culture and Architecture in Three Nineteenth-Century Utopian Communities," 219–20.

21. Ronald E. Nelson, "Progress Report" (Bishop Hill: Bishop Hill Heritage Association, 1968); accessed September 30, 2014, BHHA archives.

22. *National Register of Historic Places: Nomination Form for Bishop Hill Colony,* 3–4; accessed September 30, 2014, BHHA archives.

23. Vasa Archives, https://www.vasaarchives.org; accessed July 15, 2019.

24. "10 Great Places to Tour Swedish America," *USA Today,* September 27, 2006, http://usatoday30.usatoday.com. Accessed March 20, 2015.

25. Bishop Hill-sällskapet, https://bishophillsallskapet.wordpress.com; accessed July 15, 2019.

26. The Bishop Hill Heritage Association, https://bishophillheritage.org; accessed July 15, 2019.

27. Cheryl Hargrove, *Henry, Mercer, Rural Rock Island (HMRRI) Counties Tourism Experience Evaluation* (St. Simons Island, Ga.: Hargrove International, 2013), 1–13.

28. G. J. Ashworth, "Heritage and Economic Development: Selling the Unsellable," *Heritage and Society* 7, no. 1 (May 2014): 3–17; Regina Bendix, Aditya Eggert, and Arnika Peselmann, eds., *Heritage Regimes and the State* (Göttingen: Göttingen University Press, 2013).

29. Nelson, "Progress Report."

30. "Historic Bishop Hill: Preservation and Planning," unpublished UP320 class report, Department of Urban and Regional Planning, Urbana-Champaign: University of Illinois (Bishop Hill: Bishop Hill Heritage Association, 1976); accessed September 30, 2014 BHHA archives.

31. Isaksson, *Bishop Hill: A Utopia on the Prairie*; Olov Isaksson, "Report on Investigations Made during the Summer 1968 in View of a Planned Exhibition about Bishop Hill, Illinois, USA" (Bishop Hill: Bishop Hill Heritage Association, 1968); accessed July 15, 2019 BHHA archives.

32. Tommy Andersson, "Sweden's Bishop Hill Society Celebrates Its 30th Year, 2019," trans. John E. Norton, *Bishop Hill Sällskapets Bulletinen 1* (2019), https://bishophillheritage.org; accessed July 15, 2019.

33. Joyce Evans, "Remarks of Joyce Evans on Behalf of Rep. Lane Evans (D-IL) at the National Historic Landmark Program," April 29, 1984 (Bishop Hill: Bishop Hill Heritage Association, 1984), 1; accessed September 30, 2014 BHHA archives.

34. See, for example, Edward M. Bruner, *Culture on Tour: Ethnographies of Travel* (Chicago: University of Chicago Press, 2005), 149–50.

35. Henry County Tourism Bureau, *Uncover: 2014 Guide to Exploring Our Backroads* (Kewanee, Ill.), 12; emphasis added.

36. Emphasis added.

37. Nelson, "Progress Report."

38. Peter F. Cannavò, *The Working Landscape: Founding, Preservation, and the Politics of Place* (Cambridge: MIT Press, 2007), 6.

16

Negotiating the American Civil War

Memories and Gender in Swedish-American Civil War Reenactment

Marie Bennedahl

The reenactment of the American Civil War, with its re-creation of historical battles and hundreds or even thousands of people dressing up in uniforms, is an American phenomenon that can be dated back to the late nineteenth century. From Civil War veterans taking part in parades, it evolved over the years to become what is known today as Civil War reenactment. People meet over weekends, dress in nineteenth-century-style clothing, build and live in historical military encampments, and cook food over open fire. From sunrise to sunset the war is on with improvised skirmishes. The highlight of the event is a reenactment of a battle in front of an audience.

But even though the Civil War took place in the United States, reenactments can also be found in Sweden. The events constitute a borderland in an abstract sense, as the meeting point of two reenactment communities and their interwoven perceptions of the past. Instead of focusing on reenactment being a mediation of a national past, I will delve into the complexities of a collective memory becoming global, where the same event is reenacted in different communities, and the effects of the relationship between the two communities. More specifically, the essay shows how gender is emphasized in the Swedish reenactments of the Civil War.

The empirical material for this study consists of autoethnographic field notes and interviews with reenactors from the two major Swedish associations reenacting the American Civil War. Between 2015 and 2019 I took part in the events of Nord o Syd, the Swedish Confederate States of America Association, and Club of Western. Along with similar groups in Denmark and Norway, these associations constitute a Scandinavian-American Civil War community of about three hundred people. Although I interacted with several hundred reenactors during my research, this essay will feature only a few of them as representatives of the community, through extracts from my interviews and field notes. The associations consist of infantry, artillery, and cavalry units from the two fighting sides, along with civilians. Approximately two-thirds of the reenactors choose to portray the Confederate side, both in Sweden and in the United States.[1] The reenactment community in Sweden is small compared to the estimated ten thousand reenactors who participated at the 150th anniversary of the Battle of Gettysburg in 2013. The Swedish reenactors are in contact with American reenactors and with other Civil War reenactors all over the world through communities on social media. They have sister units in the United States and they frequently visit their American peers to take part in reenactment events overseas, including the Gettysburg jubilee in 2013.

Reenactors (both men and women) portray Confederate soldiers at an event in Norrtälje, Sweden. Photograph by Konrad Persson.

Remembering the Civil War

In the aftermath of the Civil War, four major ways of remembering what had happened emerged. These memory traditions included the Union memory, the emancipationist memory, the reconciliatory memory, and the memory of the Lost Cause.[2] All of these memory traditions are, in Astrid Erll's words, forms of *remediation*.[3] What actually happened in the past is less important than how memory influences the present, leading to an adaptation of memory. When struggling with matters in the present, people look to the adapted version of the past for guidance.

The Union memory emphasized the heroic deeds of the Union soldiers, going to war defending the Union as well as abolishing slavery. This way of remembering overshadowed contradictory parts of the past, such as racial equality in the North, and the terrors of war caused by the Union Army.[4] The emancipationist memory, on the other hand, focused on slavery and the need for change in postwar America. Here the Reconstruction period was highlighted, and eventually the emancipationist memory grew into the civil rights movement. The third memory tradition, the reconciliatory memory, was an attempt to reunite the country by disregarding the causes for war and instead focusing on uniting aspects of the U.S. population and their experiences of war.

In old Confederate states, the myth of the Lost Cause provided a way for white southerners to deal with defeat. The memory of the Lost Cause developed during the antebellum era as a romantic imaginary of the Old South with heroic gentlemen, beautiful belles, and notions of a simpler way of life.[5] After the war, the memory tradition evolved further, significantly downplaying the role of slavery by claiming that the southerners had gone to war to defend their lifestyle against industrialization and capitalism.[6]

The purpose of the Lost Cause memory was to redeem the tarnished image of the South and regain status in the Union, but it also facilitated continued white supremacy and patriarchy. Southern masculinity was a construction that enabled as well as depended on white men's mastery over women, children, and slaves. During the emasculating Union occupation, southern white males used the suppression of the role of slavery for the Civil War as a way of reasserting a patriarchal masculinity that was rooted in American racial hierarchies.[7]

White northerners did not agree with every part of the Lost Cause, but in a quickly modernizing world they saw the appeal of the nostalgic idea of a southern way of life. The conservative values embedded in the Lost Cause regarding race, politics, and gender attracted the white population, especially in the border states. The vast majority of white northerners had felt just as uneasy about freeing slaves as the southerners.[8] The Reconstruction Amendments and the emancipationist memory brought radical changes, and embracing conservative values was a way of clinging on to something familiar rather than facing the unknown.[9] Because of the popularity of those values, the Lost Cause was also used as a political tool to attract voters by the Democratic Party after the war.[10]

As a part of the reconciliatory narrative, Union and Confederate veterans came together in war commemorations. Although no one wanted to forgive, they could find common ground to remember together.[11] The commemorations and memory activities thus kept the memories of the war alive. Over time, the landscape of memory changed, and by the end of the nineteenth century, reconciliation had become the dominant theme. A "tectonic shift in Civil War memory" took place as the war became a collective American experience. The funeral of President Ulysses Grant in August 1885 is one example, where both Confederate and Union veterans paid homage to the former commanding general of the U.S. Army who had received Robert E. Lee's surrender at Appomattox.[12]

During the twentieth century, the Civil War became part of the expanding entertainment business. Novels and films became prominent parts of the memory culture with *The Birth of a Nation* (1915) and *Gone with the Wind* (1939) as notable examples. Both promoted the Lost Cause and the latter became a blockbuster with wide circulation outside the United States, including in Sweden.

The civil rights movement of the 1950s and 1960s challenged the memory of the Lost Cause. The emancipationist memory presented a different way of remembering the South that included all southerners and focused on what united rather than separated them. African Americans became active participants in the shaping of the past, which made the white separatist ideal impossible to uphold and the Lost Cause lost its appeal politically.[13] It did linger, though, as did the Union memory, especially in memory activities tied to the Civil War Centennial of 1961–65.

The emancipationist memory became highlighted in institutionalized memory activities such as museum exhibits, whereas the other memory traditions mainly became a part of popular culture.

A new form of memory activity emerged with the jubilee, namely, the reenactment of war battles. In the context of the Civil War this was something new, even though reenactments of battles can be traced back to ancient Rome. It was a part of the reconciliatory memory tradition, including both the Union memory and the Lost Cause. By focusing on the similarities between the North and South, and by introducing an element of entertainment, the memories of the Civil War regained interest among the public.[14] The reconciliatory emphasis on the universal traits of the Common Soldier also made the films about the war, and by extension the Civil War itself, more appealing to a public outside of the United States. Most notable is the film *Gettysburg* from 1993, but also *Glory* (1989), *Ride with the Devil* (1999), and the TV series *North and South* (1985). The coming of Hollywood films and TV shows, in particular the popular western genre, strengthened the ambivalent Swedish interest in the United States and American history.[15] The collective memory of the Civil War had become global with popular culture and social media, through films, TV series, computer games like *War of Rights,* and comics such as the French series *Blueberry.* Popular culture made it possible for Swedes to feel connected to the memories of the Civil War and allowed them to use remediation to adapt these memories to fit their own contemporary needs.

Martial Masculinity and Gender

The reenactment of the Civil War is a way to process contemporary topics by looking to the past for guidance. The memories are therefore adapted to be able to deal with the issues in question. In the United States, national identity and race are still questions that are being processed through reenactment, but in Sweden other topics take precedence, namely, the matter of gender.

Gender, and especially masculinity, is central to the causes of the Civil War. Two forms of masculinity were closely tied to the antebellum westward expansion, competing for precedence. The "Martial Manhood" that gave expansionists the right to seize Indigenous lands because of the perceived lacking manliness of the Native peoples, and the "Restrained Manhood" that promoted economic integration and religious conversion.[16] National politics was inextricably interwoven with notions of masculinity. The assertion of one masculine identity over another included the use of class, race, and sectionalism as legitimizing factors.[17]

Masculinity in the American nineteenth century can also be divided into a northern and a southern version, although in both cases it is limited to a white elite. In the business and professional classes in the North, concepts of manhood were influenced by capitalist economics, and economic productivity was the ultimate test of manhood. In the South, manhood was closely tied to the system of plantation slavery, emulating the English gentry in a "Southern Chivalry."[18] Both North and South had sectional misperceptions related to masculinity that escalated the alienation between the sections. Each side viewed the other as less manly and therefore no credible threat, leading to a willingness to settle their growing differences through violence, eventually erupting in the Civil War.[19]

Gender was also intertwined with racial upheaval. With the war, black men had the possibility to win their "manhood" and become equals to white men, a notion that threatened the very core of white masculinity.[20] After the war, white southerners had to find new ways to define white masculinity without the mastery incorporated in slavery. Drawing on old codes of honor and mastery, new forms of masculinity evolved, the most prominent connected to martial manhood.[21]

The memories of the Civil War promoted a masculinity that was centered on war and soldiers. The martial ideal of the hardened warrior, combined with lingering expressions of restrained masculinity, evolved with the Civil War and later blossomed with the First World War.[22] The aggressive martial masculinity was found in both the northern Union memory and the southern Lost Cause. The ideal was emphasized in the United States as well as in Europe, but during the Second World War martial masculinity became associated with fascism, resulting in its losing some of its appeal in Europe by the end of the war. In the United States, however, the martial ideal has remained an aspect of the American self-image, relating to the country's continuous involvement in armed conflicts. The image of American men as latent soldiers remains, and the "tough guy" masculinity is upheld in popular culture.[23]

The martial ideal also endorsed a conservative view of women. Drawing on Raewyn Connells's theory of hegemonic masculinity, which postulates a hierarchy of different masculinities and femininities, martial masculinity presupposes a femininity that promoted women who stayed in the home, bore and took care of children, and lived lives far from the public arena—in other words, a society with two separate spheres, one private and one public.[24] It helps us understand the memories of the American Civil War, as women took pride in their effort on the home front, and was fortified by the postwar creation of memory associations such as the United Daughters of the Confederacy.[25] In Europe, on the other hand, women who had been on the battlefront in the Second World War refused to step back to the shadows when the war ended. Consequently, in Europe the memory of the Second World War was made to include not only the soldiers' experiences, but also those of the civilians and thereby the experiences of women. This meant that the warrior ideal became void.[26]

Egalitarian values grew into an important topic in postwar Sweden through the development of the Swedish welfare state.[27] This was based on the principle that all citizens should have equal opportunities, fair wages, and that the society takes responsibility for those who are unable to fend for themselves. The welfare state introduced the possibility of part-time work, publicly financed child care, parental leave, and tax deductions for domestic services, which made it easier for mothers to handle both work and family. Women were no longer tied to the private sphere of the home, but were encouraged to take an active part in public life.[28] The ideal of the housewife taking care of the home and raising children faded in favor for egalitarian wage labor sanctioned by the state. The added two months of parental leave for fathers that was introduced in 2002 challenged the gender order further, placing Sweden in third place in a worldwide ranking of gender equality.[29]

The two spheres promoted in martial masculinity, where women inhabited the private and men the public, have thus lost much of their earlier position in Swedish society. In the United States, however, they remain prominent and the country ranks forty-first in gender equality.[30] In other words, gender is a topical subject in Swedish society and therefore something that needs to be explored, challenged, and strengthened by looking to the past. The American Civil War is a part of the past deeply rooted in issues of masculinity, providing a suitable setting for the exploration of gender. In the reenactment of the Civil War, there is a possibility to do just that.

Reenacting Martial Masculinity in the Union Army

My autoethnographic participation in the Swedish reenactment community consisted of taking on different roles while trying to adapt to the community. This meant that I took an active part in the reenactment. During my five years of research, I participated in the role of Confederate infantry private, artillery private, Union infantry private, a member of a paramilitary group, a cook, and a mourning widow. During my transition from outsider to insider, I took notes of my experiences and feelings, creating a material that goes beyond mere observations.[31]

Because of its origins in a military past, reenactment carries a legacy of upholding a male sphere. The preservation of separate spheres does not mean that women are excluded from reenactment, but it does mean that women are more welcome in some parts of the reenactment community than others. This becomes clear in the example of American reenactor Lauren Cook Burgess, who participated in the reenactment of the Battle of Antietam in 1989.[32] Because she was dressed in a Confederate uniform, park rangers gave her the choice to either change her clothes or leave the event. Cook Burgess chose to leave, and subsequently—and successfully—sued the National Park Service for sexual discrimination. Since then, women have the legal right to take part as soldiers. However, the guidelines for female reenactors in a contemporary American reenactor magazine written by the reenactors themselves show that women are still perceived as problematic in uniform, Confederate and Union alike: "The presence of a recognizable woman is going to deprive the reenacting experience of much of the comraderie *[sic]* and authenticity that makes it attractive to reenactors."[33] Authenticity is thus linked to the separate spheres promoted by martial masculinity. Karin, a Swedish reenactor, also expresses this notion when she explains her own participation as a Union civilian:

> I'm not opposed to *they* and *queer*, but I don't want to be that myself. I like the dresses, and being among other women. It feels like it was easier back

> in those days. People knew who they were. They had clear guidelines to follow. And I enjoy experiencing that at events, especially the feeling of sisterhood when we cook.[34]

Her words reveal a critique of the feminization of her society. Karin is of the opinion that Swedish society lacks guidelines and community, and that this can be attributed to contemporary gender norms. By conforming to the separate spheres, the perceived authenticity is upheld and the feeling of camaraderie that the American reenactors in the magazine mention is expressed as sisterhood among the civilian women following the Union Army.

As I took on the role of a Union infantry soldier, the other soldiers accepted my participation, but some details made me recognize that I would never fully be included in the group. Friendly reminders of the strict dress code of the Union Army made me question my own ability to portray a Union soldier. The uniform I was wearing did not conceal the shape of my body, my hair kept getting out from under the kepi, and I felt unable to take part in the macho jokes before the battle.[35] The greatest obstacle was my own body. After two days as a Union infantry soldier, I instead decided to join the civilian women making up the cooking crew. As I stood by the fire, stirring a meat stew, an officer from the Union Army came by. He was surprised to see me out of uniform and asked me if I had deserted. I laughed and told him that I had. "It's only okay because the food you're cooking is delicious," he said with a grin. Another Union soldier walked by and told me it was nice to see me where I belonged.[36] The officers' way of reassuring me that I was excelling in my new role, and the second soldier's comment reinforcing that notion, indicate that the separate spheres are just as strong in groups portraying the Union in Sweden as they are in the United States. As a part of the cooking crew and as a mourning widow, I never experienced my participation as flawed, and the same Union soldiers who had made me question myself now made me feel included.

The Swedish units reenacting the Union infantry embody a traditional martial masculinity and the women who participate are almost never dressed as soldiers, but take on the roles of wives and mothers. They do the cooking, take care of children, and watch the battles from the sidelines.

This emphasizes the separate spheres and is often justified by the notion that the reenactment of the American Civil War needs to include more dimensions of daily life during the war, other than the one on the battlefields. The Swedish reenactors portraying the Union thus conform to the memory tradition of the Union. The Union soldiers are on a heroic quest, focusing on camaraderie, protecting their loved ones, and upholding the Union. The Union memory is still valid, and therefore the reenactment of it does not need to be adapted. On the contrary, the traditional values of the Union memory are used as a critique of contemporary Swedish gender norms. Taking part in the reenactment of the Union Army in Sweden is a way of exploring traditional gender norms in a way that is sanctioned not only by American reenactors, but by the memory tradition of the Union.

A Swedish Version of the Confederacy

In some of the Confederate units in Sweden, martial masculinity is just as prominent as in the Union infantry, supporting the Lost Cause ideal of the chivalrous southern gentlemen. Several Swedish women also give the character Scarlett O'Hara in the film *Gone with the Wind* as the key reason for their interest in reenactment.[37] However, a deviation from the Lost Cause tradition is the inclusion of female soldiers in the Confederate infantry units. Although this is not a phenomenon unique to Sweden, the attitude here is inextricably tied to a Swedish national striving for gender equality. From the cooking crew, I made the transition to a Confederate infantry soldier, bearing in mind my previous experiences of the strict dress code among Union reenactors. I tried to tuck my long braid under the hat, but a Confederate soldier explained to me that I did not have to hide my hair because there had been women in the Confederate Army. I asked him if they had pretended to be men. "No," he replied, "the Confederacy needed every able soldier they could get, so they allowed women to enlist as well. They weren't forced to hide their identities."[38] This statement might be contested by other reenactors regarding authenticity, and it does not quite conform to the gender norms promoted by the Lost Cause, but it does show the general attitude among the Swedish Confederate infantry soldiers toward the participation of women.

Furthermore, it mirrors the expectations of the Swedish welfare state where the citizens not only should be given equal opportunities, but where they are also expected to contribute equally, regardless of gender.

One way of authenticating female soldiers is to emphasize the individuality among the Confederate soldiers. One of the soldiers, Bosse, defines his attraction to the Confederacy by emphasizing the Confederates' commitment to individual freedom: "They fought for one thing and that was their right to decide for themselves. And I hold that as a beacon in my life, I want the freedom of deciding for myself."[39] The notion of freedom in the Civil War is inextricably tied to the question of white supremacy, but because the Swedish reenactment of the Civil War is not part of a public expression of national history, the reenactors can choose to embrace other dimensions than slavery. This is explained by Beatrice, a Confederate infantry private:

> Slavery is all you read about in history books. But we're all aware that it was more complicated than that. There were slaves in the North as well. So, we don't talk about slavery, we focus on the freedom instead. I don't condone slavery. I just think that there are other dimensions of the Confederacy that I can still agree with. Like, wanting to decide for yourself.[40]

In other words, freedom for Beatrice is something that is available not only to white men, but to everyone, including women. In this way, the Confederate striving for freedom coincides with Swedish egalitarian values. The Swedish reenactors' interpretation of freedom is highlighted in the manner of dress in the Confederate Army. During the 1860s, the uniforms of the Confederate Army varied a lot, a fact that allows the reenactors leeway to express themselves in a way that is not granted to the Union Army soldiers. It also creates a loophole for including women participating as soldiers. The Swedish reenactors tend to focus on the possibility of women participating as soldiers during the actual war, rather than their paucity. Combining individual freedom and diversity of uniforms, Bosse concludes his view of women reenacting as soldiers: "Even though there might not have been a lot of women in the armies, there still were some. So, why shouldn't everyone be allowed to reenact and experience how it was back then?"[41] This view resonates with the contemporary Swedish aspirations of gender equality, where everyone should be able to experience camaraderie. Bosse sums up this view: "If we're dressed as soldiers, we *are* soldiers, no matter the person's sex."[42]

The Swedish reenactors draw on the perception that the Confederate soldiers were individualistic by choice and expand this notion with the help of contemporary gender norms. Not only were the reenacted Confederates individualistic, they were also protofeminist. The adapted version of the memory of the Lost Cause combines the most alluring parts of martial masculinity, such as the camaraderie and the striving toward maintaining individual freedom with aspects of contemporary gender norms such as gender equality. Even though the Lost Cause holds conservative values, the memory tradition is built on the idea that it is possible to shape the past to accommodate contemporary needs.[43] This is also the case here. The question of gender and gender equality is more pressing and in need of evaluation than the question of race among the Swedish reenactors. It does not mean that the reenactors are unaware of the controversy in their adaptation of the Civil War, but they consciously choose to focus their reenactment on matters that are essential in a contemporary Swedish context. Hence the reenactment of the Confederacy becomes a way to strengthen contemporary Swedish gender norms, especially in contrast to the conservative perceptions of gender reenacted in the Union groups.

Negotiating the American Civil War

Out of the two hundred Swedish reenactors I have met, about a third have participated once or twice in reenactment events in the United States. In addition, most Swedish units have sister units overseas. During my time in the Swedish reenactment community, several reenactors asked me if I planned to travel to the United States and take part in "real" reenactments. This very question shows that American reenactors are perceived as more authentic than the Swedish ones. One of the Swedish reenactors explained that: "Swedish reenactors are just as hard-core as American, but it's still their history."[44] Even though the Swedish reenactors are included in the collective memory of the war, the fact that remembering is also a way of processing trauma gives the reenactment in the United States a dimension that the Swedish variety lacks. On the other hand, the spatial and social distance also gives the Swedish reenactors the possibility to reinterpret the memories to fit their own context, without being limited by a desire to honor ancestors.

When the Swedish reenactor Bengt did some research about the Confederate 48th Tennessee Infantry Regiment, he contacted a group that was already reenacting that regiment, among others, in the United States. The U.S. group gave its blessing to create Company E of the regiment in Sweden. Bengt was also made an officer by the highest-ranking officer in the Pennsylvania-based reenactment group, because at that time all the Swedish reenactors were privates. The American reenactors made sure to establish a military-style hierarchy in the Swedish reenactment community, enhancing the presence of martial masculinity. This is not a hierarchy exclusive to the reenactment of the Confederacy but to all sorts of military reenactment groups. The members of the units keep in contact over social media, with the Internet being a crucial way of finding and exchanging information about the Civil War, and of locating fellow reenactors around the world. When the Swedish reenactors travel to the United States for a reenactment event, the American reenactors serve as hosts.

As the reenactors convene, their different attitudes toward the memories of the war are emphasized. When Beatrice took part in reenactments in the United States during the 150th anniversary of the war in 2015, she noticed that none of the American women among the Union groups shouldered the roles of soldiers: "They never took part in the fighting and they never wore uniforms; instead, they wore dresses and did the cooking."[45] Just as in the Swedish Union groups, the exclusion of women is justified by the claim that women are needed to portray other dimensions of the war, namely, home life. Beatrice herself took part as a soldier in different units of both Union and Confederate regiments, and explained: "For me, coming from Sweden, it's natural that I'm allowed to take part in the fighting. They never said anything against it. Since it was natural for me it became natural for them too. But their own women weren't allowed [to be soldiers]."[46] As she took part in a Confederate infantry unit, Beatrice noticed four American women participating as soldiers, but none of them were officers. The higher ranks in the military hierarchy are reserved for men.

During their visits to the United States, both Beatrice and Bengt received gifts from the American reenactors. Bengt got a leather wristband for percussion caps and Beatrice got a blue cockade. In both cases, the Swedes had expressed a fascination for the items. Bengt made a replica of the wristband that he in turn gifted to the American reenactor. The wristband is a strictly masculine and military item, whereas the cockade, although traditionally worn by men as well as women, points to a female presence connected to the item. Even the spontaneous gifts, in other words, correspond to the enhancement of separate spheres and martial masculinity.

Bosse contemplated the practice of the American reenactors and the exclusion of women: "They just don't think it's historically correct. And in a way the female reenactors today are being treated just the same way women would have been back in the days. They were sent back home if they were discovered. So, in a way they are right. But we live in the present," he adds, "which means we think in a different way. At least I do, and a lot of people with me."[47] The attitudes of the American reenactors are perceived as more in tune with the past, but the Swedes view their own attitude as being more contemporary. Beatrice was allowed to take part in the fighting dressed in uniform when she visited the United States, proving that the more inclusive version of martial masculinity of the Swedish reenactors is not disregarded by the Americans. The main difference is not the perception of the martial masculinity, but the Swedish reenactors' way of including women in that ideal.

The reenactment of the American Civil War in Sweden is an opportunity for the Swedes to explore the memories of the Civil War that are mediated through American popular culture. More important, it also allows the participants to use narratives of the past to deal with contemporary issues. Through their contacts with American reenactors, the Swedish participants define their own understanding of the memory of the Civil War. The Swedish groups reenacting the Union Army conform to the Union memory, embracing the traditional values of separate spheres and martial masculinity. Some parts of the memory, such as the conservative gender roles, can still be attractive today, as demonstrated by the contemporary reenactment of the Civil War in Sweden. Reenacting the traditional gender roles becomes a safe haven in a time of change. The reenactment of the Civil War allows the participants to explore gender relations and express a critique of the gender norms in Swedish society as a whole.

The Confederate reenactors in Sweden, on the other hand, adopt the memory of the Lost Cause, so that women can be included in martial masculinity. The memory of the Lost Cause is remediated to fit the contemporary Swedish context. The feminist approach of the Swedish reenactors incentivizes the American reenactors to promote their own understanding of the separate spheres of martial masculinity endorsed by the Lost Cause. The Swedish reenactors know that they will be evaluated when they meet their American peers, and are encouraged to be firm in their conviction of their adapted version of the Lost Cause. By reenacting an adapted version of the Lost Cause, the Swedish reenactors find support in the past for their contemporary gender norms.

The research that I conducted in the Swedish reenactment community shows that reenactment is a way for people to escape reality for a few days, while at the same time providing them with a chance to explore and adapt memories of the past to deal with issues in their everyday lives. The matter of gender is today conceived as an important topic in Sweden, overshadowing controversial parts of the history being reenacted. Lately, however, a growing far-right movement in both the United States and Sweden is forcing the communities to further evaluate their perception of the war. Jonas, one of the Swedish reenactors portraying Confederate soldiers, thinks that there is a need to find connections between Sweden and the Confederacy to justify reenacting the Confederate Army:

> If we can prove a historical link, it would motivate why we are "playing" Confederates. I didn't understand how politically charged the Confederate flag and other symbols were until I traveled through the South. The way we whitewash "Southern pride" is absurd.[48]

There have therefore been suggestions in the Swedish reenactment community to create new units that consist of immigrants from Sweden. A historical connection to Sweden would give the Swedish reenactors the same claim as the Americans regarding authenticity, but it would still not make the connection to white supremacy go away. There is a growing need to address matters of race and ethnicity in contemporary Sweden, and the centrality of slavery in the Civil War cannot be ignored. To avoid being associated with an extreme-right and neo-Confederate movement, the reenactment communities will have to be very clear about how they deal with white supremacy and the question of race. As the memories of the Civil War are adapted to process contemporary issues, the war continues to be a relevant historical narrative in the United States and in Sweden.

Notes

1. Christopher Bates, "'Oh, I'm a Good Ol' Rebel': Reenactment, Racism and the Lost Cause," in *The Civil War in Popular Culture: Memory and Meaning,* ed. Lawrence A. Kreiser Jr. and Randal Allred (Lexington: University Press of Kentucky, 2014), 193–94.

2. Robert J. Cook, *Civil War Memories: Contesting the Past in the United States since 1865* (Baltimore: Johns Hopkins University Press, 2017).

3. Astrid Erll, "Remembering across Time, Space, and Cultures: Premediation, Remediation and the 'Indian Mutiny,'" in *Mediation, Remediation and the Dynamics of Cultural Memory,* ed. Astrid Erll and Ann Rigney (Berlin: Walter de Gruyter, 2012).

4. Caroline E. Janney, *Remembering the Civil War: Reunion and the Limits of Reconciliation* (Chapel Hill: University of North Carolina Press, 2013), 9.

5. Gary W. Gallagher, "Introduction," in *The Myth of the Lost Cause and Civil War History,* ed. Gary W. Gallagher and Alan T. Nolan (Bloomington: Indiana University Press, 2000), 1.

6. Cook, *Civil War Memories,* chapter 2.

7. Bryan C. Rindfleisch, "'What It Means to Be a Man': Contested Masculinity in the Early Republic and Antebellum America," *History Compass* 10/11 (2012): 858–60.

8. Kenneth A. Dietreich, "Honor, Patriarchy, and Disunion: Masculinity and the Coming of the American Civil War," PhD dissertation, West Virginia University, 2006, 266.

9. Anne E. Marshall, *Creating a Confederate Kentucky: The Lost Cause and Civil War Memory in a Border State* (Chapel Hill: University of North Carolina Press, 2010), 5.

10. W. Scott Poole, "Religion, Gender and the Lost Cause in South Carolina's 1876 Governor's Race: 'Hampton of Hell,'" *Journal of Southern History* 68, no. 3 (2002): 574–76.

11. Janney, *Remembering the Civil War,* 162.

12. Stuart McConnell, "The Geography of Memory," in *The Memory of the Civil War in American Culture,* ed. Alice Fals and Joan Waugh (Chapel Hill: University of North Carolina Press, 2004), 230–31.

13. David Goldfield, *Still Fighting the Civil War: The American South and Southern History* (Baton Rouge: Louisiana University Press, 2002), 5–6.

14. Bates, "'Oh, I'm a Good Ol' Rebel.'"

15. Lawrence A. Kreiser Jr. and Randal Allred, eds., *The Civil War in Popular Culture: Memory and Meaning* (Lexington: University Press of Kentucky, 2014); Ulf Jonas Björk, "Stories of America: The Rise of the 'Indian Book' in Sweden 1862–1895," *Scandinavian Studies* 75, no. 4 (2003): 509–26; Ulf Jonas Björk, "Amerikansk film och television i Sverige," in *Det blågula stjärnbaneret: USA:s närvaro och inflytande i Sverige,* ed. Erik Åsard (Stockholm: Carlsson, 2016).

16. Amy S. Greenberg, *Manifest Manhood and the Antebellum American Empire* (Cambridge: Cambridge University Press, 2005), 17.

17. Rindfleisch, "'What It Means to Be a Man,'" 243.

18. Dietreich, "Honor, Patriarchy, and Disunion," 26–35.

19. Ibid., 265.

20. LeeAnn Whites, *The Civil War as a Crisis in Gender: Augusta, Georgia, 1860–1890* (Athens: University of Georgia Press, 1995), 3.

21. Craig Thompson Friend, ed., *Southern Masculinity: Perspectives on Manhood in the South since Reconstruction* (Athens: University of Georgia Press, 2009), vii–xi.

22. Michael T. Smith, "The Beast Unleashed: Benjamin F. Butler and Conceptions of Masculinity in the Civil War North," *New England Quarterly* 79, no. 2 (June 2006): 248–76; Gerald F. Linderman, *Embattled Courage: The Experience of Combat in the American Civil War* (New York: Free Press, 1989).

23. Robert A Nye, "Western Masculinities in War and Peace," *American Historical Review* 112, no. 2 (2007): 433–35.

24. Raewyn Connell and Rebecca Pearse, *Gender: In a World Perspective* (Cambridge: Polity Press, 2015).

25. Gaines M. Foster, *Ghosts of the Confederacy: Defeat, the Lost Cause, and the Emergence of the New South 1865–1913* (New York: Oxford University Press, 1987), 6.

26. George L. Mosse, *Fallen Soldiers: Reshaping the Memory of the World Wars* (New York: Oxford University Press, 1990).

27. Ronald Ingelhart and Pippa Norris, *Rising Tide: Gender Equality and Cultural Change around the World* (Cambridge: Cambridge University Press, 2003), 33.

28. Ann-Sofie Ohlander and Ulla-Britt Strömberg, *Tusen svenska kvinnoår: Svensk kvinnohistoria från vikingatid till nutid* (Lund: Studentlitteratur, 2018); Jens Rydström, *Kvinnor, män och alla andra: En svensk genushistoria* (Lund: Studentlitteratur, 2009).

29. Yvonne Hirdman, *The Gender System: Theoretical Reflections on the Social Subordination of Women* (Uppsala: Maktutredningen, 1990); Yvonne Hirdman, *Genus: Om det stabilas föränderliga former* (Malmö: Liber, 2003).

30. Anita Nyberg, "Gender Equality Policy in Sweden: 1970s–2010s," *Nordic Journal of Working Life Studies* 2, no. 4 (2012): 67–84.

31. For more information about autoethnography as a research method, see Heewon Chang, *Autoethnography as Method* (Walnut Creek, Calif.: Left Coast Press, 2008); Tony E. Adams, Stacy Holman Jones, and Carolyn Ellis, eds., *Autoethnography: Understanding Qualitative Research* (New York: Oxford University Press, 2015).

32. Eugene L. Meyer, "Judge Admits Women to the Antietam Armies," *Washington Post,* March 18, 1993.

33. John A. Braden, "Women in the Ranks," *Camp Chase Gazette,* December 2014.

34. In the original, the word *they* is the controversial Swedish word *hen,* a new gender-neutral pronoun (Marie Bennedahl, field notes, Civil War Weekend, High Chaparral, August 4–6, 2016).

35. Ibid.

36. Ibid.

37. Malin, interview by Marie Bennedahl, Järnavik, September 2, 2017; Marie Bennedahl, field notes, Civil War Weekend, High Chaparral, August 2–4, 2018.

38. Marie Bennedahl, field notes, Järnavik, September 2–4, 2016.

39. Bosse, interview by Marie Bennedahl, Norrtälje, May 25, 2017.

40. Beatrice, interview by Marie Bennedahl, Norrtälje, May 25, 2017.

41. Bosse, interview by Marie Bennedahl, Norrtälje, May 25, 2017.

42. Ibid.

43. W. Stuart Towns, *Enduring Legacy: Rhetoric and Ritual of the Lost Cause* (Tuscaloosa: University of Alabama Press, 2012).

44. Marie Bennedahl, field notes, Trapper Weekend, High Chaparral, July 3, 2016.

45. Beatrice, interview by Marie Bennedahl, Norrtälje, May 25, 2017.

46. Ibid.

47. Bosse, interview by Marie Bennedahl, Norrtälje, May 25, 2017.

48. Marie Bennedahl, field notes, Järnavik, September 5–8, 2019.

Contributors

PHILIP J. ANDERSON is professor emeritus of church history at North Park University. He is coeditor of *Swedish-American Life in Chicago: Cultural and Urban Aspects of an Immigrant People, 1850–1930, Swedes in the Twin Cities: Immigrant Life and Minnesota's Urban Frontier,* and *Norwegians and Swedes in the United States: Friends and Neighbors.*

JENNIFER EASTMAN ATTEBERY is professor of English at Idaho State University. She is author of *Up in the Rocky Mountains: Writing the Swedish Immigrant Experience* (Minnesota, 2007) and *Pole Raising and Speech Making: Modalities of Swedish American Summer Celebration.*

MARIE BENNEDAHL has a PhD in history and is lecturer at Linnaeus University. She is author of *Fall in Line: Genus, kropp och minnena av det amerikanska inbördeskriget i skandinavisk reenactment.*

ULF JONAS BJÖRK is professor of journalism at Indiana University–Purdue University Indianapolis. He is coauthor of *A History of the International Movement of Journalists: Professionalism versus Politics.*

DAG BLANCK is professor of North American studies and director of the Swedish Institute for North American Studies at Uppsala University, as well as director of the Swenson Swedish Immigration Research Center at Augustana College. He is author of *The Creation of an Ethnic Identity: Being Swedish American in the Augustana Synod, 1860–1917* and coeditor of *Swedish-American Life in Chicago: Cultural and Urban Aspects of an Immigrant People, 1850–1930*, *Swedes in the Twin Cities: Immigrant Life and Minnesota's Urban Frontier*, and *Norwegians and Swedes in the United States: Friends and Neighbors.*

THOMAS J. BROWN is professor of history at the University of South Carolina. He is author of *Dorothea Dix: New England Reformer*, *Civil War Canon: Sites of Confederate Memory in South Carolina*, and *Civil War Monuments and the Militarization of America.*

MARGARET E. FARRAR is professor of political science at John Carroll University. She is author of *Building the Body Politic: Power and Urban Space in Washington, D.C.*

CHARLOTTA FORSS is postdoctoral fellow in history at Stockholm University, Cambridge University, Oxford University, and the University of Turku. She is author of *The Old, the New, and the Unknown: The Continents and the Making of Geographical Knowledge in Seventeenth-Century Sweden* and coauthor of *Ulrika Eleonora: Makten och den nya adeln, 1719–1720.*

GUNLÖG FUR is professor of history and deputy vice chancellor at Linnaeus University. She is author of *Colonialism in the Margins: Cultural Encounters in New Sweden and Lapland*; *A Nation of Women: Gender and Colonial Encounters among the Delaware Indians*; and *Painting Culture, Painting Nature: Stephen Mopope, Oscar Jacobson, and the Development of Indian Art in Oklahoma.*

KAREN V. HANSEN is professor of sociology and women's, gender, and sexuality studies and director of the Women's Studies Research Center at Brandeis University. She is author of *A Very Social Time: Crafting Community in Antebellum New England*; *Not-So-Nuclear Families: Class, Gender, and Networks of Care*; and *Encounter on the Great Plains: Scandinavian Settlers and the Dispossession of Dakota Indians, 1890–1930.*

ADAM HJORTHÉN is senior lecturer of North American studies at the Swedish Institute for North American Studies at Uppsala University. He is author of *Cross-Border Commemorations: Celebrating Swedish Settlement in America.*

ANGELA HOFFMAN is senior lecturer (associate professor) of English at Uppsala University. She is author of *Tracking Swedish-American English: A Longitudinal Study of Linguistic Variation and Identity.*

ADAM KAUL is professor of anthropology at Augustana College. He is author of *Turning the Tune: Traditional Music, Tourism, and Social Change in an Irish Village*; coeditor of *Tourists and Tourism: A Reader*; and coeditor of *Leisure and Death: An Anthropological Tour of Risk, Death, and Dying*, which won the 2020 Ed Bruner Book Prize from the Anthropology of Tourism Interest Group.

MAARET KOSKINEN is professor emeritus of the Department of Media Studies at Stockholm University. She is author of *Ingmar Bergman Revisited: Cinema, Performance, and the Arts*; *Ingmar Bergman's* The Silence*: Pictures in the Typewriter, Writings on the Screen*; and *Ingmar Bergman y sus primeros escritos: En el principio era la palabra.*

MERJA KYTÖ is professor of English linguistics at Uppsala University. She is associate editor of *Records of the Salem Witch-hunt*; coeditor of *Corpus Linguistics: An International Handbook* and *The Cambridge Handbook of English Historical Linguistics*; and coauthor of *Early Modern English Dialogues: Spoken Interaction as Writing* and *Testifying to Language and Life in Early Modern England.*

SVEA LARSON is a PhD student in Nordic studies and folklore at the University of Wisconsin–Madison.

FRANCO MINGANTI is Alma Mater Professor of American Literature at the University of Bologna. He is coauthor of *Storia della letteratura americana* and author of *x-roads: Letteratura, jazz, immaginario*; *Altre x-roads: Modi dell'espressività afroamericana: jazz, cinema, letteratura, storytelling, performance*; *Modulazioni di frequenza: L'immaginario radiofonico tra letteratura e cinema*; and *Cool, Calm, Collected Essays: Saggi di documentate passioni.*

FRIDA ROSENBERG has a PhD in architecture and is lecturer at the KTH Royal Institute of Technology School of Architecture in Stockholm. She is author of *The Construction of Construction: The Wenner-Gren Center and the Possibility of Steel Building in Postwar Sweden.*

MAGNUS ULLÉN is professor of English at Stockholm University. He is editor and coauthor of *Våldsamma fantasier: Studier i fiktionsvåldets funktion och attraktion* and author of *The Half-Vanished Structure: Hawthorne's Allegorical Dialectics* and *Bara för dig: Pornografi, konsumtion, berättande.*

Index